Sir Arthur Bryant was born in 1899 at the twilight of the Victorian age, in a house on the royal Sandringham Estate. He served in the Royal Flying Corps in the First World War and has been teaching and writing history ever since. His reputation was established by his biography of Charles II in 1931; his biography of Pepys, his history of the Napoleonic Wars and his analysis of the Second World War through the war diaries of Field Marshal Alanbrooke, among his many other classic books, have become recognized as the standard works on the subject. Through them he has pioneered a neglected art – the writing of history as literature. Indeed Professor John Foster, reviewing Arthur Bryant's last work of medieval history, wrote 'One cannot put it down. Some men are great writers. Some are great historians. Just a few, like Gibbon, are both. And one of the few is Sir Arthur'. He has written the Diary in the *Illustrated London News* since he inherited the column from G.´K. Chesterton in 1936. He was knighted in 1954 and created Companion of Honour in 1967. He now lives in the Close at Salisbury, looking out onto the cathedral.

By the same author

Macaulay
The National Character
The Letters and Speeches of Charles II (editor)
The England of Charles II
The American Ideal

The Story of England
Makers of the Realm B.C.–1272
The Age of Chivalry 1272–1381
The Elizabethan Deliverance
King Charles II 1630–1685
Restoration England 1660–1702
English Saga 1840–1940

Samuel Pepys
The Man in the Making 1633–1669
The Saviour of the Navy 1683–1689
Pepys and the Revolution

The Napoleonic Wars
The Years of Endurance 1793–1802
Years of Victory 1802–1812
The Age of Elegance 1812–1822
Nelson
The Great Duke

The Alanbrooke Diaries
The Turn of the Tide 1939–1943
Triumph in the West 1943–1946

English Social History
The Medieval Foundation
Protestant Island

The Fire and the Rose
The Lion and the Unicorn
Jimmy
Jackets of Green
A Thousand Years of British Monarchy
Spirit of England

A History of Britain and the British People
Set in a Silver Sea

ARTHUR BRYANT

Samuel Pepys

The Years of Peril

'It is not imaginable to such as have not tried, what labour an historian (that would be exact) is condemned to. He must read all, good and bad, and remove a world of rubbish before he can lay the foundation'
John Evelyn to Samuel Pepys, 28 April 1682

PANTHER
Granada Publishing

Panther Books
Granada Publishing Ltd
8 Grafton Street, London W1X 3LA

Published by Panther Books 1985

First published in Great Britain by
Collins 1935
New edition 1948
New edition 1967

Copyright in this edition © Sir Arthur Bryant 1967

ISBN 0-586-06471-0

Reproduced, printed and bound in Great Britain by
Hazell Watson & Viney Limited,
Aylesbury, Bucks

Set in Baskerville

To
FRANCIS TURNER
Pepys Librarian, scholar and musician

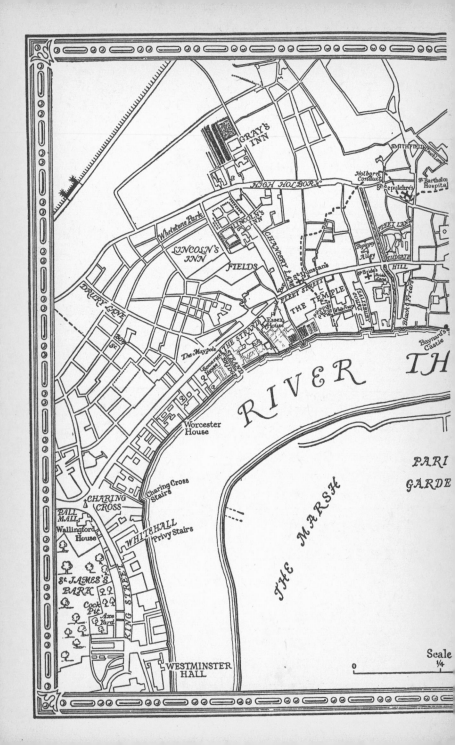

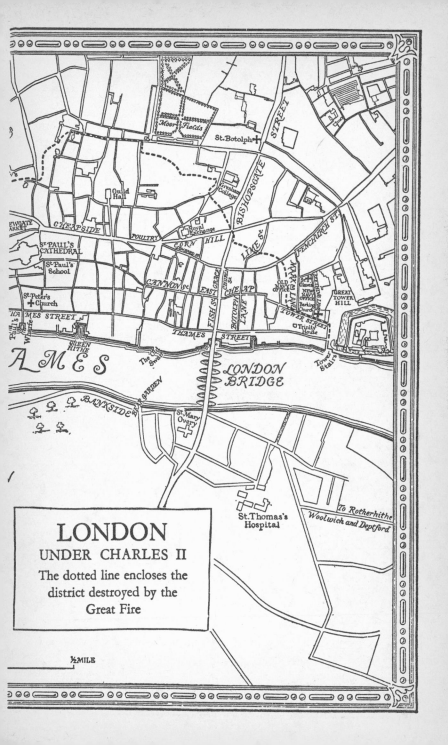

LONDON
UNDER CHARLES II
The dotted line encloses the
district destroyed by the
Great Fire

½ MILE

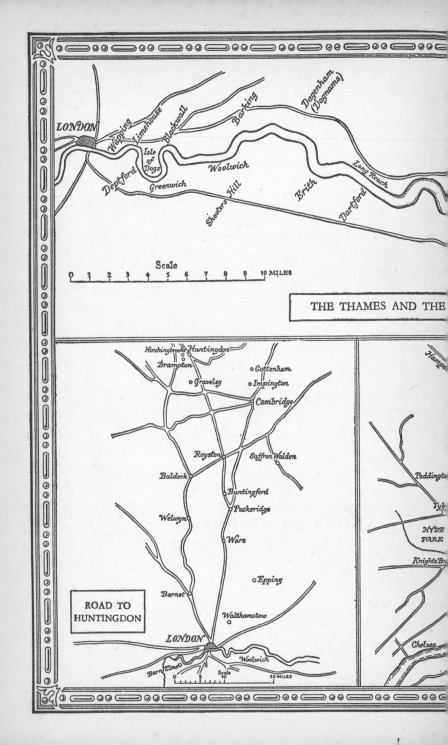

LONDON

Wapping
Limehouse
Blackwall
Barking
Dagenham
(Dagnams)

Isle of Dogs
Deptford
Greenwich
Woolwich
Shooters Hill
Erith
Long Reach
Dartford

Scale
0 1 2 3 4 5 6 7 8 9 10 MILES

THE THAMES AND THE

Hinchingbrook Huntingdon
Brampton
Graveley
Cottenham
Impington
Cambridge

Royston
Saffron Walden
Baldock
Buntingford
Puckeridge
Welwyn
Ware

Epping

Barnet

ROAD TO
HUNTINGDON

Walthamstow

LONDON

Barn Elms
Woolwich

Scale
0 5 10 20 MILES

Hampo
Paddingto
Tyb
HYDE
PARK
Knights Br
Chelsea

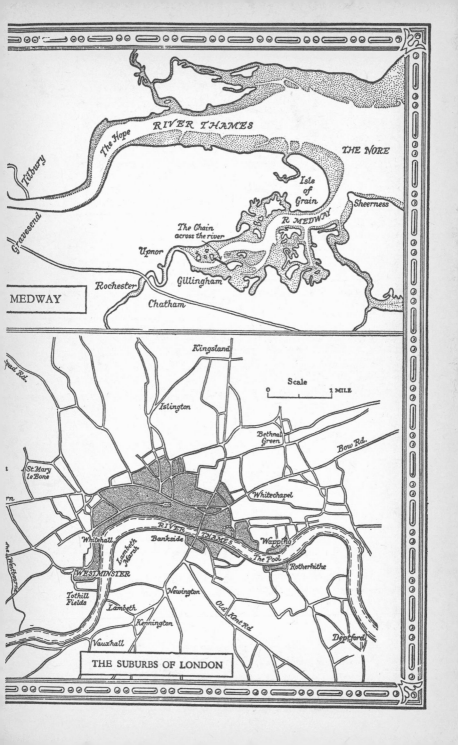

RIVER THAMES

The Hope

THE NORE

Tilbury

Gravesend

Isle of Grain

Sheerness

The Chain across the river

R. MEDWAY

Upnor

Rochester

Gillingham

MEDWAY

Chatham

Kingsland

Scale

0   1 MILE

Islington

Bethnal Green

Bow Rd.

St.Mary le Bone

Whitechapel

RIVER THAMES

Whitehall

Bankside

Wapping

Lambeth Marsh

The Pool

WESTMINSTER

Rotherhithe

Tothill Fields

Newington

Lambeth

Old Kent Rd.

Kennington

Vauxhall

Deptford

THE SUBURBS OF LONDON

Contents

Preface

The growth of our knowledge of Samuel Pepys makes a romantic story. For a hundred and twenty years after his death he was known to a few scholars and specialists as the father of the Admiralty administration and the creator of an important library. To the general reading public his name was unknown, for the historians of the eighteenth century were Whigs and only conferred immortality on such of their defeated opponents as were unmistakably villains. To many generations of English readers the best-known Tory of the later seventeenth century was Judge Jeffreys.

But in 1825, with the publication of about a quarter of his great Diary, Pepys suddenly became famous. Successive editions, culminating in the eighteen-nineties with the presentation of almost the whole Diary by H. B. Wheatley, gave the world a knowledge of Pepys' daily life and character more intimate and detailed than that of any man who has ever lived. Yet it was a curiously limited knowledge, for it was based entirely on a shorthand journal kept between his twenty-seventh and thirty-sixth years. Of Pepys' life outside those nine crowded years the world knew nothing and cared almost less. To most people his later career seemed as unreal and unimportant as that of Sancho Panza or Figaro.

Yet silently Pepys clamoured to be heard. Between the unfingered covers of hundreds of volumes in the Bodleian and in his Library at Magdalene College were the materials which he had prepared to explain and justify his career. From the walls of the Admiralty, of the Royal Society, of his College at Cambridge, the stern old face of the great Secretary looked down as though angrily seeking a champion to challenge the legend of amorous buffoon and gossip created by the publication of his Diary. He found one in a brilliant Cambridge scholar, the late Dr J. R. Tanner, who devoted thirty years of his life to expounding to the twentieth century what the eighteenth had deliberately forgotten and the nineteenth had never known, that Pepys had created the English naval machine which ultimately gave his country the dominion of the seas and the empire of more than a quarter of the world.

Dr Tanner died with the greater part of his task unfinished, for the very magnitude of the materials Pepys left behind him hid their true importance. Yet his work on the naval manuscripts in the Pepys Library provided a foundation of solid knowledge of Pepys' official career – from 1673 to 1678 in detail and from 1684 to 1688 in outline – to which historians will always remain indebted. At the time of his death, Dr Tanner was engaged on a still greater task, inherited from his fellow-scholar, H. B. Wheatley – the preparation of a full and definitive life of Pepys that should establish him in his place as one of the first Englishmen of his age.

What Dr Tanner was prevented by death from performing became my task sixteen years ago. In *Samuel Pepys: The Man in the Making*, republished by Messrs Collins last year, I covered the crowded and familiar background of the Diary years. What I had not envisaged when I began my work was that the material for the remaining thirty-three years of Pepys' life would prove, not less, but more extensive. Instead of being able to complete his biography in two volumes it has taken me three to carry the story as far as 1689, with a further and final volume still to come.

When I began work on the post-Diary period, almost all that was known of the second half of Pepys' life was contained in Dr Tanner's three volumes of correspondence from the Pepys-Cockerell archives, in his five published volumes of naval papers from Magdalene College, Cambridge, and in Dr R. G. Howarth's *Letters and the Second Diary of Samuel Pepys*, embodying the earlier publications of the Rev. J. Smith and Lord Braybrooke. For the fourteen years covered by this volume the unknown material has far exceeded the known. The greater part of it has come from Pepys' unsorted papers which after his death, instead of going to Magdalene College, passed into private hands and were ultimately bequeathed to the Bodleian Library by the eighteenth-century collector, Dr Richard Rawlinson. Their bulk and anarchical arrangement or rather lack of arrangement – in contrast to the perfect order of Pepys' Magdalene College manuscripts – explains why the details of the extraordinary and dramatic story of Pepys' part in the so-called Popish Plot remained so long unknown. Piecing together from these papers the tale of his duel with Shaftesbury and the gangster, Scott, was like tracing the story of an undetected crime from clue to clue. In pursuit of it I was enabled to discover, among Pepys' bound papers in Magdalene College, new and hitherto unknown Pepysian journals or diaries, one written by himself and the other by a member of Scott's gang at his instance. Both have been used in this book.

Since the latter was first published in 1935 much that it describes, then remote from our age, has become familiar to us. A great city in ruins and devastated by fire, a society living in suspicion and fear, men beaten up and tortured for their political opinions, the use of mob incitement, faked evidence and partisan denunciation under the forms of law are phenomena with which we have all grown a great deal more familiar than we used to be. The strange story contained in the second half of this book may seem, therefore, a little less strange today than it did in 1935.

ARTHUR BRYANT

Rapsgate
January 1948

Introduction
The Mid-Restoration Scene

The London to which Pepys returned from his foreign holiday in the autumn of 1669 and on which three weeks later his wife was to close her eyes for the last time was the London that men were rebuilding after the Fire. Already in that dismal desert of calcined stone and ashes, where over thirteen thousand houses had been burnt, innumerable islands of scaffolding were rising from the rubble lines of the familiar streets. Yet a man could still stand in Cheapside and gaze through bare ruins at the boats on the River and the wooded Surrey slopes beyond. Everywhere were wastes, dotted with wretched huts and cabins of board and canvas and gaunt skeletons of burnt churches. Over all towered the open roof and glassless windows of old St Paul's, its beautiful portico rent in pieces.

This devastated area, into which the Londoner passed as he came out of the populous streets of Tower Hill or left the prosperous western faubourgs at Temple Bar, was the keynote of more than a decade of English history. It was the perpetual reminder of all that England had suffered within the memory of man – of Plague, Fire and the shameful sound of Dutch guns on the Medway. To the plain citizen it spelt a legend of nightmarish fears, of Popes and red Cardinals, Priests and foreign dragoons threatening stake, massacre and wooden shoes to the free Protestant people of old England. And when a new city of warm-coloured brick and pleasant, ordered streets had banished the ruins, the legend persisted. On the wall of the house in Pudding Lane that arose on the site where the Fire began, the Lord Mayor of the most bigoted city in the world inscribed the words:

Here by the permission of Heaven Hell broke loose upon this Protestant City from the malicious hearts of barbarous papists.

The words epitomized the political feelings of a generation.

No man can understand that generation or the difficulty of ruling it who does not understand its fears. Popery was the bugbear with which English children were brought up by their mothers and nurses; it was a terror they never outgrew. They learnt their religion from the crude woodcuts of Protestants burning at the stake in Foxe's *Book of Martyrs* and their history from tales of the Massacre of St Bartholomew, Gunpowder Plot and the Irish Rebellion of '41. The Great Fire of 1666 was to them a further page in that bloodstained mythology, and the next – some gruesome Popish Plot of assassination, midnight massacre and invasion – might be turned by a devilish hand at any moment.

The Princes who ruled over this people did not share their fears. King Charles II and his brother, James, were the children of a French Catholic princess and of an Anglican King of exceptional tolerance. In their exiled youth they had enjoyed for many years the hospitality of the two great Catholic powers, France and Spain, and had received from their own Catholic subjects the most conspicuous loyalty: to the latter King Charles owed his life. They could, therefore, feel little hostility towards the professors of a Faith in which all but two of their own ancestors had been bred. Yet their people expected them to hate Catholics as they did themselves and to enforce the brutal laws against them that disgraced the Statute book. When they showed reluctance to do so, they were themselves suspected of Popery. James, Duke of York, in the obstinacy of his proud nature, became first a concealed and then an open Catholic; his brother the King, a thousand times more shrewd and cunning, tried for ten years to introduce a national scheme of toleration and, when his angry subjects refused it, turned to a secret alliance with his cousin of France to provide it.

Yet the France, which Pepys visited in 1669 with such delight and wonder and with whose King his master a few months later concluded the Secret Treaty of Dover, was becoming a terror to the ordinary Englishman second only to Popery. The feeling was a new one: for a century past France had been the traditional friend of England, and even the Puritan champion, Cromwell, had followed the policy of Elizabeth and sought her alliance. But with the manhood of Louis XIV the whole scene had changed. His boundless ambition, his autocratic ideals of government and the growing bigotry of his Catholicism struck at the deepest political feelings of the English – at their jealousy of foreigners, their hatred of despotism and their fear of Popery. And by threatening the Low Countries and starting to build a great Navy he wounded these feelings still deeper.

For that freedom of the trade of the narrow seas on which England had always depended for her principal source of wealth was jeopardized. In the past the very extent of that trade had been its own protection; till the days of Elizabeth the merchants of England had only to man and gun their ships to defend them. But the seventeenth century had seen the specialization of the fighting ship, and no merchantman, however large, could any longer hold her place in the line of battle. In the last resort the Royal Navy could alone defend the nation's trade. And the same century saw the creation, first by Holland then by France, of two rival Navies, occupying the whole opposing coastline of those narrow seas through which England's trade passed. To fight the Dutch at sea, the arbitrary and all-powerful government of the Commonwealth had taxed England to the bone, and the royal administration of the Restoration, dependent on a close-pursed and suspicious Parliament, had brought itself to the verge of bankruptcy. Yet the Dutch Navy remained, a standing menace to Britain's trade, and now a French Navy of equal or greater strength was fast growing up.

Here also King Charles was at variance with his people. To his clear, practical mind, backed by a knowledge both of Europe and the Navy greater than that of any of his Ministers, the immediate need of England was to destroy Holland. The sea power of France, whatever it might become in the future, was still only a gigantic shadow, for the French lacked the practical skill in seamanship of his own people and the Dutch. That France was Catholic and French did not disturb him for, unlike his subjects, he objected to neither of these attributes. Nor did he feel any jealousy of French ambitions on land, so long as he was free to pursue his own by sea. For beneath his easy, pleasure-loving exterior, Charles was quite as much an imperialist as his great predecessor. Trade and all that belonged to it – and that included colonies – he perceived to be the essential need of a commercial people. In his reign the real foundations of the British Empire were laid. And behind the Secret Treaty of Dover lay not, what his subjects came to suppose, the Catholicization of England by a foreign army, but a scheme even wilder and more grandiose, the partition of the Dutch and Spanish Empires and the cession of their vast overseas dominions to the English Crown.

But these imperial schemes – and more than Charles yet realized – were dominated by the realities of the English domestic situation.

A rough people, accustomed to governing themselves both in their parliaments and in their local communities, absorbed in their own affairs, and invincibly suspicious of new ideas, was committed to the rule of one of the quickest and most original minds in Europe, already suspect to them on account of religion. From the time of Clarendon's fall in 1667, when the King took over the real government of the country, until the final years of his reign, when steed and rider had learnt to respect each other's mettle, a duel of wit against brute force was waged between ruler and ruled. In that duel it was Pepys' lot to play an important and at times far from comfortable part.

The duel was intensified by the anachronisms of the English administrative and financial system. The innate conservatism of the race had preserved the ancient machinery of government long after the social and economic structure which it had served had passed away. The Crown, as in the Middle Ages, was still expected to maintain the essential services of government out of its semi-private, hereditary income. These services having grown out of all measure with the development of the nation, and their expenses with the fall in the value of money, this was no longer possible. But the theory and the popular expectation survived. The extra grants with which Parliament built up the royal revenue were voted grudgingly and in the teeth of faction,. and seemed to the general public wildly extravagant. In point of fact they were nearly always inadequate. During the first twelve years of the reign the ordinary revenue of the government was some 25 per cent. less than the annual sum which Parliament itself had estimated as necessary to maintain the administration. In war time the disproportion between necessary expenditure and supply was far greater. Debt, delayed payments, crazy credit and exorbitant interest were consequently the familiar burdens of English state officials.

To this must be added the fact that the growth in the national services and their necessary expenditure had proved altogether too much for the elementary public morality of the people. The government departments, particularly in their lower branches, were by modern standards inconceivably corrupt. The Crown, to which all paid exaggerated lip-service, was regarded as fair game for every kind of cheat and theft. Its servants stole the very cordage and canvas off the King's ships and sold them back to the Dockyards as new. The wastage in this way was incalculable. Moreover, it was almost impossible to prevent. What system of check there was in the departments was nullified by the fact that the salaries of most officials were years in arrears. His Majesty's property was perpetually and mysteriously passing into the possession of his subjects, a possession which it was almost impossible to make them relinquish. And public opinion was solidly on the side of the cheater. When an honest Dockyard Official visited the blacksmith's shop at Cawsham to seize on eight iron bolts stolen from the royal stores, he was beaten on the head and imprisoned by the villagers. As there was no police force, and as the King's attempts to maintain a standing army met with the fiercest disapproval, public administration in the later seventeenth century presented ceaseless difficulties. They were most marked in the Navy where Pepys' lot was cast, and which was by far the greatest of the spending departments.

All this provided constant matter for criticism from a Parliament of high-spirited and active country gentlemen, whose principal constitutional duty besides the provision of supply was the redress, by petition or legislation, of grievances. These last they found everywhere and advertised roundly. A committee of five hundred, divorced from executive responsibility and assembled to criticize, could scarcely fail to be factious.

There remain the actors for whom this stage was set. The society that was the apex of Restoration England has since become a byword for vice and cynical wit. Yet it is doubtful whether it was more vicious in practice than any other exclusive and privileged society; those born above the fear of poverty, punishment and criticism are seldom restrained in their moral behaviour. Where Restoration society was peculiar was in its unblushing acceptance of unmoral conduct, where distinguished in its very real intellectual capacity. Men who could write poems like Rochester and Buckhurst and plays and letters like Etherege and Harry Savile were no mere debauchees. Uniting the whole society of the Court and capital ran the live wire of an alert and enquiring mental virility: there was mind in it. One June day in 1669, the profligate Duke of Buckingham, the merchant John Clayton, Christopher Wren and Edmund Waller, the poet, rode up to London from Denham; they stopped to dine at Uxbridge, where, Clayton wrote, was 'nothing but quintessence of wit and most excellent discourse'. On the fringes of that society stood virtuosos like Pepys and Evelyn, philosophers like Boyle and mighty artists like Dryden and Purcell. It laid the foundations of the eighteenth century, paved the way for toleration, revolutionized taste and manners, and left behind it St Paul's, the *Principia* and the Royal Society. Yet to the nation as a whole, slow moving and traditionalist in its rustic part, Puritan in its urban, and suspicious in both, that venturesome and enquiring society was suspect from the start.

Over it, giving it pattern and unity, presided the King. He was a wit, a virtuoso and a man of affairs, and had one of the keenest minds that ever informed a throne. His morals and his shameless parade of them were at one with his Court, and his middle-class subjects, though their own coarseness of speech and habit little entitled them to cast stones at the former (which they none the less did), felt the reproach of the latter very keenly. The wits and libellers, who were mostly like Rochester of the same moral ilk as the King himself, made great play of this public feeling of reprobation –

> Most say the steed's a goodly thing,
> But all agree 'tis a lewd king –

while restless politicians used the expense of the royal mistresses* and bastards (for Charles was unusually generous to those who shared his favourite sins) as arguments for withholding supplies from his government. They failed to point out that these living witnesses of the royal indulgence, however irregular they might appear, were less expensive than would have been the normal brood of princes and princesses of the Blood Royal had the King been blessed with children.

But he was not, and herein lay the crux of the politics of the rest of the reign. By his side stood a childless Queen and a Papist successor. Already a suspected, and soon to be a professed Catholic, James,

---

* This exaggeration has been more than maintained by nineteenth- and twentieth-century historians. A classic example is that of the editor of certain official accounts published by a learned Society, who lumped all the sums paid to one of the royal mistresses over a period of many years and calmly announced in his preface that the total so obtained was an annual sum paid to the lady – an error in elementary mathematics cheerfully copied by a whole generation of historians who read the preface but never examined the figures. A more ingenuous and therefore less misleading example is to be found in the Preface of a recent volume of the Navy Records Society.

Duke of York was the chief liability of the government. To his unfortunate predilection in religion – and in the existing state of public opinion nothing could have been more unfortunate – he added the defects of his character. For where Charles was shrewd, pliant and good-humoured, James was obtuse, obstinate and morose. Those who opposed his views he regarded as evil men rooted in wickedness to be punished whenever the chance should offer. As an administrator he was capable, honest and industrious – virtues rare in the administration of the age that won him Pepys' unswerving admiration and loyalty. As a military and naval commander he had proved himself a brave man and had enjoyed a considerable measure of success. But as a politician he was beneath contempt, for he could never understand the motives or anticipate the actions of others. To most men he seemed a sinister and dangerous figure, threatening the future religion and liberty of the nation; to some who knew him intimately like Buckingham and his brilliant lieutenant, Ashley, he was a fool as well, – 'Ninny', the great 'oof, whom a ridiculous Providence had placed in the succession of the English throne.

As the King would neither divorce his Queen nor tamper with the lawful succession – and in this whatever his own inclinations and their political desires of the moment might be, he proved himself in the long run at one with the enduring instincts of the majority of his subjects – the Opposition to the government tended to centre round those who were determined at all costs to achieve James' removal.

That Opposition was comprised of many elements – of old republicans who remembered the great days of Cromwell and of new ones who fancied their own chances of ambition or revenge in the melting pot of Civil War and Revolution, of the whole Nonconformist community who, though frequently offered a friendly hand by their tolerant sovereign, were oppressed by the Anglican majority, of the sons of ruined Cavaliers who felt that the Crown had betrayed them because it had been unable to restore their fathers' broken fortunes, of the unco' guid who hated the vices and pleasures of the Court, of restless politicians and independent country gentlemen who could not brook any government, and of all restless, mutinous, dissatisfied spirits. Behind them stood the general body of the nation who feared Popery, hated tyranny and liked to avoid taxation.

In 1669 the great man who was to lead this incongruous alliance, give it unity and forge it in the heat of his own fiery spirit into a potent weapon that all but destroyed the ancient throne, was still on the side of the government. Anthony Ashley Cooper, first Lord Ashley, was at 48 one of the inner Cabal who in popular estimation controlled the policy of the Crown. Soon he was to be Earl of Shaftesbury and Lord Chancellor of England. Yet already, like his ally Buckingham, he was in alliance with the strongest of the diverse elements that comprised the Opposition – the Nonconformists by whose side he had stood in the old days of Civil War and Interregnum.

An oligarch by birth and temperament – a Venetian of the Venetians – 'the great little Lord' was the true founder of the Whig party. Under popular forms he was consistent throughout his career in extending the privileges and freedom of his class for whose vigorous virtues and talents he had a genuine enthusiasm.* Like his predecessor, 'King' Pym, he knew how to rouse the mob and appeal by rough *bonhomie* or pious phrase, as occasion demanded, to honest Smug the joiner and Mr Precisian, the Puritan merchant. Yet in his own Dorset he enclosed commons and rode roughshod over the rights of his poorer neighbours, while his facility with women was only equalled by that of his sovereign.† One of the most familiar figures of the London underworld was an old deformed knight, who was popularly known as Lord Shaftesbury's groom because he was always watering his Lordship's mares in Hyde Park on Rhenish wine and sugar, with not seldom a bait of chocolate. Yet this was the man who aligned under his banner the persecuted saints of the Nonconformist churches and the high republican zealots. A free-thinker himself, the friend of Locke and Marvell, the 'little limping peer' understood better than anyone living how to fan to cruel fanaticism the simple faith and credulity of his age.

On all he did rested the light of genius. From his very suffering – for the last twenty-four years of life he endured the constant pain of a suppurating internal cyst – he distilled acid that could dissolve the bonds of state and

* See his wonderful description of old Squire Hastings of Woodlands in his fragment of autobiography.

† 'Here comes', Charles is reputed to have said in the hearing of Shaftesbury as he passed before him with mace and seal, 'the greatest whoremaster in England.' 'Of a subject, sire,' the Earl replied.

cast the kingdoms old
into another mould.

And to the crazy tune his curled and fastidious lips piped, England, and Mr Pepys with her, were soon to dance.

1

The Second Diary

'And, therefore, resolve, from this time forward, to have it kept by my people in longhand, and must therefore be contented to set down no more than is fit for them and all the world to know.' *Diary*, May 31st, 1669.

On Wednesday, November 10th, 1669, Mrs Pepys lay dead in the comely house in Seething Lane which she and her husband had lived in and loved for nine crowded years. But, though half his heart lay buried for ever with the beautiful, jealous, foolish creature to whom he had given it, Samuel had little leisure to mourn her. Even before her body could be laid in earth beneath the stones of the church across the street and her virtues commemorated in his own flowing Latin on the wall facing the gallery where she had once sat so proudly beside him, he was writing as even he had never written. For almost on the day of his return he had been called upon to face the most serious attack he had known on his work and office.[1]

While Samuel Pepys and his 'dear and virtuous lady' had been spending their two happy, crowded months of sightseeing in France and Flanders, the Duke of Buckingham and the politicians who followed in his erratic train had been pressing home their intrigue against the Heir Presumptive and the more sober servants of the Crown, whose influence on the King they resented and whose offices they coveted. The key objective of their attack was the Navy Office, through whose misdeeds they hoped to bring down Lord Sandwich and the Duke. And the Navy Office was an easy target, for in the public eye it was associated with the humiliation of the Medway and the supposed misappropriation of the monies voted for the Dutch Wars.[2]

But there was one obstacle against which the attackers had to contend – the knowledge, ability and tenacity of the Clerk of the Acts. In nine years the junior of the seven Principal Officers and Commissioners, who had taken over the administration of the Navy at the Restoration, had by industry and force of character made his position the most important in the Service. During his absence in France his colleagues had staved off the enquiries of the Parliamentary Commissioners of Accounts, who for the past two years had been investigating the miscarriages of the war, by replying that nothing could be done till his return. Nor could it, for of those who had been in office with him during the War, none but the dilettante mathematician and courtier Lord Brouncker, and the senile Comptroller, Sir John Mennes, remained. Pepys alone could meet the storm that was threatening the Navy.[3]

Therefore, as soon as he got back to England, he sat down, without even consulting his colleagues, to draft a reply to the Commissioners' charges. There was no time to be lost, for the longer their accusations remained unanswered, the more assured country and Parliament would be of their truth. The election, which he had formerly sought with such eagerness at Aldeburgh, he relinquished without even the intervention of a personal canvass. For the very essentials of his existence were threatened, and every moment of his time was needed. Within little over a month from his return and only a fortnight after Elizabeth's death, his Answer was completed.[4]

It was a magnificent achievement. The Commissioners of Accounts had collected their accusations under eighteen heads – 'a parcel of observations', as Pepys contemptuously described them – charging the Navy Office among other sins and omissions with failure to supervise subordinate officers, corrupt purchase of goods at excessive prices and favouritism to contractors. In a document of fifty folio sheets Pepys replied with clear categorical answers that are masterpieces of administrative argument. That there had been breaches of duty by subordinate officers, he admitted, but contended that their superiors could only be charged with what it was within human power to prevent. 'For what concerns the Storekeepers not observing any order of time in their entries of provisions received', he added with biting sarcasm, 'give me leave to observe that the Officers of the Navy being incapable as a body to be present at the delivery of all stores, a particular officer is appointed by his Majesty and the Lord High Admiral by the title of Clerk of the Cheque. If', he added, 'your Lordships' meaning ... differ not from what the plain construction of the terms they here run in seems to discover, I beg I may without offence confess my present inability to discern the cogency of the said conclusions.'* And in the same grimly efficient

---

* *Pepysian MS.* No. 2554.

manner Pepys dealt with the charge that the Navy Office had bought goods at excessive prices: thanks to Parliamentary parsimony the goods had had to be obtained on credit at more than the market price or not at all, each vendor, as he said, being 'resolved to save himself in the uncertainty of his payments by the greatness of his price'.[5]

The graver charge of direct corruption Pepys met with that proud and unyielding scorn which he always reserved for such impertinences. The Officers of the Navy, he declared, could challenge the whole world to prove one instance of their ordering payment for the smallest parcel of unserviceable goods which had not been certified as fit by the officer responsible. Whatever fault there may have been in port or dock, the Navy Office was above reproach. Such was the tenor of Pepys' defence, and so closely was it argued and so amply supported by extracts from past instructions and contracts – 'not neglecting therein', he informed his inquisitors, 'the faithfullest helps I could obtain from memory, papers or books,' – that the Commissioners were left with no other choice but that of being proved either knaves or fools.

Pepys could scarcely have chosen a surer way of making enemies. Already there was a widespread feeling that the self-important, bright-eyed little man, who displayed so many treasures in his house in Seething Lane and drove abroad in a gilded coach with fine black horses, had not grown prosperous merely by upright conduct. It was not without significance that the name of Sir William Warren, the great timber merchant to whom six years before he had given his first government contract, figured so frequently in the Commissioners' charges. Nor, perhaps, had Pepys himself forgotten that among the plate, which he loved to show his guests, were the fair state dish and cup of silver, engraved with his arms, which Sir William had sent him one February morning in a box of gloves addressed to Elizabeth – 'a very noble present,' it then had seemed, 'and the best I ever had yet'. That was long ago, and he was conscious that he had not done any ill thing to deserve it. None the less he had taken office a poor man, with only £150 to his name, and now, nine years later, he cannot have been worth much less than £10,000 – a sum at least five times as much in the money of to-day.[6]

But Pepys was no longer afraid. A year before, when threatened with attack, he had contemplated resignation, now his defence had become counter-attack. A fine and stinging irony ran through his Answer to the politicians who had libelled him and his Office. He had drunk of a bitter cup and had grown bolder. Probably at no time in his cautious and far-seeing career did he write with greater scorn for material consequences.

On Thursday, November 25th, seeing that his Answer, then almost finished, was good, Pepys gave warning to the Commissioners of its early arrival – 'on Saturday or Monday morning next at the furthest' – and explained the motives which had caused him, *ex officio*, to take upon his shoulders the defence, not of himself alone, but of the whole Office. Nor did he fail, with effect damning in its restraint, to stress the difficulties under which he had laboured, telling them how he had answered their litany of complaints not only while the other parts of his Majesty's service called for his daily attendance, but during 'the sorrowful interruption lately given me by the sickness and death of my wife'.

He was as good as his word, for on the Saturday his task was done. In a further long letter to the Commissioners he explained in his stateliest language how he had made it his care 'to consider by what expedient your Lordships might (without delay) receive a competent view of the satisfaction to be expected from the Officers of the Navy, without prejudice to what answers more perfect you may hereafter ... be offered by the said Officers' – though this, being better acquainted with them than the Commissioners, he must have known would be never. And on Monday, having read his Answer over in turn to the Duke of York, Lord Brouncker, and his former patron Sir William Coventry, whose advice he had taken throughout the whole troublesome business, he took a fair copy of it to Brooke House in Holborn, where the Commission sat, and left it with the Clerk and his honest old acquaintance, Will Symons, with whom in the days when they were both young government employees he had been wont to drink at Harper's.[7]

Meanwhile to his annoyance Pepys had discovered that another of his colleagues had written a paper, full not with details of the Navy Board's past conduct but with vague criticisms of its present constitution. The culprit was Lord Brouncker, the virtuoso who presided over the infant Royal Society and whose neighbouring company and that of his mistress, Lady Williams, Pepys sometimes shared of an evening. During his absence abroad Brouncker had

secretly employed Pepys' favourite clerk, Richard Gibson, to write
down his views on the government of the Navy, and had subsequently conveyed them through his scientific friend, Sir Robert
Moray, to the King. This was the kind of thing which was always
disturbing the flow of routine under the old system of personal rule,
and, though sometimes for good ends he practised it himself, it never
failed to arouse Pepys' fury. To Brouncker, caught out in his little
attempt to procure favour for himself at Court, he administered an
unanswerable rebuke. It was eight years since he had first begun to
assert his official rights against Sir William Penn and Batten, and he
had no intention of allowing a man with half his experience and a
tenth of his industry to cheat him of his clear right of viewing every
document that issued from his Office. And in dealing with his
colleague, he gave a far homelier account of his Department's
activities than that with which he confronted the Commissioners of
Accounts. He was no enemy, he told him, to that great work of
regulating the Office but, he added, 'your Lordship cannot be less
sensible than myself that the past and present failures of this Office
are not so much chargeable on the defects of its theory as the
infirmities of the hands entrusted with the practise thereof'. The
dirty linen which he would not wash in public, he pressed firmly and
irresistibly to Lord Brouncker's nose.

It was not in that nobleman's easy nature to be angry for long nor
in Pepys' to press home an advantage so easily won. The two soon
forgot their differences in their alliance against a common foe. Here
there was no question of Pepys' right to lead and initiate: none of his
colleagues had any desire to deprive him of that. On his ready
shoulders not they only, but greater ones, laid in haste the burden of
their defence.[8]

During the second week of December the House of Commons
called for the Report of the Committee of Public Accounts, and,
urged on by Buckingham's lieutenants, fell 'with exceeding great
fury and severity' on Sir George Carteret. Though to the few who
troubled to study the evidence there did not appear to be any real
grounds against Sir George, the Commissioners' insinuations
enabled his enemies to carry a vote for his suspension from the
House.

To save him the King prorogued Parliament till February. Six
days later, he announced that, as he had received a specific Report

against the Navy Office, he would himself hear both sides, and would start with the examination of Carteret's case at the Council Board on the following Monday.

To this Pepys was summoned in person. Thus mercifully the first Christmas after Elizabeth's death was charged with excitement. And as day followed day in the gilded Council Chamber, the Clerk of the Acts managed to make himself as acceptable to his royal master as he made himself unpopular with the critics of his government. The tall dark King, who six months before had spoken kindly to him and expressed such concern for the recovery of his eyes, was amused to hear the little official, whose ability he had already apprised, contradicting the pompous Commissioners and answering their vague generalizations with a mass of detailed facts, which apparently he had at will in his head or drew on from the well-kept books of memoranda at his side. The Cheshire magnate who was wont to preside over the proceedings of Brooke House with all the bucolic omnipotence of a Chairman of Quarter Sessions,* was only restrained from violent courses by the royal presence. 'When the Lord Brereton', Pepys recorded, 'did once or twice take occasion to stop me in my discourses I ever replied that what I was doing was in obedience to the King's command, and therein appealing to his Majesty, he did always answer for me to my Lord Brereton that he had called upon me to speak and thereupon commanded me to proceed.'[9]

For once again Pepys was keeping a journal. Six months before, when his fears for his eyes had made him close his shorthand diary, he had recorded his resolve to have it kept henceforward by his clerks in longhand, setting down in it no more than was fit for them and all the world to know, and should there be anything else of a more private nature (which, at that moment of depression, he felt unlikely), adding a shorthand note in his own hand in the margin. Now for two months he kept a detailed journal of his defence of the Navy Office before the King and Council. The fair copy of it, written in a clerk's hand, covers a hundred and twenty folio pages of one of

---

* Pepys' old friend, Captain Ferrers, attending the Committee on Lord Sandwich's behalf a few months before, described the Chairman as opening his examinations 'after two or three lofty looks and wallowings in his Chair' with a 'Sir, you are one of my Lord's Gentlemen.' *Hinchingbroke MSS., Sandwich Journal* X, 38 *et seq.*

the Miscellany volumes of his library.* Its value lies in the fact that
it supplies the one thing lacking in the great Diary, which stops at
the moment when Pepys first began to become a figure of national
importance. It provides a record of his association with the King
and the chief men of his day. On its far smaller scale it is almost as
important a political document as its predecessor is a social one.[10]

The new year of 1670 opens with Pepys, as mirrored in this all too
brief journal, in daily contact with the great. On January 3rd he was
asked by Sir George Downing to draw up an answer to the now
universally believed accusation that over half a million voted by
Parliament for the Dutch War had been diverted to other ends. It
was a sign that the King had recognized his outstanding ability, for
the defence of the general financial conduct of the Crown was far
above the ordinary scope of a Clerk of the Acts. On the same day in
consultation with Carteret and the chief Treasury Officials Pepys
ran over the detailed particulars, taking minutes of them and
secretly wondering to find a business of this magnitude so little
studied and understood.†

Next morning, having spent the night in mastering his brief, he
was conducted from the Treasury into the King's presence. Here the
greatest men in the country were assembled – the Duke of York, the
Lord Keeper, the Duke of Ormonde and both Secretaries of State.
After a long discussion as to how the matter should be managed, the
King concluded by laying the conduct of it on Pepys.

But in the Council Chamber there was an anticlimax. For none of
the Commissioners of Accounts appeared but old Lord Brereton,
who announced that their chief authority on naval matters, a
Boanerges named Colonel Thomson who was always harping on the
administrative virtues of the Commonwealth days when he himself

* 'A Journal of what passed between the Commissioners of Accounts and myself at
the Council Board.' It was first mentioned by the late Dr J. R. Tanner in the first
volume of his *Descriptive Catalogue of the Naval Manuscripts in the Pepysian Library*
published in 1903 and again in his *Bibliotheca Pepysiana*. But, though Dr Tanner
discusses at length Pepys' preliminary letters to the Committee, the King and the
Duke of York, contained in *Pepysian MSS.* 2554, he does not appear to have examined
closely the contents of the Diary itself. *Pepysian MSS.* 2874, *Miscellanies* VI, 387 *et seq.*

† Dr. W. A. Shaw in his Introductions to his Calendars of the Treasury Books has
revealed how much of the misunderstanding of this period has been due to the
confused and illogical system of accountancy then in use, which has concealed from
historians the gross exaggerations in the charges of extravagance and corruption
brought against the government of Charles II by his political opponents.

had held a lucrative but not very distinguished employment at the Admiralty, had been taken ill and had gone home. The rest of them, his Lordship explained, relied for their naval knowledge entirely on the far back and now almost legendary experiences of the Colonel. The Council therefore adjourned till next day.

The Colonel having by then overcome his indisposition, the King opened the proceedings by observing that though the Commissioners had admitted in one of their private papers that the disputed £514,000 had been laid out on the Navy, their public Report to Parliament had merely stated that it had been used for other purposes than the War and so deluded the country into believing that it had been diverted, as Pepys, recording the scene, put it, 'to uses of pleasure or other private respects of his Majesty'. After their discomfiture had been still further increased by a reminder that they had also admitted that the King had not only spent the disputed £514,000 on the War but another £300,000 out of his private purse, Pepys was ordered to comment generally on their Report. This he did with damning effect, flatly contradicting them on two material points, one being their assumption that the War accounts could only be reckoned from September 1st, 1664. Money spent before that date in fitting out the Fleet, Pepys pointed out, was just as much expended on the War as that incurred later. At this Lord Brereton could not contain himself, observing that he wondered that any single Officer of the Navy should dare to take it upon himself to construe an Act of Parliament contrary to the judgment of the Commissioners appointed by that Act. But Pepys' new-found boldness was not to be snuffed out. 'I replied', he recorded proudly, 'that I looked upon this Act like all other statutes penned for the information and therefore to the understanding of every commoner, and that therefore as an Englishman and as one of the principals concerned therein I did challenge a right of delivering my sense of it.'*

A little later, while Pepys was proving the illogicality of another assumption of the Commissioners, he was again stopped, Brereton furiously interposing that 'he did believe that the gentleman would not say what he had now said in another place. Which', Pepys notes in his Journal, 'being an insolence more reflective on the honour of

* *Pepysian MSS. 2874, Miscellanies VI, 390–1.*

his Majesty and that Board than myself, I silently suffered to pass, expecting that the King would have taken notice of it'.

But Charles II, being wiser than Pepys, refrained. None the less he was obviously delighted at his little champion's boldness, and afterwards, while he dined, called him his Advocate and made much sport of Lord Brereton's manner and of his eight brethren's dismay at being corrected in the construction of their own lesson. And when at dinner next day Pepys, who on waking had felt a little abashed at his own temerity, craved the royal pardon for his overbold performance, his Majesty replied that he had behaved to his perfect satisfaction, thanked him repeatedly for the trouble he had taken and expressed nothing but resentment at Lord Brereton's ill manners.

There then ensued a delicious scene, Pepys following up the conversation, as the King resumed his dinner, by humbly advising him (and here Pepys must be allowed to tell his own story) 'to consider by what ways . . . (if possible, which I expressed my doubt of and therein was seconded both by his Majesty and the rest) to rectify the opinions of the world occasioned by this Report of these gentlemen that his Majesty had employed to his private uses of pleasure etc., not only the £514,000 here mentioned but near £300,000 more in the monies applied to the Ordnance and Guards. Here my Lord Arlington took occasion to put his Majesty in mind of what (as he said) he had the last night advised his Majesty; viz: that his Majesty would please to cause the substance of this discourse to be put into writing, and that therefore, as he did believe that Mr Pepys was the best informed of any man to do his Majesty this service, so (he added) that though Mr Pepys was by, yet he should not refrain to say that his style was excellent and the fittest to perform this work; though he would have it recommended to him to study the laying it down with all possible plainness and with the least show of rhetoric that he could, which motion the King embraced and laid it upon me as a matter much importing him'.* It must have been a proud man who returned to the lonely house in Seething Lane that evening. But the delicate flattery of the King's old friend and Minister had not altogether quenched angry thoughts of the gentlemen of Brooke House. 'I went home', the day's entry

* *Miscellanies* VI, 392–3.

concluded, 'full of intentions to send a letter to my Lord Brereton testifying a due resentment of his yesterday's challenge in his Majesty's presence, . . . but upon second thoughts suspended it until I had seen further.'[11]

Having received a check in their attack on Carteret and the Crown, the Commissioners were forced to turn their attention to Pepys' Answer to their Observations, which till now they had contrived to ignore. On January 6th Pepys had followed it up by another Memorial, 'a particular defence', as he entitled it, 'of my own single conduct . . . in diligence of my attendance, effects of my performance and uprightness'. It was a tale of almost unbelievable righteousness, of 'integrity to my master and fair dealing towards those whom his service hath led me to have to do with', of defiance to 'the whole world to allege one instance to the prejudice of the same', of 'having the comfort of being able to affirm that my conscience in its strictest retrospections charges me not with any wilful declension of my duty'.* Its effect on the already infuriated Commissioners can be imagined.

Its interest to posterity lies in its allusion to the great Diary. 'Such', Pepys wrote, 'have ever been my apprehensions both of the duty and importance of my just attendance on his Majesty's service that among the many thousands under whose observation my employment must have placed me, I challenge any man to assign one day from my first admission to this service, in July 1660 to the determination of the War, August 1667, (being a complete apprenticeship), of which I am not at this day able upon oath to give an account of the particular manner of my employing the same.' 'No concernments', he went on, 'relating to my private fortune, pleasure or health did at any time (even under the terror of the plague itself) divide me one day and night from my attendance on the business of my place.' Otherwise, he might have, he went on, 'prevented that untimely ruin of my eyes by the constancy of their night service during the War which renders the remainder of my life of much less content or use to me than can be supplied by any other satisfaction than what flows from the consideration of that duty to his Majesty to which I sacrificed them . . . To which let me add that in my endeavours after a full performance of my duty, I have neither made

* *Pepysian MSS.* 2554.

distinction of days between those of rest and others, nor of hours between day and night, being less acquainted during the whole war with the closing of my day's work before midnight than after it'. There was, of course, no mention of Mrs Bagwell.

But there was a great deal about Pepys' own salary and the modesty of his emoluments. There had been an unpleasant reference in the Commissioners' Observations to private trading by Officers of the Navy, with mention of an item of £757. 17s. 5¾d. paid to the Clerk of the Acts in 1664 for flags and cork which he had traded to the Service. Though, Pepys asserted, the burden of his place was as great as that of his colleagues', and the inferiority of his wages to theirs due solely to the prospective value of its perquisites, he 'did never . . . directly or indirectly demand or express any expectation of fee, gratuity or reward from any person for any service therein by me done or to be done him'. And he ended with a daring lie: 'in exchange for ten years' service and these the most valuable of my life, I find not my estate at this day bettered by £1000 from all the profits, salary or other advantages arising from my said employment beyond what it was known to be at my admission thereto'.[12]

This document Pepys despatched to Brooke House on Friday, January 7th, by Will Griffen, the Navy Office messenger. He then went off to dine with Sir William Coventry, who was full of gloomy predictions of the kind of usage he must expect from the House of Commons for his contemptuous treatment of their Commissioners. 'Which', wrote Pepys, who that day was feeling a little weary of the whole affair, 'I without much trouble did embrace the thoughts of, as being much more willing to be at ease than hold my employment with so much trouble as I have of long done and must still look for, while yoked to persons who every day make work for future censure while I am upon tenters in their preservation from the blame due to their failures past.'*[13]

But melancholy thoughts of retirement did not prevent Pepys from spending the weekend inditing two magnificent letters to the King and Duke of York, dealing with the popular belief that the success of the First Dutch War had been due to the administrative qualities of thrift and method. 'So much the contrary', he explained, 'that whoever shall have opportunity of taking the same leisurely

* *Miscellanies* VI, 393.

view of the management of that time, which my employment under your Majesty has led me to, will easily concur that there appears not anything in the whole conduct of that age, to which (under God) their success can be more duly attributed than a steady pursuit of all means conducing thereto, both in preference and exclusion to all impediments arising from considerations either of Thrift or Method.'* In other words, the naval chiefs of the Commonwealth had been successful precisely because they broke all their own rules and spent money like water – the very things which Brooke House was declaring had been the ruin of the royal Navy.[14]

Before the next meeting of the Council on Monday morning Pepys, walking in St James' Park with the Duke of York, expressed a wish that Sir William Coventry, whom they had just passed in the Mall, might also take a part in the defence of the Navy Office, to which the Duke replied that it would be too much in all conscience to loose both of them at once on the unfortunate Commissioners. His Royal Highness was so pleased at his joke that he repeated it to Sir William himself when they met him at the next turn. But Coventry answered that he thought they were all safe enough in Pepys' hands. Then they went up to the royal Closet, where Pepys presented the King with a fair copy of his General Answer to the Commissioners' Observations and his Particular Answer relating to himself. He even managed to read out the letter which he had written on the previous day, 'desiring', he wrote, 'that his Majesty would be pleased not to look upon me as one asserting . . . there had been no failure in our management, for failures there had been. But that . . . the greatest of them would be found imputable to the age and weakness of a servant, by name Sir John Mennes, who besides the merit of having served his Royal Grandfather, Father and himself . . . was moreover one that would be found a gentleman of strictest integrity, and that his weakness of both mind and body had been hastened upon him by his labour in his Majesty's service'.† For Pepys had learnt to deal with princes with the same easy assurance that in time past had charmed the maids of Westminster Hall, and to display his loyalty to his doting old colleague the Comptroller, in the very breath that exposed his deficiencies. 'His Majesty was pleased to own with great kindness his well-liking of all I had done and said, and, directing me

---

* *Pepysian MSS.* 2554. S. Pepys to the King, Jan. 8th, 1670.
† *Miscellanies* VI, 393–4.

to act accordingly, he went forth' (one suspects, at his wonted large pace) 'and so to the Council Chamber.'

For old Mennes' drivelling incompetence was as great a handicap to Pepys as ever. Two days later, at a special examination of the Navy Officers at Brooke House, his senile eagerness to justify himself had proved a great embarrassment, for when the Commissioners enquired in whose hands the despatch of Warren's accounts lay, 'Sir John Mennes answered that it lay in his, and that he had taken much pains therein, and employed two of the ablest accountants in London about them, and that he had also made several objections long ago to the Account . . . and that he could never get Sir William Warren to satisfy him therein. And so was running on (God knows whither) when Sir William Turner' – brother-in-law to Pepys' cousin and old friend, Mrs Turner of Salisbury Court – 'desired that he might have a plain answer'. Even dictation did not always rob Pepys of his old style.[15]

On Monday, January 17th, the Council met again and Lord Brereton rose to prove the first of his eighteen Observations about improper contracts. After he had read a paper on Sir William Warren's contract for Gottenburg masts, Pepys took it upon himself to speak and did so at great length. Once more he drove Lord Brereton into a towering rage and caused a scene which ended in the Duke of York's rising to rebuke the old gentleman for unfit language. And when the Commissioners referred to the great charge the Crown had been put to provide a convoy to bring the masts home, the King reminded them (as everyone, including Pepys, had forgotten) that the convoy had been sent not only for his own goods but for those of his merchants who had specially asked for it.*

On every front Brooke House was routed. When Colonel Thomson ignorantly urged that there was more use for great masts than small, Pepys, appealing to Sir Jeremy Smyth as a seaman, 'ran him down so as to make him laughed at'. And when the Commissioners produced an Affidavit by Peter Pett that Warren's contract had clogged the stores with useless masts, he rose to complain of the injustice the King's Officers lay under, 'beyond any of his Majesty's

---

* 'Which answer was not only useful, but wholly new to me, and what Sir William Warren tells me is true.' Journal of what passed between 'the Commissioners of Accounts and myself at the Council Board'. *Pepysian MSS.* 2874, *Miscellanies* VI, 385–504. Jan. 17th, 1670.

servants triable in any other Court, where as Englishmen they have a right of confronting their accusers'. After which he trumped Brooke House's card by producing Pett's own signed certificate of the due performance of Warren's contract. The discomfiture of the Commissioners was again completed by the King, who, when it was being urged that Warren's rivals had been ready to supply the service with masts on cheaper terms, contributed the information that they had indeed been so but only upon condition that they might have secret leave to trade with the enemy. 'Which stroke from the King himself', Pepys notes, '(being new I confess to me as well as them, but very seasonable) struck them dumb.'[16]

In the next day's proceedings, which were unexpected, Pepys took no part. He had gone out early to see Du Vall the highwayman executed at Tyburn* and so missed a sudden summons to the Council table. But his reply on January 24th to the Commissioners' 3rd Observation was devastating. The crime they charged upon him and his colleagues, he observed, was their not doing 'what in no age was ever practised, what we could not have attempted to have done without unfaithfulness, and what in itself is impossible'. And once more the Commissioners had to listen to their sovereign's biting observations about people who made hasty judgments without hearing the defence, and about the liberty taken in every coffee-house to declare how much better things were done in the Navy in the late times, 'those pure Angelical times (saith the King), to which', the well-read Pepys interposed, 'I added those times concerning which people discourse in matters of the Navy as historians do of the primitive times in reference to the Church'.[17]

But just when Pepys' old tormentors seemed to be routed, there was a setback. At the last Council meeting in January the Commissioners presented a rambling paper about their misrepresentations which, though full of fair professions, made no real amends for the injustice they had done the government. Pepys, with his own paper in his hand, was all ready to annihilate them when, to his mortification, the Solicitor-General, Sir Heneage Finch, rose and delivered an eloquent and elaborate harangue, full of compliments to Brooke House and completely missing the point. 'I confess', wrote Samuel,

* Here lies Du Vall; Reader, if male thou art,
  Look to thy purse; if female, to thy heart!'
                                    Stone in Covent Garden Church.

'I was extremely sick of this day's passages and particularly the Solicitor's speech, blessing my fortune that happened not to begin the day, my discourse being likely to have been of a sense so much contrary.' Later when Lord Ashley moved that some further apology should be demanded, the timorous Finch merely shook his head and whispered that he did not think it expedient that the gentlemen should be teased with any ungrateful questions. The only consolation, before that barren meeting broke up, was that the great Ashley, now one of the inner Cabal who controlled the national destinies, leant over to Pepys and with an oath declared that he thought the Solicitor was mad.[18]

On February 1st, in his reply to the Commissioners' charge that the Navy Office had received goods without contract, Pepys ventured to embark on impromptu oratory without first reading his Reply. It was not a success, for he forgot several telling points, 'which inconvenience', he noted in his Diary, 'I must hereafter labour to prevent by reading always my written answer'. The King, however, was as usual a great standby, for when Pepys asked him what he would have said if the Navy Office had failed to provide the Fleet with some essential in an emergency merely for want of a formal contract, he 'answered readily and as happily as I could have wished that he would have said we deserved to be hanged'. The Clerk of the Acts, who, like many others, had once set his sovereign down as one who minded nothing but pleasure and hated the very sight and thought of business, was learning to revise his opinions.

The day's proceedings ended with a row. Old Colonel Thomson, apropos of nothing, broke into a sudden diatribe against the Navy Office for having used foreign plank to build ships, 'with some insultingness', Pepys noted tartly, 'that for his part he had served in the Navy and that he ever was and should still be for the good English plank. I replied that we had also served in the Navy as he, and were as much in love with English planks as he . . . and should give him thanks to direct us where, for a considerable advance of price, we might be furnished with 2000, or but 1000, or 500 loads at this day of English plank . . . With which his mouth seeming to be stopped',* the Council, one imagines thankfully, broke up.[19]

Nearly another week passed before on Monday, February 7th,

* *Miscellanies* VI, 452.

Pepys stood again in the presence of the King and Council. On this occasion he was able to score, a little irrelevantly, over his old foe, Thomson, by proving the complete falsehood over his boast that the Navy Office officials under the Commonwealth had had their parish dues and the cost of their stationery and candles paid by the State. He then read his reply to the Commissioners' 8th Observation, and launched forth on an interminable oration on the complicated business of balancing Storekeepers' Accounts.

In the end it became absolutely necessary to stop him, and this his sovereign, with much tact, did. 'The King', Pepys wrote happily that night, 'was so fully satisfied with the reason as to prevent any enlarging of mine thereon by taking it upon himself in his own vindication as well as ours (as he was pleased to call it) the giving a summary account of the success of our endeavours in the late War, which he was pleased to say was such as, but for the unhappy business of Chatham, we had no reason but to own to come up to the utmost of what was performed in the First Dutch War . . . and so of his own accord run over several instances of despatch given by this Board in the fitting forth and the refitting forth of the Fleet before and after fights always sooner than the enemy could do . . . To which I humbly took leave to offer the consideration of the difference between the charge which the late War is owned to have cost them and us.' But this financial exercise was not permitted, for again the King tactfully interposed and 'very readily took upon him also to speak to, by saying that he had made it his work to inform himself in the expense of the Dutch in the late War and finds it upon very good information to have amounted to eleven millions, whereas ours does not . . . exceed six'.[20]

On Saturday, February 12th, the debates waged round the 11th, 12th and 13th Observations and the question of payment by ticket. The day was not without the usual passages between Pepys and Lord Brereton. The latter plainly thought that at last he had got a trump card, for, observing that large numbers of seamen's tickets had been found entered as paid to the late Surveyor, Sir William Batten, who had been notoriously corrupt, he went on to insinuate that the same offence could be proved against other members of the Board. Upon which Pepys rose in his place and took the boldness, as he put it, 'to tell them that whatever they would have the world think as to others, I did desire the whole world to show me to have been concerned directly or indirectly in one ticket . . . At which', he continued, 'my Lord Brereton, with a look full of trouble and malignity, answering, "How, Mr Pepys, do you defy the whole world in this matter?", I replied, "Yes, that I do defy the whole world and my Lord Brereton in particular". At which I could perceive the whole Board shaken with the surprise thereof, and my Lord Brereton himself strook dumb'.[21]

The Council did not take the Commissioners' further charges into consideration until after the opening of Parliament. Before the next hearing on February 17th Pepys was four times warned, by Brouncker, by Mr Slingsby, by Lord Lauderdale and by the King himself, that Brereton had publicly given out that he was going to make good his challenge of proving that he had dealt in the purchase and sale of seamen's tickets. But it was not till February 21st, after Pepys had demolished Brooke House's 15th, 16th and 17th Observations, 'to the satisfaction of his Majesty and the total silence of those Commissioners', that Lord Brereton suddenly and dramatically produced a ticket for £7. 10s.* made out to one Capps of the *Lion* and bearing the ominous words – 'Paid to Mr Pepys'. The implication was that the dignified Clerk of the Acts had used his official position and the broken credit of the government to buy a ticket cheap off some poor seaman and then cashed it at its face value for himself. The offending slip of paper was offered in silence to the King and then to the Duke of York, after which the King handed it to Pepys. While he was examining it, Colonel Thomson observed that they would not have troubled his Majesty with such a trifle, had not Mr Pepys been so positive in his denial.

But Pepys continued passionately to deny all knowledge of the thing and to defy mankind to prove that this or any other ticket was ever paid him. 'It is not by any presumptuous guess but by a firm knowledge', he said, 'that I do take upon me to assert in defiance of the whole world my uninterestedness in anything of this matter, and doubt not . . . but I shall be able . . . to show the little truth lying in this. Which having said,' he recorded, 'the King with a smile and shake of his head told the Commissioners that he thought it a vain thing to believe that one having so great trust, and therein acting without any exception in matters of the greatest moment, should

---

* By some curious error the amount is stated to have been £9. 7s. in Pepys' letter to Anthony Stephens in his letter-book. See Tanner, *Further Correspondence*, 263.

descend to so poor a thing as the doing anything that was unfit for him in a matter of £7. 10s.' And there, for the moment, the matter ended.

The proceedings closed with Pepys' speech on the Commissioners' 18th and final Observation, in which he commented with scorn on the poor shabby proofs which were all they could bring to support the accusations of nearly two years. 'At this the King and the whole Board and all bystanders discovered by their murmur a disdainful resentment of those gentlemen's proceedings, and the King and Duke after their being up took notice of it in like manner publicly at supper as of a matter most enormous and oppressive.' Samuel in fact had crowned his earlier achievements against the unfortunate Commissioners by proving, in the most public manner possible, that they were not even gentlemen. There were some who never forgave him.[22]

He had no opportunity of clearing himself in public in the matter of John Capps' ticket, for the Council did not meet again, and after the adjournment of Parliament in April, the Brooke House Commission died a natural death. But he took the trouble to write to his old acquaintance, Anthony Stephens, Carteret's former clerk, telling him how during his defence of his office against the 'vanity, frowardness and injustice' of the Commissioners he had 'proved so happy as to leave his Majesty and my Lords of the Council under a satisfaction' too great for his accusers to admit of his going quiet away with, and how they had used his name to support their charge that a ticket had been paid to Pepys – 'a particular I knew most false'. And he asked Stephens for an immediate explanation, and in writing.[23]

So ended, as he called it long after, 'the ridiculous success of that terrible Commission to Brooke House' – on the one side in ridicule that left behind it a bitter sting and on the other by false legend that the lapse of two and a half centuries has not fully dissipated. So ended also Pepys' second, though not his last, diary. On March 3rd, the pressure of his labours relaxed, he wrote to his late agent at Aldeburgh to thank him for his help during his unsuccessful election and to apologize for not having written before; 'nothing but the sorrow and distraction I have been in by the death of my wife, increased by the suddenness with which it pleased God to surprise me therewith, after a voyage so full of health and content, could have forced me to so long a neglect of my private concernements'. For the support Captain Elliott had given him he was as grateful, he assured him, 'as if the business had succeeded to the best of our wishes'. As for those who had opposed him and so shown disrespect for his patrons, the Duke of York and Lord Howard, they would 'meet with a time of seeing their error therein'. It was a foolish threat to make in free and Protestant England, seeing that of his patrons one was a professed and the other, though Pepys did not yet know it, a secret Catholic. But, for the moment, this matter like others could rest, and there was time, and time to spare, to mourn Elizabeth.[24]

2

The Man Made

'Mens cujusque is est quisque.'
Pepys' motto.

The Samuel Pepys who gazed out over the roofs and treetops of
London that Spring was a different Samuel to the young clerk of ten
years before. What the outside world saw was a little, squat, dark
man,* incessantly busy, self-important with the additional and
slightly ludicrous dignity common in men of small stature, and, were
it not for the life and brightness of his eyes, decidedly ugly. Those
who were lazy were apt to find the Clerk of the Acts officious and
over-anxious to impress others with a sense of his own splendid
devotion to duty (and, as often as not, of their own neglect of it).
Refined folk, though they shared his tastes which were already
princely, and relished his company, which was entrancing, were
sometimes apt to think him pushing and even vulgar – the result,
doubtless, of his humble origin; he had once, it was rumoured,
carried the homely wares of his father, the tailor. And though he was
now at the age of thirty-seven the recognized driving force of the
Navy Office, Treasurer of Tangier, and a man of great influence and
authority with a house full of fine things and a banking balance at
Alderman Backwell's that ran into many thousands, Pepys' contemporaries had not altogether forgotten the lowly source from which he
sprang. In quiet ways they liked to remind him of it.

Yet nearly all those who knew him intimately liked and admired
him. It was not so much that he was industrious, true to his word, a
great outward respecter of virtue and the conventions, a loyal and
courageous upholder of his office and his colleagues. He was
magnificent company. No one in all that high-spirited England had
a greater zest for life or was more good-humoured, and the hard
struggle by which he had won and retained his place and dignities
had not left any alloy of bitterness or disillusionment. He loved

* 'I asked him what was that Mr Pepys; he said he was a low squat man.'
Information of Spackman, *Pepysian MSS., Mornamont* I, 38.

company and company loved him. And his admirers included most women. He was compact of vitality and eager to relish every experience, and had all the child's sense of enjoyment that prompts a woman to spoil a man. And almost as dear to the other sex, he loved things of good report: was discreet, honoured the respectabilities, and liked to see all around him neat and ordered.[1]

This was the surface: there were deeper waters beneath. To what are we to look for the core of the man? – and the answer must be to that intangible, illusive quality, character. It was bred of the sturdy Fen stock from which he came, nourished in his youth by the homely Puritan precepts and example of his parents, and developed by the constant friction of a powerful ambition on the rough surface of life and work. When he chose there was no limit to his capacity for labour, and he could work as quickly as he could persistently and doggedly. To put his great powers to their full stretch, he generally needed some special occasion: an attack on his office or honour or a shattered fleet crying to be refitted in the teeth of urgent time. Yet he had shown that he could force himself from idleness or pursuit of pleasure to a course of unbroken diligence with no other stimulus but the prick of conscience or ambition. This too he had found easier with the passage of time, and, whenever he achieved it, a source of happiness.[2]

For pleasure had often called him and at thirty-seven must call him again. He loved good food and wine and women – too well these, perhaps, for there was something pathological in his craving for the excitements of sex; – he was avid for every new sight and experience, full of inextinguishable curiosity and infinite capacity for being pleased. His mind delighted in curious speculations and problems, and he, who ten years before had eagerly contemplated 'a pretty trick to try whether a woman be a maid or no, by a string going round her head to meet at the end of her nose', could now show an equal zest for the learned propositions and wonders that tickled the intellectual palates of the Arundel House philosophers in whose company he was so proud to count himself. Mathematical propositions and mechanical instruments, the power of spirits to animate dead bodies, the intricate niceties of the Law, were all canvassed by that restless mind. And the soul moved with it. Beauty was with him an unconscious passion; when he looked at one of the stately palaces by the Thames side, it thrilled him to see 'the remains of the noble soul of the late Duke of Buckingham appearing in his house, in every place, in the doorcases and the windows'. Some of his descriptions of scenery are among the most moving things of their kind in our literature – the summer drive with his family on the Banstead Downs or the glow-worms shining in the fields under the walls of Tangier.[3]

His home was a treasure-house of seemly and beautiful things, and it was his taste, not Elizabeth's, for all her wifely zeal in sewing and fringing, that made it so, for it continued to grow in beauty after her death. Even now, after the lapse of two and a half centuries, the bindings of his books and the cases that house them reflect the spirit of the man who chose to have them so: there is nowhere, not even in the great Diary itself, that one can come so near to the heart of Pepys as in his little library at Magdalene. 'My delight', he once said, 'is in the neatness of everything, and so cannot be pleased with anything unless it be very neat.' It had to be beautiful, too, though with him, as with nearly all the great men of his age, beauty and order went hand in hand and were scarcely separable.[4]

He found their union most in music – a lover of harmony and music, John Evelyn once called him. 'Musique', he himself wrote, 'is the thing of the world that I love most.' No reader of the Diary is likely to forget the passage in which he described how the sweet sound of the wind music ravished his soul and made him afterwards feel physically sick as he had once been in the ecstasy of first love for his wife. He did not only love music, but understood its niceties; he was an accomplished and always happy performer on the flageolet, the lute and the bass viol; he had learnt the technical art of composition and had composed at least one excellent song, 'Beauty Retire', which is very much more than the dilettante achievement of an accomplished amateur. And he could sing it in a voice that gave his friends pleasure and himself more. The older he grew, the more Pepys loved and practised music. 'A science', he wrote of it in his last years, 'peculiarly productive of a pleasure that no state of life, public or private, secular or sacred; no difference of age or season; no temper of mind or condition of health exempt from present anguish; nor, lastly, distinction of quality, renders either improper, untimely or unentertaining.' He always found it so, and it was a happy gift of the gods that brought him a measure nearer the angels than he would otherwise have been.[5]

To some, perhaps, he seemed rather too near the angels – but they judged him by his public appearances, and not as we can and those who knew and loved him did, by his easier, less righteous moments of intimacy. After the manner of the Puritans among whom he had been brought up he was much given in his bilious hours to deploring the 'vanity and disorders of the age', and, what was a great deal more annoying, the more particular frailties of those of his contemporaries with whom he chanced to come into conflict. He possessed in a very peculiar degree the gift of making other people seem small. With this he combined an intensely irritating habit of calling attention to his own virtues, which partly arose out of an excessive sensitiveness to criticism, particularly to criticism in its most common terrestrial form, unjust criticism. And it also arose from a very real and ever-abiding sense of what he once described as 'God's great mercy to me, and His blessing upon my taking pains, and being punctual in my dealings'.[6]

For Pepys was both sensitive and self-confident – a paradoxical mixture of character not quite as uncommon as it seems and one that helps to explain the apparent discrepancies in his temperament. He could not bear to have people think or speak ill of him (though as time went on he grew more accustomed to it), was as eager to vindicate himself of every charge as a passionate child and had a wonderful and quite womanlike capacity for fretting and worrying. It was this that accounted for his occasional and rather petulant impatiences. Yet with all this he never doubted his capacity to achieve what he really set himself to attain; and he was perpetually choosing goals that would have daunted any other man. 'I thank God', he once wrote, 'I have always carried about me such a watchfulness and integrity as will support me . . . against anything that the Malice of Mankind can offer to my prejudice.' There were, perhaps naturally, some who thought him arrogant and a hypocrite. Yet they were usually of the baser sort.[7]

Under Pepys' outward arrogance was a gentleness of feeling towards others that may not have been bred in him, but which arose from his sensitiveness and grew with his always deeply felt experience of life. To those who were unassuming he was generous and even extravagant to give praise, and ready to admire in others virtues which he was then charmingly able to forget in himself. The jealous, self-assertive, bourgeois temperament that strangers saw in his worse moments and resented, was only a shell: fundamentally he was a gentleman in a sense that perhaps few men are. And he did not only wish that others should love him, but was capable of deep affection towards others. When he was far from his friends, he could not always keep back the tears when he thought of them; his experience, influence and industry were perpetually at their disposal, and his delight in their conversation and society constitutes one of the most moving features of his correspondence. Nothing could be more tender than his attitude towards those to whom he had given his trust and heart. They repaid it by an almost passionate affection and loyalty; to those who served and understood him, such as Will Hewer and Morelli and his clerk of later years, Lorrain, scarcely anything seemed too good for him. He was their adored master and all that they had was at his service.[8]

To his family and all those who had claims on him, like his old servants the Edwardses whose children he continued to befriend when their parents were dead, he was most loyal. It cannot always have been easy to be a careful, successful, fastidious man to own and take responsibility for the rather helpless and down-at-heels relations whom fate had chiefly bestowed upon Samuel Pepys. But he did so, and gave them love as well. Gratitude and loyalty, almost the rarest of human qualities, he was blessed with to a fortunate degree – fortunate to those to whom that gratitude and loyalty attached, but most fortunate of all to himself. In the whole of his life there is no record that he ever betrayed a trust.[9]

To others less dependent on him he could be very charitable. His correspondence is full, not only of references to the complaints of angry men, but of palpably sincere testimonies of the deeply felt thanks of grateful men. 'Honoured Sir and my worthy good friend,' wrote one of them, 'I thank God he hath given me discretion to be sensible of the kindness you have so frankly done me. I beseech the same God to make me capable (in some measure) to retribute the courtesy ... which I am fearful I shall never be able to requite. However, my wife and children and I am bound to praise God that hath sent us such a friend.'* Many another of his countrymen, and many a distressed foreigner (for whom he always had a tender place in his heart) shared the same grateful prayer. Most of all were the

* Capt. T. Guy to S. Pepys. Dec. 14th, 1670. *Rawl. MSS. A.* 174, f. 191.

ingenious and industrious sure of Pepys' charity, whether they were learned scholars or humble craftsmen. That it was sometimes a carefully modulated charity, no one can blame him, for the calls on his well-filled but not boundless purse were perpetual, and, as is always the case when such calls are answered, for ever increasing in number.[10]

Moderation, that classic quality, he learnt to practise with the years; for one as sensitive and passionate as he it was the one certain salve that life offered. Long ago, while still a lad, he had been struck by the beauty of Epictetus' rule – τῶν ὄντων τὰ μέν ἐστιν ἐφ' ἡμῖυ τὰ δὲ οὐκ ἐφ' ἡμῖν – a saying of great reason, he thought it, that he should not vex himself over what he could not control. In his passionate youth and early manhood he had found it hard to practise; but every year made it a little easier. To it he added another rule – *est modus in rebus*. After Elizabeth's death it became the regimen of all his domestic affairs: 'having not in my nature', as he told a friend, 'any more aversion to sordidness than I have to pomp'. To avoid extremes, that must be the secret of life, and he made his home a cool and temperate place where the storms of the outside world could not reach him. The desire for the happy mean saved him from the excess of his passion for perfection – that dangerous impulse which, urging him to great heights, carried him also along the brink of precipices.[11]

The bent of his mind, whenever he could escape from his too eager passions, tended to moderation. He was by nature exceedingly just, and, despite the occasional lapses caused by his ambition, was often so against his own interests – probably too much so for him ever to attain to the highest pinnacles of public life. Readers of the Diary will recall how unflinchingly he could hold the scales against himself. It was the source of his honesty and of that stern sense of duty, which if too anxious to impress on others he always kept doggedly before himself. But he was not only honest in the smaller punctilios of life (though not quite always, it must be confessed, in the greater ones), but honest in his mind in a way uncommon among Englishmen of his stamp, though perhaps more so in his England than it is in ours. He may have been, as Coleridge called him, a pollard man, but he was not easily deceived by intellectual conventions, whether of his own or of other men's making. His habit of seeing through his own motives was often disconcerting, and he had an unexpected talent for philosophical reflection which was not the less distinguished for being generally couched in quaint and rather ingenious language. His frequent gaiety and love of fun were on the surface and declined with age; his sense of humour was of a rarer, grimmer kind that if anything grew with experience; without its brilliant flame, it had more than a touch of his sovereign's mordant wit. 'Do an oyster gape and shut according to the tide when it is out of the water?', he jotted down among his notes during a period when the Admiralty was enjoying the most ignorant and incompetent rule that it had ever known; 'if so, a better oracle for the sea than any of our present Commissioners of the Admiralty.'[12]

Pepys never lost a fastidious sense – it became keener as he rose with age into a sort of innate aristocracy of mind – of constantly comparing his high sense of what things ought to be with what they were. Sometimes it made him inclined to retire out of the world and abandon in disgust the obstinate pattern of things that would not set to his hand and desire. For Pepys could sulk. But from this he was always sooner or later saved by his courage and force of character. Smaller men seeing his pleasures or his labours, sometimes mistook him for a dilettante or a mere boneless man of routine; but, when they acted on the belief that he would sacrifice essentials to love of comfort or office, they found themselves deceived. He never sacrificed a single one. In the waiting, anxious hours before a fight he could suffer agonies, but when the necessity for it arose he fought gloriously.[13]

Once, in the autumn of the year that saw his brush with Brooke House, Pepys was almost betrayed into a duel with the Swedish resident, Sir John Barckman Leyenbergh, and was only prevented by a hasty order from the King and Lord Arlington, that he was on no account either to send or accept a challenge. It was possibly a dispute about his privateering accounts with the estate of his former partner, Sir William Batten, whose widow Leyenbergh soon afterwards married; one can feel quite certain that he believed wholeheartedly and passionately that he was in the right. A year or two before he had described Leyenbergh as 'a cunning fellow' and noted that he wore a fur cap and mittens in bed. But Leyenbergh was a man of learning, a member of the Royal Society, with a house in the fashionable piazza of Covent Garden, where he kept very agreeable company, and Pepys does not appear to have borne him any permanent grudge nor he Pepys, for among the books in the

Pepysian Library is a folio history of Sweden with a flattering Latin inscription presented to him by Leyenbergh in 1687 in memory of twenty-six years of happy friendship.[14]

Not that he was reckless. There was a nicely calculated prudence in his ordinary actions whereby he laid up treasure for himself against the day of trouble. His worldly goods continued to increase for a long time after the Diary ended; and his integrity and very real courage when the hour of sacrifice struck never made him a poor man. Nor was he without a certain cunning. 'What cares I am in', he once told a friend, 'to keep myself having to do with people of so different factions at Court, and yet must be fair with them all'; indeed he seemed to take a pretty content in doing so. He knew from A to Z the art of suggesting nobility or disinterestedness of motive while pursuing very effectively some advantage of his own. And he sometimes practised with equal skill the craft of deliberately, though with an appearance of dignified innocence, shutting his eyes to something that he did not wish to see. He acquired, as the years went by, a very serviceable stock of worldly wisdom, which he was always ready to place, with some display, at the disposal of his younger and less experienced friends. And more than one knave was to find this man of probity a match for him.[15]

His religion had more than a touch of the same worldly sense; at least he was never taken in by its professors. 'A cunning fellow,' he wrote of his parish priest, 'and knows where the good victuals is and the good drink.' In fact his opinion of parsons was generally anything but flattering. He particularly disliked the more enthusiastic variety, whose canting sermons had been so much in vogue during his youth; everyone recalls his disgust when 'a simple bawling young Scot preached'. But it was not really the enthusiasm he disliked, but only the simulated appearance of it; a man of genuine saintliness, of whatever profession, always won his respect. And for unrepentant wickedness and debauchery he had a real horror: religion to him was the means by which divine order reassumed its rule over chaos, and his Father in Heaven was like himself a benevolent, though stern, administrator. He set His Commandments up at his private expense in the winter of 1670–1 in Chatham Church, to stand, as one of his correspondents put it, as a durable monument of his pious generosity. He had little belief in dogma or persecution – a tolerance which in that most intolerant age placed him constantly under suspicion. But he had been brought up a Puritan and remained a Protestant, though a very broad one, was constant in his attendance at divine service, which he plainly regarded as one of the guiding rails of an ordered life, and was too shrewd and had too much reverence for the nobility and beauty of life not to be a believer. 'If faith be the evidence of things not seen,' he once wrote to a friend, 'infidelity must be a non-discerning of things visible.'[16]

Order, dignity and strength that springs from order, a comely and seemly rule in all things, there lay the motive springs of Pepys' career. He was a monarchist, and, as the years went by an increasingly strong one – (he who, as a boy, had rejoiced when the axe severed Charles I's head) – because to him monarchy stood for external order and the decencies of life, which deserved respect and loyalty even when its representatives were personally unworthy of their trust. Once, when he was quite a young man, he heard an irreverent Scottish Colonel speaking of the Emperor as a sot because he neglected his duties and was led by the Jesuits; 'Mr Progers', he recorded gratefully, 'told him that it was not a thing to be said of any Sovereign Prince, be his weaknesses what they will, to be called a sot, which methinks was very prettily said.' And into the service of order, all his energy, vast ability and passion for detail were enlisted. In due season they bore a great fruit, not for himself alone nor for the Stuart kings whom he served with flawless loyalty but could not save, but for the island State he loved and which still lives by the service he did her.[17]

For the rest he still inhabited the house in the Navy Office in Seething Lane, with its courtyard garden and its pleasant walk on the leads to repair to on spring evenings, when the first blossom of the city fruit trees peeped out of the dark tunnels of alley and lane. There was no Elizabeth to share it with him now, and there is no evidence that he ever so much as thought of marrying again. That he continued to have affairs with women is likely enough, though, being a thoroughly discreet man and no longer keeping a shorthand diary, the knowledge of them is as remote from us as it was from his contemporaries. We do know, however, that not long after Elizabeth's death he formed a connection with a young lady of good family called Mary Skinner, the daughter of a respectable but declining city merchant who lived in Mark Lane in his parish and

sister to a young Westminster and Cambridge scholar who had had
the then rather invidious distinction of having been John Milton's
last amanuensis. Her parents, who, like most who knew him well,
had a great admiration for Pepys, were shocked, as well they might
be, when they realized the passionate nature of the relationship
which had sprung up between their young and witty daughter and
the charming, worthy and, as they had supposed almost awe-
inspiringly virtuous, public man whom they were so proud to know.
Pepys, in his love for Mary, had befriended her clever but erratic
young brother, Daniel, but when the truth was realized, the good
relationship between the two families was severed. Yet only temporarily, for after a few years the younger generation of Skinners were
once more looking to Pepys as their patron, and he and Mary's
mother became close friends. And as neither Samuel nor Mary ever
married, and as a quarter of a century later she had returned to him
as the respected mistress of his household and the loved consoler of
his old age, it is certain that their enduring flame was no mere light
of love, however bright and perilous the spark that first lit it. She
was a clever and charming woman, with all Samuel's own love of
order and beauty, and a serene instinct for bringing it into the lives
of those who were happy enough to know her. Almost Pepys' last
words were of her: as he lay dying he called her, what she truly was
to him, his dear child. Yet though Samuel lived perhaps a happier
and less hysterical life after his wife's death, something in him that
neither time nor any other woman could take away belonged to
Elizabeth, and he carried it with him to the grave.[18]

To his dead wife's memory Pepys dedicated his care of her
poverty-stricken parents and her feckless brother, Balty St Michel,
whom he had provided with the post of Muster Master at Deal.
Three years after her death Balty, whose family also Pepys sheltered
and to whose eldest son he stood godfather, wrote to him:

> You daily and hourly so comble me with (not only expressions but also)
> deeds of your worthiness and goodness, as well to myself as the rest of your
> most devoted humble creatures here, that I am as well as my poor drooping
> mother (whose continual illness since the death of my father gives me but
> little hopes she will survive him long) . . . a living witness of your dearness to
> her poor child your late dear consort, my beloved sister.*

* B. St Michel to S. Pepys, Aug. 14th, 1672. *Rawl. MSS. A.* 174, f. 235. (Printed
Braybrooke, Chandos Library Ed. 607.)

There is a charming postscript, too, to the letter, which gives a glimpse of another side of Pepys' character,

> Little Samuel (who speaks now very pretily) desires to have his most humble duty presented to his most honoured uncle and god-father, which please to accept from your most humble little disciple.[19]

His own younger brother, John, also claimed Pepys' care. His father had let Brampton and was living with his daughter Pall and her husband, John Jackson the grazier, and their two infant children at Ellington, a few miles away. John Pepys, who with his University education and bookish tastes must have felt a little lost in this bucolic atmosphere, was temporarily helping Jackson with his not very prosperous farming affairs, when in March 1670, the Clerk of Trinity House died, and Samuel, who was a younger Brother of the Corporation, seeing his opportunity of providing for him, hastily summoned him to London:

Brother,
Something hath offered itself which may prove of advantage to you, that makes it necessary for me to have you here on Tuesday night next. It is an employment into which some or other must be elected on Wednesday morning. If my endeavours for you succeed, it will be a good provision for you. If it do not, it is very well worth a journey to attempt it.

I am sensible this may be inconvenient to my brother Jackson; but I hope some way or other may be found to put off the meeting on his business for a few days. For whether this succeeds or not, you shall be at liberty in a few days to return for a little time. Therefore pray fail not to be here on Tuesday night next.

I beg my father's blessing and rest
Your loving brother,
S. PEPYS.*

In pursuit of this pious plan Pepys canvassed the Duke of York, Lord Sandwich, Lord Craven and his friend Evelyn's father-in-law, old Sir Richard Browne, one of the most influential of the Elder Brethren. 'I have a sudden occasion offered me of asking your friendship', he told the latter, 'as well as a full assurance that I shall not want it. 'Tis this; Mr Ascew, Clerk of Trinity House, is dead. I have a brother of my own, whose relation to me could not tempt me

---

* 'To my loving brother, Mr John Pepys at Ellington, near Huntingdon.' S. Pepys to J. Pepys, Mar. 26th, 1670. *Rawl. MSS. A.* 182, ff. 475–6.

to this motion, were it not that his sobriety, diligence and education (being a scholar) . . . doth lead me to think it a service to the Corporation to offer him to them. I aim not so much at the salary for him, as the opportunity by this means of introducing him to that sort of business for which I have for some time designed him. He is about thirty years of age, unmarried, his life that of a scholar's . . .' Four days later Pepys appeared before the Corporation to plead his brother's cause. He was successful. The Pepysian trinity of brethren in the service of the sea was now complete.[20]

After nearly a year of abnormal happenings – his foreign holiday, his wife's death, his exhilarating duel with the Commissioners before the King and Council – Pepys settled down in the spring of 1670 to the normal routine of office. Yet that he could do so at all, in a work which entailed perpetual perusal and preparation of memoranda, contracts and letters, is a remarkable instance of the determination of his character, for since the breakdown of his eyesight a year before, he had been unable to read or write without rendering himself blind.* Every attempt to do so was followed at once by intense pain and a blindness so complete that he could scarcely grope his way out of the office. The only exception, he told his physician (and it was one that he could in no wise comprehend) was when he was at a public audience before the King and Council, where he was not at liberty to consider the burden on his eyes, and even then after half an hour or so the suffering became intolerable. This apparently insuperable disability he conquered by making his clerks his eyes, so that they both read to him and wrote for him. He even taught them to counterfeit his hand. So long as he followed this practice, his eyes gave him little pain and appeared to be completely restored, so that his vision for distant objects was as good as any man's. But when the necessity of the Service, as it sometimes did, drove him to write and read with his own eyes, resort to spectacles or mathematical tubes of oiled paper as he might, he underwent a veritable martyrdom. His achievement in overcoming such a handicap is as heroic as anything in the annals of administration.[21]

Of the problems of the Office, of which as Clerk of the Acts and by far the most experienced member, Pepys was virtually the working

* This, I think, has never been realized before. For Pepys' own account of it see the long memorandum on 'The Present Ill State of My Health' (*Rawl. MSS. A.* 185, ff. 206–13) printed in the Appendix.

head, the familiar one of lack of money was still first. At the beginning of 1670 the Navy debt stood at £458,991 or half a million less than it had done at the end of the War. But the nicely calculated plan which William Coventry – Charles II's 'visionaire' – had proposed for limiting the Fleet to ten ships in winter and twenty-four in the summer at a total annual cost of £200,000 had never been even approximately realized, partly because it was dependent on the existence of a large preliminary sum of ready money, which the King could not and Parliament would not supply, to pay off surplus ships and workmen, and partly because the growing needs of the merchant marine, particularly in the Mediterranean, would not admit of so small a force. The estimate for 1670 was £363,120. 4s. for a fleet of fifty ships, manned by 5279 men, with a further £84,061 for repairs to ships in the Yards and replenishing stores.

But in the Stuart administrative machine it was one thing to estimate, another to obtain money. In May Pepys was busy preparing a statement of the nine hundred thousand odd pounds needed by the Navy Office to pay off current charges and old debts. A little later in the summer he made a 'discourse' on the same subject to the King and Lords of the Treasury. Yet despite his oratory, which one can only hope that Charles enjoyed as much as himself since he was called upon to hear so much of it, only two-thirds of the naval charge that year was met in cash.

None the less, a favouring wind was beginning to blow what money there was towards the Navy. That May Lord Sandwich sailed from Greenwich in the *Anne* yacht to fetch the King's sister, Madame of France, to Dover, where the Secret Treaty was signed and those far-reaching plans launched for the acquisition by England of the colonial empires of Holland and Spain. Of these Pepys, like others, knew little or nothing. But the policy of the great men who controlled the Government turned once more towards a new naval war with Holland and, as a consequence, a better supported Navy.[22]

It was perhaps this that sent Pepys out that autumn on a visit of inspection to Chatham. The Yards were growing busy again. At Portsmouth, his protégé, the great naval architect, Anthony Deane, was laying down new ships. In May Pepys had had to rebuke him for making experiments in shipbuilding without the leave of his superiors; he half apologized for doing so, 'being very desirous to give you all the ease and furtherance within my reach towards the great work you are upon'. But it had come to the knowledge of the authorities, he continued, 'that you have of your own head, without precedent, as well as without the advice, or so much as the privity, of this Board or the Commissioner upon the place, presumed to lay aside the old secure practice of fastening your beams in your new ships with standards and knees, and in the room thereof taken upon you to do it with iron'. But Deane stood up for his iron dogs; not only were they the strongest means of fastening beams, but, he added, 'between you and myself, the King must build no more great ships, if nothing can be invented but knees . . . we having not one knee in the yard'.* When the King saw this letter, he was so impressed that he overruled the objections of his more cautious experts, and Pepys became the announcer of the pleasing news that his Majesty had 'replied that he would as soon believe his own eyes and Mr Deane's as any of them all'.[23]

Pepys was constantly in the royal presence during 1670: even at Newmarket where like his friend Evelyn he saw the jockeys breathing their fine barbs and racers on the Heath. He also visited Windsor, where he must have been keenly interested in the preparations going forward to repair the Castle, and in the martial furniture – pikes, muskets, pistols, bandoliers, holsters, drums and breast-plates – with which rough old Prince Rupert, the Constable, was festooning the walls. The King seemed less busy, passing his time mostly in hunting the stag and walking in the park, which he was planting with rows of trees. Perhaps it was on such a walk one misty autumn morning that the Clerk of the Acts, walking at his side, discussed with him the important matters he had come down to transact.[24]

Pepys' own worldly affairs were prospering. Under Will Hewer's businesslike supervision he was growing a rich man. Altogether that year over £43,000 passed through his banking account at Alderman Backwell's, the great banker who did business at the sign of the 'Unicorn' in Lombard Street. On January 1st, 1671, his credit balance with Backwell alone stood at £6855. And he had other investments, and there was still money coming in from the prize awards arising out of the now forgotten depredations of the *Greyhound* privateer.[25]

* S. Pepys to Capt. Deane, May 2nd, 1670. Tanner, *Further Correspondence*, 264–5. Capt. Deane to S. Pepys, May 5th, 1670. *Rawl. MSS. A.* 174, f. 179.

The winter of 1670–1 saw the death of two old colleagues, Penn at the beginning and Mennes at the end. In the early morning of February 18th Samuel wrote to the Duke of York to tell him that by the time his letter reached his hands, the Comptroller – 'that doting fool', as he had once termed him – would be no more. Not that he had any ambition, he assured the Duke, to recommend a successor, much less of being thought fit for it himself. But, recalling the drawbacks of Mennes' infirmities, he could not do less than remind him that there was no employment in the Service that called for 'a greater measure of integrity, experience, vigour of body and vivacity of mind with a disposition to the taking pains in both'. Yet it was not Pepys, but Sir Thomas Allin, a distinguished flag-officer who had just returned from a campaign against the North African pirates, who was appointed to the vacant Comptrollership.[26]

On the day after he wrote this fruitless letter, Pepys had a pleasant experience, dining with the Surveyor General, Christopher Wren,* as the guest of his cultured friend, John Evelyn, at Sayes Court, Deptford. After dinner the latter took them to a poor, solitary, thatched cottage in the neighbouring fields and showed them a great wonder – a Crucifixion of Tintoretto's – such a work, Evelyn thought, that for the curiosity of handling, drawing and studious exactness as he had never seen before. But the greater wonder was the carved frame, 'being nothing in nature so tender and delicate as the flowers and festoons about it'. And Evelyn told them how a few weeks before, walking in these fields, he had seen it through the window, and so for the first time met that incomparable young man, Mr Gibbons, its creator, who had come here to this obscure place that he might apply himself to his profession without interruption. He proved to be a young man very civil, sober and discreet in his discourse, and a lover of music. For two of that distinguished company thus brought together in that humble cottage – the Surveyor General and the young wood-carver – it was the beginning of a famous partnership.[27]

During those last four years as Clerk of the Acts, we have less knowledge of Samuel's private life than at any other time of his career. His official correspondence affords an occasional glimpse – a

---

* 'Two, extraordinary, ingenious and knowing persons', Evelyn called his two guests. Evelyn, *Diary,* Feb. 19th, 1671.

friendship formed with Monsieur Mignon, the French Ambassador's Secretary, the gift of an Italian guitar and a bundle of musical cards from the English Consul at Leghorn, or of a cask of Mountaigne Allicant and of a tun of Barcelona wine from his old clerk, Richard Gibson, now serving as Sir Edward Spragge's secretary in the war against the Algerine Turks. Gibson wrote frequently with many tender messages for old Mr Pepys, for Tom Hayter, Will Hewer, Tom Edwards (Samuel's former singing boy who had now become his clerk) and other familiars whom he had met at the hospitable table in Seething Lane. Absence had not quenched Gibson's passion – almost equal to Pepys' own – for writing interminable memoranda on naval matters: a report on the island harbour of Minorca, whose 'poor but shuffling people' he found very friendly, and a scheme for placing the victualling of the Mediterranean Squadron in the Admiral's hands, both found their way to the busy Clerk of the Acts. A little wearily the latter replied that, though he knew no objection to the idea of victualling the Fleet by commission instead of contract, he could not see his way to do anything for the present in the matter, partly because he did not know when the war would end and partly 'from a backwardness of burthening myself any more with the care and envy of carrying on things against tide whilst those who are more properly concerned to do it either neglect' or oppose it.

Happily Gibson was not easily put out; he had been encouraged, he told Pepys, by the Admiral 'with so great freedom as to lay and write in his State Room and be as bold as at home'. But there was a slight *fracas* a little later on, when the Admiral laid all the blame of an accident to the mainmast of one of his ships on its architect, Anthony Deane, who in his hearty, salty fashion he declared was a great malicious knave. And when his secretary took it upon himself to tell him that Captain Deane was his friend, Spragge replied, 'a turd in his teeth that would not join with him to declare the truth'. But the gallant officer was soon appeased, drank Pepys' health next day in his cabin and told Gibson to present his service to him. And the faithful fellow's happiness was crowned soon after by an exceedingly kind letter from Pepys himself, 'which put me in mind of a speech of Dr Donne's, Dean of St Paul's, in a sermon there; viz. that the goodness of God was not so much seen in our creation as redemption, nor so much that we are his, as that nothing can take us

out of his hands'.* Such was the impress of Pepys' rule on those who
served him.[28]

Others, whose work brought them into contact with him, felt the
sterling worth of the man and grappled him close to them. One of
these was Sir John Bankes, the great East India merchant, whom he
had first met on the Exchange seven years before. A dispute had
arisen between the Crown and the East India Company over the
freight of a ship seized by Dutch traders in the Far East, and Pepys
was asked by the Treasury to report on the whole affair. For several
months Pepys and Sir John, who was delegated by the Company to
represent its interests, were in almost daily communication. Bankes
was in many ways a man after Pepys' own heart, with a noble
mansion in Lincoln's Inn Fields and an estate in Kent, princely
tastes, a charming wife and a family of clever children such as
Samuel loved to jest with and instruct. He too had started life in
humble circumstances, but by tireless energy and assiduity in
business had acquired a vast fortune and a seat in Parliament. In the
interstices of their official contacts, amid the clamour and urgency of
great affairs, a friendship grew up between these two busy men.[29]

There were other ties that Pepys' work brought him. Requests for
help were the most frequent, and some, rarer, were letters of thanks
for help given. Anne Pett, widow of the Master Shipwright at
Woolwich, who long ago had given him a Japan cane with a silver
head and a ring of Woolwich stone, wrote to thank him for his
'careful and vigilant successful services' to her and her fatherless
children and asked him to accept a pair of china flower-pots.
Thomas Pointer of Radcliffe testified how Pepys had raised him
from the dunghill and worse than nothing, though he would like, he
added, a little present money for his work for the Service. And his
erstwhile ally at Aldeburgh, Captain Elliot, begged him to secure
the discharge of one of his late supporters who had been pressed into
the *Mary Rose*. Some of his petitioners were very humble folk, like the
poor woman whose husband had lost his pay ticket and who came to
the Office to beg his help, having heard that the Clerk of the Acts
was a just and kind man. Among others was young William Penn,
son of his old neighbour, the Admiral, whose Quaker enthusiasm
had been getting him into trouble, to beg his 'parfyet charity' for a

---

* R. Gibson to S. Pepys, Aug. 17th, 1671. *Rawl. MSS. A.* 174, f. 372.

'grey headed man'. 'Wm. Penn to S. P. in a Quaker's style', was the recipient's businesslike endorsement.[30]

The noblest service Pepys performed for the poor and needy was his work for the Chatham Chest, established by Francis Drake and John Hawkins after the defeat of the Armada for the support of aged and maimed seamen, and towards the maintenance of which every serving sailor contributed 6*d.* a month out of his wages. Generations of high-placed officials had abused the trust, and its funds had been wasted by every sort of petty peculation. For years Pepys had been trying to restore order and honesty to the Chest's management, and now, in the summer of 1671, he was forced to urge the late Navy Treasurer, the high-placed Earl of Anglesey, to disgorge £3000 of its money which he had improperly retained in his hands, and for want of which the Governors of the Chest had had to defer the annual pay, though the Pensioners had made weary journeys from every part of England to receive it. A year later, Anglesey, whose piety was equalled by his cunning, was still being dunned for £1200, and was writing suavely of his regret that there should be any delay or disappointment in so good a work, caused solely, he assured the impatient Pepys, by the failure of his own creditors. To secure that the pay should not be delayed again, Pepys engaged himself personally to the Chest on Anglesey's behalf for £800: 'more than this', he wrote, 'I am not in a condition at this time to do; but do hope (and heartily pray) that one or other of the helps your Lordship hath before you will take place. If it do not, I know not what I can possibly add to what the Board hath said in theirs, but that I do most heartily condole, not only the Chest's and the King's Service but your Lordship's particular misfortune in this matter'.* The courteously veiled threat did its work, and that evening Pepys received a note from his Lordship to say that the money would be forthcoming next day.[31]

Pepys' administrative zeal did not always bring a shower of blessings on his head. In September 1671 he was the recipient of some very sarcastic letters from the occupant of the Navy Treasurer's house at Deptford, Madam Howard, whose unauthorized repairs at the Service's expense he had had in the course of his duty to suspend until a formal warrant could be procured from the Navy

* S. Pepys to Earl of Anglesey, Aug. 4th, 1672. *Rawl. MSS. A.* 172, ff. 75–6. Printed *Smith*, I, 136.

Board. The masons, Mrs Howard bitterly informed him, had already taken up all the stones in the kitchen and half the tiles, kind Mr Wren had been civility itself and, if it had not been for his interference, the work would have been finished. 'I am sure', she went on, 'I have had as great a regard to the King's expense as I could have for my own, . . . but if I must seek for new orders for every nail and tile this house wants, I believe the Board would be as weary of my requests as I am of seeing the house when rain comes.'* The claims of duty and of courtesy to ladies were not always compatible.[32]

Preparation for war, and shortage of money for almost every purpose called for by it, were the two motifs which kept recurring in the administrative annals of 1671. As early as March 23rd Anthony Deane was writing anxiously about the supply of the Yards should hostilities break out. Here the very workmen were tramping out to seek their bread elsewhere. And, though the Government was deflecting to the Navy every penny it could from the other Services, the national revenues were mortgaged to the bankers to such an extent that very little cash could come in. At the end of May, of the £660,000 allocated to the Navy for the year, only £110,000 had been paid. Pepys' talents for oratory and exposition, though several times exercised before the King and the Lords of the Treasury, could avail nothing.[33]

Yet the Government was straining every nerve towards setting out a fleet in the spring. For, though few knew it, the King and his ministers were now committed to an alliance with France to destroy the Dutch republic at the first opportunity, the English part being to sink the Dutch fleet and seize her colonies, while the French armies invaded her by land. Mr Evelyn was instructed by his sovereign to make his history of the late War a *little keen*, and Lady Temple, wife of the English Ambassador at the Hague, and by posterity remembered as Dorothy Osborne, narrowly escaped a heroic death as the tiny yacht on which she was being borne to England fired at the anchored Dutch flagship for its failure to salute the English flag. All this affected the Clerk of the Acts, who was constantly summoned to Windsor and other summer retreats to discuss matters with his sovereign and the Lord High Admirals. In October he attended

* Madam Howard to S. Pepys, Sept. 27th, 1671. *Rawl. MSS. A.* 174, ff. 197–8.

them at Newmarket, where according to Evelyn all the jolly blades were racing, dancing, feasting, and revelling, and later through watery roads to Lord Townsend's house near Norwich where, owing to an indisposition of the Duke's, Pepys had had to wait three days before he could get the royal brothers together to listen to what he had to say.[34]

But before that Pepys had made another journey. In July, with Lord Brouncker and Commissioner Tippetts as his companions, he travelled the familiar road from London to Portsmouth, sleeping a night at Guildford, perhaps at his old inn the 'Red Lion', where ten years before he and Creed had had such fun jumping over the wall of an old well. At Portsmouth all was in confusion, for the King who was to 'coast it in his pleasure boat to Plymouth', had arrived several hours before he was expected and no one was ready to receive him. Thence the travellers crossed to the Isle of Wight, and embarked on the *Henrietta* yacht, one of the little squadron of yachts and frigates that accompanied the King on his western pilgrimage. The voyage being very stormy it is more than probable that Pepys was sick.

At Plymouth he stayed with Mr Lanyon, his Tangier agent, and then, when his Majesty set out home by coach, took horse with Brouncker, Tippetts, Anthony Deane, and four clerks, to make a tour of inspection of the royal forests. They stopped at Ashburton where their bill was £1. 6s. and at Exeter where it was £3, with an extra 2s. 3d. for sugar, dined one day at Taunton, slept at Bridgwater and so came to Bristol, where Samuel's thoughts must have strayed a little wistfully to his former visit with his wife and Deb. Here they spent a day or two, for their bill came to £5. 8s. 9d. with six shillings more for servants, six for claret and another six for the waterman, three and six for a trip down the river and half-a-crown for having their linen washed. The hire of eight horses from Exeter to Bristol cost £8.

Thence, with their horses and clerks and three bottles of cider, they were ferried across the Severn to Wales, where they stopped at Chepstow and Newnham and visited the iron works. The bill for one of their meals has been preserved – a leg and neck of mutton with carrots five shillings, a couple of rabbits two and eight, fruit and cheese tenpence, a bottle of claret one shilling, a pint of white wine one shilling, and bread and beer four and twopence. At another meal they ate a leg of mutton and cauliflower, a breast of veal, six chickens, artichokes, peas, oranges and fruit and cheese with a modest three and sixpence worth of wine to wash down £1. 9s. 7d. of food.

So they came to the Forest of Dean, where they stayed at Micheldean and took a survey of the Forest. Their Report, which Pepys afterwards presented to his Majesty, was not encouraging. Of ten thousand trees, about half were oaks, most of them wind-ridden or cup-shaken and not more than eight hundred of them fit for the service of the Navy. The beeches were in better condition: taking twenty-four average trees scattered over the whole forest and to fell which they gave the Woodward £2. 5s. for an encouragement, they found them all sound and good for making four-inch by three-inch planks, though of no use for any other purpose. A great many trees, too, were lying on the ground, having been felled for the building of a new warship at Bristol, but of these few were worth the transporting and all were likely to be useless if they lay much longer.*

With a guide and a shilling's worth of beer, they went on to Gloucester where they stayed a night and collected their letters from the post-house. There, wearying of riding, they hired a coach for £6 and jolted over the bare pleasant Cotswolds to Oxford *en route* to the great midland forest of Whittlebury. A day in Oxford proved expensive, but it was probably worth it (and, anyway, his Majesty paid) – £2. 5s. 9d. for the tavern bill, 5s. 6d. for the servants, £1. 0s. 10d. for fodder for four coach horses and the clerks' four saddle-horses, 1s. for the ostlers, 10s. for seeing the new Theatre (newly built by Samuel's friend, Mr Wren), 8s. for tips in the College cellars, and another 2s. to the fellow who showed them the Divinity Chapel, and 1s. for the poor. Next day they went on to Brackley where they stayed and whence a guide led them through the intricate ways of the forest and where – for what purpose it is impossible to say – both Pepys and Lord Brouncker spent a pound.

From Brackley their coach bore them next morning to Buckingham where they dined and took a guide to bring them down the old bridleway across the rolling green hills and the great vale that led to Aylesbury. The lumbering coach, with the bewigged faces of the four great men peering out at the unfamiliar sights of the countryside and

* The accounts for this journey will be found in *Rawlinson MSS. A.* 174, ff. 402–7. The survey of the Forest of Dean is contained in *Pepysian MS.* 2265, Paper 36.

their four clerks riding beside them must have passed by the stone-mullioned house in East Claydon, where fat, lazy, good-humoured Mun Verney dispensed good French claret to his country neighbours. So they came to Aylesbury, its vaned church jogging before them against the far blue line of the Chilterns all a summer's afternoon and evening. Another night passed at Uxbridge, and the next day, August 4th, saw them at the Navy Office again, where the Clerk of the Acts took horse for Windsor to report their doings to the King.[35]

That was a summer's idyll of a vanished England; but the sands were now running out fast. All that autumn, with the utmost secrecy, the royal ships and dockyards were made ready for war. It was uphill work, for the shortage of money was as bad as ever. Poor Beckford, the slopseller, was tens of thousands of pounds in debt for clothes supplied to the Navy, and no one knew how to find money to meet his present necessities and enable him to raise credit to equip the new men whom the Office were drafting into the ships. But Charles and his fiery adviser, Sir Thomas Clifford, had a plan of their own. In December the bullying Sir George Downing – '*le plus grand querelleur de la diplomatie Britannique*' – was sent to the Hague to make demands of the Dutch so high-handed and peremptory that they could scarcely do anything but refuse them. And when the republican chiefs of Holland, realizing their peril, humbled themselves to conciliate the revengeful English, Downing's demands were only heightened. The bells that rang out the old year sounded amid storms and tempests. On January 2nd, the day before the Victuallers announced their long-anticipated inability to supply the Service further without ready money, the Council decided to suspend principal payments from the Exchequer and to resume possession of the incoming revenues which were by now almost entirely mortgaged to the bankers. Pepys' own banker, Alderman Backwell, lost £296,000 in Exchequer bonds* and a little while after was forced to close his doors, but Pepys, who throughout the year had been buying bills of exchange, payable abroad, had reduced his credit balance of £6855. 0s. 1d. to an overdraft of £17,666. 13s. 4d. so that Backwell's necessities scarcely worried him. A few days later orders

---

* Evelyn records that Sir Thomas Clifford, the Treasurer, gave him a hint of what he was about to do. Evelyn, *Diary*, March 12th, 1672. It is possible that Pepys also had some such premonition.

were given to set out the largest force England had ever put to sea with all conceivable diligence, and Sir Robert Holmes wrote urgently from Portsmouth for leave to seize homecoming Dutch merchantmen. It was granted.[36]

3

The Third Dutch War

'*The King*. "Send immediately Purveyors to know what stores are in town, and where to be had for money."
Sir T. Allen. "It is my place, but I am going down the River. Let Mr Pepys enquire."
Mr Pepys. "In a day or two your Majesty shall have a sufficient account of whatever is to be had in town."' *P.R.O. Foreign Entry Book* 177, May 9th, 1672.

On January 21st, 1672, Pepys presented, written in his own neat hand, a confidential analysis of the needs of the Navy if the task before it was to be fulfilled. £1,337,292. 9*s*. was needed to pay off the debts of the past year and to maintain a personnel of 23,000 men for eight months. But for once, thanks to the Secret Treaty of Dover, cash, though not enough of it, was at hand. It came before the end of January from the French King, 600,000 pistoles, rumbling up to London from Rye in country carts between the files of his Majesty's horse guards. It was just in time. On February 5th, while snow lay thick outside the Office windows, Pepys was writing urgently to the Duke of York's secretary to obtain that afternoon what was so desperately needed from the Treasury.[1]

All the 1st, 2nd and 3rd rate ships, the full line of battle, were accordingly ordered out. 'Never', wrote a correspondent, 'was so great cheerfulness known in the seamen as how to enter into that service, everyone freely offering themselves to it and pressing who shall get first in.' But this proved to be far too roseate a view of the situation. A few weeks later information was coming from every port of a shortage of men so serious that riggers and labourers were being taken from the very Yards to get the ships down the river. In Cornwall the fishermen of Newton and Mousehole dangled ropes in front of the government's agent, beat him with clubs and threw his servant over a cliff. None the less the work went forward. By March 3rd, Holmes at Portsmouth had eleven ships ready with an early expectation of six more. The government thereupon issued orders that all Dutch vessels were to be seized, and on the 13th Holmes was able to send in two prizes laden with wine and oranges. Next day, too greedy to wait for reinforcements, he engaged the home-coming Smyrna fleet off the Isle of Wight. From Portsmouth, from Beachy Head, from the Downs came a train of rumours as the running fight between his light squadron and the Dutch merchantmen passed up Channel.

But when the official report arrived on the 19th, it was known that the Dutch had defended themselves so stoutly that only six prizes had been taken. The chief honours of this not very honourable affair went to an English merchantman outward bound, who, hearing the guns, joined in and captured two Dutch vessels. Other fruits of the fight were less pleasing to the authorities – ships 'notably torn', with masts and rigging shot away, and mangled seamen stacked in the streets of the Kentish coast towns before the Commissioners for the care of the sick and wounded were ready to receive them. 'The hardest duty I was ever engaged in, making bricks without straw', the Surgeon-General reported. It was then that Evelyn, one of the Commissioners, hastening to the spot, saw a chirurgeon cut off the leg of a wounded sailor, 'the stout and gallant man enduring it with incredible patience, without being bound to his chair, as usual on such painful occasions ... Not being cut off high enough, the gangrene prevailed, and the second operation cost the poor creature his life. Lord! What miseries are mortal men subject to, and what confusion and mischief do the avarice, anger, and ambition of Princes cause in the world!'[2]

Yet, while the Channel resounded with guns, and Pepys at his office grappled with the ceaseless routine of wartime administration, the peaceful world of England went on much as before. John Pepys, from his new-found glory at Trinity House, sent his father and sister oysters, with straw hats for little Samuel and John Jackson, and Pall wrote back to say that the old man was in good health and her boys thriving bravely. Samuel himself was chosen an Elder Brother of Trinity House – an honour which showed his rising place in the world – and his father down in Huntingdonshire made his will, dividing his little personal property among his three children.[3]

On March 15th all England was astounded, and not a little shocked, by the Declaration of Indulgence – the King's bold and final bid to achieve a scheme of toleration for all sects including the Catholics. It won little support. The Church of Christ in Exeter hailed its broad-minded sovereign as the breath of its nostrils and a repairer of breaches, with a supplementary petition that Lewis Stuckley might be its teacher, but scarcely anyone else said so much as thank you. Even the tolerant Evelyn was shocked, 'papists and swarms of sectaries', he noted, 'now showing themselves in their public meetings'. It is probable that Pepys as well as he witnessed the open 'fopperies of the Papists' that tense Easter in the Queen's Palace of Somerset House – 'our Blessed Saviour at the Paschal Supper with his disciples, in figures and puppets made as big as the life, of waxwork, curiously clad and sitting round a large table, the room nobly hung and shining with innumerable lamps and candles'. But to most Englishmen there was only one candle of this kind for which they had any use – that lit by Latimer and Ridley a century before on the martyr's stake at Oxford.[4]

Most of the spring Pepys spent at his desk in the Office; others were to do the fighting, it was for him to labour that they might fight. From the ports came a stream of demands. 'We have no flags, cotton or kerseys in store,' wrote Commissioner Tippetts from Portsmouth: 'the ships gone out went without them, except colours, one of each, and so ragged as would hardly hang on the staff. Very little timber is in store, and what you will do with the workmen three weeks hence I would gladly know.' Even Pepys could not inform him, but he supposed what they had done before – live from hand to mouth, and coax, cheat and drive work out of men and credit out of contractors.

More than ever his had become the controlling hand at the Navy Office. In April he was writing to the Duke of York, relying on the 'accustomed liberty your Royal Highness has been always pleased to indulge me, of offering my humble opinion in matters relating to his Majesty's service within my observation . . . and with an assurance of my continued industry by night and day to discharge my own duty' – to urge the transference of the Surveyor, Middleton, to the Commissionership of the Chatham Yard and the elevation of his assistant, Tippetts, to his place. Though he had to write again before his purpose was achieved, his recommendation was adopted. And his protégé Deane was promoted to the rank of Commissioner in charge of the Portsmouth Yard – as great a blessing to Deane, who had a large family, as it was to the Service. A further administrative change, though not of Pepys' making, had taken place a little earlier, when Sir Thomas Osborne, a hard-headed Yorkshire Cavalier, had succeeded to the Treasurership of the Navy.[5]

Throughout the spring the press went on furiously. Balty wrote from Deal to beg a protection for the four men who rowed him to and from the ships; 'sometimes at my landing (having but four men) I have been overwhelmed with the boat and almost drowned; other times not being able to fetch Deal have been driven one time almost as far as Dover'. And if any of these four were taken from him, Pepys was left to infer, his brother-in-law would be lost beyond retrieve.

Though many of the ships were only partially manned the Fleet was made ready in time, and on April 22nd the King went down the river to see it riding at the Buoy of the Nore and wish it God Speed before it sailed for Portsmouth to join its French allies. The Duke of York was in command, with Lord Sandwich as Admiral of the Blue.[6]

Meanwhile the Dutch, also, were preparing. Some supposed that, terrified by the size of the forces that England and France were arming against them, they would never leave the shelter of their sand dunes, but the King, who knew them, did not share these views. Though like the English they had some difficulty in manning their fleet, for which they had largely to rely on the seafaring population of North Germany, by the end of April De Ruyter with seventy ships of war appeared off the mouth of the Thames to engage the English fleet before it could join the French. He was just too late. On May 3rd, King Charles inspected at Spithead a joint armada of nearly a hundred ships of war, with 34,000 men and 6000 guns.[7]

While the rival fleets were manoeuvring for position, Pepys with Hewer at his side sat at his desk dictating continuously. In the Duke's absence at sea Prince Rupert had gone to the Admiralty, and on top of all his other duties, the Clerk of the Acts was obliged to satisfy his perpetual demands for statistical information. Early in May he was faced with the additional anxiety of a first-class crisis. As he had long foreseen the old Surveyor's estimates of the state of the stores had proved wildly optimistic, the heavy demands of the Fleet suddenly revealing to the higher authorities that the stocks of hemp, pitch, tar and canvas, which the ships would be in urgent need of after the first action, were practically exhausted. The King acted promptly and the matter was examined by the Committee for

Foreign Affairs. As usual the task of defending his erring colleagues against some very angry strictures of Clifford and Rupert, fell on Pepys' shoulders. The enquiry ended characteristically, as recorded in the minutes of his Arundel House friend, Mr Williamson, the new Secretary of the Council:

> *The King.* Send immediately Purveyors to know what stores are in town, and where to be had for money.
> *Sir T. Allen.* It is my place, but I am going down the River. Let Mr Pepys enquire.
> *Mr Pepys.* In a day or two your Majesty shall have a sufficient account of whatever is to be had in town.*

It was an extra burden taken on without a murmur, at a time when Pepys was under such constant applications for one thing or another that he knew not how to leave the Office.[8]

Another of Pepys' wartime tasks was the collection of intelligence. From Captain Langley, Master of the Packet Boats at Harwich, came a stream of information about the movements of the fleets, all of which had to be sifted and transmitted to the ports. Here Pepys had to wage war on his own account – against the authorities of the Post Office. On one occasion five of his outgoing despatches were sent by a stupid postmaster down the wrong road and, after being returned to London and sent out a second time, were again returned, with an insolent letter because they had not been delivered at the General Post Office. This maddening emanation of official pomposity reached Pepys when he was in bed at midnight. What made it worse was that the Office messenger had actually proffered the offending despatches at the General Post Office, where he had been told that it was no one's business to receive them and that he ought to take them to the Barbican, 'where it seems', wrote the angry Pepys, 'letters and expresses are despatched the Northern road'.[9]

On May 16th, a glorious day, Evelyn watching from Dover saw the allied fleet of over a hundred and fifty vessels passing eastwards from the Straits – 'a goodly yet terrible sight'. At dawn next day a watcher on the Essex coast counted the Dutch eighty-eight strong off Harwich, 'looking very terribly'; 'we expect now very shortly to hear

---

* *P.R.O. Foreign Entry Book* 177. May 9th, 1672.

the guns'. But the allied fleet missed them in a fog and, contrary to the King's advice, put into Southwold Bay to careen.[10]

Here, as both the King and Lord Sandwich had foreseen, the Duke of York was caught napping on a lee shore. At dawn on May 28th the Dutch fleet was discovered standing into the Bay from the north-east, with a fine fighting south-easterly gale behind them. At that moment many of the English seamen were sleeping in ale houses ashore, and the drums were hastily beaten to bring them to their boats.[11]

All that day over many miles of peaceful countryside the guns could be heard – some said even in London. Balty, listening at Deal, on the other side of the Thames estuary, could hear the thunder of the broadsides quite clearly. Nearer at Landguard Fort the windows shook continually. Pepys in the quiet of the Navy Office never stirred, and for two anxious days continued, as was his unheroic duty, to despatch away men, stores and ships and to perform the thousand and one tasks of his post. But his heart, one can well guess, was with the Fleet, and most of all on board the *Prince* and the *Royal James*, the great ships which carried the Duke of York and Lord Sandwich.[12]

For the latter he was particularly worried. The sensitive, retiring, heavy-figured man had been strangely melancholy of late; there had been murmurs, especially from the fiery Clifford, who was now carrying all before him at Court, that his past prudence had been nothing but cowardice. A few days before he left Whitehall to join his ship, Sandwich, visited by Evelyn at his lodgings in the Privy Garden, had shaken the gentle virtuoso mournfully by the hand and told him that he believed he would never see him again. And a short while previously, walking in Lord Burlington's garden and leaning his gouty, unwieldy frame on the shoulders of his young adherents, Charles Harbord and Clem Cotterell – son of the Master of Ceremonies – he had spoken bitterly of the management of affairs, observing that, though he was Vice-Admiral of England, he knew nothing of the plans for the summer's campaign. 'This only I know,' he had added, 'that I will die and these two boys will die with me.'[13]

Thus it came about, that when on May 29th rumours reached London that Sandwich had fallen in action, Pepys' fears were but confirmed. By next day it was known for certain that the *Royal James* had been lost. But for some time it was impossible to obtain definite information, though Pepys, tied by his work to his Office, wrote anxiously to Williamson to obtain it, for, as one correspondent put it, 'after sea fights the spirit of lying is very predominant'. On the 31st it was still uncertain whether the Earl had escaped or not.[14]

The authentic account of what had happened on the 28th did not reach London till the first day of June. The Fleet, caught on the careen, had weighed at sundown and stood north to engage, but there had been a serious lack of co-ordination, the French Admiral disregarding his orders and partially turning out of the battle. The Dutch with the weather gage had concentrated their main force on the leading ships of the Red and Blue Squadrons of the English, which bore the flags of the Heir Presumptive and Lord Sandwich. By seven o'clock the latter was seen to be surrounded, the Dutch sweeping round the *Royal James* 'like a torrent'. Then the mist had fallen and the wind had dropped.

Thus for some hours the Dutch were able to concentrate on the two flagships, and with what was left of the wind loose their fireships on them. These the beleaguered English had constantly to beat off. By ten o'clock, two hundred men in the *Prince* had fallen, her sails and rigging were gone, and the Duke was forced to shift his flag to the *St Michael*. Meanwhile Sandwich, in still worse plight, was fighting the *Royal James* against a whole squadron. After two hours the Dutch Admiral, Van Ghent, tried to board. But though the *Royal James* had by that time lost three hundred men, Sandwich resolved to 'cuff it out to the last man'.

While the stricken ship was still struggling with Van Ghent's boarders, the ghostly masts of Sir Joseph Jordan's* squadron appeared out of the mist. But though Sandwich had already sent to summon it to his aid, it was only to pass by, apparently on its way to join the Duke of York. Then said the English Admiral: 'we must do our best to defend ourselves alone'.

After that no other hope of help came near. Sometime after midday a great fireship, disguised as a battleship with blue guns and dummy men, came flaming alongside. That was the end. 'So brave

---

* 'He is a person I know not,' wrote one who watched the engagement from the Suffolk shore, 'but I like not his fighting nor conduct. I wished myself on him to have saved that brave Mountague, for he was in the wind of him and might have come down to him . . . I was so near as I saw almost every broadside and was in hearing and whistling of the shot.' T. Lucas to N. Herne, May 29th, 1672. *C.S.P.D.* XIII, 1672:9.

Mountagu', wrote one spectator '(I shall ever honour him) being all in fire and smoke, that nothing but his flag was to be seen from seven till about one, was fired by a pitiful fireship, having sunk a great Dutch ship and three fireships before, and let the whole squadron taste of his valour.' Towards two o'clock the *Royal James* 'flew into the air'.

Meanwhile the ships of the Red Squadron and the remainder of the Blue, which all this while had been struggling to get into action, engaged. The fight now became general. And though at about six the *St Michael* dropped out of the line and the Duke for the second time was forced to shift his flag, the enemy had no longer things their own way. At dusk they turned towards their own coasts. But though the English followed them next day almost to Zeeland, fog and lack of shot forbade any further engagement, and in the evening the Duke, half blind with smoke and with his wig singed by fire, led the Fleet home. Though the losses both of ships and men had been fairly evenly divided, the Allies had entirely failed to win the victory they had anticipated, and Holland had still a fleet in being to defend her coasts from invasion. Lord Sandwich was missing and, though it was reported that he had been seen getting into a boat just before the *Royal James* blew up, few doubted but that he was dead.[15]

No certain news came for ten days. Then on June 10th a ketch, sweeping for anchors lost in the battle, picked up the Admiral's body, swollen with wind and scoffed by porpoises, but with the George and Star of the Garter still shining on his breast. For a week he lay at Landguard Fort, until a yacht could bear him to Deptford, there to lie till the day of the splendid interment which the King had ordered.[16]

On July 3rd the barges left Deptford to bring the dead Admiral to Westminster. With Standard and Guidon, trumpet and drum, the velvet pall adorned with scutcheons, he passed up the familiar river, with the King, the Duke of York, and all the principal nobles and officers of England following after, while the Tower guns sounded a last salute. About five in the evening he came to Westminster pier, to be carried through a double file of the King's guards to the west door of the Abbey, where the Dean and choir were waiting to receive him. In the pomp of that solemn procession Samuel Pepys bore his part. First marched the twelve Earls who were the principal mourners, among them the Lord Chancellor, the great Lord Shaftesbury, then the supporters of the pall, and bearers of the Standard, Guidon and Great Banner, and then the proud, sad Clerk of the Acts with his five fellow Bannerolles, Talbot Pepys his cousin, Sidney Pickering, the two fathers, Sir Charles Cotterell and Sir Charles Harbord, whose sons had fallen by the Admiral's side, and Harbord's other son William. There were others in that procession with whom Pepys had long ago been familiar and with whom he had grown up in the dead Earl's shadow – Creed, whom he had once envied and whose cunning wit he had despised but enjoyed and who had now grown rich, and poor Captain Ferrers, who in the old days at some hopes Pepys had once given him had fallen so mad with joy that he had leapt out of a window and broken his leg. It was the end of a chapter in Pepys' life that had begun in poverty in the little garret in the turret of Cromwell's Whitehall, where Elizabeth had washed his 'foul' clothes with her own hands and worn her old gown 'Kingdom' that had so pleased him, and which now after nearly twenty years was closing in national pomp and majesty and sorrow.[17]

While he was still mourning Sandwich Pepys suffered a bitter disappointment. Among those wounded at Sole Bay was Matthew Wren, the Duke of York's secretary. Once before, when the office of Secretary to the Lord High Admiral had looked like becoming vacant, Pepys had nursed fearful hopes of it; now he set himself in haste to obtain it. On June 3rd he secured William Coventry's promise to write at once to the Duke. But early next morning he heard from Coventry that his hands were tied by the appointment as Wren's deputy of his nephew, Harry Savile, against whose interest he could not with decency act. Savile was a cheerful humorist and something of a contrast to his fastidious brother Lord Halifax, a wit, an accomplished linguist and one of the very best letter-writers of his day: he had just written an admirably official account of the battle. But he was fundamentally careless and lazy and blessed with a genius for getting himself into scrapes; a few months before he had had to go into a disgraceful retirement, from which only the War had saved him, on account of an injudicious attempt on the chastity of a great lady who was his fellow guest at Althorp – a nocturnal escapade that had set every bell in the house ringing and every fashionable tongue in London wagging.

Being on the spot, Savile was left in possession. Pepys accepted the disappointment with grace, and sought his rival's friendship.

'How unnecessary soever it be', Coventry wrote at his request to Savile, 'for me to desire your kindness to a good correspondence with Mr Pepys, whome you know so deserving it . . . yet since Mr Pepys hath been so obliging to me as to give the opportunity to be instrumental in an affair so much to be desired by your friends, I willingly embrace it . . . You may receive more help and learn more of the Navy affairs from him than from any man living.'*[18]

As many, thinking that Pepys had received the appointment, wrote to congratulate him, he had the mortification of explaining that the flattering rumours about him were untrue. A still worse humiliation followed when, Savile's appointment proving temporary, the reversion was granted to John Werden, a young diplomat wholly inexperienced in naval affairs. 'I cannot but advise you', Samuel wrote mournfully to Balty, 'that even diligence and integrity itself is not always defence enough against censure, nor can be while envy remains in the world, and therefore you are by all honest improvements of your time to provide against a day where possibly I in my place may not be able to help you . . . a very serious reflection upon what you may very possibly find my condition to prove.' And he urged his brother-in-law to prepare his mind to meet adversity – the more so 'from the trouble that it in some degree gives me that I had no sooner learnt it myself'.[19]

But there was no time for philosophy or even regret. A battered Fleet had once more to be put to sea. The King went down to the Nore to meet it before dawn on June 5th. Allin, the Comptroller, writing next day from the Swale voiced the attitude of the Navy Office when he demanded that everything should be done to provide good bread and fresh beef for the seamen 'who, although unwilling to venture their limbs, yet, when at it, have behaved like Romans'. Provisions and stores of all kinds were needed; 'to-day', he wrote, 'we want nails, spikes, . . . and oak-timber'. The worst lack of all was masts and spars, but happily Deane, who was on the spot, was 'a great contriver'. Back in London Pepys ordered, urged and entreated, working ceaselessly to get whatever the Fleet needed despatched down the River. The Navy Board was sitting twice daily, in the mornings at Whitehall to be near the King and Prince Rupert, and in the afternoons in Seething Lane, so that office work had to be

---

* Sir W. Coventry to H. Savile, June 11th, 1672. *Rawl. MSS. A.* 174, f. 239.

crowded into the early mornings and nights. But by June 10th Deane could write that the hulls and rigging of five of his 'lame geese' would be ready that night and another nine in a day or two.[20]

On the 17th the King again went down the River to view progress. Pepys went too, though he was clamoured for at the Office all the time he was away. He was back on the 21st, well – 'saving some little disorder an uneasy lodging for so many nights hath given me' – and glad to find the Navy Office was still standing after its escape from a fire that had broken out in Crutched Friars. Before the end of June the Fleet was once more at sea and hastening towards the Dutch coast.[21]

For an extraordinary thing had happened. The Dutch resistance to the French on land had completely crumbled. Louis' armies were carrying everything before them, town after town surrendering without a struggle. The first feelings in England were of delight that the proud 'Hogen Mogen' were brought low, and then of wonder that so potent, rich and well-governed a commonwealth should so easily be subdued. Soon these gave way to alarm at the triumph of a Catholic despot over a nation of free Protestants.

As the French armies advanced across the Dutch plain, 'all Protestant hearts trembled'. Envy and insular hatred of the French fanned the flame; by the early days of June a 'fearful murmur' was abroad that England's allies had behaved ill at Sole Bay. Admiral Spragge voiced the rough prejudices of his race when he wrote: 'the French who will never be as they ought to be'. Within a few weeks they had become everywhere, except at Court, intensely unpopular. Never had the jealous English passion for the balance of power offered so swift and startling a demonstration. Even the King was alarmed, and on the day before the Fleet sailed for the Texel Lord Arlington and the Duke of Buckingham were despatched to Louis' camp with suggestions for a general peace. At that moment the surrender of De Ruyter's fleet was hourly expected, for its own ports seemed likely to be closed in its face by the French armies.[22]

Again the unexpected happened. For the first three weeks of July the Allies cruised off the Dutch coast in constant storms. During that time they never so much as saw a Dutch ship. They then stood off for the Dogger, hoping to meet their victualling ships and to intercept the home-coming Dutch East India fleet. All they got for their pains was one prize. Crowded with soldiers whom it was intended to land in Holland, the English ships were rotten with sickness, while the perpetual storms to which they had been subjected had played havoc with anchors, cables and bowsprits.

In the first week of August, the victualling ships not having appeared, the Fleet, seventy-three strong, left the Dogger and stood in for Burlington Bay, and after a few days on the Yorkshire and Northumbrian coast took advantage of a northerly wind to run for the Thames. On the night of August 23rd, the disappointed King went down to the Buoy of the Nore to greet his brother, the Admiral. The ships were no longer in a state to keep the seas and their crews so decimated with sickness that they had scarcely men enough to weigh anchor. 'I never saw people so intolerably weary as they all are of being at sea', wrote an eyewitness. So wet and stormy a summer had not been known in human memory.[23]

For a few days, while there was still talk of getting the Fleet out again to land troops in Holland, Pepys and his fellow Officers were kept busy hustling fireships and victuallers' barges down the River and hurrying out caulkers and shipwrights from the Yards. But it all ended in nothing, for the stores were empty, and the Victuallers, whose unpaid account stood at over £110,000, refused to move without cash. The wastage in material had been appalling, the rough and ready extravagance of the fighting men having contributed to it as much as the storms. Middleton told his colleagues at the Navy Board how one captain had ordered his carpenter to cut two hundred and forty yards of canvas out of the maintopsail in order to make extra cabins, and then had calmly demanded a new sail in its place from the hard-pressed stores. 'I fear your multiplicity of business will make you forget this great and unpardonable sin,' wrote the grim old Commissioner, 'which if you do may God forgive you, but I never shall.' Rebuked by his colleagues for his disrespectful language, Middleton remained unrepentant, promised to try to be a good boy and learn such a style as would give no offence, and suggested that, if his letters were not fit to be seen, they should have them burnt, though not, he hoped, by the common hangman.[24]

With a wages bill of £340,000 to meet at Michaelmas, the naval administration was in no mood for further adventures that year. Nor was the nation. The press-gang was drawing little now but the dregs of the sea-ports, *Poca Robor*, as Middleton called them, 'naked, pitiful souls, such as I would not give bread and water to for their labour'.

And when the Press-Master, scouring the city with forty seamen with drawn cutlasses, broke into the house of a worthy citizen 'of sober life and known repute among his neighbours' and bore him off from his wife and family, Pepys, Brouncker and Tippetts, who at the time were carrying on the work of the Navy Office, had to eat humble pie and order his immediate release. On September 23rd, the Council resolved to pay off Fleet and Yards for the winter.[25]

Worst of all the Board's cares were the sick and wounded. Every south-eastern port was full of them. Evelyn, on a tour of inspection in Kent, wrote to his friend, the Clerk of the Acts, of his difficulties at Gravesend, where he had to quarter eight hundred people in a town that could only hold five. And the cursed people of the place, he complained, had no bowels and swore to receive no more wounded till their arrears were paid. He had done everything he could, and the clamour against him and his fellow Commissioners notwithstanding, there was not a man who was not decently quartered or provided for. 'But', he added, 'when all imaginable care is taken as to our part, unless you be pleased to allow some covering to the poor creatures, who are (many of them) put stark naked and mortified on the shore, multitudes of them must perish, and therefore (presuming on your charity and indeed humanity) I have adventured to give way, that some of the most miserable should have shirts or stockings according to their needs.' It was Pepys' business to find the means.[26]

Faced by this prodigious inflow of wretched humanity, only Balty down at Deal remained serene. The more wounded that came there, he declared, the better, 'where our cleanly nurses and houses are ready now to receive them, being now empty, I having pretty well cleared this town and consequently eased his Majesty's charges by returning them as fast as possible I could to their respective ships; . . . better, I say, than to be thronged up and indeed partly murdered (as at Gravesend)'. One can picture the expression on Pepys' listening face as this epistle was read him, but perhaps the grim smile relaxed a little when the postscript came, 'with little Samuel's humble return of thanks for your most kind remembrance of your little disciple'.*[27]

A more valuable document on the same melancholy topic came to the naval authorities from a surgeon, John Reade, who stated that

* B. St Michel to S. Pepys, Sept. 11th, 1672. *Rawl. MSS. A.* 187, ff. 357–8.

there had been more sickness in the Fleet than he had ever known before. He gave his reasons: the unusual number of land men and soldiers on board 'unacquainted with the ways of keeping themselves clean at sea', the long sojourn in the North Sea, 'in which gross air our English bodies are always subject to the scurvy', and the tempestuous weather, which had kept the port-holes closed and prevented the ships from being aired and cleansed. In the French Fleet there had been far less sickness because the ships, having no cabins between decks, were far more airy, and the crews followed a more wholesome diet, especially in their resort to wine and water instead of beer, and to garlic, 'which is the poor man's treacle'. Reade recommended that the holds should be washed after every voyage, that captains or pursers should be given money to buy fresh beef, herbs and fruit two or three times a month, that brandy and lime juice should be served out every morning, and that the Lord High Admiral should enjoin the regular eating of garlic. His document impressed the Clerk of the Acts so much that he preserved it among his papers.*[28]

While fate had dealt thus unkindly with their enemies at sea, the Dutch had not been swallowed up by the French on land. At the eleventh hour, a heroic people had regained their ancient courage, and casting off their republican rulers and calling on the young Prince of Orange to lead them, let in the sea, 'resolved to die in the last dyke'. Nor would Prince William listen for a moment to his Uncle of England's suggestion that he should secure his family's status at the expense of his patriotism. The hard-pressed nation responded to the call of his calm heroism, and everywhere the French encountered resistance. Nor did the English escape. Into Pepys' unwilling ears there began to pour a tale of impudent little Dutch capers and picaroons, who played havoc with commerce and brought ruin to English shipowners. The trade routes were infested, and the very fishermen as they put out into the placid waters of the Wash had their nets taken from them. But when the naval authorities put forward suggestions for convoys, a liberty-loving trading community rejected them with impatience; the foolhardy colliers would still venture out, one official complained, if the Devil himself were in the way.[29]

* *Rawl. MSS. A.* 187, ff. 345–6.

The real working head of the chief branch of the English bureaucracy, Pepys had little time during that troubled summer for a private life of his own. His very nights were public property, and often he was roused from his sleep by some urgent despatch. But the national crisis did not prevent the death of Uncle Wight – the pious, rather revolting, old fishmonger who had once proposed to poor Elizabeth that together they should furnish her unsuspecting husband with an heir – nor the litigation in which the disposal of his estate involved Samuel and a good many other hopeful and ultimately disappointed relatives. Nor did it prevent Balty from writing long, almost passionate letters of love, hope and entreaty about himself and his dependants. 'I have perused and studied your most dear and more than fatherly, kind advices', he told his brother-in-law, 'for which you may, Sir, believe and know how much I find in my very heart and soul that I am obliged to your goodness . . . not only to myself, but also to the rest of your humble creatures, my relations.'*

It is at least pleasant to know that Pepys sometimes found a leisure moment for other, less humble, creatures. The Duke of Richmond, husband of La Belle Stuart and English Ambassador at Copenhagen, sending him forty gallons of Rhenish wine of the year '60, wrote that he envied him the happiness of having the pleasure of so many fine women – 'whilst poor I know no such thing'. There was no Elizabeth to be jealous now. But perhaps his Grace's allusion was by way of jest and referred to Samuel's charming cousins and companions, the two sisters of Portugal Row, Mrs Stewart and Lady Mordaunt.† He had first met the latter, in her salad days with her aunt, kind Mrs Turner of Salisbury Court, and set her down then – that was six years ago – as 'a most homely widow, but young and pretty rich and good-natured'. She was now, in the opinion of her friends, 'the best humoured woman in the world'. Both these witty and fascinating ladies swore they were desperately in love with Samuel, and 'sighed out their passions so charmingly', as one mutual acquaintance wrote to him, ''tis hard to know whether to

* B. St Michel to S. Pepys, Sept. 11th, 1672. *Rawl. MSS. A.* 187, ff. 357–8.

† Elizabeth Mordaunt was a niece of Sir William Turner, the Lord Mayor, who was brother to John Turner, the Sergeant, of Salisbury Court. She had married Sir George Mordaunt Bart. of Massingham, Norfolk, but had been early left a widow. Pepys in his Diary of Dec. 11th, 1666, wrote of her: 'which was Betty Turner', but this was a mistake for her maiden name was Johnson.

envy or pity you. Your enjoyments in their conversation can nowhere else be found, and theirs is so great when you entertain them they all acknowledge your humour the best in the whole world'.*[30]

Such delights must have gone some way to compensate for laborious days and public mortifications. Ever since his great speech at the Bar of the Commons Pepys had hoped to enter Parliament, where his oratorical gifts, he believed, would bring glory to himself and repute to his Office. The chance seemed to have come, when in the middle of August he heard from Harry Savile that the Duke, remembering his desire to enter Parliament, had recommended him to his friend Lord Henry Howard, a great Catholic magnate, whose pocket borough of Castle Rising was expected to fall vacant through the rumoured elevation of its member, Sir Robert Paston, to the peerage. But where Catholics were concerned the electorate was not what it had been, and it soon appeared that there would be many obstacles. Before the end of the month, Thomas Povey, who was a friend of Howard's, warned Samuel that there was a good deal of ill-feeling among the Norfolk gentry at the idea of the seat being given to a courtier and a stranger. Moreover Howard, who was an obliging man,† had already engaged himself to the King for one candidate and to the Duchess of Cleveland for another, as well as to the Duke for Pepys; he was anxious to help, he said, but found himself 'oppressed with his prerogative of recommending on elections'. And in the end nothing happened, for Sir Robert was not promoted after all, and the only elevation to the peerage that autumn was Lord Henry's own to the Earldom of Norwich.[31]

So for the moment Pepys had to content himself with the work of a mere Civil Servant, for which he was better fitted than any man in England. Paying off the Fleet, because it could not be supported during the winter, and manning and equipping it again against the spring – rather as the farmers killed their cattle each Michaelmas and raised a new stock at Lammastide – was his chief business for the next six months. The usual lack of money and a too lavish use of

* 'Long', Mr Hill continued, 'may you enjoy these happinesses, which I should envy in my King, if he were so fortunate, but not in my friend.' Thomas Hill to Samuel Pepys from Lisbon, April 4th–14th, 1673. *Howarth*, 41–3.

† He allowed the Royal Society to meet at Arundel House, his palace in the Strand, and at Evelyn's request gave the Society his library. Evelyn, Jan. 9th, 1667.

tickets, confused by thousands of hasty transferences from ship to ship, made the former almost as hard as the latter, and there was bitter ill-feeling among the seamen, with whom Pepys could not refrain from sympathizing, at the harsh and ungenerous rules laid down for their pay by the new Lord Treasurer. Nor did Pepys' own rules escape criticism. When he asked the Commissioners for Sick and Wounded for alphabetical lists of all their charges, that bluff country gentleman, Colonel Bullen Reymes, replied that it was quite impossible to supply them. For who, in the meantime, he asked, should quarter the sick and wounded? Who should enter tickets and discharges? Who give passes? Who make enquiries after runaways? Who pacify mutinies? There was no one to do all this, and much more besides, but one poor deputy, and he without even a clerk. Besides, the Colonel added, the thing was impossible in any case. But there were few who worked under Pepys' surveillance who dared to take such a line. In his own limited world the 'Squire', as one of his humbler correspondents termed him, was fast becoming an autocrat.[32]

He was certainly learning to present rather an unbending countenance to the world. At the end of 1672 his old friend Thomas Povey, who by their original agreement of 1665 was entitled to half the profits of the Tangier Treasurership in which Pepys had succeeded him, ventured to enquire after the terms on which he was transmitting money to the garrison. He received a very unprofitable answer. 'It would very much unbecome me (I grant)', Pepys replied, 'to deal in anything darkly with you; nor do I see how I could in the particular you enquire after – since the account of all my proceedings therein must appear, and that upon oath. But because that may not be so soon as you seem desirous to have it, you may please to know that the £3000, which I told the Lords then I had remitted by Bills of Exchange to Tangier do (after the best means used I could find to get them in cheaper) cost me neither more nor less than four shillings and fourpence per piece . . . I thought I had done very well for the King now, I not remembering that the King was ever yet served . . . with such money so cheap. However I am glad to be instructed how it may be done cheaper, and do desire you to go on with the merchant you mention at four shillings and twopence or under, for I am at this day furnished with very good Tallies on the Excise, wherewith to supply the garrison with another quarter, and shall with the more content embrace the opportunity of doing it by your hand, that you may be a witness of my doing the best I can for the King's advantage . . . without the least advantage to myself.'* As usual the portrait Pepys painted of himself was one of flawless, and to more ordinary and frail mortals, of almost insulting integrity.[33]

During the early months of 1673 the War went on in the desultory fashion common to seventeenth-century wars in winter. The French armies wearily faced the dismal waters that stood between them and the last but now secure remnants of free Holland, while the battle fleets remained in their harbours. Only the Dutch capers continued to vex the Navy Office with their ceaseless depredations. Not only did they play havoc with the Newcastle colliers and send London's fuel prices soaring, but they lay off almost every harbour in the West of England in such numbers that it was impossible for the frigates of the Winter Guard to deal with them all. In November a Dutch privateer actually came into Plymouth Sound and spread her colours in the faces of the infuriated townsmen. 'I with many other English hearts', wrote Pepys' correspondent, Philip Lanyon, 'am sorry to see such things.' But there was only one way for English merchantmen to elude these 'nimble gentlemen', which was by submitting to the restrictions of a convoy system. And this they still refused to do.[34]

With the coming of the New Year, the work of getting the Fleet out again overshadowed everything else. There were ships to be stripped and resheathed, deals and masts to be sent to the Yards, broom and reed to be bought for cleansing the hulls. In all this, Deane, now Commissioner at Portsmouth, was a tremendous standby. Nor did he, like other officials, constantly bombard the Navy Office with demands for the impossible. Ready cash he needed as much as any of them, yet, he wrote, 'if not in your power, I urge it no further'.

Often there were maddening set-backs in the work. In January 1673, an accident to the *Resolution* nearly deprived the Admiralty of one of the finest third-rates of the line. Just as she was about to sail from Portsmouth under Deane's motherly eye, the Yeoman of the Powder Room elected to inspect the powder chest which he

---

* T. Povey to S. Pepys, Dec. 23rd, 1672. *Rawl. MSS. A.* 172, f. 93.

erroneously believed to be empty. The unexpected arrival of the
ship's cat in pursuit of a rat caused him to drop the lighted candle he
was carrying into the chest, and thereby proved it not empty after
all. Amid a series of explosions the crew took to the water, while the
Commander heroically staved the beer and flooded the powder
room just in time to save the ship.[35]

A few days later a more serious disaster befell the naval administration. January 29th, 1673, was a windy, overcast day, following a
bitterly cold month. In the course of it the Prerogative Court of
Canterbury made an order giving half Uncle Wight's £4000 estate to
his widow and the other half to old John Pepys, Uncle Thomas and
Aunt Mary Day, who had been suing for a distribution. That night a
fire broke out in Lady Williams' closet in Lord Brouncker's lodgings, burning the Navy Office and thirty other houses. Samuel lost
his fine heads by Nanteuil and many another noble treasure which
he and Elizabeth had collected; but his Diary and probably most of
his books* were saved. The closet he loved so much – 'as noble a
closet as any man hath' – the dining room with its panelled pictures
by Danckerts of the royal palaces, his fine room with the hangings of
the Apostles on the walls, were gone for ever.[36]

Thus, in the midst of the War, the Administration that fed the
Navy was driven into the wilderness. Fortunately the greater part of
its papers and records were saved, but in a condition which it is easy
to imagine. Temporary and very cramped quarters were found in
the Old Trinity House in Mark Lane, until more adequate accommodation could be provided a few doors away in a house hitherto
occupied by the Prize Office. Here additional rooms were taken by
the Crown, at a rental of £260 a year, for Pepys to live. These
probably were his 'fusty old lodgings' in Winchester Street, or more
correctly Winchester Lane (which backed on to Mark Lane)
referred to long after in a letter of Sarah Houblon's and which have
been commonly assumed to have been in Great Winchester Street.[37]

Burnt out the Navy Board might be, but the demands for stores,
provisions and money continued to pour in as before. The ropemak-
ers wanted hemp and the victuallers money, and it was for Mr Pepys
to see to all. And how to pay the seamen after the next campaign

* There are many in the Pepysian Library that were plainly purchased before
1673, and two of the presses which still house them are almost certainly those which
Sympson, the joiner, made for him in 1666.

there was no saying. In the midst of so much want, came the still voice of Balty, asking for a little smack or hoy to attend him and save him from the danger of landing at night in bad weather.[38]

There was an evil genius in the air of England that winter. Rain fell incessantly, aguish fevers rose from the earth, and the troubled farmer –

> As th'other day in bed I thinking lay,
> How I my rent could to my landlord pay,
> Since wool nor corn nor beasts would money make,
> Tumbled, perplext, these thoughts kept me awake –

turned angry, suspicious eyes on the great men at Court and spoke of the secret Cabal of Ministers who were leading all to ruin. The War, the French Alliance, the Declaration of Indulgence to Papists, and, worst of all, an unholy, mysterious, widely rumoured plot hatched in the highest quarters to make England Catholic, were grievances that were on every tongue.

When Parliament met in February, though Lord Chancellor Shaftesbury's *Delenda est Carthago* speech won a grudging supply for the War, the Commons insisted that the King should withdraw his Declaration of Indulgence. And by placing on the Statute Book a Test Act, which compelled every office holder to receive the Sacrament according to the Church of England and take an oath against the doctrine of Transubstantiation, they made it impossible for any Catholic to hold public office. The political power of the great Papists crumbled away in a night. On Easter Sunday a crowded auditory waited breathlessly in the Chapel Royal to see whether the Duke of York received the Communion by his brother's side. To the grief of good men and the joy of restless spirits, he did not. Revolution, Civil War and a Commonwealth were once more among the possibilities of practical politics.[39]

A few weeks elapsed before the Duke of York and the Lord Treasurer laid down their offices for their faith. Meanwhile Prince Rupert, with a Commission as General under the Lord High Admiral, was given orders to embark troops, engage the enemy, and effect a landing on the Dutch coast. To the burgesses of such sea towns as he should capture he was to offer the option of retaining their old form of provincial government under the suzerainty of the British Crown or of being incorporated with England with the right of sending members to Parliament. Pending the fulfilment of these lofty conceptions, there floated back to the Navy Office from the Prince's flagship a continuous stream of complaints; everything an Admiral had a right to expect in his Fleet was wanting, those who supplied it were idlers if not knaves, and the Duke of York and his agents were deliberately stinting him and putting obstacles in his way. The latter's orders, Rupert informed the Secretary of State, he had made bold to put into his pocket.[40]

But it was the beginning of May before the fiery old General and his ships could be got out to sea to seek De Ruyter in the Schoneveldt. Nor did he achieve anything when he got there. For, though, with the auxiliary French Squadron, he had eighty-one ships of the line to De Ruyter's fifty-two, he was no match for his adversary. Twice, on May 28th* and on June 3rd, the great Dutch Admiral, choosing his own time, sallied out from his shoals, both to suffer and inflict severe losses but without question to save his country. Meanwhile Prince Rupert's litany of wants continued unabated; so many were they, he said, that his captains came on board every morning with tears in their eyes. 'The truth is,' he told Lord Arlington, 'as I foresaw long ago, this fleet was merely whodled out': that it had survived at all was to be attributed only to his own capacity. He brought it home to re-fit at the beginning of June.[41]

All this may well have seemed stale and unprofitable to Pepys. He had fitted out so many fleets, only to see them return shattered, with their high hopes unfulfilled. The dykes he had built and repaired so industriously were constantly crumbling away through circumstances over which in his still subordinate position he had no control. His attempts to obtain the Comptrollership of the Navy and the Duke's Secretaryship had failed, and he had twice been disappointed in his hopes of a seat in Parliament. Now the seemly and gracious home, whose making had been so intimately associated

---

* On this occasion, Rupert had endeavoured unsuccessfully to put into practice a project of Captain Richard Holland's, the skilled renegade navigator who had led the Dutch up the Medway in 1667 and had since received the royal pardon. Holland's plan, had it succeeded, would have repeated the tactics of Gravelines by offering the anchored enemy the alternatives of being burnt by the English fireships or of being driven on the sands to leeward. But Rupert by delaying four hours launched the operation on an ebb instead of a flood tide, and De Ruyter was left free to counterattack on a windward tide. *Rawl. MSS. A.* 189, f. 251.

with his work at the Navy Board, had crumbled in a night to ashes, and he was left in his fusty lodgings and cramped office to the thankless drudgery of slaving in a failing war. And his old patron, the Heir Presumptive, whose aid and confidence he had so laboriously won, had been driven from office and was fast becoming the most unpopular figure in England.

In this dark and disillusioned hour a great call came to Samuel Pepys. On the 13th day of June he wrote on the Board's behalf to Lord Anglesey about the residue of his debt to the Chatham Chest –some £6800 'under which the Poor of the Chest . . . hath for so many years languished'. He was in no mood to mince his words but spoke out his mind boldly – 'the soliciting your Lordship with all decent plainness', he called it. 'Your Lordship became Treasurer of the Navy in July 1667, and continued in the execution of that office till November 1668, during which time you were pleased (differing from the practice of any other Treasurer past or present) to take to yourself the benefit of the allowance made by the Chest to the Paymaster . . . which being the case . . . we do once more make it our humble suit to your Lordship that the day being near on which the many cripples of this Society will . . . resort from every part of this kingdom to Chatham in dependence of that yearly relief, which (without the help of this money) we shall not be in any condition to give them, you will be pleased, after so many years' forbearance of it and its interest, to find some present means of helping us; the distresses of the Poor not only requiring it, but to prevent the ill consequences of their coming up hither and . . . the reproach which might justly be esteemed the greatest the Navy hath ever yet met with; namely that while his Majesty labours under the wants of his seamen serving him abroad occasioned by their arrears of wages not yet paid, those who lie maimed at home should perish for want of what hath so long since been both by his Majesty and themselves actually paid, and is or ought to be now remaining in your Lordship's hands to their use.' It was a tremendous broadside,* and the last that Pepys ever fired as Clerk of the Acts.[42]

* Anglesey was very angry. In his reply he referred to the letter (*Rawl. MSS. A.* 172, ff. 81–2) as 'unjustly scandalous', and added: 'If there had as great care to provide for the necessity of the Chest as there hath been art used by strained and mistaken inferences to reflect causelessly on me, that letter might have been spared; and things cleared by discourse which will hardly be by writing.' *Rawl. MSS. A.* 172, ff. 83–4.

On the same day the King in Council adopted the new instructions for the Admiral's Office, which Pepys had secretly drafted and which henceforward were to control the higher command of the Navy. At all times, it was laid down, the Lord High Admiral must be able to give the King a perfect account of the state of his Navy, ships, yards, stores and personnel; must meet with the Principal Officers and Commissioners of the Navy at least once a month and receive a weekly report of their proceedings; must obtain from the Comptroller preliminary estimates of all work to be done and with the Treasurer of the Navy present them to the King 'for the obtaining seasonable and sufficient supplies of money'; and must see that a fair Register of all naval proceedings was kept in an office by a permanent Secretary of the Admiralty. It was the end of the old, personal, half-irresponsible rule of the King's Navy; henceforward there was to be order, method and precedent. Two days later the Duke of York, in accordance with the terms of the Test Act, resigned his office as Lord High Admiral.

No successor was appointed. On June 22nd a warrant was directed to the Attorney General to prepare a bill appointing fifteen of the greatest men in the Kingdom Commissioners for executing part of the Office of Lord High Admiral, leaving a residue, including the disposal of all places and offices, in the direct control of the Crown. The new Commissioners included Prince Rupert, the Dukes of Buckingham, Monmouth, Lauderdale and Ormonde, the Lord Chancellor, Lord Treasurer and Lord Keeper and the two Secretaries of State. But even before the warrant went out, his Majesty called Samuel Pepys, Esquire, 'the only survivor of the first ... set of officers of the Navy at his Restoration' to the place of Secretary to the Office of Lord High Admiral of England. His brother John and his old clerk Tom Hayter succeeded him as joint Clerk of the Acts.[43]

4

Called to the Admiralty

'I hear you have a task set you.' James Houblon to S. Pepys. *Pepysian MS.* 2865, Paper 95.

In the middle of the stream the King had changed horses. For, though men knew it not, the Cabal and all the ambitious, secret designs it stood for and the still more secret hopes it hid, were gone for ever. Clifford, the fiery champion of a lost cause, laid down his Treasurer's staff, packed up his vast pictures of lion hunts and wild beasts and went down to the lonely, lovely home of his ancient race to die. York, betrothing himself to a foreign and Catholic princess, took up his position openly as the head of the Catholic faction and therefore, to nine Englishmen out of ten, as the most dangerous and feared man in the country. Buckingham and Shaftesbury, with their rats' sense of a sinking ship, hastened to make secret overtures to the ultra-Protestant, anti-Court parliamentary Opposition. Only the courtly Arlington and Lauderdale, the tough, coarse, red-faced Scottish Viceroy, remained.

In three vital points the old administration had failed – in its control of public opinion, in finance, and in the management of the Fleet. In the first it was to go on failing until the King himself in his closing years applied his latent political genius to counteract the results of his earlier mistakes. In finance, the promotion to the vacant Treasury in June 1673 of Sir Thomas Osborne, the hard-headed Yorkshire squire who, since 1671, had been Treasurer of the Navy, gave the control of the national purse to a practical financier of the first order. And in naval matters, the elevation of Pepys at the age of forty to the Secretaryship of the Admiralty Office, though little noticed at the time, ultimately produced results which affected not England alone, but the whole world. For by his precept and example Pepys was to transform an inchoate and ill-directed service into the most enduring, exact and potent instrument of force seen on this disorderly planet since the days of Imperial Rome.[1]

Nobody guessed this at the time, least of all Samuel, who could no more envisage the ultimate stranglehold on the trade routes of the world of the naval machine he was so painfully to create, than he could the spectacle of a million heads bowed over the pages of his Diary. All he knew was that he had served his full apprenticeship and that the work of his heart had at last come to his hand.

For the moment there was no time to think of anything but the conduct of the War. Though it was no longer Pepys' part to fit out the ships, it was his duty now to see that others did so, and a week after his appointment he was writing sternly to his old colleagues at the Navy Office to urge them to 'the despatch of all things requisite for putting the Fleet into a speedy condition of going to sea' – especially men, who, after the mistakes of the previous year, had been almost impossible to procure. One of his first achievements as Secretary was his discovery that the River was full of well-manned naval tenders whose crews by pretending service on the Fleet had escaped attention. With Pepys' elevation an ill day had dawned for malingerers.

For several weeks after his arrival at the Admiralty, Pepys was kept busy writing to Press-Masters at the ports to spare no effort to obtain every man available. Often he had to urge discretion on them also and to demand the release of forbidden persons seized by the gangs – his Majesty's Dutch baker, the waterman of the Clerk of the Cheque at Gravesend, the sanctified barge-crew of his Grace the Archbishop of Canterbury. Even his Majesty's foreign mails were delayed by the excessive zeal of the Press-Masters; the King, Pepys wrote to one offending salt, did not think it sufferable that his very packet boats should be rifled and his whole service disappointed at the pleasure of a single disorderly officer.[2]

Driven as he was, Pepys still managed to derive a good deal of content from the grandeur of his new position. The great Committees of State in the seventeenth century were wont to meet with pomp – a vast board covered with green cloth and silver standishes with an attendance of obsequious clerks; a tall porter with staff and messengers at the door; fine furniture and rich hangings, with an imposing array of atlases, maps, charts and globes. Round that Board which was now Pepys' very own, sat the greatest men of the kingdom, and in the chair the King's Majesty himself. The attendance of some was more formal than regular – the Duke of Monmouth for instance only attended three times in six months – but this was if anything an advantage, for it left the more power in Pepys' hands. The Board met on Mondays, Wednesdays and Fridays, at eight o'clock in the morning, and, until a separate office of its own could be found for it, in the Council Chamber at Whitehall.[3]

For Pepys it meant a big increase in power and prestige. His salary, which as Clerk of the Acts had been £350 per annum, was raised to £500 per annum – say £2500 per annum in modern money – with substantial travelling allowances, while he was also entitled to considerable emoluments in the way of fees, which amounted in popular estimation to several thousands a year and on his own public admission to at least another thousand.* And he still retained his lucrative appointment as Treasurer of Tangier. His power to grant places to others was very large, and none the less so for being exercised indirectly in the King's name. Almost the first letter of congratulation he received – from his old chief, Sir William Coventry – begged a job for a protégé: 'I know you and the place you execute too well to think it fit for me to recommend an unfit man.' Coventry was careful to add that as he was now living in remote Oxfordshire, he could not make a suitable return unless Pepys should ever want to keep a running horse at Burford – an unlikely contingency. Yet the favour of one of Coventry's influence and connections was no small matter. Even the ladies, after the manner of their sex, had more occasion to be nice to Mr Pepys now that he was so great a man; a few weeks after his appointment Lady Mordaunt was being entreated for her intercession with her kind friend, the Secretary.[4]

But to Pepys the pleasantest part of his new influence was his power to do good acts. For some time he had been maturing in his head a noble scheme for improving the trade of his country. Nearly two years before he had suggested to Lord Sandwich the benefits that might accrue from the erection of 'a nursery of children to be educated in Mathematics for the particular use and service of navigation'. Now that he was in almost daily attendance on the King, Pepys was able to persuade him to embrace a scheme so congenial to both their minds. On August 1st the Attorney General

* He was, for instance, entitled to a fee of £1 for every protection granted to merchant ships or fishing boats, £5 on the renewal of every commission to Vice-Admirals of Counties, £2 on the renewal of those of Admiralty Judges, Registrars and Marshals. *Rawl. MSS. A.* 171, f. 137.

was directed to prepare a bill for the establishment of a Mathematical School for forty picked boys, chosen for their wit and scholarship from the general body of the old charitable foundation of Christ's Hospital, to be instructed in arithmetic and mathematics and the science of navigation, until old enough to be apprenticed to the sea. Towards it the King promised a grant of £1000 per annum for seven years, the equivalent to a sum of £7427 formerly left to the Hospital and unwisely invested and consequently lost in Commonwealth state securities.* Twenty beds were provided for the children and a competent mathematician, one Mr Leake, specially recommended by the Royal Society, chosen as master, while the King at Pepys' request graciously promised that no petitions for admission to the foundation save under its own proper rules should be received. And Mr Hooke, the architect secretary of the Royal Society, was commissioned to design a special badge, to distinguish the mathematical scholars from their fellows, which he very magnificently did, in the form of 'a prospect with a crown over and a label under, enclosing a bluecoat boy attended by Geometry, Arithmetic and Astronomy'. At a distance could be seen the Herculean pillar, with a ship passing through it, and far off *terra incognita*.[5]

These were the by-products of a busy life. For the first eight months of Pepys' Secretaryship England was still at war. In July there was Rupert and his Fleet to be got to sea again; after many delays and complaints, the impetuous old soldier sailed for the Dutch coast on July 19th. The day before, Pepys had accompanied Charles down the River and in the great cabin of the *Royal Sovereign* had taken down in his own hand the resolutions of the Council of Flag Officers which were to be Rupert's instructions. The King and Schomberg, the soldier of fortune who was in command of the troops, believing that De Ruyter would otherwise decline a decisive action, were in favour of attempting an immediate landing on the Dutch coast, but Rupert was so opposed to such an attempt that it was decided that the soldiers should be deposited at Yarmouth until the sailors had tempted him out of the shoals to his destruction.

---

* The late E. H. Pearce, the historian of Christ's Hospital, from this infers that Charles II was thus only giving back to the Hospital a part of what he had already stolen! Fantastic as so much of the historical interpretation of this period has been, no one else has suggested that Charles was accountable for the bankrupt finance of the Commonwealth.

But it was not easy to destroy De Ruyter, who, choosing his moment carefully as usual, gave battle off Kijkduin on August 11th, an indecisive engagement in which the finest flag officer in the English service, Sir Edward Spragge, was drowned gloriously while shifting his flag for the third time to a less damaged ship, that he might the more effectively prosecute his contest – 'all fire and flame' – against his old adversary, Tromp. 'Here', wrote Pepys, to a Norfolk correspondent who had kept him on tenterhooks with misleading intelligence, 'let me take notice of the good ears of your neighbours of Blakeney and Wells, that could hear the guns so plainly all Tuesday, on which there was not one shot.'[6]

The only result of the engagement was still further to embitter relations between the Allies. The French part had not been a glorious one, and the English seamen from Rupert to the meanest cabin boy were furious – 'the plainest and greatest opportunity ever lost at sea', was the former's comment. It was the final battle of the triple sea duel between England and Holland, the greatest naval adversary she has known. And when Rupert's ships returned to the River and Pepys with the King went down to meet them, it was the last time he was ever to welcome home a British fleet after a great naval action. His supreme service to the Navy was to be of another kind.[7]

For the Secretary of the Admiralty Office the remaining months of the War, while the two maritime powers were negotiating a peace that had become essential to both, were concerned chiefly with the protection of English commerce from the Dutch capers, whose veto on the freedom of the seas was now as complete as that of the German *unterseeboote* of two centuries later. That veto Pepys challenged, and defeated, with a convoy system. Shortly after his arrival at his new Office, the East India Company, whose ships were being snapped up as they entered the Chops of the Channel, submitted a plan of its own to the Admiralty. Ten of the nimblest frigates in the service were to be stationed at Plymouth; of which two were to patrol the waters between the Deadman, Isle of Wight, Ushant and the Land's End, two, 'ranging thirty or forty leagues to the westward', to ply between Scilly and Ushant, two between Scilly and Cape Clear, and two sixty or seventy leagues into the Atlantic between the latitudes of 48 and 50, while two more took it in turn to tallow and careen at Plymouth. 'Set these ships in their stations upon a Platt', the proposal concluded, 'and your Lordships will see how they guard the Sea, hunt the capers, make strangers talk how many English men-of-war they see in such a latitude and give our own people . . . protection and convoy.'*[8]

With certain modifications Pepys and his Admiralty Board adopted these proposals. As early as July 19th he was writing that the King was 'sending as much force as conveniently he can immediately to the Soundings', and by August Captain Tyrwhitt was ranging the mouth of the Channel with the *Adventure, Morning Star, Norwich, Dragon, Speedwell, Hunter* and two other frigates extracted, with many angry protests, from Rupert's fleet. But, as Pepys saw, the scheme did not go far enough. In the home-coming merchant flotillas from Virginia, the East Indies, the Straits, Barbados and the Canaries, the King depended for his customs and the nation for its trade. The first of these fleets arrived at Plymouth on September 21st having lost twelve ships to Evertson in the Atlantic. Two days later Pepys was instructing the best of the younger officers in the Service and his particular protégé, Captain John Narbrough, to send out frigates and sloops 'with all possible earnestness' to the westward. His measures proved effective. But his principal achievement was the formation of convoys for the great outgoing merchant fleets, who were to carry England's trade overseas in the early winter months and bring it back again before the spring that the seamen who manned them might be available to re-man the Battle Fleet before the summer's campaign.[9]

On October 8th Pepys' orders went out in the name of the Admiralty to the Navy Board. On St Crispin's Day seven frigates, victualled for five months, were to assemble at the Buoy of the Nore to escort all out-going merchantmen bound for the Straits. Seven more were to be in waiting for the Canaries. By November 10th three more, victualled for three months, were to be ready for the Bordeaux fleet, and three armed merchantmen, carrying thirty-six to forty guns apiece, for the West Indies fleet. A further squadron was to escort another Straits fleet out before the end of the year. At the same time embargoes were placed on all ships bound for these places until the convoys were ready. And though there were considerable delays in the execution of Pepys' schedule, due to 'the jealousies of particular interests' and the dilatory behaviour of the merchants, the plan worked, and each of the great convoys went out

* *Rawl. MSS. A.* 185, f. 346.

to their destinations through seas infested with capers. Pepys' fine achievement was accomplished with under half the force and expenditure which others had supposed essential to make it feasible. 'I cannot but be glad', he wrote with justifiable pride, 'that the continuing of trade abroad, the stopping the clamour of the poor workmen at home, and the securing to his Majesty the Custom that will arise by so considerable a fleet, will be compassed with the absence of about 3000 men.' It was an interesting object lesson to his countrymen of the economic benefits arising from a proper application of the principles of sea power.[10]

The year 1673 was a red-letter one for Pepys, for it saw not only his appointment to the Admiralty Office but the fulfilment of his ambition to enter Parliament. That autumn the long-awaited elevation of Sir Robert Paston to the peerage took place. Even before that happy event, Pepys had applied himself to the Earl of Norwich, informing him with ostentatious delicacy of the King's and Duke's wishes on his behalf. A further letter, extravagantly polite, and assuring the Earl that only the Duke, his master's desires could have justified his presumption, produced an encouraging answer. 'You may depend upon it as done', the great nobleman assured him, 'though unluckily the Mayor (a perfect creature I could depend upon) dying, will put us to a little trouble extraordinary.'[11]

This was too optimistic. It was seven years since Pepys had described in his Diary how Bab May had gone down to Winchelsea with the Duke of York's letters, not doubting to be chosen, and how the people of that place had elected a private gentleman in spite of him, declaring they 'would have no court pimp to be their burgess'. And now as then the country was seething with discontent against the government, and terrified by the fear of Popery. And the Duke of York being a Papist himself, it was not unnaturally supposed that those he favoured were also Papists.[12]

The writ for the election was issued on October 27th. A few days before a carpet-bagger called Offley – 'a person of no name, estate or interest in the county' – had appeared in the borough and, by a liberal distribution of wine and the friendly offices of one Mr Stringer, 'a good-fellow and parson of Sandringham', procured a petition, signed by the Mayor and two burgesses and attested by the marks of seven others who were unable to write, requesting the Earl of Norwich to assent to his election. This Offley tried to present to the Earl, who was sick in bed at his London house, but was sent about his business by his Grace's steward. However, when on November 1st Pepys appeared at Castle Rising, he was greeted by the Mayor and burgesses with anxious questions about his religion, and by the populace with the coarsest expressions of dislike. For it appeared that 'Mr Offley had . . . infused it into the whole country . . . that Mr Pepys was a Bluddy Papist, by which Mr Pepys at his first appearance and during his whole staying there was saluted by the public cries of the Rabble, Mr Offley himself being sometimes in the head of them, with the name of Papist as often as he appeared abroad'.* For a dignified man of position who liked to stand well with his fellow men it was most distasteful. On one occasion the insufferable Offley even marched through the little town with a band of disorderly soldiers from Lynn headed by drums and trumpets.

Fortunately the Earl's letter of recommendation, and a testimonial to his nominee's orthodoxy signed by several neighbouring divines, quieted the scruples of the more reputable inhabitants who alone had the right to vote. On November 4th Pepys, elected by twenty-nine votes to seven, started home for London a member of Parliament.[13]

But his troubles were far from over. On the day of his election, Parliament, after refusing to grant a supply for the prosecution of the War until the country had been secured against the dangers of popish counsels, had been prorogued till January 7th. Next day 'the Burning of the Whore of Babylon was acted with great applause in the Poultry' by the mob. Hatred of Popery was in the very air. And it was a hatred that was fanned by the folly of one of the stupidest men in the kingdom. Against the advice of his best friends and the protests of Parliament, the Duke of York had just married the fifteen-year-old daughter of a petty Italian prince, Mary of Modena, a foreigner in the French interest and a Papist. It was an opportunity that was not missed by his two bitterest enemies and rivals, the Duke of Buckingham and Lord Chancellor Shaftesbury. The latter, deprived of his Seals on November 19th, now became the acknowledged leader of the anti-Court, anti-Papist party. Except perhaps the King himself, there was no more skilful politician in the country, and none more unscrupulous. It was Pepys' lot to cross his path at the very outset of his parliamentary career.[14]

* *Rawl. MSS. A*. 172, ff. 141–6.

Meanwhile the refusal of supply had made it clear that the Battle Fleet could not be set out in the coming spring. The Navy Board was over a million pounds in debt, and the seamen, unable to get their tickets discharged, were threatening to pull down the office and burn the books and papers. In his own hand Pepys drew up for the private consideration of the King and Duke of York a plan for defending the mouth of the Medway.* But he had no faith in it nor had anyone else. To his brother-in-law at Deal, struggling with householders clamouring to be paid for the sick seamen long quartered on them, he wrote earnestly that it were better that he should get himself discharged of his employment 'seasonably and decently, and thereby eased of the fears of any further inconveniences that may arise to you and your family from it, than continue to hold it upon terms dishonourable to the King, unsatisfactory to the poor seamen, injurious to your poor neighbours, and unsafe to yourself'.[15] 'This brother', he concluded, 'is the sum of what I shall say to you upon this subject . . .; therefore, in a word, let me persuade you to make it your business to be as serviceable to the King and careful of yourself as you can while you are in it, and . . . labour with as much decency, prudence and speed as you can to get out of it, and so God bless you.'

At this inauspicious moment Pepys took his seat in Parliament upon its reassembly on Wednesday, January 7th, 1674. At the same time an election petition from Offley was laid on the Clerk's table, complaining of undue influence on Pepys' behalf by a Catholic nobleman. It was referred to the Committee of Elections.[16]

Twelve days later, Pepys underwent his baptism of fire in debate. The House was discussing the popular grievances of the past year, one of which was the provision of naval materials to the hated French auxiliary squadron. Eight cables and anchors, it was said, had been supplied to the French at a time when the King had none in the Stores for his own ships, and a member rose to ask Mr Pepys whether it was true. It must have been a particularly galling question, for at the time Pepys had strongly opposed their issue.†

* *Rawl. MSS. A.* 191, ff. 114–15.
† On October 4th, 1673, Pepys had written to Deane that he was heartily sorry the French were 'forced still to hang upon our coasts, lest their necessities may drive them to call for further supplies, while God knows in how ill condition we are to answer our own wants, therefore much less theirs'. *Cat. Pepysian MSS.* II, 90–1.

The actual number of cables supplied, he replied, was thirty-one or two with fifteen or sixteen anchors; it had been done at the King's command and he, as Secretary of the Admiralty Office, had countersigned the Warrants.[17]

Two days later, on Wednesday the 21st, Pepys was again under fire – this time on account of the most unpopular of all naval activities, the press-gang. A leader of the anti-Court party, Lord Cavendish, presented a petition from several Masters and Officers of merchant vessels who, he declared, had been pressed contrary to the law which excepted them. Pepys flatly denied it; if it could be proved, he desired to be punished for it himself. Some rather irresponsible speeches about the injustice of pressing followed. Again Pepys was on his feet: if the course taken since time out of mind should now be altered, no fleet could be set out. After that there were several scornful references to the cocksure Secretary of the Admiralty, especially from Sir Thomas Lee and Mr Child, the East India merchant, who asked for a Committee. But Pepys would not be put down. Whatever the consequences were, he told the House, he would ever bear about him, speaking the truth. If any Master or Officer illegally pressed had complained to the Admiralty or Navy Board, he had at once been discharged; of the truth of that he would be eternally accountable. Again when he sat down there were many angry speeches. At his first entry he had already made himself unpopular in a House that had not forgotten his treatment of the Brooke House Commissioners.[18]

It was not till February 6th that the Commons had time to turn from public business to a more private concern, when the Committee of Elections and Privileges reported that Pepys had not been duly elected for Castle Rising. It was thereupon resolved to debate the matter at 10 A.M. on Tuesday, February 10th.[19]

Pepys took hasty measures to defend himself. Offley's champion in the Committee of Elections, Sir Robert Thomas, one of Shaftesbury's lieutenants, had extended the vague charge of undue influence into an irrelevant but, in the existing state of public opinion, far more damaging one of Popery itself. Pepys, he declared, was a typical Duke's man, a concealed Papist who had converted his wife to Catholicism and in whose house decent men had been shocked to discover crucifixes and altars. As his wife was dead and his house burnt, this seemed a safe line of attack.

To confute the charge Samuel wrote to Balty, who replied on February 8th in a long and passionate letter. 'I wonder, indeed, that you, whose life and conversation hath been ever known to be a firm Protestant, should now be called in question of being a Papist; but, Sir, Malice and Envy will still oppress the best of men; wherefore, Sir, to the hazard of my life I will prove (if occasion be) with my sword in my hand . . . that your competitor is a false liar.' And Balty went on to describe how his father had given up everything for his Huguenot beliefs and how glad he had been when his daughter had married such a Protestant as Samuel, believing 'that she had by matching with you, not only wedded wisdom, but also one who by it, he hoped in Christ would quite blow out those foolish, Popish thoughts she might in her more tender years have had of Popery'.[20]

Armed with this awe-inspiring testimonial, Pepys met his accusers at Westminster on February 10th. There information was given that certain members had been told by a Person of Quality that he had seen an altar with a crucifix upon it in his house. It was at once moved by Garroway, one of the leaders of the Country Party, that the members who had made this charge should be allowed to give it to the House in their own words. But at this there was some protest, even so strong a hater of the Court as rough old Colonel Birch declaring his conviction as an Englishman that all this was mere hearsay and that before Pepys were judged he had a right to be confronted with his unnamed accusers. In this he was strongly supported by Sir William Coventry.

However, Sir Robert Thomas proceeded to repeat what he had said in Committee: that Pepys had had an altar and crucifix in his house and had been heard to say that the Church of England had come out of Henry VIII's codpiece. And he added that he had made a ridicule of Lord Brereton and the Commissioners of Accounts at the Council Table and had challenged an Act of Parliament. But despite the protests of Sir Thomas Meres and Garroway, who again dragged in the business of the anchors supplied to the French and hinted that Pepys had broken his wife's heart because she would not turn Catholic, the Speaker insisted that Sir Thomas should undertake to produce his informants.

Pepys was now allowed to reply. He stood up in his place and heartily and flatly denied that he had ever had any altar or crucifix, or the image or picture of any saint whatsoever, in any part of his house.

Sir Robert was then formally asked to name his accusers. The Country Party leaders did everything they could to evade this fatal issue, but Sir William Coventry fought manfully for Pepys and in doing so had the sympathy of every just-minded man in the House. For some time Sir Robert delayed, but in the end the question was put and it was ordered that all who had given in information against Pepys should name their informants.

On this Sir Thomas revealed that it was no less a person than the great Lord Shaftesbury who had seen an altar and crucifix in Pepys' house; he had heard too that Sir John Bankes had said that he had seen it. It was therefore ordered that Bankes should be called to the Bar of the House, while a Committee consisting of Coventry, Garroway and Meres was appointed to wait on Lord Shaftesbury, who, as a member of the House of Lords, could not be compelled to attend. Thanks to Coventry Pepys was given the right to be present at this interview, though Garroway protested vigorously.[21]

Even before the Committee had waited on Lord Shaftesbury, that great man, growing apprehensive, had written to Meres that it was so long since he was at Pepys' lodgings that it would be impossible for him to give evidence on oath before the House of Commons. Confronted in person by the Committee he denied that he had ever seen the altar. As to a crucifix, he had some imperfect recollection of having seen something very like one. Asked when, he replied before the burning of the Navy Office. Whether it was painted or carved he could not remember, or what kind of thing it was; his memory of it was too imperfect to give testimony upon oath. This Coventry reported to the House on Friday the 13th, and was grudgingly confirmed in it by Garroway. Meres tried to make out that there was nothing in Shaftesbury's reply that contradicted his original statement, but as Coventry observed a great many more men would be Catholics than were, if merely having a representation of a crucifix could make them so.*

Shaftesbury had treated the whole affair with that rather brutal but disarming *bonhomie* which was one of the secrets of his hold over

---

* By 'crucifix' the seventeenth century meant a picture or other representation of the crucifixion. That Pepys had possessed something of this kind is quite clear from his Diary entries of July 20th and November 3rd, 1666. It appears to have been a print of the Passion.

his countrymen. As the still indignant Secretary of the Admiralty Office had taken his leave with the other members of the Committee, he had turned on him with a jovial, 'Mr Pepys, the next time we meet, we will remember the Pope!' But Pepys was not the man to be mollified in this way, and next day he had waited on his great accuser at the House of Lords to demand an explanation. Shaftesbury merely sent out Lord Anglesey with a verbal message to say that he could not see him. What he was not allowed to do by word Pepys then did in writing and composed an epistle which, whatever may be thought of its literary merits, ranks very high as a monument of injudiciousness:

My Lord,

I shall rest upon your Lordship's nobleness for the expressing my taking this way of supplying what your Lordship thought not fit to admit me to do yesterday by word of mouth; namely, the observing to your Lordship the injurious consequence of that ambiguity, under which (for reasons best known to your Lordship) you have been pleased to couch your late answers to the Questions brought you from the House of Commons, touching your having declared to some of its members (said to be ready to justify it) your having seen an Altar with a Crucifix erected upon it at my lodgings.

Concerning which, as I must take leave of asserting by being in no wise chargeable with either, so while your Lordship would yourself seem to acquit me of the former (as a thing too signal, if seen, to have been forgotten) you are pleased nevertheless (though with a voluntary unbespeaking of any credit to your testimony therein) to own some imperfect impressions sticking with you (and thereby giving grounds to some doubtful suggestions in others) touching the latter, I mean, the Crucifix; which cannot (I presume) be held a thing less signal than the Altar, as being of a figure not so much akin to any other object as an Altar is to every table that stands against a wall, differing only (I think) in furniture.

With all the earnestness therefore that can become, and may be forgiven one used as I am, I do both desire and conjure your Lordship by all that is honourable in itself and just towards me, to perfect your recollections so far as to give the House (in what method you shall think fit) a categorical answer one way or t'other to-morrow morning in this business of the Crucifix. Which whether it be Aye or No, I do hereby declare I will hold myself equally (and but equally) obliged to your Lordship for it; as being one who has always directed myself in my duty both towards God and my Master, with such open blamelessness, as not to leave either my security or good name therein to depend upon the single Aye or No of any one, friend or enemy. Which plainness in a circumstance of this moment to me, I doubt not but after the twenty years observances I have paid your Lordship on all other occasions, you will be pleased to take in good part from, My Lord, Your Lordship's most obedient servant,

S. PEPYS.*[22]

On Monday the 16th Sir John Bankes was called to the Bar of the House. He declared that he had known Pepys for several years, that he had often visited him at the Navy Office and that he had never seen any altar or crucifix in his house. Nor, he added, did he believe him to be a Papist nor the least that way inclined.

After Bankes had withdrawn, Pepys asked to be heard. As so much, he said, had been spoken of his religion, he would like to give a short account of himself and his life. He would only go back twenty years; for his earlier deportment at Cambridge, he could refer the House to his chamber-fellow there, Mr Sawyer. From thence he had made but two steps in his life; first when he was invited to serve as Secretary to Lord Sandwich, in which trust he had shown himself a good Protestant of the best kind, regularly attending the proscribed churches of the Anglicans; and second when by Lord Sandwich's favour he was preferred to the Navy. What more, he asked, could he say? In his own parish he had not been absent from church in fourteen years. He had been there twice every Sunday and for twenty years had received Communion seven or eight times annually. As for his official conduct, having heard insinuations that there were Catholics in the Navy, he had obtained authority to proffer every Master and Captain the Oaths of Allegiance and Supremacy. He himself had duly conformed with the Test Act, and had even taken out a certificate to that effect from the Bag Office. He challenged the whole world to prove that he had ever once in his life attended Mass or had had a priest or a Popish book in his house. And he could show members several churches – a new window here, a pulpit cloth there – which had benefited by his pious generosity.

Could he believe, he went on with rising indignation, that Lord Shaftesbury really imagined him a Papist, when, on his coming to him in the royal presence for his last commands before going down to Norfolk he had wished him good succession in his election? for, even though his Lordship had afterwards treacherously written to Lord Townshend on Offley's behalf, he would never have wished success to one whom he believed in his heart to be a Papist. He

* S. Pepys to Earl of Shaftesbury, Feb. 15th, 1674. *Rawl. MSS. A.* 172, f. 135.

should not care to say more against a man of Lord Shaftesbury's quality, yet he would not be thought to be too phlegmatic a Protestant – and here Pepys poured out the whole passionate story of his vain attempt to speak with Shaftesbury and of the letter he had written him after his rejection, subsequently reading it to the House. After that he became almost incoherent in his anger. Perhaps Lord Shaftesbury had written some other member of the House an answer to his letter: if so let it be produced. He had exposed himself to conversation as much as any man. Not being able by reason of his work to go much abroad, he had made his house as pleasant as he could, embellishing it with paintings. It had been seen by hundreds from top to bottom; the doors were all unlocked and were of glass; there were no secrets anywhere. The minister of the parish where he lived, Mr Mills, as learned a man of fame and function as any in London, could testify to all this. In his closet there was a small table, with a Bible and a Book of Common Prayer upon it, a basin and an ewer, and over it his wife's picture by Lombard. If there was anything more except a cushion, he would lie under all their aspersions. After which Pepys withdrew.

In the general discussion that followed many reproaches were cast, but the general sense of the House was that either Shaftesbury or his allies in the Commons had exceeded the latitude usually allowed to gentlemen. In the end the debate was adjourned till February 28th. By that day, the House itself prorogued and no Vote having been taken, Pepys was left in possession of his seat. But it had cost him £700 to win and retain, more than ten times as much as he had been led to expect.[23]

He never quite recovered from the impression produced by this attack, and from henceforward always appeared at St Stephen's in the guise of a righteous public servant defending himself against malicious or treasonable falsehood. In the assembly in which above all others natural good humour and sociability are passwords, nothing could have been more unfortunate. Nor did Pepys ever forgive his accusers. Six months later, when his good-natured friend James Houblon, a lifelong Whig, tried to compose the matter, with an offer from the Opposition leaders to prevent any further attempts of Offley's to unseat him in return for his benevolent interest in their mercantile concerns, Pepys flatly refused; he was not one, he said, to lick the stone that had been intended for breaking his head. 'I shall take leave to say', he told Houblon, 'that the success of that openness and simplicity of dealing, which I have ever hitherto preserved, has not (I thank God) been such as that I should need at this time a' day to resort to any new methods of practice . . . In a word then I must beg your forgiving me this one piece of (I hope innocent) obstinacy.'* Innocent it was.[24]

While Pepys was bearing the brunt of a false public charge, he was repelling a private one with equal vigour, though with less justice. On the day of his great speech, his old acquaintance Thomas Povey wrote, reminding him once more of their ancient agreement to share equally in the Tangier profits and asking for some account: 'to which I have sometimes moved you, but have received no other satisfaction than a sullen and uncomfortable return that you have made no other profits but from the bare salary. An answer which neither satisfies me', Povey remarked, 'nor will I suppose any other persons that shall be judges between us, it seeming to be a very unfortunate and improbable thing that what afforded in my unskilful hands some measure of honest advantage, should yield nothing being transferred to yours, and that every one of those particulars should cease to be beneficial whilst they receive their better conduct from your providence and dexterity, which I may believe have seldom had so ill success in other cases, your felicity and improvements following you as closely as my ill-luck and declensions do me . . . I cannot doubt but a considerable sum will be found in your hands to which I have a right, as being received to my use for virtue of your faith given as a gentleman and a Christian'.† As during the tenure of his Tangier Treasurership Pepys had sums impressed to him to the extent of £852,573. 1s. for the pay of the garrison, and on his own showing was owed £28,007. 2s. 1d. by the Crown on this and other accounts, there appears to have been some justification for Povey's claim.[25]

But Pepys was furious. After several delays, which he attributed to Parliamentary business, he wrote his old friend the kind of letter which the Idle Apprentice (which in a sense poor Povey was) might have expected from the Industrious one. That he had made some trifling profits, he admitted, 'though not so considerable as to make me think myself at this day your debtor, nor any at all of those of

* S. Pepys to J. Houblon, Oct. 6th, 1674. *Rawl. MSS. A.* 172, ff. 155–6.
† T. Povey to S. Pepys, Feb. 16th, 1674. *Rawl. MSS. A.* 172, ff. 100–1.

that sort which you expect from I know not what negotiating of the King's money, which my dealing shall never be blemished with. I must therefore resort to what I said in my last . . . which is that, till I have stated my whole account to myself, . . . it is impossible for me to offer at any adjustment with you, but what must expose me to the danger either of wronging myself or (which I would less do) of injuring you'.

'Pray therefore,' Pepys concluded in a more forgiving vein, 'let us have no more of this sort of correspondence between us, for as I am one too stubborn ever knowingly to endure being imposed upon, so shall I with much less willingness be ever willing to violate the known simplicity of my dealings, especially with one from whom I shall always own my having received such civilities as may challenge and shall meet with all expressions of gratitude on this side admitting of manifest wrong.'* A fortnight later he sent Povey fifty guineas on account.[26]

Before this had happened the War had come to an end. On February 9th, 1674, the articles of peace were concluded at Westminster. The Dutch were to pay an indemnity of 800,000 patacoons and to strike flag and lower topsail to the King's Jack between Finisterre and Norway. Hostilities were to cease within twelve days after publication of the Treaty in the home seas, with six weeks' extra grace between the Soundings and Tangier, four more between Tangier and the Equator, and eight months' south of the Line. Pepys promptly instructed Captain Herbert to seize a Dutch merchant ship, which had been driven into the Shetlands, before it was too late. On the 28th Peace was proclaimed by the Heralds in the streets of London.[27]

* S. Pepys to T. Povey, March 15th, 1674. *Rawl. MSS. A.* 172, f. 107.

5

The Squire of Derby House

'I shall never think the Navy capable of doing any great matters unless officered with sober, discreet and experienced seamen . . . and that men may see advancement plain before them when they deserve it, and that instead of being industrious only to get friends to recommend them . . . the officers and seamen shall be brought to an emulation who shall do best as being sure to be preferred that way and no other; when this is everyone will do his duty.' J. Houblon to S. Pepys, April 23rd, 1675, *Pepysian MSS.* 2265, Paper 95.

At the beginning of 1674, Pepys removed his Admiralty Office from its temporary quarters at Whitehall to Derby House in Channel or Cannon Row, a few hundred yards southwards up the river. Here, where in less reputable days he had given Betty Lane lobsters, he now set up in state at the very heart of the national administration, half way between the Palace and the Parliament house, and within a few yards of Westminster stairs. £150 was allowed to his chief clerk, William Hewer, to buy furniture, maps and other necessities. On January 3rd the Secretary's first letter was dictated from Derby House.[1]

Here Pepys moved his personal belongings and took up his permanent abode. There was a great room above stairs with windows looking on the river, where his clerks could work, and lodgings for himself, where he could display his books, his prints and his gilded models, of ships, his scriptor and his presses and the long mirrors in which his small energetic form, crowned with its vast periwig, was so frequently reflected. Below was a sheltered garden, on which two men were at once set to work to make order out of chaos, and where before long Samuel was setting out orange trees.[2]

Here was the background where a great work was exactly performed. The duties of the Admiralty Office were the general supervision of the building, manning, provisioning, discipline, upkeep and finance of the Navy (the details of which were carried out by the Navy Board), the formal control of the jurisdiction of the Admiralty Courts, and the actual execution of the more peculiar functions of the Admiral – the appointment of officers, the issue of orders and warrants and the direction and movement of ships. Hitherto the Lord High Admiral's control of the Navy had been more or less a personal affair, and in peace time had usually dwindled into an occasional inspection of the work of the Navy Board, a spasmodic visit to the ports to launch a ship or inspect a new battery and the appointment (often with a good deal of Court intrigue) of flag officers and captains. Pepys set out to render the 'Admiralty' a single controlling force for the whole Service, and to make himself a sole interpreter of, as he was the sole link between, the limited and carefully defined functions of the new Admiralty Board and the more general powers which the King did not delegate to the Lords Commissioners but retained in his own hands.[3]

Even before the War ended the new Secretary had begun to make his purpose felt. A month after his appointment he issued orders to the Navy Board to attend the Admiralty at 8 o'clock every Saturday morning, and set his late colleagues to work making statistical returns of the state of the Stores, the wages bills of the Yards and the debts of the Service. When the Muster Masters were slow to send up their books to Mark Lane, he intervened in person. Having served a thirteen-year apprenticeship as Clerk of the Acts, Pepys knew the practical business of the Navy Officers by heart, and was able, as no Lord High Admiral or his Secretary had done before, to keep an exact check on the performance of their duties.[4]

Nor was it only the Board and the officials of the Docks and Stores who felt the firm controlling touch of a master hand on the rein. In the King's ships at sea it was felt also. Command of a quarterdeck often makes a man resentful of external authority; in the Stuart Navy, recruited in its higher commands for the first time by courtiers and independent gentlemen, who felt that their sovereign's enthusiasm for the sea had given prestige to its service and gentility to its emoluments, this impatience of rule had become a source of perilous weakness. And it was Pepys' creed that power rests on unity of control and purpose, and sea power most of all. He did not therefore look favourably on well-connected courtiers who supposed that honourable birth was a sufficient passport to command at sea. When someone importuned him to find employment for a cadet of honourable family on the grounds that he had always behaved like a gentleman and an understanding man, Pepys replied that the character lacked downright diligence, sobriety and seamanship. 'For as no man living', he continued, 'can be more inclined than myself to favour a gentleman that is a true seaman, so neither is there any man more sensible than (after many years' observation) I am, of the ruinous consequences of an over-hasty admitting persons to the office and charge of seamen upon the bare consideration of their being gentlemen.'[5]

To apply the rules, first taught in his Puritan youth, by which he had governed his own life, to every activity of the Navy, was the essence of Pepys' work. 'Little care', he jotted down among the rough notes on naval matters which he kept for his guidance, 'goes to the making officers of the Navy for their own preservation to put in very wholesome words and cautions in their orders for any service to be done, such as words of Dispatch, Efficacy, Good Husbandry, etc.' He himself never failed to insert such words in his orders nor to insist that they were observed. Henceforward, in the Service, there was to be a rule for everything, and an unsleeping authority to see that it was obeyed or punished when disobeyed.[6]

But it was an Augean stable that Pepys set himself to cleanse. Ever since it had grown up in the remote mists of the Middle Ages, the Navy had conducted itself on a rough and ready method of living with as few rules as possible and of disregarding these whenever it could. Occasionally some great seaman, a Drake or a Robert Blake, had enforced a stern discipline on those under his immediate command, but, when once that personal rule had been removed, this had quickly vanished in the general atmosphere of corruption, laissez-faire and boozy optimism which was the tradition of the Service. 'Your observations about the intemperate use of brandy in the King's ships', Pepys wrote to a correspondent, 'seems very seasonable, and too justly grounded.'[7]

Pepys began his reforms at the top; if he could only establish discipline there, it would follow naturally throughout the Service. He therefore issued orders that captains, as well as subordinate officers, were to be subject to the periodic musters of the Clerks of the Cheque and Muster Masters, whose duty it was to see that all those drawing pay were in actual attendance. In defiance of the 7th Article of the Admiral's Instructions, commanders were constantly leaving their ships and going on shore on their private occasions to the detriment of all good conduct. Sometimes they even abandoned their stations and brought their ships unexpectedly into harbour; on one occasion after giving orders that a warship should put in to Portsmouth for repair, Pepys ran into her commander, Captain Priestman, sauntering up and down Covent Garden. He at once addressed to that high-placed officer such a letter as he can never before have received, and certainly not from the son of a tailor. 'To which', he concluded, 'I must take leave to add that . . . your forbearing to give your attendance on board to the despatch of your ship . . . (as appears by the Clerk of the Cheques' Muster books) seems to imply such a deportment towards his Majesty's service and the instructions of the Lord High Admiral, as . . . I shall not without manifest unfaithfulness be able to omit the making known both to his Majesty and my Lords, and to his Royal Highness also' (Priestman's particular patron) 'who, I am sure, expects a better account of the diligence of every person he favours.' And all Priestman could do was to confide to his friends that the Secretary was a scoundrel and swallow his ungentlemanly observations. Yet the necessity of the letter shows clearly the limitations of Pepys' position and the difficulties under which he had to work during the ill-defined, go-as-you-please, administrative regime of Stuart England.[8]

For as soon as such well-connected offenders began to realize that the little Secretary at Derby House meant business, there was trouble. All their influential relations in Court or Parliament were called into action, and Pepys had constantly to leave his desk to repel ill-informed and often revengeful attacks. The very interest of his sovereign in the Navy was here a handicap, since every captain who appeared at Whitehall could obtain easy access to the royal ear and, often enough, favours that ought, as Pepys wrote, to have been 'duly considered in their proper place'. Fortunately Charles, though far too compliant and easy-going, never objected to his sea Secretary's calling him to order.[9]

Worse even in its effects than native idleness or quarterdeck pride, Pepys soon found, was the practice of using men-of-war for the carriage of bullion. It had long been a recognized custom of the Navy to transport gold and silver for British merchants trading abroad, and in days when the sea swarmed with pirates it seemed on the face of it a reasonable one. But the consequences of 'plate-carriage' on discipline were disastrous. For commanders who had precious metals in their holds thought twice before engaging in any perilous duty, while merchants, accustomed to sending their gold and silver in the King's ships, soon went further and offered their captains bargains to carry other commodities. And now that England was sending her fleets regularly into remote seas, the opportunities for carrying freight were almost unlimited. The Spanish and Mediterranean stations proved a gold mine to naval officers. The scandal was so universal that many captains actually advertised their terms of freight in foreign ports. Not only did this throw the whole economy of the Service into confusion, but, through undercutting by captains whose overhead charges were all paid by the Crown, seriously injured the carrying trade of the nation.[10]

The autumn of 1674 saw the culmination of Pepys' first attempt to attack the abuse, in the court martial of Captain Haddock for conveying merchants' goods 'on terms of freight for his own benefit'. Haddock was sentenced to six months' imprisonment and ordered to pay all his profits to the King, who at Pepys' request allotted them to the Chatham Chest. A few weeks later Pepys heard that an important dispatch to the Commander-in-Chief of the Mediterranean station had failed to arrive because Captain Anguish of the *Deptford* ketch, who had been posted at Marseilles to carry it, had sailed off on some trumped-up excuse to Leghorn. Examination of the printed bills of lading in the Leghorn Customs House showed the real nature of Anguish's errand. Worse followed, for on his way back to his station, Anguish, still carrying merchants' goods, ran on to a rock, 'at which (accompanied by so many aggravations)', Pepys reported, 'his Majesty was so moved (and I cannot say but with much reason)' that the captain was at once superseded.[11]

At the beginning of 1675 Pepys was presented with a strong argument for ending the practice, when the Grand Duke of Tuscany demanded that the English government should pay customs duties on the naval stores and provisions which it kept at Leghorn. 'Occasion was hereupon taken by Mr Pepys', ran the minutes of the Board, 'of observing to his Majesty and my Lords the ground of these innovations, rendering them in some sort reasonable on the part of the Grand Duke, namely, our commanders turning his Majesty's ships into merchantmen by taking in of merchants' goods . . . and thereby putting themselves into the condition of merchantmen and exposing themselves to the being treated as such.' But though the King and the Lords of the Admiralty declared their intention of stamping out the abuse, and though Pepys wrote to the English Consuls in the Mediterranean to report all cases of royal ships carrying merchandise, the evil continued, for so much money could be made out of even a single 'good voyage' that captains were ready to run the risk of being cashiered, knowing that they could always retire on the profits. And those who were well placed could generally wheedle their way back into the Service. A classic example was that of Captain Poole, an excellent commander, as Pepys willingly testified, who after transporting the new Governor to Barbados remained on that station without leave for no less than six months, 'without one hour spent in the service of the King'. To pass over an offence of this kind, Pepys informed the offender, 'could be construed no other than the delivering up his Majesty's honour, service and treasure (by the example of it) to irrevocable ruin'. Yet so popular was Poole at Court that the most Pepys could obtain against him in the way of punishment was the choice between a court martial and the forfeiture of his pay for the voyage. Poole chose the latter and in the end contrived to get even that refunded.[12]

The jealousy of martial law shown by a suspicious and liberty-loving race made Pepys' work of giving discipline to the sea service more difficult. At Common Law, the most serious naval offences like desertion and disobedience to orders were merely breaches of contract and could be punished as no more. A curious case arose in 1675 when the mate of the *Wivenhoe* guardship, a seaman named Northall, with a fine record, obeyed his Captain's orders by firing at another naval boat whose crew, 'with provoking language', refused to give an account of themselves. In doing so he mortally wounded the carpenter of the *Oxford*. On landing to get help for the wounded man, Northall was arrested by the civil authorities of Portsmouth. His captain, frightened by the possibilities of the situation, tried to get him acquitted on the ridiculous ground of his being short-sighted, but Pepys with his usual clear grasp of principle refused to allow the basis of defence to be shifted in this way, 'you seeming to desire', he told the Captain, 'that his killing the carpenter of the *Oxford* should be judged accidental, whereas the former part of your letter and the whole tenour of the Mayor's would have it was in performance of his duty and obedience to your orders'. It was a great pity, he confessed, that so good a man should remain under any unnecessary charge from a crime arising in the execution of his duty; 'but, on the other hand, the death of one of his Majesty's subjects must also be duly enquired into and therefore some inconvenience must be borne with by him'. In the end Northall was acquitted, Pepys providing £10 towards his expenses out of his own purse.[13]

It was no pleasant part of Pepys' duties to have to force a merciful sovereign and a generous and sociably-inclined Service to punish the offences which wrecked its efficiency. Where the death sentence was involved, his humanity sometimes became too much for his administrative zeal; one suspects his hand in the royal order that the sentence of death passed by court martial on Captain Joseph Harris, for striking his topsail to a Spanish man-of-war in the Bay of Biscay should, after 'all appearance of its being purposed to be really executed, even to his being brought on board the *Anne* yacht before the musketeers', be reprieved at the eleventh hour 'upon considerations of his former good services and known proofs of courage'. But where the penalty was less than death, Pepys never allowed his sympathies to interfere with his duties. Thus when the *Rose*, Captain Ashby, bound for Virginia 'came to an untimely disaster by breaking her rudder in running aground as she was going through the Narrows', he insisted that the Lords of the Admiralty should not let a miscarriage of such a kind pass without enquiry and censure. It was the establishment of a wise usage which the passage of two and a half centuries has not seen abandoned.[14]

The ill-discipline, which Pepys made it his life work to expel from the higher ranks of the Service, made itself felt in the lower. Officers insulted their own captains, intrigued against them on shore and threatened revenge against them whenever their authority galled. In their turn commanders often turned the enforcement of discipline among their subordinates into a personal vendetta. 'Nothing', Pepys wrote to one captain, 'will give so great an authority to the credit of your lieutenant's ... complaints than if ... you should by any expressions of revenge or other passion give him the advantage thereof for proving any part of the allegations he hath lately exhibited to my Lords of the Admiralty concerning you.'[15]

On the lower deck, where punishments were stern and often brutal, bad discipline was too often the result of tardy payments. The pay of 24*s.* a month for an 'able' seaman, with a daily victualling allowance of a gallon of beer, a pound of biscuit and two pounds of beef, was not ungenerous according to the values of the time. But when men saw their families starving because the government was months and sometimes years in arrears with their pay, they were apt to turn their rough native courage and love of independence against their own officers and make the lower deck a rude commonwealth of their own. And as, in its lower ranks, the navy and the merchant marine were interchangeable, the bad discipline of the one reacted on the other, shipowners whose wages were certain and whose rates of pay, as Pepys thought, excessive, finding their tarpaulins as hard to control as the King's captains. 'A vice', Pepys noted, 'which I pray God I may see rectified before it prove too fatal, not only to his Majesty's service, but the whole navigation of our country.'[16]

Schoolmaster in sea matters to the nation in general and the Navy in particular Pepys for the remainder of his life became. And though the office was unpopular, it was needed. Once he even had to teach one of the King's captains to read and write; for when the commander of the *Ann and Christopher* fireship excused his failure to comply with the Admiral's Printed Instructions on the grounds that he was unable to read them, the Board resolved that he should be 'admonished from his Majesty and my Lords by Mr Pepys to apply himself to the learning (as late as it is) of both'. Even the King had to be instructed and gently admonished for breaking the rules which the Secretary of his Admiralty Commission made for his service, it being 'humbly offered to his Majesty by Mr Pepys' – so the latter's minutes of one Board meeting ran – that the master shipwrights, when questioned for excessive and unauthorized charges in carving and gilding yachts, 'do generally pretend his Majesty's verbal command'.[17]

To the axiom that the King's navy must be disciplined within, Pepys added the corollary that it should be respected without. Not the King himself had a greater sense of the deference due to the outward and visible signs of his authority.* At sea this was the flag. Pepys never ceased to assert its dignity and the sacrilege involved in any abuse of it. In June 1674 he delivered a lecture to the Court of

---

* Long before, in the September of 1665, going down the River to meet Lord Sandwich's fleet, Pepys had been struck by the beauty of '100 ships, great and small, with the flag-ships of each squadron distinguished by their several flags on their main, fore, or mizzen masts.' *Diary*, Sept. 18th, 1665.

Trinity House – the virtual headquarters of the Merchant Marine of England – on what colours were proper for merchantmen; the King, he told his audience, would have none but his own ships wear the Jack. This was followed by a proclamation forbidding merchant ships to carry any ensign but the flag of St George, with a red cross in a white canton in the upper corner next the staff. Captains of warships were strictly enjoined to see that this was enforced and that merchantmen made the traditional obeisance to the Jack whenever they passed a King's ship. 'And here we begin our warlike achievements,' wrote Henry Teonge, bound down the River for Tangier, 'for, seeing a merchantman near us without taking the least notice of a man-of-war, we give him a shot, make him lower his top-gallant (*id est*, put off his hat to us), and our gunner presently goes on board of him, makes him pay 6*s*. 6*d*. for his contempt, abating him 2*d*., because it was the first shot.'[18]

Pepys was equally insistent on the salutes due from foreign vessels to the King's flag as Sovereign of the Narrow Seas from Finisterre to Norway. Whenever news came that this formality had been neglected he was quick to demand satisfaction for the affront – from the King's officer who had allowed the neglect and from the proper authority for punishment of the offender. At the end of 1674 he proudly informed a learned friend that he was about to attend the Sessions House at the Old Bailey, where 'a cause relating to the Flag will be publicly and with no less solemnity handled, where I expect will appear all that law or learning can furnish the Judge of the Admiralty with on that subject'. The offender, the captain of an Ostend pirate who had failed to strike to the *Woolwich* sloop, paid the penalty both for his contempt and his piracy, and Pepys had the solemn and mournful satisfaction of waiting on the Chief Justice of the Common Pleas for his advice on the form of warrant required for his execution and of obtaining from the Lieutenant of the Tower three files of musketeers to keep order at the riverside gallows at Wapping.[19]

One weapon the Secretary of the Admiralty Office possessed in his battle to impose his will on the Navy – the power of appointment. That right the King had not vested in the Admiralty Commissioners but retained in his own hand. In practice, as his sovereign came more and more to trust him and to accept, with good-humoured resignation, his rules, it was exercised by Pepys, though there were many exceptions, disturbing to his administration and maddening to his dignity. Pepys was always careful to explain to his subordinates the theoretical limitations of his authority and the principle that governed his system of awards and promotions. He could not, he told one aspirant, remember promising an employment to any man: that the King alone could do. All he could do was to present his Majesty with 'the certificates by which persons recommended for employments are to have their different qualifications and merits made known to him'. Nor was there any need, he constantly repeated, for them to haunt the Admiralty or the royal presence, 'I being the King's remembrancer no less in behalf of the absent than those that are daily soliciting'.[20]

Just occasionally, and, of course, without breaking his own rules, Pepys was able to do a kindness to a relation or friend. When his cousin Tom Alcocke was fit for it, he told Deane that he would be glad of an opportunity to do him right, though naturally, he explained, he would do nothing without his advice, 'as well believing that some years' practice at sea is no less than necessary to confirm a shipwright in the principles of the theory he learned on shore, as also to qualify him thoroughly for a land employment afterwards in the King's Yards, without which, were his relation ten times nearer to me than it is, I hope I should never be guilty of looking out for anything for him'. Several of Evelyn's poor neighbours – all of them 'very diligent and able workmen' – found themselves in the King's Yards at Deptford, while in a somewhat loftier sphere Pepys was able to do a good turn, and a richly deserved one, to the little Captain who had once, long ago, carried him to the Sound, and whom he preferred, in the teeth of powerful competition, to the comfortable sinecure of gunner of the *Royal Charles*.[21]

In recommending for appointments Pepys frequently consulted the Duke of York, who, though deprived of his office, had still, as Heir Presumptive, a powerful influence on the affairs of the Navy. It was to the Duke that Pepys wrote in the spring of 1676 one of the most valuable of his letters, explaining the principles on which naval appointments of responsibility should be made. The Storekeeper of the Yard at Chatham had died, and, knowing that there would be many pretenders to it, Pepys had made haste to reinforce his own official influence by the still more potent word of the Duke. 'I have not – may it please your Royal Highness – at any time hitherto, nor shall now take upon me to become a recommender of any particular person to the employment, but content myself with the doing my duty of being his Majesty's and your humble remembrancer, that the office of a Storekeeper in the Navy is an employment of very great trust, and such a one as, whatever it calls for of integrity, calls for no less experience in the business and methods of the Navy, and therefore do with all humility hope on his Majesty's behalf that, with the regard his Majesty may be pleased to have to those who by many years' education and labour in his service have qualified themselves above others for his favour herein, your Royal Highness will be pleased to bring to his mind that Article which (among others) was at your Highness's motion about three years since established by his Majesty in Council for the direction of future Admirals, declaring that utmost circumspection should be used in the choice of every office according to the knowledge which should be had of each man's deserving in former employment, either from the Lord High Admiral's own observation or the Report of the Principal Officers and Commissioners of the Navy.'*[22]

Sometimes, as was natural, the great man relaxed. Once, when the Duchess of Portsmouth, the King's reigning favourite, chose to recommend a young man, Pepys was enough of a courtier to write, at her especial desire, to Sir John Berry to receive him on board his ship. His age, he admitted – he was under sixteen – did not render him capable, by the rules lately established, of recommending him to the Admiral by the King's warrant; 'but', he added, 'I find such a report of the sobriety and diligence of the young man, and have received of himself such assurances of his resolution to apply himself studiously to his work and duty of seaman, that I cannot decline the accompanying him to you with this letter from myself'. One likes to think that it was not entirely the fact that a beautiful woman had the King's ear that made Pepys glad to stretch a point to do her a service.[23]

There were other times when an attempt to influence Pepys' judgment brought down on the offender a terrible tirade. William

* S. Pepys to the Duke of York, April 10th, 1676. In the possession of the Countess of Gainsborough. The letter, which is copied from one in the Admiralty archives, is endorsed by Sir Charles Middleton, June 14th, 1787, with the words: 'This letter may equally apply now to every officer in his Majesty's Yards and confirms the Article of recommendations in the Navy Board's Instructions.' It is also printed in *C.P. MSS.* III, 185–6. See also *Rawl. MSS. A.* 185, f. 392.

Harmon, son of his old acquaintance the Admiral, desiring the command of a yacht, had the tactlessness to promise a present of a hundred guineas, should his application be successful. 'The fullest expression I can ever give you of my good will', replied the offended Secretary, 'lies in my forgiving you your late mistake . . . it being what I have not done elsewhere . . . Adieu.' And in April 1675, the Lieutenant of the *Phoenix*, in need of a small favour, sent Pepys a small 'neager-boy' with a hope that he would find him 'well seasoned to endure the cold weather and live in England' and a promise of more worthy presents to come. Pepys replied that the favour he asked was a reasonable one, so much so that without his requesting it, he had already moved his Majesty for it. 'But that which I have reason to take amiss from you is your thinking that any consideration of benefit to myself or expectation of reward from you should be of any inducement to me. Therefore pray reserve that sort of argument for such as will be guided by it, and know that your meriting well of the King is the only present that shall ever operate with me.'

But Pepys' masterpiece in this kind belongs to the December of 1678 when an official of the Chatham Yard offered him a bribe. 'I have your letter of the 12th inst.', he replied, 'and could not have believed the method of my proceedings in the Navy could, after near twenty years' public observation, be so ill understood by any one man therein as it seems to have been by you, when you would think any offer of money or any other argument can obtain anything from me that bare virtue cannot.' It must not, however, be supposed that Samuel was too rigid to receive occasional gifts of a more domestic kind from friends and admirers in the Service – a present of red sprats from the Captain of the *Anne* yacht or a tun of the best Rhenish wine from the grateful acquaintance whom the yacht had carried over. Once he was given a tame lion cub by Mr Martin, the Consul at Algiers, who was addicted to presenting these useful pets to his friends in England – a gift, which Mr Martin explained, he had taken the boldness to send as the only rarity the place offered. It must have required even more boldness to receive it, but Pepys wrote soon after to assure his benefactor that the lion was comfortably installed at Derby House – 'as tame as you sent him and as good company'.[24]

The sixteen little yachts which lay in the River off the Palace wall at Greenwich, or coasted between England and the continental ports, were another means by which Pepys could sometimes do a favour to a friend or win the good will of a powerful enemy. Their ordering was part of his regular routine, and, as they offered by far the pleasantest as well as the cheapest means of crossing the Channel, there was a constant demand for them. Ambassadors and highly placed officials travelled in them more or less by right, and most noble lords visiting or returning from the Continent expected to be so accommodated. So did Pepys' friends – his old tutor, the pious and learned Mr Joseph Hill, now minister of the English congregation of Rotterdam, or Balty on his occasional visits to France. 'We intend, sir, on Tuesday next', wrote James Houblon, 'to set out for Rochester and Chatham by land and so meet the yacht at Sheerness on Wednesday; if there be any need you will please to mention that in the order, lest the Captain be scrupulous. Thus you see, sir, what a perpetual trouble I and my friends are to you. God grant we may make a good use of all your favours, and that one day at least you may have cause to believe that you have not obliged the most ungrateful people upon earth.'* Some of Pepys' clients were not so appreciative; in September 1676 he was forced to apologize to his old antagonist, Lord Anglesey, because a noble lady friend of his had been incommoded in her passage; 'not', he added with a characteristic touch of self-explanation, 'that either the perfection of courtship is to be looked for from a tarpaulin, or the fullness of accommodation from so small a ship.' As some consolation for the complaints of this tiresome woman, he had several times the pleasure of obliging Nell Gwynn with a yacht. She, at least, one feels, was not so exacting.[25]

As Secretary it was Pepys' lot, not only to keep the minutes of the Board and the office at Derby House, but to attend the King on his naval occasions. In the spring of 1674 he was with him for some days at Chatham and in the same June on board Sir John Narbrough's flagship at Spithead. He also waited on him during the summer months at Windsor and Hampton Court, and in the spring and autumn at Newmarket. One Saturday evening in the August of 1674, after a visit to Windsor, he witnessed, in company with his friend, Mr Evelyn, the seventeenth-century counterpart of a torch-

---

* James Houblon to S. Pepys, Sept. 21st, 1676. *Rawl. MSS. A.* 185, f. 253.

light tattoo. At the foot of the long terrace below the Castle, works had been thrown up to represent the fortress of Maestricht, then newly taken by the French. There were bastions, bulwarks, ramparts, palisadoes, horn-works and counter-scarps, which were dramatically stormed by his Majesty's eldest son the Duke of Monmouth, who had just returned with young John Churchill from the siege. Trenches were opened, batteries raised, grenadoes shot, great guns fired, mines sprung, while the heroic attackers amid a blaze of noise and light swept forward to victory; 'in short', as Evelyn put it, 'all the circumstances of a formal siege, . . . and, what is most strange, all without disorder or ill accident, to the great satisfaction of a thousand spectators'. Afterwards the two friends returned together to London, which they reached at three in the morning, and late as it was one feels that Pepys must that night, at least, have once more gone 'with great content to bed'.[26]

A few days later, Pepys paid his second and last visit to France and Flanders. It was only a brief one – far briefer than he had intended – but he had as travelling companions the charming ladies of the Houblon family, who had long been trying to persuade him to accompany them. From August 25th to September 7th he wrote no letters, the faithful Will Hewer deputizing for him at Derby House. The travellers visited Dunkirk, where the English merchant colony made much of them, and Mardyke, where they were very civilly entertained by little Captain Country in the *Roebuck*. They also inspected Gravelines and listened to what Pepys, recalling it in later years, described as a 'wretched choir of repining nuns'. And on September 8th, after a treat at Dover by Sir John Narbrough and the principal officers of the borough, Pepys was back at the Office.[27]

Though Derby House claimed three hundred and fifty days of the year, Pepys was very welcome whenever he could find time to pay any of his friends or relations a visit – particularly to their wives and daughters who were charmed by the bright-eyed little man who took such a vivid interest in everything he saw, told such satisfying tales of great events and persons and was so visibly delighted by their company. Cousin Roger Pepys, the squire of Impington, wrote to tell him how much the present of wine he had sent them had pleased his daughters – 'those creatures here whom you are pleased to style with the name of ladies, having none such, but honest country girls . . . And if a glowing cheek did not tell you that upon the receipt of your letter, they drank your health . . . they have commanded me to you that they did it'. Dross for gold, Roger said they returned, for they sent him in exchange a tierce of Cambridgeshire cider.* Nor was there anywhere Pepys loved more to turn his feet for an evening than to those doors where there were clever and pretty women to welcome him – his cousin Roger's daughter, Barbara Gale, that fine woman who had just married the High Master of St Paul's, or Sarah Houblon, the wife of James Houblon's son, Wynne, with whom he so delighted to sing and play of an evening.[28]

For music remained for him the same delight that it had ever been. To those friends who practised it with him, he clung with particular tenderness, even when they were far away. Thomas Hill the merchant – the little 'master in music' of Diary days – wrote to him from Lisbon of a young Fleming, bred to music at Rome and employed by a Portuguese nobleman, who had a rare skill in reading difficult pieces at sight and sang exquisitely to the theorbo – a most ingenious person, too, who spoke Latin, Italian, French and Spanish. Hill suggested that Pepys should take the young man into his employment: the pair of them, he pointed out, would make a ravishing choir when joined with 'our ladies'. The idea of having a trained Italian singer, especially one who was also a linguist and a virtuoso, appealed greatly to Samuel, though he was a little afraid he might increase his expenses and unduly unsettle his household.

Pepys thought the thing over, and after some delay wrote to Hill that he was ready to take the young man into his household, feed and house him and pay him £50 a year, in return for his services in languages, reading, writing and translating as well as what he described as the 'satisfaction to my sense in his excellent qualifications in music, in which my utmost luxury still lies and is likely to remain so'. But, remembering the Portuguese nobleman, Pepys added, 'if my silent and unencumbered guise of life will sort with him'. For nothing, he explained, 'which has yet or may further happen towards the rendering me more conspicuous in the world has led or can ever lead to the admitting any alteration in the little methods of my private way of living, as having not in my nature any more aversion to sordidness than I have to pomp'.[29]

So in the spring of 1675 Caesare Morelli arrived with his lute and

* Roger Pepys to S. Pepys, Impington, Dec. 14th, 1674. *Rawl. MSS. A.* 185, f. 30.

theorbo by the *Suadados* yacht and took up his residence at Derby House. Samuel was charmed with him, a modest and gentle-hearted creature who did as he was told, offended no one and pleased equally with his music, languages and sobriety. It was Morelli's engaging practice to rise at dawn and sing Italian psalms for an hour or two in the fresh air before completing his slumbers. And sometimes in the evenings and on Sundays Pepys would join him in this pleasant pursuit. His only drawback was that he was a Catholic, which made the rest of the household rather suspicious of 'Monsieur', as they called him. But Pepys, with that delicacy which with all his self-importance was part of his nature, treated the young foreigner with the most flattering ceremony and made his servants do the same.[30]

It was, indeed, the part of Samuel's servants to do as he chose. His household was as strictly ruled as the Office next door. Over it presided his housekeeper. What was expected from her can be gauged by a letter recommending a candidate for the post as 'very just, sober and virtuous, and, though very well extracted, as humble as the meanest servant'.* A butler, a footman and a coachman, a fluctuating number of young clerks who, like Will Hewer and Tom Edwards in earlier days, shared the duties and amenities of the household, a cook and a maid or two and at one period, at least, a small black boy named Jack, made up the household. Pepys sometimes complained that he was unfortunate in his servants, but this was because he expected perfection from them and was therefore inclined to view the too warm peccadillo of a maid-servant or a footman's susceptibility for the bottle as a kind of trial expressly sent from Heaven to test his virtue. On the whole his employees were very faithful to him.[31]

To the home so governed Pepys would often bring his friends to dine after a morning at the Admiralty Board, where perhaps James Houblon, Sir John Bankes or his old colleagues of the Navy Office had been in attendance. It was a pleasing affectation of his to pretend to be unable to offer anything but humble fare; 'you shall find me attending the King at his dinner, and a piece of ling at my house afterwards for you', runs one Lenten invitation. Yet one knows that whatever was offered at that seemly and orderly table

* Mrs Hannah Rushworth to S. Pepys, May 18th, 1676. *Rawl. MSS. A*. 185, f. 155.

was of the very best. Here Samuel's guests could look with pleasure on his splendid possessions – the engravings and maps he was buying from Paris through his old friend at the French Embassy, Monsieur Colbert's secretary, the cabinets that Sympson, that master-craftsman, built for him, the ranged silver dishes, ewers and flagons, the glittering glass, the clocks that Tompion made. Afterwards they might be taken to his closet with the long mirrors and shown his books and engravings – the Bible cuts, and vellum-bound volumes of old illuminated pages, the naval manuscripts, calligraphical specimens, black letter ballads and all the other rarities and oddities that he was beginning to collect. And there on the shelves of his tall presses were all the finest books of his day, the treasures of Mr Herringman's and Mr Nott's bookshops (for Pepys like his acquaintance Mr Hooke, often 'rambled about books'), bound in his binding and stamped with his own golden arms. Then there was his microscope and the mathematical curiosities bought from Mr Winne's shop; sometimes, perhaps, his more privileged guests might even be shown the sweating chair, that throne of a virtuoso's home, that he had bought to cure his carefully recorded complaints. And to give lightness to it all there would be Mary Skinner's guitar, the yellow and bright-coloured fringes she sewed on the chairs, and the canary birds which he so loved to have singing in the house.[32]

To the outward world – that is to all but the very great and to those who knew him intimately – Pepys seemed a very great man. Whether he still dressed, as he did in his Diary days, in such glorious apparel as a flowered tabby vest and coloured camelot tunic with gold lace on the sleeves, we cannot be certain. But when his portrait was painted and sent to Mr Hill at Lisbon, the latter could scarcely contain his admiration: 'the picture is beyond praise, . . . it's so stately and magnificent a posture, and hits so naturally your proportion and the noble air of your face, that I remain immovable before it, hours together.' As for his coach, with its paintings of fair harbours, forts and ships a'fighting on all its panels, it was so plainly that of an Admiral riding the seas that irreverent and envious souls were apt to jeer. And to base eyes, the beauty and symbolic dignity of the Secretary of the Admiralty's barge seemed much of a sort – with its damask curtains and cushions and painted seas: far too much, many felt, for a tailor's son. Yet to Pepys himself it was all part of the seemliness and outward perfection he liked to have in everything about him. That, and not sinful pride, was what had caused him to ask his friend, the Master Shipwright to Woolwich, to convert his open boat into a barge, or better still, if it could be done without loss to the King, to build him a new one,* with panels and elegant windows that 'slide up and down in grooves, as your glasses in coaches do, as being safer, closer and more handy than the hanging them upon hinges.' And a very elegant gentleman he must have looked sitting in it discoursing with his inferiors as his watermen rowed him up and down the River.[33]

---

* 'Though I have done all I can in fitting my oiled cloth to my iron bails, yet I find it troublesome in the opening and shutting.' S. Pepys to Phineas Pett, June 22nd, 1677. Tanner, *Further Correspondence*, 296–7.

6

The Thirty New Ships

'What is our land force if we be not defended by a strong Navy, and what is the Navy without sufficient money to discharge it?' A. Deane to S. Pepys, Feb. 23rd, 1674. *Pepysian MSS.* 2265, Paper 63.

For some months after the end of the Third Dutch War retrenchment was the predominant note in the government of the Navy. The discussions at the Admiralty Board ranged round such questions as 'the cutting off of the growing expense of the growing charge upon seamen's wages', while Pepys kept the Navy Board busy preparing estimates of the number of workmen in the Yards and the ways by which their numbers could be reduced. The difficulty as always was lack of ready money, for until it was available seamen could not be paid off and until they were the monthly charge of the Fleet could not be reduced. Pepys solved the difficulty by proposing that cash should be paid on all arrears up to a certain date and the residue in tickets, though he would have been glad, he said, of any other means of paying 'the poor seamen without being driven to any longer use of that fatal way of discharging them'. But there was no help for it.[1]

By the summer of 1674, the Fleet was reduced to 8200 men. Under the influence of the new Treasurer, Osborne, now Lord Danby, it was again proposed that Coventry's scheme of six years back for reducing the annual charge of the Navy to £200,000 should be put into force, though this chimera however proved no easier of realization in 1674 than it had done in 1668 and 1670.[2]

Therefore, when the irrepressible Deane, impervious to the needs of the hour and as enthusiastic as ever for increasing the Service, wrote in the spring of 1674 to urge the laying down of new ships against the next War, Pepys had to reply that he found the King 'so full of the thoughts he is now under of stopping of all things that look like occasions of laying out money, that I perceive he is more thoughtful of getting out of debt for what is past (wherein God bless his endeavours) than willing to entertain any proposition that may tend to the increasing of it'. None the less, Pepys continued – and here he was going a great deal further than his Board could have dreamt of at that moment – though no man more heartily wished the King success in his economical resolutions than he, he agreed that there was a vital need to provide his country with a Fleet strong enough to fight the Dutch without the aid of the French ('which with sorrow we must acknowledge ourselves unfit to do this day'), and expressed a hope that before long 'our prospect of things in the Navy will become a little more pleasant, and his Majesty be in condition to entertain with more satisfaction the discourse of building of ships'.[3]

Pepys made it his business to hasten that day. His chance came in the autumn of 1674, when the growing restiveness of the Dey of Algiers, under the restrictions imposed on the piratical activities of his subjects by Sir Edward Spragge's treaty of three years before, began to alarm the merchants of the City. For some time past Pepys on his visits to the Exchange had been bearded by his friends of the East India and Turkey Companies with complaints of depredations by North African corsairs, a sign not so much that the Navy of England was growing weaker – for actually the regular protection, poor as it was, offered by the King's frigates in the Mediterranean, was greater than it had ever been before – but that the maritime needs of the nation were increasing. It was therefore resolved to reinforce the two or three small ships plying in the Straits and bring the Dey to his senses by the presence of a strong English squadron off the town. In September Sir John Narbrough, who though still only thirty-four was in Pepys' estimation the first officer in the Service, was given orders to hoist his flag in the *Henrietta*, one of the few remaining ships of the line in commission, and proceed to the Straits.[4]

Throughout the early months of 1675 Narbrough was ransoming English slaves from Algiers and negotiating with the Dey of Tripoli. But in the middle of March news that the Tripolines were still defying the King's demands made an immediate decision of war or peace essential. Pepys left on the same day for Newmarket where the King and Court were in vacation. A racing government acted promptly, and two days later Pepys was back in London, despatching instructions to Narbrough to deliver an immediate ultimatum, on refusal of which he was to commence hostilities. 'You may easily believe', he wrote, 'that at this time a war of no kind can be very acceptable and least of all one so far from home.' But there was no alternative, and immediate orders were issued to fit out eight frigates of the 4th and 5th rate to reinforce Sir John.[5]

All this, however inconvenient, helped to strengthen the demands of Deane and Pepys for new ships. Already the King and Admiralty Board were convinced. Twenty of the old ships were in need of total or partial rebuilding, and even when this necessary work had been completed, the total effective strength would be little more than a third of the maximum Dutch force and three-fifths of the French. All through the Christmas season Pepys was busy drawing up figures and estimates, often till long into the night. By the time Parliament was due to meet, he was armed with what he regarded as an unanswerable case for the rebuilding and modernizing of the Fleet, and the due provision, as a sound and indeed essential measure of national economy, of an adequate sum for the purpose.[6]

But Parliaments are not always easy to impress with unanswerable cases. The King met that body on April 13th with a strong recommendation to look to the condition of the Fleet. Eleven days later Pepys, who had been a little troubled by a further though unsuccessful threat to his seat from Offley, gave in his account of the ships and stores. The total strength of the Fleet was seven 1st rates, five 2nd rates and eighteen 3rd rates, or thirty ships of the line, with thirty-six 4th rates, besides a number of smaller vessels and fireships. Many of these were antiquated and in bad repair. To be stronger than either Holland or France, both of which were building rapidly, it would be necessary to build two new 1st rates, seven 2nd rates, twenty-seven 3rd rates and four 4th rates. 'Our neighbours' strength', he said, 'is now greater than ours, and they will still be building, so that we are as well to overtake them for the time past as to keep pace with them in the present building.' Moreover their ships, being built on modern lines, were stronger and more durable, and it would be necessary to lay down vessels with thicker sides, greater breadth and guns higher above the water line.[7]

The debate that followed was not promising. Almost at once exceptions were taken to Pepys' rather portentous insistence on the secrecy of the figures he had revealed. Garroway remarked that there were lists of the Navy in public circulation every whit as good as that given in by Pepys; these things were known all over Europe and needed no concealing. Another old foe, Sacheverell, argued that from the figures given there was nothing wrong with the Navy at all.

And when a member of the Court Party offered a loyal observation that, since the French were increasing in shipping, it was high time for members to lay their hands on their hearts and purses, Sir Thomas Meres replied that he proposed to lay his hand on his purse, like a sensible man, to keep his money in it. The general contention of the Opposition was that the defects of the Navy were so small and the revenue so large that there was no need for any grant at all. And, despite all attempts of the government spokesmen to keep the House to the matter in hand, the debate rambled off into a proposal, not to vote more money, but to appropriate part of the existing revenue, the Customs, to the express use of the Navy.[8]

Owing to a dispute between the two Houses, Parliament was soon after prorogued till the autumn without any progress being made. In the meantime, Pepys, who had made several speeches to prove that the King was spending every penny of the money derived from the Customs on the Navy,* continued to accumulate facts and figures, and prepare them (including a grand Alphabetical Register of all the ships in the service with tabulated details of the tonnage, manning and guns) against the inevitable triumph of reason and oratory which he counted on in the next session. At midsummer he was with the Fleet at Portsmouth, when the King was all but lost in a storm while sailing from the Downs to Spithead to watch the launching of a new ship. When Pepys arrived at noon on June 29th in perfect time to see Deane's *Royal James* take the water, there was no sign of the *Greyhound*, the little 6th rate of 180 tons in which Charles was sailing. A day later the Duke of York, separated from his brother by the storm, arrived in the *Anne* yacht with a load of very disconsolate courtiers – 'our landmen who have had enough of the sea this bout', as Pepys termed them. But his apprehensions of the 'too great adventure his Majesty was running without other security on board than his own seamanship and poor Clements" was still unrelieved that night, when darkness found the anxious company of cravatted, periwigged grandees still waiting, and it was not till next morning that fires on the low hills beyond the Solent announced that the royal truant had appeared on the coast of the Isle of Wight, rather hungry but in his usual good spirits. During his adventures he had

---

* The actual figure as worked out by Pepys, taken over the years 1660 and 1674 was £11,677,227 or an average of £464,276 for each of the peace years and £1,041,648 for each of the war years. *Pepysian MSS*. 2265.

been much sustained by a courtly and, as it turned out, very timely present of lamb and fish made to him at Deal by Balty.[9]

When the King reached Portsmouth on Friday July 2nd he showed great satisfaction with all he saw, especially with the *Royal James* – so much so that as he walked along the walls he knighted its architect Deane and Commissioners Haddock and Tippetts. Pepys was not knighted, probably because he no longer coveted the honour: the less he had in this way, the more disinterested must Mr Pepys' service of the Navy appear in the eyes of the world. Instead he sat down to describe it all to his friend, Sir Joseph Williamson, the Secretary of State, but just as he got to the bottom of the first page he was summoned to attend the King to dinner at Mr Noel's house at Titchfield. Afterwards he saw his Majesty embark for Spithead where he was to join the *Harwich* 'with purpose of making the best of his way this evening towards London, the wind blowing at WSW and very fresh and the weather fair. God give him a good passage'. Pepys himself returned to London by *terra firma*.[10]

Among the things that delighted Charles II at Portsmouth were two little yachts which Deane had built for the French King's lake at Versailles. One of them, weighing about 42 tons, had been wheeled on a cradle to the sea side and there, fully rigged, lowered by a crane on to the water, where it cruised about all afternoon to the applause of all who saw it, particularly of Pepys who thought it out-did anything that ever swam.

At the beginning of August, Deane took the two yachts to France. He was accompanied by Will Hewer, Pepys' chief clerk, who before sailing made arrangements for his uncle Blackburne, the Secretary of the East India Company, to supply his master's financial needs in his absence. From his correspondence it appears that Hewer at this time possessed £8500 in cash, £3000 in monies owing him and another £5000 in banker's notes held by him for Pepys. Sancho Panza, as Pepys' chief clerk seemed to many, was growing as rich as his master; soon he was to start buying land at Clapham and to purchase the finest of the new houses then building above the river on the site of old York House. The shrewd business acumen of Samuel's former servant-boy was only equalled by his loyalty; 'the kindness you are pleased to express towards me and more particularly your regard of my mother', he wrote, as the *Cleveland* yacht bore him across the Channel, 'is such that I want words to express my thankfulness . . . Living or dying I shall remain to the end your faithful servant'.*[11]

Even at the time this voyage of his two closest lieutenants to France gave Pepys fears of any ill-construction of it by malicious enemies: later it was to play a highly important part in his life. During their trip, both Deane and Hewer sent him letters regularly, describing all they saw – the journey through Rouen to Paris, where they passed the two yachts on the road, the generosity of their French hosts who accompanied them everywhere defraying all their expenses (somewhat to the embarrassment of Deane who was much hampered in the confidential enquiries he was making at Pepys' request on the state of the French Navy); their noble entertainment by Monsieur Colbert and the Marquis de Seignelay, the Secretary to the French Admiralty, and the wonders they saw at Paris and Versailles – 'so fine and magnificent', wrote the entranced Hewer, 'that . . . I do believe there cannot in the whole world be anything that is finer'.[12]

With the autumn came a renewed duel with Parliament. When the Houses met on October 13th, the King once more asked for money to build ships. But the Commons, in spite of all Pepys' carefully prepared figures and Danby's more effective offers of posts and pensions, reverted to their plan for appropriating the Customs of the Navy, in the insulting belief that the King had misappropriated the money voted for the service of the Fleet. The Opposition's point of view was, in Sir Thomas Lee's words, 'we are told that there's always spent yearly upon the Navy £400,000, and yet here is no Navy'. Against this kind of committee logic, the Secretary of the Admiralty Commission's figures were useless.[13]

But on Friday, October 22nd, Pepys made a great effort. After Sir John Cotton, declaring that our ships were our walls, had moved that the House should vote £500,000 for building new ones, and the Opposition, speaking through Meres, Vaughan and Garroway, had demanded a detailed statement of why they were wanted, Pepys rose to supply it.

It was the greatest speech he had yet made. He began by saying that he was sorry that there should be suspicions in the House of any member's good intentions; he had none and would give none. To

* W. Hewer to S. Pepys, Aug. 9th, 1675. *Rawl. MSS. A.* 185, f. 58.

follow he had carefully prepared an historical preamble, a protestation of the plainness and truth with which he proposed to speak, and an offer to have the crime punished on himself if he were found to have concealed anything. And then, his notes ran, 'proceed to the giving as welcome, and as unwelcome, an account as ever was yet given of a Navy of England'. But the debate had already begun, and in the presence of that curious and electric assembly of which he never quite felt himself to be a part, it was impossible to keep to the exact terms of a lecture prepared in the study.

So he went on to tell them, that at his Restoration the King had found a Navy of 157 ships, a force fair in appearance but in shocking disrepair, destitute of stores and burdened with a debt of nearly £700,000 – and here he looked at Birch and recalled that troublesome veteran's own Report of fifteen years back. And though subsequently Parliament had made provision for its wages and victualling it had made none for replenishing the stores or repairing the ships, all of which the King had taken upon himself as well as the year-by-year building of new vessels. Since his Restoration King Charles had actually built 90 ships, great and small, thus exceeding all that any of his royal predecessors had done or, for that matter, the much vaunted Commonwealth men, 'notwithstanding what their public revenues enabled them and the necessities of their violent government urged them to'. Thanks to the royal building programme England, 'after the injuries of two of the severest wars that ever the Sea yet knew', now enjoyed a Fleet of 150 ships, superior in tonnage, force and condition to that of 1660. And here Pepys paused to speak of the King's other services to the Navy – the new docks, the provision for flag and superannuated officers and their widows and orphans, the voyages of discovery in distant seas, the Mathematical Foundation at Christ's Hospital and his 'personal knowledge and labours in war and peace, and enquiries after everything advantageous to Navigation'.

But though, Pepys went on, there was nothing seriously wrong at home, it was another matter, 'when we consider the condition of our neighbours, who never till now since the memory of our dominion at sea ever had pretended to any equality, but now do to a considerable superiority to us in naval force. Of which', he observed, 'I had occasion of giving the House information in April last, and have since had the disquiet of understanding that disproportion to be risen to our greater disadvantage'. Then, reading the Abstract which he had drawn up on the relative strength of the three Navies, he declared that now was the only time and the House the only hand for remedying matters against the envious Dutch and the imperious French.

One small concession Pepys made to the Opposition – an admission that more might have been done with the money supplied, had it come more seasonably. He closed with an assertion of the truth of everything he had said and an offer of delivering it all in writing so that, should there be found the least mistruth in it, his hand should bear witness against his head.*[14]

Though the Opposition remained critical, the House was frankly impressed as it nearly always is by anyone who presents a difficult case to it with sincerity. In spite of Garroway's contention that Pepys' figures were exaggerated and Birch's bold murmurs that there was once a time when the French had been told to build no more ships or we should burn them ('hopes we may see that day again, but we shall sweat for it first'), most members after hearing his speech accepted the necessity of strengthening the Fleet. The debate that followed ranged round the question of whether money should be voted for a long period building programme or whether the Government, as the Opposition contended, should be confined to what they could actually spend in a year with the necessity of coming back to Parliament for more at the end of it. To show the impracticability of this last suggestion, Pepys spoke again; to build ships, he explained, three things were necessary, places, hands and materials. Places and hands could be calculated – fourteen docks available at Chatham, Portsmouth, Woolwich, Blackwall and Deptford, and 305 shipwrights required to build one ship of each rate a year – but materials were hard to come by and harder still to estimate. At home and abroad there was a dearth of plank, and timber would have to be felled. To build twenty ships in the next

---

* 'I closed with these very words, which Colonel Birch afterwards repeated with some expressions to my advantage.' Grey, who seldom does justice to the speeches of the Government's supporters (though unfortunately he is almost our only source for the parliamentary debates of the period), devotes twelve inadequate lines to this speech against the twenty-nine given to Birch's rambling commentary on it, but its structure is given in Pepys' own 'Notes for my Discourse in Parliament introductory to the Debate of the Business of the Navy. The 22nd Oct. 1675'. *Pepysian MSS.* 2266, Paper 119.

year, as members were now proposing, must be to build them all of green timber. The only sensible way was to estimate, as he had done, the number of new ships needed to secure parity with France and Holland, and then to vote an adequate sum to build them over a number of years. Of ships of forty guns and upwards France had twenty-two more than England, and Holland thirty-seven.

On that day at least the Opposition contended against Pepys' oratory in vain. Sir Thomas Clarges asserted that the royal revenue was ample to support the government and build ships as well, and Sir Thomas Lee anticipated the twentieth century by arguing that armament programmes merely caused wars and that if England were now to lay down twenty ships, France would build forty. But for the moment the waverers were convinced and the debate ended with a Resolution in Committee that twenty ships of the line should be built.[15]

A few days later when the House came to consider Ways and Means, the leaders of the Opposition threw the whole business into the melting-pot by an apparently ingenuous suggestion that the money to be voted for the new ships should be lodged, not in the royal Exchequer, but in that of the City of London and that no payment should be made without an order of the Lord Mayor and Common Council. This was not only an insult to the Crown but nothing less than a constitutional revolution.*

Pepys, who spoke last in the debate, again turned the scale. He would have been silent, he began, but for the fact that no man could say what he had now to say but himself. Of all men he knew that the money would be best spent if placed in the King's single hand. A recollection of former ill-managements had perhaps caused this jealousy of the Crown, but was it justified? Was the state of the Fleet worse now than when the King came in? It was better in quality, rates, burdens, force, men and guns. It was the best Fleet the kingdom had ever known. There were eighty-three sail, more than any of his predecessors had possessed, and the most beautiful were those of the King's own growth and building. Why, therefore, should the House mistrust him? He himself had the honour of a near attendance upon his Majesty by virtue of his office, and he could assure them that not one of his subjects took such pains for the Fleet

---

* As Sir George Downing put it: 'You are the restorers of the government, but this about the Chamber of London is setting up a new government.' Grey, *Debate* III, 360.

as 'this master of ours'. The King, if he might say so, had actually been in a conspiracy with the Officers of the Navy how to get money for ships. When the question was put, the proposal to lodge the grant in the Chamber of London was defeated by eleven votes.[16]

But the money had still to be voted. A week later with the House in Grand Committee a fierce debate raged all day as to the exact number, rates and burdens of the ships. Pepys, who had brought a book of statistics, spoke no less than five times on the proportionate advantages of the various rates, while the Opposition, who complained that the ships were 'every day enlarged and girdled' in Pepys' papers, contested every point he made – 'fighting from dock to dock and slip to slip', as Sir Thomas Meres called it. This debate on naval technicalities continued for a week. Once it was even proposed, by Meres, to limit the grant to the building of the hulls, leaving the Crown to find the sails and rigging, a suggestion, Pepys commented, like giving someone a coach without any wheels. In the midst of this cloud of ill-informed oratory and argument, Mr Waller was observed sitting on the steps of the House instead of on his seat and was called upon by the Speaker to resume the latter. This he refused to do on the grounds that in the days of the Long Parliament steps were seats and seats were steps as in an amphitheatre, and the Rump by putting backs to the seats had confused the whole issue. Meres, on the other hand, contended that a man ought not to be disquieted in his seat, and that a step in a gangway could not therefore be a seat. The interruption was symptomatic of the whole debate. It ended on Saturday, November 6th, with a Resolution that one 1st rate of 1400 tons, five 2nd rates of 1100 tons and fourteen 3rd rates of 900 tons should be built on a computation of £14, £12.10*s*. and £9. 10*s*. a ton respectively, and that a sum of £300,000 should be raised for the purpose.[17]

But the King and Mr Pepys never got the money. For in the following week the Opposition succeeded in the end in tacking on to the Bill of Subsidies an appropriation of the Customs. On November 16th in despair the King admitted his defeat and prorogued Parliament. The most he could now look for was a small subsidy from Louis to bridge the gulf between current income and the normal national expenditure, in return for keeping England out of the European Alliance against France. There was nothing left for it but a further spell of economy. Sadly Pepys produced a plan by which all the 1st, 2nd and 3rd rates were to be laid up and the active naval force of the country reduced to a winter and summer guard of three frigates and thirteen yachts in the Downs, a frigate at Portsmouth, another at Sheerness, two in Ireland, four in the Straits, two off Newfoundland, one at Jamaica and two on the herring fisheries.[18]

Once again economy proved impracticable. Narbrough was still blockading Tripoli with a dozen ships, almost as many again as the whole of the projected peace-time establishment, and the beginning of 1676 saw him embarking on a cutting-out expedition on the shore forts. A young lieutenant called Cloudesley Shovell, who had begun his career under the heroic Myngs (and was ultimately to end it under what must be almost the ugliest and largest sepulchral monument in any English cathedral), led the boats, burning four Tripoline vessels of war and a large quantity of stores. All this a middle-aged Warwickshire parson, who had left home to escape from his creditors and was now serving as Chaplain on board an English frigate, sang in crude but spirited verse:

> The Turks they took it in great snuff,
> And sorely were offended;
> But we did carry off their stuff,
> And so the battle ended.

> God bless King Charles; the Duke of York;
> The Royal Family;
> From Turks and Jews that eat no pork
> Good Lord deliver me!

The boisterous days of Elizabethan England that old Colonel Birch was always lamenting were perhaps not so far away after all.[19]

The news of 'that great and happy action of Sir John Narbrough's', as Pepys proudly called it, reached London at the beginning of April 1676. It was highly satisfactory to be able to write to one's own protégé of how all England was ringing with his praises; 'my Lords', he told him, 'have commanded me to signify to you the extraordinary content they take in the effects of that action of yours . . . perfected with all the acceptable circumstances that can attend any attempt of that kind – namely, the being effectual, speedy and not chargeable to his Majesty in his treasure nor to his subjects in their lives'. Narbrough in fact was exactly the kind of seaman that

Pepys had been so long looking for – as industrious and enterprising on the water as Will Hewer in an office or Anthony Deane in a dockyard. And, like everyone else, Pepys was delighted with the reports of Cloudesley Shovell's gallantry, though less so when the young man, working through unauthorized channels, persuaded his sovereign to grant him a medal worth £100, nearly double as much as that allocated for medals and chains for his seniors.[20]

Unfortunately one pirate led to another. Though in the spring the Dey conceded a peace more profitable and honourable than any obtained from that nation by any prince, his subjects, taxed to pay an indemnity and deprived of the right of preying on English ships, promptly turned him out and enthroned another in his place. Narbrough was accordingly forced at some expense to bring the second Dey to reason also. And when, at last, the triumphant Admiral was returning home, news came that the neighbouring pirate state of Algiers had seized a ship of the Houblons on the grounds that she was not able to show a Pass, though the Anglo-Algerian treaty of five years before had expressly excepted English ships entirely manned by English subjects, as this was, from the necessity of carrying one. On July 13th Pepys sent orders to Narbrough at Cadiz to return to the Mediterranean. But by the time they reached Sir John, both he and the government at home had received further information that Pepys' lion-collecting friend, Mr Martin, the Consul, with the timely help of some presents to the authorities had secured the discharge of the captured vessel. The Admiralty Board and its harassed Secretary breathed a sigh of relief at escaping another chargeable war, while Narbrough, holding that the situation on which his instructions were based no longer existed, came home. For this he was commended by a broad-minded Admiralty, Pepys being the first to welcome him home with his 'affectionate respects and congratulations'.[21]

But in the autumn of 1676 far more disquieting news arrived from the Mediterranean – nothing less than the surrender of an English ship of war by Captain Charles Atkins, son of the Governor of Barbados, who had calmly allowed himself to be towed into Algiers by a couple of corsairs, in the hope of saving the bullion which in defiance of orders he was carrying. Mr Martin was almost distracted, and the English government, on receipt of his anguished communication, resolved that, cost what it might, the insult must be

avenged by war. Immediate orders were given to fit out a powerful
squadron, including three ships of the line, for Narbrough to lead
back to the Mediterranean. But a further complication ensued, for
no sooner had the orders been given than Pepys' merchant friends
appealed to him to get them respited until their ships had had time
to get out of the danger zone. It was therefore decided to wait until a
reply could be received from Algiers. In the meantime the strictest
secrecy was ordered about the whole matter. Picture therefore
Pepys' fury when the pioneer journalist, Mr Muddiman, in his
weekly paper of *Intelligence,* published the full story, 'containing
matters not only untrue but expressly contradictory to his Majesty's
last determination'. Nor could the Secretary of the Admiralty Office
be appeased till the enterprising news man had been haled before
the Council for his 'vanity and presumption'.[22]

Fortunately Algiers made amends for the affront, and it was not
till the following year that Narbrough's squadron sailed again for
the Mediterranean. But hardly was the affair of the *Quaker* ketch
resolved – the thorn, in Pepys' words, out of that foot – but the
Admiralty was called upon to equip another naval expedition for
operations across the Atlantic. On the last day of September news
arrived from Virginia, where trouble had long been brewing, that a
force of rebels under one Bacon had overthrown the administration.
Next day orders were issued for transporting twelve hundred
soldiers to America under an escort of frigates. Pepys spent the next
six weeks collecting vessels capable of carrying them – a difficult task
in a time when few ships had a burden of over two or three hundred
tons – sending yachts out to bring in soldiers from garrison ports and
seeing that the expedition was adequately victualled. For every
soldier there was to be a three months' allowance of bread and
cheese and a gallon of brandy, with a store of rice (a hasty
afterthought) 'as a relief to such of them as shall be sick in their
passage', while certain favoured ones like Sir Charles Wheeler's
two sons, whom their father specially requested might accompany
the expedition, were to be given an additional runlet of brandy, a
hamper of wine, a firkin of butter and a cask of cheese and biscuit.
The care of these homely details fell principally on the shoulders of
the Secretary of the Admiralty Office, who felt unable to leave them
to the more dilatory methods of the Navy Board. By November 5th
the troops were all on board, saving only some 'little parcels of men'

who had been forgotten and had to be fetched from Windsor and Rochester at the last moment. A fortnight later Sir John Berry with the advance guard was well on his way, eighty leagues beyond the Lizard.[23]

These hasty arrangements proved effective and the rebellion was suppressed. Pepys' naval year closed with no worse anxiety than that caused by the intense cold, which necessitated moving the yachts down to Gravesend lest they should be frozen in and drove a most unwelcome squadron of Dutch warships into Portsmouth, where they were regarded with the utmost suspicion by the dock-yard officials, who tried in vain to coax them on to Plymouth. It was the Christmas when the snow lay so deep that Evelyn was prevented from going to church and the King drove about St James's Park in a sleigh.[24]

The New Year brought the reassembly of Parliament after a fifteen months' prorogation, and with it a resumption of Pepys' great plan to rebuild the Navy. On February 15th, 1677, the King met the Houses with an appeal for the immediate construction not of twenty but thirty new ships, the least which in Pepys' considered view would now suffice against the building programme of France. The Chancellor followed with a speech in which he said that there was no more commendable jealousy in an Englishman than that of a foreign prince at sea. Frightened by the growing power of France, the House was in a much more favourable mood, which was much enhanced by a tactical blunder by the two great peers, Shaftesbury and Bucking-ham, who directed the Opposition. For having carefully secured control of the corrupt electoral machinery, the 'great Electors' tried to force a general election by arguing that the present Parliament, having been prorogued for fifteen months, was *ipso facto* dissolved under a forgotten statute of Edward III – a suggestion which caused their own House to imprison them and enraged the Commons. Though there was talk of foreign counsels and refusing supply till grievances were redressed, the general feeling, potent in a House of country gentlemen, was that no good patriot could now be against giving something. Sums ranging from £800,000 to £400,000 were spoken of in debate, and on Wednesday the 21st, the Secretary of the Navy, as the House called him, rose to give his account of the state and needs of the Service.[25]

It was universally admitted to be a great speech. After a

preliminary discussion with the Navy Office Pepys had arranged his notes under thirteen exhaustive, and to some who heard him possibly exhausting, heads.* Together they constituted a complete lecture to an as yet unmaritime people on matters of vital importance to their interests. There was the familiar confession of faith and integrity – his head should be at stake for every syllable of fact he uttered – and the usual historical introduction on the state of the Navy before the Restoration.† Since then, Pepys declared, not one year had been entirely free from War, and yet the King had built more ships from the stocks than all his predecessors put together. This year he had spent on the Navy not less than £400,000 – here Pepys was embarrassed by a previous careless ministerial claim of £450,000 in the Lord Chancellor's rhetorical address – and he would give it in writing, that his hand might be witness against his head if it were not so.

Why was it necessary, he continued, to ask for more ships than two years before? Because our neighbours had continued and were still continuing to build, so that we had now to overtake them for lost time as well as to keep pace with them for the future. Since 1674 the French had laid down nineteen great ships and were building seven more. In vessels of over twenty guns they exceeded us by twenty-four and the Dutch by forty-four. How had this disproportion arisen? It had begun even before the Restoration, for during the Commonwealth the English had had to hire fifty merchant ships to equal the Dutch and our victories in that War had been due, not to superiority in numbers, but to the great ships built by Charles I, whose superior gun power had done the real business against Tromp. Since that time the Dutch had been steadily building large vessels, and had 'got before us by a constancy of disbursing money in building ships both in war and peace', while we, though we had laid down more merchant ships in the past ten years than ever before, had stood idle in the Navy for long periods of enforced economy. Nor was the size of the French Fleet to be wondered at considering the vast superiority of its revenue.

* 'Heads of a Discourse in Parliament upon the Business of the Navy.' *Pepysian MSS., Miscellanies* II, 453–69. The detailed materials for this are to be found in *Pepysian MSS.* 2265.
† '151 sail the King took possession of, but should be sorry it were now in so foul a pickle.' Grey, *Debates* IV, 116. 151 is a mistake for 157.

Pepys then went on to discuss the size, strength and rates of the proposed ships. Here the extent of his knowledge made him for once a little indecisive. 1st rates could stand battery better than any other, but 2nd rates needed fewer men, smaller draught and less weight of ordnance, and with their three gun decks were equally 'terrible to the enemy . . . playing down upon them'. Against the Dutch, whose shallow harbours forbade them to build three-deck ships, no new 1st rates were needed; the French, however, had harbours which enabled them to build any size of vessel: they had already four larger than any of the English. On the whole he inclined to the three-deck ships of the 2nd rate. 4th rates, on the other hand, were not needed; as they could not stand in the line of battle, they were useful, like the 5th rates, only for convoy and for warfare against the African corsairs; there were already thirty-six of them, and if at any time more were wanted, they could be reinforced by converted merchant ships.

After explaining the highly technical reasons why the difference in price was greater between 3rd and 2nd than between 2nd and 1st rates, Pepys turned to the question of how and where the ships should be built. Timber was bound to be a difficulty; in Commissioner Deane's expert view all the royal and private timber within transportable distance – roughly twenty miles – of the Thames and the coast would not furnish enough knees, breast-hooks, standards and compass timber to build two 1st rates and six 2nd rates in four years. Foreign material would therefore have to be bought. And as, in view of the size of the French ships, it was particularly important to build heavier vessels less penetrable by shot, the King's Yards were better for the work than those of private contractors, for the latter, not daring to buy more timber than was absolutely necessary, were always inclined 'to build slight'.

Pepys closed with a peroration on the service of the Stuarts to the Navy. The King had consistently 'outbuilt' the sums voted him and had frequently started to lay down vessels against the entreaties of his Lord Treasurers, in the belief that money would ultimately be forthcoming. By his personal application to shipbuilding, a skill in that art had been advanced to a degree beyond the memory of man, and perhaps beyond all possibility of improvement. No other age had known such encouragements to navigation. There were the new docks, the provision for flag-officers, the wonders of Trinity House, which had grown from a little hospital into the greatest charitable foundation in the country; very august, he declared with emotion, was the King's seminary for seamen. He ended by moving that provision should be made for building thirty ships.[26]

Pepys' speech would scarcely have seemed complete had not Colonel Birch followed it. While he spoke and during the subsequent debate, Pepys sat making rough, fragmentary notes in shorthand in his pocket book. Birch both praised and blamed him, generously declaring that his opportunities for knowledge were as great as his abilities, and then advancing his old thesis that in the time of the Commonwealth naval expenditure had never exceeded £4 per head per month. Garroway followed with a sneer at little people who made irresponsible overtures in default of a Lord High Admiral whom the House could have recourse to and trust, and other members of the Opposition spoke of the poverty of the nation and of a secret alliance with France that carried the Pope in its belly. But by six that night the House had resolved to grant the sum Pepys needed. 'I doubt not', he wrote proudly to the Navy Board, 'but 'ere this you may have heard the issue of this morning's debates . . . touching the Navy, wherein I thank God the account they received from me of the past and present state thereof . . . was so received as that the debates arising therefrom terminated in a vote for the supplying his Majesty with a sum of money for building ships not exceeding £600,000.'[27]

On February 27th the House went into a Grand Committee to consider Ways and Means. During the next few weeks Pepys, as full of Parliament business as a man could be, was perpetually on his feet answering some captious criticism or explaining some misunderstood technicality, and at constant pains to prevent his opponents from fastening upon him promises which he might not be able to fulfil, such as having the ships built in a limited time or within too closely specified a sum. All he would undertake was that the materials should be bought and the work set in hand as cheaply and as quickly as was compatible with efficiency. Among his most persistent critics was William Harbord, son of Sir Charles Harbord, Lord Sandwich's old friend, who in one speech recalled how a great and wise Lord who had since died in the King's service – meaning Sandwich – had once promised to secure England against the French at sea if someone would but secure her against them at Whitehall.

In all this worrying business Pepys received little or no help from any of the King's ministers, the whole business of the Navy being left on his hands. But his knowledge, sincerity and oratory carried the day, perhaps because for once in his dealings with the House they were reinforced by his enchanting good humour – a quality which he usually kept for anywhere but Westminster. When old blustering Sir Harbottle Grimstone, arguing for another appropriation of the Customs to the Navy, declared that he thought it as proper to think of keeping his young as of getting them, Pepys remarked cheerfully that it would somewhat lessen the pleasure of getting children to think of the cost of maintaining them. The House finally resolved to build one 1st rate of 1400 tons, nine 2nd rates of not less than 1100 tons, and twenty 3rd rates of not less than 900 tons. £600,000, payable quarterly over the next two years, was allocated for this purpose.[28]

Yet Pepys had to pay a price for his triumph. Early in March, the Commons fell to discussing grievances and chose as one of them the necessity of merchants' taking out passes from the Admiralty to secure immunity from seizure by North African corsairs, as laid down by the treaties with Algiers and Tripoli. In most respects these passes were a great benefit to English merchants, on whom they conferred immunity from attack in places where in time past the English Crown could never have protected them. But they necessitated delay and trouble in the taking out, and, according to the universal bureaucratic practice of the day, the payment of fees to the Admiralty Office. Pepys had acted personally with scrupulous care and, after investigating the question, had actually reduced the fee of 30*s.* a pass received by his predecessor to 25*s.* But this had not prevented merchants from reproaching him and his Office, even when, as in some cases, he had actually for friendship's sake waived his whole fee. 'One piece of easiness indeed they met with . . .' he had written to James Houblon of two ungrateful acquaintances, who had had to pay no other fee but ten shillings to his clerks – 'a penniworth to be had in few offices in England but mine, I fear. And with very good will they shall have it so, provided that while I am contented to forgo my profit they will not make me a further sufferer by turning that to my prejudice, which I labour most to merit by – I mean the easiness, civility and despatch which I pretend to give to all that have occasion of applications to my Office. But if the reward I am to have for it must be to have those simple methods of mine interpreted for perfunctoriness and want of scrutiny, 'tis twenty to one but my invention might serve me to make my Office as troublesome and chargeable as others . . . You will forgive me for appearing a little touched with this usage.'[29]

All this and much else was now brought against Pepys by his enemies in Parliament and by disgruntled merchants who readily lent themselves to their purposes. On Wednesday, March 7th, he was forced to sit for some hours, taking occasional shorthand notes on his knee, while one unjust, angry or malicious speech after another was made about him. Passes, it was said, had cost £80 a piece to obtain; £10,000 a year was paid for them to the benefit of particular persons, for whom the whole device had been invented; they were absolutely unnecessary and an infringement on the right of the subject and the freedom of trade. Three times Pepys rose to defend himself and with a complete denial of every charge. He had ever despised, he said, the thought of any undue profit; he had never taken a farthing more for any pass than 25*s*. – less than any of his predecessors (and his pains and diligence had deserved as well as any of theirs) – he had written himself blind in the King's service. He was concerned, not for his fees, but for his good fame in the world, and would have the affair referred to a Committee.* It was referred to a Committee.[30]

Two months later, following on the Commons' resolution, the matter came before the Admiralty Board. On May 19th Pepys rose to defend himself in the presence of the King, Prince Rupert, the Lord Treasurer, the Dukes of Monmouth, Ormonde and Lauderdale and half a dozen of the greatest men in the kingdom. He was able to show that it was through the exactions of others and not himself that the charges of taking out passes were so high, and that the 25*s*. he claimed as his due was lower than the fee taken out by any of his predecessors. On which Seymour, the imperious West Country magnate, who combined the functions of Treasurer of the Navy and Speaker of the House of Commons, observed that it was taken for granted in the House that 4000 passes went through Mr Pepys' hands in a year and that some put the figure as high as 8000;

---

* '. . . comme il se défendit parfaitement bien (car c'est un des hommes d'Angleterre qui parle le mieux) on nomme des commissaires pour examiner tout ce qui avoit esté allégué . . .' Courtin to Louis XIV, March 8th/18th, 1677. *P.R.O. Paris Transcripts*, No. 135.

he proposed therefore a reduction of his fee to 10s. But Pepys would have none of it; whatever the number of passes, his right to the fee was neither more nor less, but in any case the annual number of passes since his coming to the Admiralty had never exceeded a thousand. And his labour in the issue and scrutiny of passes would be increased fivefold by the new rules proposed by the House of Commons. He therefore humbly submitted himself to his Majesty for the continuance of his fee or for compensation if it was to be taken away. 'Upon which', Pepys triumphantly minuted, 'his Majesty was pleased to say that he saw no reason to have it taken away.'[31]

But whatever people might say against the little autocrat of the Admiralty Office, the £600,000 for the new ships had been voted, and nothing could rob him of that glorious fact. Thirty ships of the line, laid down on the finest and most up-to-date lines, would give his country the first fleet in the world. Even before the money was voted, he had instructed the Navy Office to put out all necessary enquiries both at home and abroad for materials, so as to be ready to buy the moment funds were available. All the while the debates on Ways and Means were continuing, he was making enquiries on his own, even in Parliament, where he was much solicited by disinterested members who had heard of some worthy merchants, complete strangers, they always assured him, who wished to sell him some commodity. On the evening of Monday, April 16th, after a further hard tussle at Westminster, he was able to tell Commissioner Tippetts that 'the Money Bill, blessed be God, passed this night' and that he and his colleagues could now go full speed ahead on the great work.[32]

With the old ships to be repaired and thirty new ones to be built, a tremendous strain was put on the ship-building resources of the country. For sooner than 'expose them to contractors', the Admiralty resolved to build all in the royal yards save one 3rd rate at Bristol. Pepys was actually forced to ask leave to impress carpenters, shipwrights and caulkers. In view of the growing likelihood of a war with France, work was started at once on the 1st and 2nd rates, leaving any delay necessitated by the slow coming in of the parliamentary subsidies to fall on the 3rd rates. The King, insisting that the ships should be made as big as possible, made Pepys send back the schedule of burdens and dimensions of each rate to the

Navy Officers for revision and, when they pointed out the heavy increase of cost that must follow, replied that 'he would make it good out of his own purse rather than hazard the wronging the ships for want of it'.* To their further query how they should be indemnified for not keeping a separate account for each of the thirty ships, as the Act required, this being impossible since they must all be built out of the same materials bought at varying prices, his Majesty answered briefly 'that things impossible do excuse themselves'.[33]

---

* Compare a later note of Pepys' on this very subject: 'How can King Charles 2nd be supposed an enemy to his Navy that out of his own purse enlarged the dimensions assigned by the Parliament itself to the 30 new ships, by virtue whereof they became of so great consideration for the strength of England as they are now found in our war with France, 1693?' Samuel Pepys' *Naval Minutes*, 318.

'The Envious Name of Admiral'

'The life of a virtuous Officer in the Navy is a continual war defensive, viz. against the Ministers of State and in particular the Lord Treasurers in time of peace, and all prejudiced inquisitors and malcontents with the Navy management in time of war.' S. Pepys, *Naval Minutes*.

While Parliament was debating Pepys' right to his fees, his only surviving brother John died. Like Thomas before him, John left few assets and many liabilities, which it became the business of Samuel, his reluctant administrator, to meet. Even Trinity House asked his harassed brother to account for the deficit their late Clerk had left behind him. After wearily going through his bills and his statements of official expenditure, which appeared to be chiefly 'laying out upon Trinity Dinners', with vast items for oranges and lemons, rum, runlets of sack and Rhenish wine, Pepys deposited £300 on account with the Wardens until a final adjustment could be made.[1]

One liability that accrued to Samuel through his brother's death was a closer responsibility for the perennially confused affairs of his father in Huntingdonshire and the failing fortunes of Pall and her lazy, improvident husband. These John Pepys had affectionately, though not very competently, supervised, appeasing their quarrels and sending them the news of the town and an occasional present of claret, sturgeon, or clothes for little Samuel and John Jackson. Now all this humble but necessary labour fell on the overburdened shoulders of the Secretary of the Admiralty Office – the care of his father's health, for which he took advice from his old surgeon, Thomas Hollier, the despatch of the wine that gave the old man such pleasure, the little law suit over the Brampton land with Thomas Pepys, the turner, on which he took legal counsel on behalf of his sister's children, 'that I may', as he told his father, 'as much as it is possible secure myself against any imputation of doing anything misbecoming an honest man towards my cousins . . . But', he added, 'if my sister should be prevented in this, I shall be able by God Almighty's blessing to make her children as good a provision in another way.' He had travelled a long road since the day he had made Pall stand in his wife's presence lest she should grow too proud. And to his father the great Secretary ended his epistle – 'So craving your blessing, and with my kind love to my brother, sister and children, I remain your ever obedient and dutiful son.'[2]

Perhaps it was the thought of these accruing responsibilities that made Pepys in the summer of 1677 anxious to increase his estate. What he described in after years as his exactness to see the King's business well carried on, even to the offence of his great Ministers, proved rather a handicap here, his many representations to Lord Treasurer Danby on the wants of the Navy having made him unpopular in that quarter. In August he heard how a certain Francis Gurney of Malden had drowned himself in his well and begged the Duke of York to secure him the grant of his estate which as a suicide's was forfeit to the Crown – 'the value of which', he wrote, 'I have no knowledge yet of, but suppose it cannot be great, the highest quality of the said person being that of his having served as Bailiff of the said town'. A few days later a caveat was issued at his desire that no grant should pass of the estate. But he was less fortunate in an attempt to obtain the galley which the Grand Duke of Tuscany had given the King for use at Tangier, for to his chagrin it was granted to two other favourites of the Duke's, George Legge, the Governor of Portsmouth, and Sir Roger Strickland.[3]

On the whole, office, though it brought to Pepys all the wealth he had, never made him a really rich man as it did his friend, Sir Stephen Fox, the Paymaster General. Primarily he valued office for what he put into it and not for what he took out of it. In this his country was the gainer. 'You', James Houblon wrote to him in the May of 1677, 'are above those petty advantages and sneaking perquisites your predecessors did stoop to and which you have to your hurt rejected, though the King and the Kingdom hath had the benefit of it.'[4]

But if Pepys never became a very rich man, he was becoming known in the world of learning and culture as a worthy and distinguished one. Men like Evelyn, Sir William Petty and Sir Robert Southwell loved to number him among their friends and to share with him their learned and curious speculations on art, history and natural philosophy; they were always sending the discerning Mr Pepys their disquisitions for his nice appreciation, and could generally count on the compliment of being asked permission to take a copy for his library. Sir Samuel Morland, the famous inventor, begged him to stand god-father to his child and postponed the day that he might be present, and the ingenious Henry Shere, part-maker of the great Mole at Tangier and once beloved by Elizabeth for his poetry and delightful conversation, dedicated to him his Discourse touching the Currents in the Straits of Gibraltar. And when Pepys told his learned friends that he intended, when the day of leisure came, to write a history of the Navy, and possibly of the world's navigation, they all vied with one another in contributing materials for it.[5]

Such a man was naturally picked for those honourable but rather costly distinctions that are conferred on public men who patronize the arts and sciences – to serve his year from August 1677 as Master of the Clothworkers' Company, who commemorated his princely gift of silver* by placing his arms in their windows; to stand Steward in the same September at the Feast of the Honourable Artillery Company in Merchant Taylors Hall, with the Treasurer of the Royal Household and one of the Secretaries of State as his fellows; to become a governor of Bridewell; to subscribe to the erection of a new building at his old College at Cambridge, begun in 1677 and where to-day his library is housed.[6]

But perhaps the distinction that Pepys valued most was that which came to him in May 1677 when he succeeded Lord Ossory as Master of Trinity House. He had been a Warden two years before and an Elder Brother since 1672. Every Trinity Monday he took his place at the annual sermon and feast of the great charitable Corporation at Deptford, returning in state by barge and dining magnificently on pottage of duck, salmon whole with fried fish and roast turkey, Westphalia ham, Lombard pie, lobsters, prawns, creams and silla-bubs, washed down by claret, champagne, Rhenish and Canary. And whenever any matter affecting the privileges of the King's most august 'seminary for seamen' or the general interests of navigation arose, Pepys' official influence was used to do the Corporation right. He was several times successful in opposing private projects for erecting lights without proper authority, and received on one occasion the public thanks of the City of Newcastle for so doing.[7]

* A large silver gilt bowl and cover, ewer and rosewater dish, still preserved. They weighed 362 ounces and were apparently of John Heriott's making. *Rawl. MSS. A.* 172, f. 25; *A.* 190, f. 99.

Any attempt to improve the navigation and sea-borne trade of England was dear to the heart of Samuel Pepys. He was always lending his aid to such schemes as the discovery of the true longitude, and took a personal interest in the appointment of John Flamsteed as first Astronomer Royal at Greenwich. And amid the pressure of his business, he found time to frame rules and establish a table of rates for pilots in order to encourage the breed of them in England.[8]

Another project dear to Pepys' heart was the attempt to find a passage to the East round the northern coasts of Scandinavia and Muscovy. In February 1676 he arranged a meeting between his city friend, Sir John Bankes, and Captain John Wood, the explorer, to discuss its financial possibilities, and induced the King to set out a frigate at his own cost for a sixteen months' voyage to penetrate the North-East Passage and to seek out 'what trade can be found upon the coasts of Tartary or Japan'. Pepys invested money in the scheme, becoming with the Duke of York, Lord Berkeley, Sir Joseph Williamson, Sir John Bankes and three others, a part owner of the *Prosperous* pink and a 'joint adventurer for the discovery of the said passage'. But his hopes of becoming a great merchant and of opening up a new trade route for his country foundered in the ice of Nova Zembla, where the frigate had to be abandoned. The little *Prosperous* pink survived to bring back Captain Wood and his entire crew, her captain, 'in consideration of his extraordinary humanity, care and courage' being granted the value of the anchors and cables which he had saved. Pepys secured for himself and his fellow owners compensation for the victuals and medicines supplied to the ship-wrecked company.[9]

It was about the time of this ill-starred expedition that Evelyn dining with the Secretary of the Admiralty Commission met at his house one Captain Baker, who had just returned from a similar attempt on the North-West Passage, and heard him talk of the wonders he had seen – the prodigious depth of ice, blue as sapphire and as transparent, and the thick mists which had been the cause of return. Of such voyages Pepys delighted to accumulate records, binding them nobly as they deserved and placing them among his treasured books and manuscripts.[10]

No work that he did for the navigation of his country seemed more vital to Pepys than that which concerned the Mathematical Foundation at Christ's Hospital. In the autumn of 1675 the first batch of boys received their certificates from Trinity House, and on September 13th, accompanied by the President of the Governors and several of the most important citizens of London, he had the satisfaction of escorting them into the presence of their sovereign who spoke kindly to them and promised them his further care. This Pepys subsequently obtained in the shape of an additional grant from the Crown of £300 a year towards their apprenticeship. Henceforward, he hoped, ten future navigators would be set out yearly.[11]

On February 1st, 1676, Pepys was appointed a Governor of the Hospital, and also took his place on the Mathematical School's Committee. For some time he was almost religiously consulted on all matters by the Hospital authorities, who took a solemn resolution not to set out any boy as apprentice without first taking his advice. But in this world perfection is seldom maintained. On October 22nd, 1677, Pepys delivered a speech at the Mathematical Committee which expressed his deep sense that things were far from being well with his cherished foundation.

The trouble was that the boys were not being properly taught. It was not enough, he said, that they should be qualified to become mere ordinary seamen; the object of the royal charity was rather that they should be trained to serve the King 'in any negotiation at sea or in foreign parts, to treat with foreign governors, to reside as Consuls, to keep accounts as Pursers, clerks or other officers of the Navy; to serve as Secretaries to Admirals and ... dictate orders, letters, instructions, articles of treaty and other works of secretaryship – a negotiation beyond what the ordinary education of a bare tarpaulin can ever arrive at'. In fact in his passion for perfection he wanted to turn out a whole corps of marine Pepyses.

Yet this was just what the Mathematical children were not. Their writing was bad, their English grammar worse, while the Trinity House examiners reported that they were so ignorant of Latin that they might never have heard a word of it. 'I find (by all my informations)', Pepys went on, 'that our mathematical boys spend their time idly without control, without correction, without any awe to their present Master, or any memory of respect for their old ones, ... above receiving any admonition, accustoming themselves to liberty and idleness, corrupting by their examples the rest of the children and in short rendering themselves every day less and less fit for the calling they are designed for.' In other words, they were boys.

To remedy this Pepys in his speech – a lengthy one* – proposed that the school should be subjected to a public visitation at least twice a year, that the maximum number of boys receiving instruction should be reduced to twenty, and that as their master was no seaman, 'a method of mathematical learning' should be prescribed, which at his request, his friend, Sir Jonas Moore, the great mathematician, had been preparing. To keep up their Latin, the boys were to be provided with Erasmus' *Colloquies*, Cicero's *Epistles* and a dictionary or two that they might, when their mathematical studies were over, resort to 'nightly exercises in Latin' under the Grammar Master of the old Latin School. And to all this Pepys proposed to add a sort of competitive examination, 'not only in Latin, Writing and Arithmetic, but growth, health, age and morality'.†[12]

Having delivered himself of this homily, Pepys had it bound into a book and presented to Sir John Frederick, the President of the Hospital. The latter acknowledged it humbly and gratefully,‡ and the chastened Committee returned him thanks for his great pains. Mr Leake, the mathematical master, was 'remonstrated with', and forbidden to take more than the specified number of pupils or teach in his private room, and one boy was given corporal correction by the Steward of the Hospital in the presence of his companions in the great hall.[13]

Unfortunately all this proved more than Mr Leake would stand. Though the Committee offered to raise his salary from £50 to £70 per annum and pointed out the impossibility of his being able to observe the misdemeanours of the children if he persisted in

* A year earlier one who had heard him speaking on the same subject recorded 'Mr Pepys . . . made a long speech to no great purpose'. Robert Hooke, *Diary,* Dec. 19th, 1676.

† *Pepysian MSS.* 2612, ff. 238–67.

‡ 'For, Sire, if you had only shewed us our defects and not applied a fit remedy, it would have been a long time before we could have come into a way to have answered his Majesty's intentions. Sir, God has bestowed upon you great parts, and you have taken notice of that in our Hospital as to this affair more than any person has done. I shall with all speed communicate the whole contents of the book to a Committee, and with all convenient speed will call a Court to settle the whole affair, at which I pray you to be present, and I am sure that the said Court will give you public thanks.' *Rawl. MSS. A.* 185, f. 103.

teaching as he did in his private closet, the injured scholar declared roundly that 'he would not for £200 p.a. be obliged to sit publicly in school'. Expostulation only produced from him a melancholy assurance that he would carry out the orders of the Court for so long as he stayed and an uncompromising reply, when asked how long that would be, of till Lady Day and no longer. There was therefore nothing for it but to find a successor.[14]

The task of procuring a suitable one kept Pepys busy for some weeks. A long procession of aspiring mathematicians duly stressed their Latinity, Loyalty and skill in Arithmetic, Logarithms, Planimetry, Stereometry and Trigonometry, though one more modest than the rest admitted to an ignorance of Architecture and Algebra. In the end a Mr Peter Perkins was chosen and Mr Leake, who changed his mind at the last moment, was told to provide for himself forthwith.[15]

The apotheosis of Pepys' establishment of the Mathematical Foundation at Christ's Hospital occurred on New Year's Day 1678 when he presented several of the Governors and all the children of the School to the King, the Duke of York and the Lord Treasurer. It was this scene which at the Mathematical Committee a week later he proposed should be commemorated by a life-size painting upon the wall of the great Hall, 'representing his Majesty and some of his Ministers of State, the Lord Mayor, the President and some Governors with the children of his Majesty's new Royal Foundation, a ship, globe, maps, mathematical instruments, etc.' But even while he was enlarging on this picture, there entered Mr Holmes, the Grammar School Master, complaining bitterly of the behaviour of the mathematical boys, who, on the previous evening, when he had attempted to put into practice Pepys' well-planned scheme of Latin exercises, had made 'unruly noises' at him and gone deliberately to bed. Pepys, who was in the chair, asked the angry pedagogue if he had corrected the boys, and on his answering No – 'which the Committee took very unkindly from him' – had five of them brought in then and there and whipped by the Steward. The sequel followed a few days later when Pepys secured the insertion in the school's prayers of some 'pathetical expressions for a blessing upon the King's Majesty, his royal consort, James Duke of York, and the rest of the Royal Family, for the Clergy and Gentry, for the prosperity of this City and the Magistration thereof, and for the President and

Governors of this Hospital', with a special mention of their Benefactors. And for the performance of this salutary exercise, it was laid down that the children should for the future kneel together in the middle of the great Hall, 'and turn their faces to him that is to read in the pulpit, and not to use any irreverent gesture or ill behaviour'.[16]

That the young should grow up in godliness and sobriety was an abiding passion in Pepys, and he visited both his ever-thwarted passion for human perfection and his own childlessness on the children of his friends and relations. Evelyn's son and Sir Robert Southwell's, the young Houblons and the Bankeses, alike found in him an unwearying expositor of righteousness, albeit sometimes a very human and lovable one. When his old friend John Pearse, the Surgeon-General and now his neighbour at Derby House, wished to dispose of one of his ten children at sea, it was to Pepys the young man was sent to receive his appointment as a purser and with it those excellent maxims which alone could enable him to turn his good fortune to account. And when he showed the least dereliction of duty, Pepys was quick to give him, as he put it, those 'cautions which I should with more severity give a child of my own (and did to my only brother to the last day he lived in the Navy), namely that you do never entertain one thought of any indulgence from me under any neglects of business, for I am one that will never be guilty of contributing to the advancement of any man that will not be contented to rise by the same steps of diligence and faithfulness which have (by God's blessing) raised me to this capacity of doing good offices . . . and so God bless you'.[17]

Mary Skinner's brilliant, ne'er-do-well brother came in for the same salutary course of instruction. After obtaining a junior Fellowship at Trinity he had deserted Cambridge and applied for help in a long, sycophantic Latin letter to the man who a little while before he had been abusing as his sister's seducer. Pepys gave him an introduction to his friend Sir Leoline Jenkins, then Ambassador Extraordinary at Nymegen, describing him as 'an ingenious and in every way hopeful young gentleman' with a reputation for sobriety, parts, learning and Latin style, and begging a post for him in his office. But it turned out that Skinner, who took six months to acknowledge Pepys' kindness, had also gone to Holland with the idea of printing a political paper of that dangerous though now defunct poet Milton, and of subsequently dispersing copies in England. At least so it seemed to Sir Joseph Williamson, his Majesty's Secretary of State, who both wrote to Ambassador Jenkins and spoke seriously to Pepys about the matter. And though the young man swore to Heaven he had never had the least thought of prejudicing either King or State and that his acquaintance with the republican poet had been solely due to an 'ambition to good literature', Pepys was forced to warn him that some time must elapse before he could reasonably expect to have this unfortunate concernment with Mr Milton and his writings forgotten. He recommended him, therefore, instead to apply himself to the study of French and Dutch.[18]

The man who advised others so confidently on their course of life was all too frequently driven to consult others about his own health. The old trouble with his eyes persisted, and the growing necessities of his work made it impossible for him always to use another's eyes to save his own. During the debates on the building of the new ships he had again resorted to taking shorthand notes. In the November of 1677 he set down on paper his symptoms and the causes to which he attributed them. The worst pain came whenever he was forced to read or write, but he was also troubled with headaches and inflamed eyes in the early morning and whenever the weather was wet. Neither spectacles nor paper tubes gave him relief, but he appears to have found some comfort from a soothing recipe, preserved among his papers, of:

Green Hazel Nuts, less than half ripe, split and distilled. To each pint put 2 ounces of Lapis cahminaris. In the application every night and morning, drop 4 or 5 drops from a spoon into each eye.[19]

In the long analytical document, which he dated November 7th, 1677, and entitled 'The Present Ill State of my Health',* Pepys defined his other maladies. They were many and various, but he was writing on a gloomy November evening and had just come out of the crowded Council Chamber into the cold night air, and he may have felt unduly depressed. Scurvy and wind colic were his principal complaints. From the first he suffered, he said, shortness of breath, constant pain in legs and joints, swellings in the thighs during wet

---

* *Rawl. MSS. A.* 185, ff. 206–13.

weather, and 'retching and spitting' accompanied by loss of voice. This last also attacked him whenever he came out of a warm place, such as a church or playhouse, into the cold, or 'out of a cabin when I go up upon the deck, or upon my first entrance on the road in the morning at my first coming out of an inn'.

Then there was the wind colic. Ever since he could remember he had been subject to the most intense pain in bowels and bladder, whenever he took cold – an agony, like the great Secretary's other attributes, 'so certain and orderly that I never have a fit thereof but I can assign the time and occasions of it'.* The best prevention, he had discovered, was to keep his feet warm and his stomach full.

Pepys ended his medical confession with an account of his general condition. 'I am at this time in the 45th year of my age ... I have during my whole life been in a constant heat of body little below a fever. My life has been wholly sedentary without any opportunity for seasonable exercises, the pain of the stone preventing me therein before I was cut and business constantly since as it doth at this day.' Because of the wind colic he found it advisable at all times to wear 'something extraordinary for warmth before my belly'. He also suffered from 'a mighty drought during intent speaking', a furred mouth in the morning, and dizziness at night due, he believed, to his practice of supping at midnight. But, having lately discontinued this last habit, ('the nature of my present employment admitting it'), the dizziness had vanished.[20]

As for food, Pepys stated that he had small appetite or sense of taste. He made no distinction of meats, though he preferred salt, and seldom made a full meal save when tempted by sitting long in good company. Wine he drank temperately and principally at dinner, and he preferred the stronger sorts – Greek, Italian, Spanish and Portuguese – and seldom meddled with the thinner French variety, which he believed occasioned the moisture he so feared in his eyes and body. Twice a year, though not at stated times, he was bled in his arm. 'Courses or seasons of taking physic I never knew nor my employment since my manhood ever allowed me time for, more than sometimes on my occasions of crossing the sea between this and France or the like sea trip has given me occasion of being seasick, which I am to the utmost extremity.' He did not add, though we

---

* Cured always, he found, whenever he could 'break wind behind in a plentiful degree'. *Rawl. MSS. A.* 185, f. 210.

know it from another source, that, to find air and a little occasional quiet he rented a villa at Parson's Green to the west of the riverside village of Chelsea. Here in the summer he would repair on Saturday nights for brief weekends of peace and recreation.[21]

But Pepys' meticulous concern for his own health weighed little or nothing when set in the scales against the welfare of the great Service to which he had dedicated his life. For the Navy of England he was prepared to contract all the diseases expounded in the Schools of Medicine. In the same cold and gloomy November and December that saw him brooding so anxiously over his own bodily ills, he brought to completion three far-reaching schemes for the reform of the Service. The first, formally adopted on November 3rd, 1677, laid down what Pepys called 'a solemn, universal and unalterable adjustment of the gunning and manning of the whole fleet'. It reversed the recent tendency to increase the number of guns in favour of the older dictum of Raleigh that ships should not be 'over pestered and clogged with great ordnance', fixed the size of each ship's company by the number and quality of guns carried, and rigidly limited, in the teeth of bitter opposition from angry admirals, the retinues allowed to flag-officers.[22]

Pepys' second achievement was his Establishment for naval chaplains. For long past he had been perturbed by the inadequacy of the ministers serving with the Fleet.* As the seamen contributed 4*d.* a month out of their pay towards their provision this was hard. Such chaplains as there were, were often men of notoriously loose life, such as the Reverend George Bradford who, on one occasion, after drinking six pints of beer, and throwing another at the coxswain's head, went ashore for more and there 'took off his clothes, and swearing, God damn him, he was a man of war, . . . leapt over a wall and tore his shirt almost from off his back, running up and down swearing and staring as if he was a madman'.†[23]

Pepys made a point whenever he could of persuading captains when commissioning their ships to take a godly divine with them

* 'Mr Pepys took an opportunity from thence to move the Lords that they would be pleased to take . . . into their consideration the business of the Chaplains of his Majesty's ships: how few commanders take any; the ill choice generally made of those that are entertained, both for ignorance and debauches, to the great dishonour of God and the Government, and the encouraging of profaneness and dissolutions in the fleet.' Admiralty Journal, Dec. 2nd, 1676. *Cat. Pepysian MSS.* IV, 383.

† *Rawl. MSS. A.* 181, f. 365.

and, what was more, to pay him 'as much respect to his function as could be shown without increase of charge to his Majesty'. He was at pains to discover the practice of other nations and included in the long catechism of questions about the state of the Dutch Fleet, which he gave to his old tutor, Mr Hill, on his return to Holland, a special query about the number and kind of ministers the 'Hogen Mogen' carried aboard their ships. He even took the trouble to study the sermons of eleven clergymen, candidates for the chaplaincy of Bridewell, and for ten successive Sundays in the autumn of 1676 made a comparative table of their respective merits under the heads of Prayer, Text, Apposition of the Subject and Application, Action, Voice, Tone and Style; Countenance, Length, Learning, Latin, Conformity and Orthodoxness. His opinion of this great flow of sacred oratory was not particularly favourable; the delivery of one divine was dismissed as 'stiff and schoolboylike, always in a tone, looking one and the same way, his finger in his book constantly', the application of another 'none, it being all upon the subject of distinguishing and mortifying our darling sins', while the learning of the whole company ranged from 'not much' to 'none'. Only their countenances were satisfactory and were set down as 'good', 'grave', and 'tolerable'.[24]

Pepys' standard in these matters was embodied in the Regulations which he presented to the King and Admiralty Board in December 1677. It was laid down that henceforward the Secretary of the Admiralty Office was to notify the Church authorities of every ship ordered to sea that there might be a chaplain appointed to each, properly equipped with the King's warrant and a certificate from the Archbishop of Canterbury or Bishop of London. Fruits of this happy dispensation were to be seen a year later when one of the flag-officers sent Pepys the manuscript of a sermon preached before him by his chaplain, with a proud request that he should forward it to the Bishop of London. But the implacable Secretary was still critical. 'As for your chaplain's sermon,' he replied, 'were it fit for me to give him advice, it should be that he would not have it exposed to my Lord Bishop's perusal and censure till it were fairer writ and writ more correctly, this being done so slightly as to its manner of writing and with so many blots, interlineations, false spellings and wrong pointings . . . that I doubt besides the prejudice the author may receive to his credit, the Bishop may think himself a little neglected in his having it presented to him in no better dress.'[25]

Most far-reaching of Pepys' reforms, since in time it was to recruit the whole service with trained professional officers, was the Establishment for Lieutenants. Since the King and Duke had made the sea-service fashionable, the ships had been invaded by an army of well-born amateurs who were too high-spirited to condescend to learn the seaman's trade but not too proud to take his pay when they could procure commissions, until which time they were wont as Reformadoes to use the King's ships as clubs, 'pestering' them, as Pepys put it, 'with cabins' and undermining the morality and discipline of the Fleet.* From these gentlemen, rather than from the old rough tarpaulins who had been schooled under Blake or learnt their hard craft before the merchant mast, the Officers of the Navy were being more and more recruited; 'if this course holds . . .' Pepys wrote to Sir John Kempthorne, 'bethink yourself what sort of Captains the honour and safety of the Crown and Government will have to rely upon for support at sea, when the few commanders (for God knows they are but few) that are now surviving of the true breed shall be worn out'.[26]

It was to remedy this and turn young gentlemen, since gentlemen in the Service there must be – and for this Pepys was not sorry† – into good officers, technically fitted for their profession, that he tendered to the Board on December 1st, 1677, his project of an 'Establishment for ascertaining the Duties and Trust of a Lieutenant'. Henceforward every candidate for that office must have served three years at sea and at least one as midshipman, must produce a certificate from his Captain as to his sobriety, diligence and obedience, and pass a solemn examination at the Navy Office in navigation and seamanship. There was some opposition to the clause about midshipmen, the three paladins of seventeenth-century chivalry, Prince Rupert, the gallant Earl of Ossory and Lord

* Of the excess of Reformadoes, or young Gentlemen drawing victuals on board ship without pay, Pepys had written in April 1675: 'The King will soon find it intolerable, it seeming to me to be for the most part but the drawing upon himself the constant charge of maintaining so many persons out of his own purse, to the ruin of the Service they pretend to be maintained for.' *Cat. Pepysian MSS.* III, 29.

† '. . . as it is not only likely that younger sons of gentlemen will still be put forward in sea employments, but very desirable also with respect to his Majesty's service that they should be so, provided they would but set themselves early to it and pass through the same necessary methods of knowledge and practice which the true bred seaman doth.' S. Pepys to Sir John Kempthorne, Dec. 1st, 1677. *Admiralty Letters* IX, 242–3. Cit. *Cat. Pepysian MSS.* I, 203.

Craven, declaring it 'a service beneath the quality of a gentleman'. But the King and the Flag Officers were on the Secretary's side, and the Establishment in its entirety was adopted by the Board on December 15th. It was a great triumph for Pepys, and the beginning of a rule that still stands.[27]

Pepys wasted no time in putting the Establishment into being. On January 24th, 1678, the first Certificates signed by the Navy Officers, approving the qualifications of four candidates and disapproving those of five others, were read at the Admiralty Board, 'to the great satisfaction', the happy Secretary noted, 'of his Majesty and my Lords'. The effects of this were soon seen. 'I thank God', he wrote in March 1678, 'we have not half the throng of those of the bastard breed pressing for employments which we heretofore used to be troubled with, they being conscious of their inability to pass this examination.' For Pepys had constructed a rudimentary hoop through which henceforward gentlemen must pass to preferment. In the womb of time, fired by his germinal power, an examination-recruited Civil Service, the public school and the crammer's establishment began to take embryo shape.[28]

But every kind of creative achievement has to be paid for by its creator, and the usual price for administrative creation is loss of friends. One of those whom Pepys was proudest to know was his fellow virtuoso George, Lord Berkeley, whose wife and daughters had begged him during a recent visit to their house to obtain a Lieutenant's commission for a favourite. Pepys had not let a day pass without soliciting the King and Duke, and had actually secured a signed commission from his Majesty. But under examination it appeared that the young man, however charming to ladies, had an inadequate knowledge of the theory of navigation. The commission had consequently been withdrawn.

Imagine Pepys' horror when a short while afterwards rumours reached him that the Berkeley House ladies, mortified at the failure of their influence, had been saying unkind things about him and had even gone so far as to hint that their protégé's lack of success had been merely for want of a little timely expenditure – 'a reproach', the injured Secretary wrote to his Lordship, 'lost upon me, my Lord, who am known to be so far from needing any purgation in the point of selling places as never to have taken so much as my fee for a commission or warrant to any one Officer in the Navy within the whole time, now near twenty years, that I have had the honour of serving his Majesty therein'. Lord Berkeley hastened to reply; neither he nor his wife had ever charged him in word, thought, or deed, and, though his daughters had been puzzled, having heard that the Navy Officers had passed their friend, they now realized they had been misinformed. Possibly pretty Mistress Henrietta, his youngest child (who, a few years later, was to figure in a *cause célèbre*), had let slip some hasty expression: but if she had said anything that gave offence, she had never intended it and begged his pardon. 'And now my good friend,' Lord Berkeley added, 'though I am not under an accusation and therefore need not say anything to vindicate myself, yet give me leave upon this occasion to assure you that there is no person has a better opinion of you than myself . . . And give me leave to add further, without flattery to you and with great sincerity, that I believe our Gracious Master, his Majesty, is so fortunate in employing you in his service that if he should lose you it would be very difficult for his Majesty to find a successor so well qualified in all respects for his service, if we consider both your integrity, vast abilities, industry and zealous affections for his service. And if his Majesty were asked the question, I will hold ten to one his Majesty declares himself of my opinion.' He could scarcely have said anything more acceptable.[29]

The qualities which the discerning Lord Berkeley saw in Pepys were displayed during the closing months of 1677 in a new Victualling Contract – the supplement to his great triple Establishment for Manning, Gunning and Officering the Service. The partners who since the close of the Dutch War had held the contract, had been gradually failing for lack of credit. Indeed Pepys' old friend Sir Dennis Gauden had fallen on such evil days that the Navy Office, to save its own face, had had to protect him from arrest by his creditors.[30]

At the beginning of the winter of 1677–8 new tenders were therefore invited for the contract – the greatest that could come the way of an English merchant. Pepys used the opportunity to establish firm and permanent rules for the future. To these the new contractors, Messrs Brett, Vincent and Parsons, were compelled to agree. The rules, which were very complicated, were laid down with the utmost precision. Henceforward, on a payment to the Victuallers of 6*d*. per diem for victuals in harbour, 7¾*d*. at sea and 8*d*. south of

Lisbon, every seaman was to have a daily allowance of a gallon of beer, brewed under clearly defined conditions, a pound of clean, sweet wheaten biscuit, and two pounds of English salted beef, or of bacon and pork on four days a week, with cod, haberdine or Poor John, and two ounces of butter and four of Suffolk cheese on the other three. For ships south of Latitude 39N. there was an alternative diet of flour, rusks, raisins, currants, sweet olive oil, pickled suet, stockfish and rice, with a quart of wine or half a pint of brandy instead of beer. 'Englishmen', Pepys jotted down in his rough notes, 'and more especially seamen, love their bellies above anything else, and therefore it must always be remembered in the management of the victualling of the Navy that to make any abatement from them in the quantity or agreeableness of the victuals is to discourage and provoke them in the tenderest point, and will sooner render them disgusted with the King's service than any one other hardship that can be put upon them.' For he was not only a great administrator, but a very human one.[31]

Discipline and rule in all things was the unceasing burden of Pepys' administrative creed. In the autumn of 1677 hostilities, long averted, had broken out with Algiers, and Narbrough had again been despatched to the Mediterranean with a powerful squadron of nearly thirty ships. But while he was chastising the Algerines, his captains fell to their old courses of going from port to port in search of freights. Such was the cost of this abuse that Pepys declared angrily that for every penny gained by a commander in this way it would be cheaper for the King to give him twopence out of his own purse. Nor were 'good voyages' the only crimes against discipline with which he had to contend. In the summer of 1678, he poured out his heart to his old colleague, Sir Thomas Allin, about the way in which captains left their ships to hover round the Court:

I would to God you could offer me something that may be an effectual cure to the liberty taken by commanders of leaving their ships upon pretence of private occasions and staying long in town ... it seeming impossible as well as unreasonable to keep the door constantly barred against commanders' desires of coming to town upon just and pressing occasions of their families, and of the other hand no less hard upon the King that his gracious nature as well as his service should be always liable to be imposed upon by commanders, as often as their humours, pleasures or (it may be) vices shall incline them to come ashore. Pray think of it and help me herein, for, as I shall never be guilty of withstanding any gentleman's just occasions and desires in this matter, so shall I never be able to sit still and silent under the scandalous liberties that I see every day taken by commanders of playing with his Majesty's service, as if it were an indifferent matter whether they give any attendance on board their ships, so as they have their wages.*[32]

But however discouraging his progress in putting down the abuses of the Service may have seemed to Pepys, there were others, better able to take a detached view, who could well see what was happening. One was his Huguenot friend of Winchester Street, James Houblon. 'I know your great wisdom is such', this good man wrote to the overburdened Secretary whom he had learnt to love and respect, 'as . . . you will at last do the great work which all honest men would rejoice in, that is that the management of the King's Fleet in all particulars may be executed by sober, discreet and diligent persons and men of business, and that all drinking, swearing and gaming and expensive and sumptuous eating may be banished the Fleet, and particularly that the King's ships may not be made bawdy-houses nor the captains publicly carry and entertain their whores on board as some of them have formerly done, and that from port to port in the Mediterranean to the great scandal of our religion and government both amongst Turks, Jews and Christians.' Only by such redeeming work, he declared, could the Navy become what he longed to see it – 'a protection to the nation and a terror to our enemies, which without a strict discipline and real sobriety in officers and seamen it can never be'.[33]

Not all English merchants were so discerning. Though Pepys did his best to dispose the scanty ships of the peace-time guard where they would best protect the nation's trade against the anarchical conditions of violence and piracy which still prevailed at sea, many traders abused him perpetually because he did not do more. They accused him of denying them protection until they took out passes at exorbitant fees, and even of secretly financing Dunkirk and Ostend privateers to vex their ships. His master, who had long learnt to be cynical about all men, took the abuse with indifference, 'as having been too acquainted with the merchants' censures on other occasions to wonder at anything they say'. But Pepys felt the abuse

---

* *Admiralty Letters* VII, 296, June 29th, 1678. Cit. *Cat. Pepysian MSS.* I, 197.

bitterly, strained every nerve till he had had Ostend blockaded and persistently worried the Admiralty Board for convoys.* Yet the ungrateful ones remained as ungrateful as ever.[34]

The year 1678 saw the new naval machine and its creator subjected to violent strain. For some time past the relations between England and France had been growing steadily worse. In November 1677 Pepys witnessed the celebrations that attended the marriage of the Princess Mary, the Duke of York's eldest daughter, to King Louis' most determined foe, the Prince of Orange. By December the international situation was so critical that Pepys took counsel with the Navy Office as to how soon the battle fleet could be set out. At that moment there were in commission only two 3rd rates or ships of the line, fourteen 4th rates, five 5th rates and ten smaller craft, with three more 3rd rates, six 4th rates and one 5th rate fitting out for the war against Algiers. At the same time Pepys obtained from a secret source an alarming list of the French Fleet, which revealed a paper strength of eighty-five ships of the line, including twelve 1st rates.[35]

Such was the condition of affairs when on January 8th, 1678, Pepys was informed that a rupture with France might occur at any moment and was directed to give all merchants trading in the Mediterranean a secret warning of their danger. Three weeks later the King, armed with Pepys' estimate for setting out ninety ships of war and sixty-two other vessels for ten months at a total cost of £1,083,860, met Parliament with a request for a million pounds to support his alliance with Holland, preserve Flanders and enforce peace between France and Spain.[36]

Once again, therefore, Pepys found himself at his old task of coaxing money for the fleet from Parliament and meeting the captious attacks of the Opposition on its administration. Already those who had been most furious for a Dutch alliance and a French war were declaring that supply was neither necessary nor desirable, because it would be used to establish a military despotism. On February 5th Pepys dealt with such insinuations in his most pontifical style; who, he would like to know, did most to set up arbitrary government? – those who opposed the royal measures against the French peril or those who promoted them? The truest

* If the Canary merchants were to have a convoy, the Duke of York replied to one such solicitation, they must 'be more orderly than the last time they had one'. S. J. Davey, *Catalogue* (1889), Item 2896.

mark of a Prince's greatness was to take good counsel; the King had done so and taken theirs, and it was now for them to enable him to follow it. It was noticeable that in addressing the House Pepys used the word 'you' and not 'we'.

In the same grand manner he rebuked those who had criticized the naval administration. Did they imagine that the Lords of the Admiralty had been asleep and done nothing? Their Lordships' work had borne such fruit as England had never seen. Some of the new ships would be launched that very year. Ninety sail could be afloat by the spring by God's blessing and the House's concurrence.[37]

When Pepys sat down the Opposition fell furiously upon him. 'Twas said, sneered Sir Thomas Lee, who now knew how to sting Master Secretary to a nicety, great things had been done in the Navy: for his part he thought the Victualler was asleep, for in his country beef was never cheaper. Pepys sprang to his feet: 'I challenge any man alive, and his books to help him, to show me that in January there were ever more stores in the Victualling House than now.' Next day Colonel Birch took up the familiar tale of the good old Commonwealth days, when the Fleet had never cost a penny more than £4 per head per month and every ship had been paid off as soon as it came in. How, Pepys answered, if the ships were so well paid off in Birch's time, was it that the whole Navy was four months in arrears of pay when the King came in? 'If Birch talks of £4 a head, so will I too. We set not ships out now to ordinary errands. We set them out to war, I believe and hope. To them must be appendages, of ships of advice, tenders for wounded men, and other things attendant as necessary as guns themselves. What I say is not for money. I handle none of it, but I will not betray you by my silence. I would not come here to have Brooke House Commissioners of Accounts to make enquiry, and to make attendance here to answer their objections; and by all their enquiry, there was no fraud found in the accounts of the Navy to pay for their wine and biscuits.'* The brisk boys of the Opposition had their fun. But the House, having so frequently addressed the King to contract an alliance with Holland, could scarcely refuse all supply now that he had done so, and voted by a majority of forty-two that the cost of

* Grey, *Debates* V, 107–9.

setting out ninety ships would be what Pepys' figures stated – £1,448,681 for thirteen months.[38]

But long it was before the money was voted and still longer before a penny found its way into the Treasury. In the meantime Pepys, on whose tired shoulders the ultimate responsibility of setting out the Fleet fell, had to meet a ceaseless bombardment in Parliament from the Opposition leaders, who, fortified by French money,* maintained a prolonged and cheerfully rowdy obstruction to everything the government proposed.[39]

Pepys was appointed a member of the Committee, set up to consider the charge of fitting out the ninety ships, which met every afternoon after the House rose in the Speaker's Chamber. So also were his enemies Sacheverell, Garroway, Birch, Littleton, Powle, Meres and Thomas Lee. The latter had himself demanded the Committee with an insulting observation that the House should not be forced to take the bare word of one member. And after the House had at last voted a million to enable the King to raise sea and land forces, Lee tried to get the proud Secretary to commit himself to some date by which he would have the Fleet ready, believing with some justification that it would prove impossible. Pepys replied that he would venture his head upon it, provided his tormentor would do the same if he proved him wrong.† 'But', he added, 'Lee loves his head too well.'[40]

During March Pepys and Birch had two further duels about the relative costs of the present occasion and the First Dutch War, the one armed with facts and the other with what is usually far more acceptable in England, a robust determination to stick to his prejudices whatever facts and figures might prove. Birch declared breezily that it would be impossible to spend more than £300,000 on the Fleet before Michaelmas. Pepys showed that during the First Dutch War – 'in that husbandly year of 1653' to which Birch never

* Pepys' principal foe, William Harbord, had 500 guineas from Barillon, as also had Littleton and Powle. *Dalrymple* (1773 ed.) II, 386.

† 'And as another instance of the scandalous ignorance of the gentlemen of England in this matter, it is worth noting how stupendous an undertaking they took mine to be to set out ninety ships of war within so little time as I proposed; they often pinching me upon it while it was in doing; and Sir Thomas Lee by name asking me whether I would venture my head upon that too (as I had formerly upon good grounds and with good effect in another case), and had for answer that I would if he would venture his on the contrary; my success herein afterwards justifying me to the utmost, even beyond my undertaking.' *Naval Minutes*, 358–9.

tired of referring – the stores alone had cost £600,000, while the total expense for a fifteen-months' naval war had been as much as £5,707,000, or nearly four times more than the King was asking to set out a Fleet against a far more dangerous neighbour. The delays so skilfully brought about by the Opposition were holding up all his plans for buying stores cheaply: 'it will be an unfortunate War', he told them, 'if you go not early to market for stores ... and a contemplation of joy to your enemies abroad'. But though money was needed for the most vital services, even an advance of so small a sum as £20,000 was refused by a House composed of country gentlemen utterly ignorant of everything to do with the sea and manipulated by a determined and well-organized group of skilful politicians.[41]

When at long last the Poll Bill passed, the Opposition leaders, in daily conference with Louis' agents, concentrated their energies on turning every warlike action of the Executive into a national grievance* – the recruitment of the army for Flanders, the rising cost of the Fleet – and even the delays which they themselves had made in setting it forth, and the use of the press-gang. Pepys, harassed by the thousand and one details of equipping the Fleet and distracted by a series of mysterious robberies that had been going on in his own office, found it harder and harder to keep his temper. Least of all could he be patient at the constant insinuations that the war scare was a mere ruse to get money. What greater proof, he asked, could the King have given that he intended war, if Louis would not yield, than to have gone so far without parliamentary aid? Recalling Charles' insistence at the cost of his own pocket on the increase in the original dimensions of the new 1st and 2nd rates – a measure needless against the Dutch – it is difficult not to believe with Pepys that at the beginning of the year the King had genuinely contemplated hostilities.[42]

But by April Charles contemplated them no more. To declare war on France, as the Opposition were now urging him to do, without the money to support a long campaign and with the moral certainty that Parliament would harass his every action and make a

---

* In March Barillon reported to Louis how Ruvigny had been giving money to the Opposition leaders and how 'they are resolved to seek for everything that can give the Court vexation'. *Dalrymple* (1773 ed.) II, *Appendix* 163–4). And see *Rawl. MSS. A.* 175, ff. 179–82.

humiliating peace inevitable would have been virtual suicide. Pepys, though he almost certainly knew nothing of the King's secret measures, himself shared this view: writing long after in 1693, when England was at last at war with France, he noted in his book of Naval Minutes: 'Nor after the proof which we have made of the consequences of a French war, and particularly as to the strength of France by sea, in opposition to the united forces of England and Holland, will it be doubted whether King Charles could have taken a shorter or surer course to destroy the Navy of England and put the Dominion of the Sea into the hands of the French King if that had been his desire and aim, when our Parliament voted and gave money for an actual war with that kingdom, labouring by all arts, fair and foul, to drive the King into it.'[43]

For Charles had already taken his own measures and opened up negotiations with Louis, who was sufficiently frightened by the speed of his preparations for war to accept his suggestions for peace that would still leave Flanders intact. And though almost every subsequent historian has blamed Charles for having done so, no one has suggested what else he could have done.[44]

With troops pouring across the Channel to Flanders, with Narbrough's squadron threatening French ambitions in the Mediterranean, and Pepys, despite all difficulties, hastening out the battle fleet and pressing forward the completion of the new ships,* Louis accepted Charles' terms. In May he agreed to a truce with his enemies pending negotiations for a general European pacification. But the Opposition leaders, loyal to their French paymaster, offered him a new chance by persuading the House, still haunted like the nation by fears of a standing army, to vote for an immediate demobilization of all the forces raised.[45]

In the troubled debates of that unhappy spring Pepys took a prominent part. His proud omniscience on naval matters won him among his angry fellow-members 'the envious name of Admiral'. 'Pepys', one of them once taunted him in debate, 'speaks rather like an Admiral than a Secretary, *I* and *We*. I wish he knows half as much of the Navy as he pretends'. Against another member, who had dared to accuse the Admiralty of exorbitant charges, he was so

* The first batch were launched that summer, two 2nd rates, the *Vanguard* and *Windsor Castle,* and six 3rd rates, the *Anne, Captain, Hampton Court, Hope, Lennox* and *Restoration. Cat. Pepysian MSS.* 1, 223.

transported* that Garroway moved that his words should be written down. They were, and Pepys was forced to beg the House's pardon. Had he, he subsequently said, behaved himself with disrespect to the House, he heartily begged pardon. Only the tenderness he had for the House had constrained him to say what he had. 'Pray, sir,' he begged, turning to the Speaker's chair, 'forgive me if I was transported to hear the same thing said over and over again here.'[46]

Yet all the while that Pepys was fretting at the ignorance or malice of his enemies, he was straining his poor eyes by jotting down in shorthand his views on the parliamentary scene. With the clear vision that he brought to bear on all things, he saw the weakness of his political colleagues, the strength of his enemies, and the beginning of the party system. On the Opposition benches, he noted, there had come into being a new power – a corporate body of men who regarded the manipulation of parliamentary and public opinion as a profession, who always made themselves masters of the matter under discussion and came to the House with their brief prepared and digested, who understood to a nicety the rules of procedure so they could hasten or impede business as they chose, and who never failed to rally their full forces when an important debate was due. That party was both an autocracy and a republic, directed by a single clear mind and yet with the ultimate strength that came from mutual trust and companionship; however implicit the obedience of its members to the edicts of the great little Lord in the Upper House, on their own benches and in the 'Whig' taverns and clubs where they mingled every evening, there was an unrestrained social equality and good fellowship and an absolute freedom to every member to speak out his mind as he chose. Whereas on Pepys' own side of the House, the supporters of the Court were without leadership or cohesion; their leaders were great Ministers with their heads full of their own business and the defence of their private interests, or pensioners and kept men. Not that Pepys set much store on debate, a bribe being in his realist view normally more efficacious than any amount of oratory: 'but then', he noted, 'we must be sure

---

* 'Sir John Knight, in the heat of this debate, had poured out much of his indignation upon the exorbitant accounts of the Navy, unto which Mr Pepys made reply, and in demonstrating of his gross mistakes, did so handle him with that severity that he was fain to beg the pardon of the House for his being so far transported.' June 8th, 1678. *H.M.C. Ormonde n.s.* IV, 431. See also Grey, *Debates* VI, 74–5.

to bribe voices enough'. And of those who defended the affairs of King and Court, not one had any proper comprehension of parliamentary method: every courtier or place-holder envied some rival and was glad to see him worsted in debate; and no one knew who was appointed to lead or was prepared to pay him any allegiance. The Court Party were always on the defensive, always surprised and always worsted in Committee, which they seldom troubled to attend.*[47]

But when on June 17th the Committee which the House had set up for lessening the charge of the Fleet made its report to the House, it paid an involuntary tribute to Pepys' work. At the time that the House had formally resolved to set out the Fleet for war, there had been in actual commission only thirty-five ships of war with twenty-eight other vessels, manned by 6334 men. Three months later when the House resolved on demobilization, there were eighty-nine ships of war with thirteen fireships and fifteen other vessels manned by 15,609 men. Seldom if ever had a great fleet been put to sea more quickly. And when at the end of June Parliament's ill-timed precipitancy caused Louis to repudiate his former terms and Charles was forced to bring him to reason by suspending demobilization, Pepys' preparedness still did the country's business. The machine he had created with such difficulty stood the test. The first part of his great work was done; the coming years were to see it undone and its necessity made only more manifest.[48]

* Pepys' Shorthand Parliamentary Observations in *Rawl. MSS. C.* 859. For the transcription of these I am indebted to my friend, Mr W. Matthews, who imposed his eyes to almost as severe a strain as Pepys'.

8
The Great Plot

'A fair attempt has twice or thrice been made
To hire night murderers and make death a
trade.'

                    Dryden, *The Spanish Friar.*

The August and September of 1678 were apparently months of
exceptional placidity. The King, pleased with his success at
Nymegen, went down to Windsor to hunt and fish, and Pepys
himself drove down there once a week, crossing the ferry at
Datchet in the hot summer haze to attend Admiralty meetings. In
London his business was chiefly concerned with paying off the
Fleet and transporting troops back from Flanders. Only in the
Straits, where Narbrough with a squadron of 3rd and 4th rates was
still blockading the Algerine pirates, was there any sign of warlike
activity.[1]

Though himself unable to share in the almost universal holiday
of those about him, Samuel contrived to take a trip abroad by
proxy. His friends Sir John and Lady Bankes, at whose country
home in Kent, Olantleigh Towers, he sometimes spent a brief
holiday, 'noiseless and thoughtless', had sent their son travelling on
the Continent in charge of John Locke, the philosopher. To them –
'my beloved Mr Bankes' and his 'excellent friend and director' – he
wrote many a letter full of fatherly advice and childlike enthusiasm
in their journeyings. He was torn in two by a desire to extend the
young man's travels as far as possible and to relieve the natural
anxiety of Lady Bankes and give her what he called 'the just
satisfaction of contemplating him with his face homewards'. In the
end, backed by the travellers' entreaties, he succeeded in persuading Sir John and Lady Bankes to let the young man proceed, first
as far as Bordeaux and then, after a tremendous tussle with his
own humanity and Lady Bankes' fears, to Italy. Only, he insisted,
there were four conditions: he must be careful of his health; must
write home at least once a week and never let 'my Lady, the best of
mothers, labour under a dearth of letters'; must rely in all things

upon the advice of Mr Locke; and be back by the spring, 'which . . . is not to be strained beyond the latter end of April or beginning of May'.[2]

While the virtuous Secretary of the Admiralty Office was writing thus placidly to the Continent or begging a powerful city acquaintance to help a poor kinsman* – 'once an able citizen but brought low by God Almighty's hand in the late Fire of London' – another man of a very different stamp, who called himself Colonel John Scott, was lodging with a Presbyterian haberdasher in Cannon Street. He had begun life as the son of a poor Kentish miller, whose widow had taken him while still a child to New England. Here he had lived miserably poor, until the death of a young girl with whom he was out 'a'birding' necessitated his removal to Long Island, where he looked after hogs in the woods, learnt the Indian language and 'convert with the women even to scandal'. By trading with the Dutch settlers of New York (then New Amsterdam), he made enough to return to England, where being a handsome young fellow with a 'nimble genius' he established himself in the household of a Kentish Quaker called Gotherson. This gentleman's wife, who was herself given to preaching in a conventicle,† was the heiress of the Scotts of Scott's Hall, and on her yielding spirit her good-looking namesake played with such effect that he not only debauched her but induced her to part with several thousand pounds (her whole fortune) for an imaginary estate in Long Island. Having thus perpetrated the earliest recorded swindle in American real estate, he returned to Long Island with the proceeds, taking with him Mrs Gotherson's jewels, her eldest son and several other young men and women whom their over-enthusiastic parents (one of them rejoiced in the name of Hallelujah Fisher) entrusted to him to apprentice and whom he subsequently disposed of in his own inimitable manner by selling the boys and seducing the girls. Equipped with the proceeds of his ingenuity and a forged royal commission, he informed the English colonists who had just taken over New York from the Dutch that he was the rightful heir of the Buccleuchs, tricked out the simple

* His cousin Porter, the turner. See *Diary*, Aug. 10th, 1665.

† As she first met Scott at Whitehall about the year 1663, it is not inconceivable that she was the pretty Quaker whom the King, in Pepys' presence on January 11th, 1664, was so merry with, telling her that old Sir John Mennes was the fittest person for her quaking religion as his beard was the stiffest thing about him and that if her desires were as long as the paper she carried she might well lose them.

country girl whom he had formerly married in the finery of a grand lady, and, displaying his Quaker's garter (for he was greatly given to boasting) in every company, laid toll on the country with a troop of very troublesome retainers. His splendour, however, was short-lived for, after all but involving the young colony in a war with the Long Island Indians on account of the swindles he had perpetrated on their Queen, Sunk Squaw, he had to leave in a hurry and was next heard of, loaded with chains, in the gaol of Hartford, Connecticut. Thence he escaped through the woods to the coast and reappeared as a very personable young Quaker at Barbados, to whose Governor he proceeded to sell some more Long Island land. After that he was forced to transfer his activities to St Kitts, where he murdered his master and actually got as far as the gallows with a rope round his neck before his 'hopefulness and brisk parts' saved him once more and established him as an officer in command of a company against the French. But war was not his real *métier*, for being ordered to lead his men against the enemy, he had hidden behind a rock. This and their subsequent loss led to his being court-martialled for cowardice.[3]

Having exhausted the resources of the New World, Scott tried his hand at the Old. After a brief visit to England in 1671, where he had posed as an expert on America and deceived no less a person than Lord Sandwich, who then, as President of the Committee of Trade and Plantations, was investigating transatlantic conditions, he repaired on the eve of the Third Dutch War to Holland. Here he appeared as Major-General Scott of Scott's Hall, Kent, Shield Bearer and Geographer to the King of England, one of the greatest engineers in the world who had made charts of all the islands and fortifications in the West Indies and a man 'capable to do much good or hurt to the States of Holland'. De Witt, delighted to find that this distinguished stranger shared with him a great love for republican institutions and a hatred for the house of Stuart, gave him the command of a regiment, and for a while the ex-miller's son had a glorious time, marrying a second and possibly a third wife – his first was still living in Long Island with three children, 'a civil, harmless woman' – making very bad maps of England and its coasts and winning the hearts of the good people of Bergen-op-Zoom by telling them with what ease he could bring their ships up the river of London, what plunder there was to be got there and how he would 'make England dance'. But when he forged a deed, cheated all the tradesmen, and absconded with the regimental funds, their feelings underwent a change, which they expressed as best they could by hanging his effigy on the gallows.[4]

In Flanders, where he took refuge, Scott continued making maps and charts which he sold to a number of eminent and very stupid people, and robbed a nunnery. He then, about the year 1675, moved to France, where he opened up new veins of undeceived and well-endowed humanity, exhausting them however with the same prodigal genius, selling charts to the French King that no one could sail by and new model guns that only blew up themselves and their possessors, and a scientific process for blanching copper into silver which transmuted nothing but the faith of its purchasers. It was quite extraordinary how rapidly his friends and patrons became soured.[5]

But happily his native country still offered an almost virgin soil for his gifts. And a time was at hand when they could scarcely fail to bear fruit there. Some time in the year 1677 his talents became known to the restless and brilliant Duke of Buckingham, who having failed as Prime Minister was now bent with Lord Shaftesbury on subverting the State which he was unable to rule. Through Buckingham's rather ghoulish agent, Sir Ellis Leighton,* Scott became acquainted with a whole circle of interesting notabilities of the republican underworld, including old Major Wildman, later to figure as the first proposer of the plot to assassinate the King at Rye House, and a mysterious individual who travelled under the name of Benson, alias Wilson, alias Harrington, and acted as Shaftesbury's Paris agent. To such he posed alternately as the son of Colonel Scott, the Regicide, and a gentleman of fortune, who had been unjustly turned out of his command at New York by the malice and ingratitude of the King and Duke of York and upon whom he was now resolved to have a gentleman's revenge.† His wide experience of life made him peculiarly at home with the diverse social elements out of which the Whig party was then secretly taking shape,

---

* '. . . the most corrupt man then or since living . . . But his own recovered him at last, that is the jail, where he died miserably.' R. North, *Examen*, 488.

† . . . 'He swore, God damn his body and soul, the King, the Duke of York and the Kingdom should repent it. For, says he, I am about a thing here will make them all repent the injustice they have done me.' Mr Fielding's Paper, June 10th, 1680. *Rawl. MSS. A.* 194, ff. 163 v.–5.

for he was equally happy debauching with the rakes and praying with the sectaries.[6]

The years 1677 and 1678 Scott passed between England and France, collecting information – parliamentary intrigue, naval statistics, charts and anything he could pick up or invent – and selling it to his paymasters. The threat of an Anglo-French war and the clandestine relationships of the Opposition leaders with the French King enabled Scott to make himself useful in many ways, and his poorer acquaintances were astonished to see how often his poverty would be changed to sudden opulence, followed by a gorgeous display of guineas and fine clothes until the splendid extravagance of a week or two restored him to his normal state. Others who knew him during his hours of good fellowship (which were many) were shown maps of the English coast, drawings of ships and forts, 'very neatly and curiously drawn' and full of elaborate details about harbours, rocks and sands, and statistics of the crews, guns and stations of the King of England's ships; sometimes they were also shown noble presents which he told them King Louis had given him for them. He travelled much, avoiding ordinary routes, between Paris and London, where he lodged at Newman's coffee-house in Talbot Court, Gracechurch Street, and at Hill's, the iron-founder's, in Houndsditch, interviewed great personages and distributed state libels in coffee-houses and taverns. It is pleasant to know that his employment had its softer side, for among the more respected figures in the republican camp was the widow of Sir Harry Vane, who had perished on the scaffold in 1662. This lady was moved to an indescribable and romantic tenderness in the company of Scott, for he was a lusty, tall, full-bodied man, at this time about forty-five years of age; the very sight of him, she used to say, fed her soul, and she wrote him long letters in a very high style of love and romance, called him 'Artaban', 'a person that lived a great while a private man but afterwards proved a Prince', dated her letters from 'Suspendence' and signed herself 'Constantia'. He returned her affection in the same vein, for she was a widow with a fortune and he was at home with all women. He even composed poems for her.[7]

The summer of 1678 that brought his wandering feet to good Mr Payne's, the dissenting haberdasher of Cannon Street, saw Scott busied in many quiet and useful ways. In June, when war with France was still threatening, he had spent a fortnight on Brownsea

Island at the entrance to Poole Harbour with the ostensible purpose
of inspecting the progress of some works there belonging to Major
Wildman and Sir Robert Clayton, the great Whig merchant, from
whom he bore a letter of recommendation to their foreman, Dragett.
But Scott never looked at the works and spent his time viewing the
island and making notes in his chamber, whiling away the evenings
in trying to seduce Dragett's maid. It was remembered afterwards
that he was very flush of gold and that on leaving he went towards
Lord Shaftesbury's house at St Giles'. Shortly afterwards he was
reported by Colonel Blood (who, since being pardoned for his
assault on the Crown Jewels, had been employed by the Government to keep an eye on the activities of his old republican friends), as
very busy with Aaron Smith, Sir Robert Peyton, the rich City
republican who was one of the founders of the Green Ribbon Club,
'and the rest of the crew', contriving an assassination, though whose
Blood was unable to say.[8]

Up till now the lives of this extraordinary person* and Samuel
Pepys had been as far divided as those of any two human beings
could well be: they were now to meet. During the autumn vacation
while the Government were languidly speculating on the reasons for
the Duke of Buckingham's last mysterious visit to France, and the
Dover Castle authorities were looking out for his agent, Sir Ellis
Leighton, strange rumours of a Catholic plot to assassinate the King
and overthrow English liberties and religion by setting up a Papist
successor began to circulate in London. Unhappily for himself, the
Duke of York, against whom all these stories seemed directed,
demanded (as those who invented them had probably calculated) a
public enquiry, and on his return from Windsor the King, who had
hitherto pooh-poohed the whole matter, agreed to have them
examined by the Council.[9]

At eight o'clock on the morning of Saturday, September 28th,
Pepys took his familiar place at the Admiralty Board, assembled for
the first time since the vacation at Whitehall. The King, Prince
Rupert, the Lord Chancellor, Lord Treasurer Danby, and the Duke
of Monmouth were all present; the usual report from the Navy

* His rich life-story, it should be remembered, we owe entirely to Pepys, who
collected it and left it to a neglectful posterity scattered among his vast accumulation
of papers at Oxford and Cambridge. As a picture of the underworld life of the later
seventeenth century it is almost as remarkable as the *Diary* itself.

Office on the progress of the new ships was read and there was a discussion on the traditional limits of the herring fisheries, on which the Secretary was asked to make himself acquainted from 'ancient papers' and report to the Board on Monday. But the Lords of the Admiralty were not to meet again that year. The King then passed on to the Council, before whom there was called a certain Ezrael Tonge, a hare-brained London clergyman, much given to finding terrifying Popish designs, who asked leave to introduce the discoverer of a most extraordinary plot. Titus Oates was then called in. And as his vast brazen mouth opened – in the very midst, it seemed to onlookers, of his round face* – the mouths of the King's Protestant Counsellors opened too at the tale he had to tell. The Jesuits, in whose designs he had been steeped till horror at their wickedness had caused him to reveal all to good Dr Tonge, had for long, he said, been making arrangements to burn down London, massacre its inhabitants, land a French army and assassinate the King. Their plans were now complete: on any day the Queen's physician, Sir George Wakeman, might slip the fatal potion into his Majesty's drink or Coniers the Jesuit plunge the foot-long knife he had consecrated for that purpose into his breast as he walked in the Park. The heads of the new Government were all chosen and waiting to take their places, among whom were the chief Catholic noblemen of the country and the Duchess of York's secretary, Edward Coleman. If the Duke himself would not agree to their plans and take his place on the throne, he would be killed too.

It was true that the bull-necked, bow-legged young man who unfolded this gruesome story had already three times changed his religion – he had begun life as the Anabaptist son of an Anabaptist preacher – that he had been expelled from school and university, had been dismissed from a naval chaplaincy for unnatural vice and from a Jesuit seminary in Spain for the same reason. It was true also that he had perjured himself on his own admission again and again. He was now to be given wider opportunities of doing so. For the tale he told was exactly attuned to the fears of Protestant England,

---

* 'Sunk were his eyes, his voice was harsh and loud,
   Sure signs he neither choleric was nor proud.
   His long chin proved his wit; his saint-like grace,
   A church vermilion and a Moses face.'
                                   Dryden, *Absalom and Achitophel.*

haunted as it was by the terrifying shadows cast, a hundred times larger and more awful than the reality, by the Secret Treaty of Dover. And there were one or two circumstances in Oates' narrative which tallied almost exactly with facts known only to a very few, and which such an obscure creature could never have guessed had he not enjoyed the confidence of some very great personage.[10]

On the night of September 28th Oates left the Council Table armed with warrants for the arrest of the less distinguished persons he had named. Next morning, with many of his Jesuit victims in Newgate, he returned to renew his charges. Charles, who alone seemed to disbelieve the whole story, cross-examined him and caught him out in lie after lie. But Oates still showed the same knowledge of secret matters concerning the very great, and the seizure of Edward Coleman's letters revealed how deeply that busy, foolish intriguer, whom Charles had again and again begged his brother to dismiss, had committed himself to designs against the established religion of the state. As the story spread, first London with its mob fed with ever-growing rumours, then all England, broke into unreasoning panic. On those who were Catholic or who stood near the hated Duke of York, the fury of a rough and cruel people fell. But the King as usual went to Newmarket.[11]

Thither, summoned by his Majesty, Pepys also set out before dawn on Friday, October 11th.* It was perhaps well for him that he did so. A day and a half later, an acquaintance of his, Sir Edmund Berry Godfrey, a popular London magistrate, left his house in Hartshorn Lane and was never seen alive again. By that evening it was being rumoured round the town that he had been murdered by Papists. On the following Thursday, the day after the King got back to London, his body was discovered in a ditch at the foot of Primrose Hill with his sword run through him. But there was no blood on the sword or body, though there were bruises on his breast and round his neck were marks that suggested that he had been previously strangled. Two fields away the track of a coach or cart was found. And at the inquest it was disclosed that the state of his body showed that he had not eaten for about two days before his death.[12]

Who had murdered Sir Edmund Berry Godfrey? For though the Catholics, terrified at the clamour raised against them, seized on the

* He remained there till the 14th, reaching London very late that night. *Pepysian MSS., Admiralty Letters* VIII, 231–3.

fact that the money and valuables on his person were untouched to declare that he had committed suicide, the evidence produced at the inquest soon showed that they were wrong. For how, the triumphant Protestants asked, could he have conveyed himself to so obscure and dirty a spot as Primrose Hill with shoes untouched by mud or dust? Indeed they had obviously just been polished! And how could he have run a sword through himself after he was dead, for it had passed through his body as dry as a butcher's knife through a well-hung carcass? And on his breast was another and apparently earlier wound and a great mass of cruel bruises; and round his neck the tell-tale marks of strangulation. After the inquest no one but a child could maintain the charge of suicide. Yet it almost looked as though someone had intended unwary Catholics to make it.[13]

Immediately everyone, knowing their love of mysterious deceptions, declared that the Jesuits had committed the murder. At once the Plot which had been languishing a little on account of the King's repeated exposure of Oates' lies in the Council,* was on its feet: the fury of the mob and the insane panic of the public left no doubt of the matter. The fact that Oates had attested the truth of his story to Godfrey before he revealed it to the Council confirmed these suspicions. Godfrey had known too much and plainly had been put away by the wicked Fathers. In the general uproar that ensued nobody thought of asking why the Jesuits should have gone to the trouble of polishing the dead man's shoes and providing other irrefutable evidence to disprove their own allegation of suicide.

Indeed the Jesuits, who were no fools, had everything to lose by Godfrey's murder. As their own chief modern accuser Mr John Pollock, has written: 'from that moment the Popish Plot was rooted in the mind of the nation'. Nor had they had anything to gain by the poor magistrate's gruesome end. For there was nothing in the depositions that Oates had made to Godfrey which was not already in the possession of the Council.[14]

But there were other men, who had long been trying to throw the country into a ferment with the bugbear of Popery and who before many weeks had passed were to reveal themselves as stopping at no

* 'The truth is, after searching over every man's sack of papers (to a degree that we are all harassed) there is but little found to corroborate Mr Oates' assertion as to the point of killing.' Sir Robert Southwell to Duke of Ormonde, Oct 15th, 1678. *H.M.C. Ormonde* IV, 458.

villainy, however horrible, to attain their ends – the destruction of the Catholics, of the Catholic Heir Presumptive and the Catholic Queen. These ends were immeasurably advanced by Godfrey's murder. Nor was any murder ever more industriously or brilliantly made public. On the very day of his disappearance it was bruited round the town that he had been done to death by Papists and the newsletters of that Saturday carried the tale of his disappearance into the country. And if (in an age when news circulated slowly and the absence of a London magistrate from his home was unlikely to become public knowledge for some time) that swift and prophetic rumour was not the design of someone with close knowledge of his movements and the organization to spread a tale quickly, it was an exceedingly fortunate coincidence for the republican leaders.[15]

It was not the Papists who had had most reason to fear Godfrey. For though to the ignorant populace he stood as a brave Protestant magistrate who had stuck to his post during the Plague and never flinched from doing his duty against the great, the Opposition chiefs well knew that he was no inexorable enemy to the unhappy Catholics. One of his closest friends had been Edward Coleman, the Duchess of York's secretary, the discovery of whose foolish, intriguing letters to the French King's Confessor constituted the principal evidence for popular belief in the Plot. When on September 6th Oates first swore the truth of his depositions before him, he had secretly warned Coleman of his danger. And when three weeks later, on the day of the official exposure of the Plot before the Council, Oates delivered his full depositions to him, Godfrey had not only again warned Coleman but sent him to the Duke of York with a copy. But for Coleman's careless failure that night to destroy the whole, instead of only a part, of his incriminating correspondence, Godfrey's prompt act of friendship might have nipped the Plot in the bud.[16]

From that moment Godfrey had shown unmistakable signs of fear. Something, he seemed to know, was coming to him. He had been blamed, he told his friends, by some great men for having done his duty and by others for having done too much. He told them also that Oates, the saviour of the nation, was forsworn. 'If danger there be', he said to his sister-in-law, 'I shall be the first to suffer.' The melancholy of his mournful countenance, as with downcast eyes and tall thin stooping figure he glided ghostlike* down the City lanes, bore eloquent testimony to his sense of that danger. On the evening before his disappearance he had burnt a great mass of private papers; on the same morning an unknown and mysterious messenger had called for him.[17]

Mr John Pollock, in a brilliant study of the Popish Plot made thirty years ago, suggested that in those secret interviews between Godfrey and Coleman, the latter blurted out the fatal truth that Oates' charge of a Congregation of Jesuits on April 24th at the 'White Horse' tavern was a lie because the Congregation had met, not at a Strand tavern, but in the private apartments of the Duke of York at St James' Palace. Had this fact been established the almost certain exclusion of the Duke from the succession must have followed. Therefore, Mr Pollock argued, the Catholics must have discreetly done away with the magistrate who had become the repository of such embarrassing knowledge. But if Godfrey, with a meeting of Parliament imminent, was ready to court the hatred of the most powerful men in England by warning the Duke of his danger, he was scarcely likely to undo so perilous a kindness by revealing a fact that must almost inevitably have destroyed him. And even if Mr Pollock's surmise were right and the Jesuits were seeking to put Godfrey and his secret out of the way for ever, they would presumably have done so directly and not have kept him in duress and without food for two days before killing him. The facts revealed at the inquest suggest that it was someone who wished to obtain a statement from him rather than someone who wished to destroy him promptly who covered his breast with bruises and, after holding him captive without sustenance, strangled him.[18]

It is not inconceivable that those who brought about Godfrey's death did so by accident while pressing him with fiendish cruelty to swear to that which they wished. If those who had him in their clutches were the republican leaders, such an hypothesis is not out of keeping with their proved methods of proceeding. After Godfrey's body had been brought back to London with all the circumstances of horror and clamour that skilled mob-management could give it, Shaftesbury used his terrifying powers to extract admissions that

* He was sometimes known as the Ghost. *A Sober Discourse of the Honest Cavalier with the Popish Covenanter*, 1680, p. 7.

might inculpate the Papists from men whom he knew to be innocent. One wretched hackney coachman was offered £500 by him to swear that he had carried the corpse to Primrose Hill and threatened with being rolled down a hill in a barrel of nails if he refused. When the poor man, ignorant of the whole affair, refused, the great apostle of English liberty had him committed to Newgate and kept in a filthy dungeon loaded with heavy chains until, after many weeks and repeated threats, the murder was fastened by false evidence on some obscure Catholics associated with the Queen's Palace, Somerset House. Two other men who had been present at the finding of the body were imprisoned at the command of the Lords' Committee, closely examined in private by Lord Shaftesbury and Major Wildman, Scott's republican friend, and alternately cajoled* and threatened by them to declare that they had been set on by some great Roman Catholic to find Godfrey's body. One thing, at least, is certain, that the Opposition chiefs were determined to fasten the murder on someone as quickly as possible.[19]

But most of all did the champions of freedom reserve their menaces for those whose proffered evidence suggested that the unfortunate magistrate had died by any other hand than the Papists'. In the midst of the outcry after the murder, the wife of one of Godfrey's kinsmen, Mrs Mary Gibbon, had the courage to record on paper how shortly before his death he had come to her in a state of great distress and, after barring the door, had asked her if she had heard that he was to be hanged, confiding that he was in dire disgrace because he had never told Sir William Jones, the Attorney-General, of Oates' deposition. This paper she delivered to Pepys' City friend, Sir John Bankes, who passed it on to Lord Shaftesbury as the Chairman of the Lords' Committee then examining the circumstances of Godfrey's death. Shaftesbury promptly sent for her and laying aside all ceremony (for she was a gentlewoman) addressed her roundly as 'Damned woman' and 'Bitch', and swore that if she would not confess that she had been set on to write it by Mr Pepys

---

* 'Lord Shaftesbury took him into a by-closet, and with a pleasing countenance said, "Honest Smug, the Smith, thou look'st like an honest fellow; thou shalt shoe my horses and I'll make a man of thee. Prithee tell me who murther'd this man, and who set thee to find him out? What Papist dost thou work for?" This was after the poor man, John Walters, had lain in fetters in a dungeon for many days.' Archdeacon Echard, *History of England* (3rd ed., 1720), p. 961. See also L'Estrange, *Brief History*, Part III, 100.

and Monsieur de Puy, he would have her torn to pieces by the multitude, as dogs worry cats, 'insomuch that she fell into fits upon it'.[20]

If, as Mr Pollock supposes (and no other satisfactory reason has been adduced for saddling the Catholics with anything so embarrassing to their own cause as his murder), Coleman ever confided to Godfrey the perilous knowledge of the Jesuits' meeting at St James', it is likely that he revealed to him an even more damning fact: that Shaftesbury's chief lieutenants, including Pepys' sworn foe Harbord, had been receiving at his hands secret pensions from the French King in return for their Navy-wrecking activities of the previous summer. If so it lay in Godfrey's power to bring against these men, who posed as patriots and sworn foes of France, charges that amounted to High Treason, and no one who knew his courage and probity of character could doubt that he would do so. Those who had taken Coleman's bribes served on the Committee that soon afterwards sent him to the gallows: they kept him closely from all contact with the world and reported to the House that he had confessed to having converted to his own use the £2500 intended for their own share. But the French Ambassador's accounts tell another story, and two years later Harbord, speaking in the House, let the cat out of the bag by admitting that the Committee had been careful to take no names from Coleman, 'it being in his power to asperse whom he pleased, possibly some gentleman against the French and Popish interest'. It may well have lain in Godfrey's power also.[21]

One thing is certain that whatever Coleman confided to Godfrey, the leaders of the republican party had many reasons for hating this too honest magistrate. Like the Council he had received Oates' wild tale with caution and had privately expressed his disbelief in it – a crime for which others beside himself were soon to suffer. Still worse he had warned Coleman and the Duke of York of their peril. And one of Shaftesbury's closest followers, and a homicidal maniac to boot, the young Earl of Pembroke, had a cause of his own for detesting Godfrey, who that very spring had been the foreman of a Grand Jury of London Justices who had presented him for a particularly brutal murder. Pembroke had subsequently been convicted by his peers of the lesser crime of manslaughter and, on claiming Benefit of Clergy, had been discharged, and Godfrey had seen fit to take a prolonged holiday out of England. It is not without

significance that among Lord Shaftesbury's MSS is part of a letter –
the rest is missing – from a magistrate reporting that he had received
information that Godfrey had been traced on the day of his
disappearance to a house in St Giles', close to Lord Pembroke's
mansion in Leicester Fields. Shaftesbury, usually so furious to
pursue every charge, never followed up this clue or took any steps
to trace a butcher of St Giles' named Linnet, who had been the first
to report the discovery of the body.*[22]

One man at least, now known to have been in dependence on the
republican chiefs and mentioned a short while before by Colonel
Blood as planning an assassination, behaved in a most mysterious
way. On October 15th, two days before the body was discovered,
Colonel Scott left his lodgings at the haberdasher's, telling him that
he was due to leave town that day and would be back in about a
month. He added that should he be asked for by Major Wildman or
Mr Wentworth, a young Whig member of Parliament in whose
company a little while before he had given out that he was being
poisoned by Jesuits, he was to say he would be back in four or five
days. For some reason he wished to abscond, and to conceal from his
republican associates that he was doing so. He did not, however, do
as he had announced, for he was seen in town on the following day.
The next news Payne had of him was a letter purporting to come
from Bridgwater in Somerset and dated Saturday, October 19th.
Yet early that very afternoon, Scott, passing under the name of
Godfrey, appeared with his horse all covered with lather at
Gravesend.[23]

It was perhaps not surprising that a local dealer in butter and
cheese at first mistook him for a highwayman: 'a proper well-set

---

* My friend, Professor J. W. Williams of St Andrews University, in a brilliant but
as yet unpublished paper, has advanced an alternative solution. Godfrey, he points
out, could not have committed suicide, or been murdered by the Papists or have died
a death of ordinary violence at the hand of footpads. But, being already a sick man, he
might have died of natural causes, precipitated by excessive anxiety, at a secret
consultation with the King, Duke of York and the Catholic chiefs at Somerset House,
who thus confronted with the appalling problem of explaining his body and their own
presence, hit on the clumsy device of staging a pretended suicide. This does not,
however, altogether explain the bruises on Godfrey's breast. And James II's
subsequent statement that Charles II had mentioned his being at Somerset House at
the time Bedloe swore to the murder being committed, though not essential to the
thesis, is manifestly incorrect, since both Charles and the Duke of York were at
Newmarket at the time of the murder.

man in a great light-coloured periwig, rough visaged, having large hair on his eyebrows, hollow-eyed, a little squinting . . . full-faced about the cheeks, about 46 years of age with a black hat, and in a straight bodied cloth coat coloured with silver lace behind'.* He made his way to the house of John Skelton who sold drink during Gravesend Fair, and stabled his horse, a large black nag, with a good saddle, holsters and pistols, in the cow-shed. After a meal of pork and sausages, he went into the Fair and bought an overcoat, which he was without though the previous day had been extremely wet. It happened that the salesman was normally employed at the 'Leg' in Cannon Street just opposite Mr Payne's shop, and recognized him.

By this time the traveller had aroused the suspicions of one of the subordinate officials of the Clerk of the Passage, who henceforward had him watched. As soon as it was dark he was seen to sally out and call on one of the Searchers named Cresswell, with whom he appeared to be familiar, afterwards enquiring at the 'King's Head' for the master of a ship, the *Assistance*, outward bound for Lisbon.

Later that night in his cups at Cresswell's house, he became very communicative, saying that he had been fourteen days out of London travelling the coasts of Sussex and Kent seeking a yacht and staying with Sir Francis Rolle,† a local republican member of Parliament. A health having been drunk to the Prosperity of Old England, he called for another for the noble Duke of Buckingham. But when someone proposed confusion to all who had a hand in the Plot, he was observed to hold the glass long in his hand, and only drank when a fight was threatened.

Next afternoon, giving his shadower the slip, Scott vanished. Leaving his horse behind him, he bargained with a waterman to take him out with some sailors to the *Newcastle*, but when once on the water insisted on boarding the *Assistance*. Meanwhile his behaviour had so alarmed the town that a search was made for him. But by the time his flight had been discovered, the *Assistance* had sailed, Mr Cresswell having cleared her privately without the knowledge of his colleagues.‡[24]

* Mr Gibson's Notes from Gravesend. *Rawl. MSS. A.* 188, ff. 114–19. Also in *Pepysian MSS., Mornamont* I, 113–17.

† A Whig member of Parliament to whom Scott had written on March 11th, 1678, about Parliament and its plain dealings with France. *Rawl. MSS. A.* 175, ff. 179–82.

‡ All outward bound ships at Gravesend had to be 'cleared' by officials called Searchers before being allowed to proceed.

At this point the life of John Scott first impinged on that of Samuel Pepys who, like the rest of the official world, was occupied in searching for escaping Jesuits. At midnight on October 25th Pepys was informed by a letter from Gravesend of the events of the weekend. Having already had orders to close the ports, he wasted no time and wrote an express to the Commander-in-Chief in the Downs ordering him to overtake the *Assistance*, and arrest 'a tall thin-faced man, squinting with both eyes, about 50 years old, with a dark brown periwig'. He also wrote other letters, seeking every circumstance that might throw light on the identity of the fugitive. The letter from Gravesend he gave to the Duke of York who, almost frantic to prove his innocence, handed it next day to the Committee of the Lords examining the Plot. When Pepys was called to give his evidence, Titus Oates, who stood by and knew everything, declared that the fugitive was Father Simons, a notorious Jesuit and one of the chief instruments of the Plot.[25]

But Pepys found out the real identity of the wicked Father so quickly that the great men examining the Plot had reason to be grateful that their old employee was not brought before them as a Jesuit and a murderer. Already Sir Ellis Leighton, believed by the English colony in Paris to be implicated in the Plot's contrivance, was lying in Dover gaol, and the capture of another of Buckingham's agents, and particularly of one so liable to peach on his friends,* might well have proved fatal to their whole design. But Scott, as Pepys soon discovered, had left the *Assistance* at Margate and, riding by night, had secretly sailed for Dieppe from Folkestone in a fishing vessel, whose owner knew him only as the Duke of Buckingham's man John.[26]

On October 28th, in the presence of the rough-tongued Recorder of London, young Sir George Jeffreys, Pepys took down from the lips of Mr Robert Payne of Cannon Street, haberdasher of hats, all that that worthy knew of the doings of the mysterious traveller whose lodging had been traced to his house. From Payne Pepys learnt how Scott had slipped away before dinner on the 15th, saying he would be away a month, how he had returned next day to bid him lie to his republican colleagues, Wildman and Wentworth, and how – presumably for their deception – he had falsely dated his letter of

---

* As in after years Scott was to do. See *Rawl. MSS. A.* 190, f. 56.

October 19th from Bridgwater, the very day on which he had ridden so hotly to Gravesend. Pepys did not, of course, know more than this – that Scott was a secret agent of his great enemies, Lord Shaftesbury and the Duke of Buckingham, and an arrant poltroon who might well wish to fly the country for a while after a deed of darkness to which he had been privy and to deceive his paymasters as to the cause and nature of his flight. But one curious circumstance Pepys did notice, that during Payne's examination the great City magnate, Sir Robert Clayton, seemed to betray a knowledge of Scott. Next day, the last in October, Pepys delivered to the House of Commons a collection of republican pamphlets, army and navy estimates and papers about the state of the Fleet, which had been found in a little trunk in the absconded man's lodgings.[27]

But while Pepys, with his habitual mastery of detail, was striking blindly at the unknown, the enemies of the Government were closing round him. If, as his contemporary Roger North, the lawyer, always held – and few men were better equipped for knowing – the original plan of the contrivers of the Plot was to accuse Pepys directly of Godfrey's murder in the belief that being 'a known, faithful and professed servant of the Duke of York . . . who had known softness and the pleasures of life', he would accuse his patron to save his life,* they had been defeated by this eleventh-hour summons to Newmarket on the night of the 10th, which provided him with a perfect *alibi* and, of which in the conditions of the seventeenth century, they might well have known nothing until it was too late. But there were other and less direct ways of reaching him.[28]

---

* 'For what will not human nature in its weakness do to avoid torment and save life? . . . And it is probable that persons, conscious of small disposition towards martyrdom in themselves, might think the reasonings . . . hinted would be very powerful over others.' North, *Examen*, 243–4.

9

The Trial of Atkins

'For certainly no youth of his wit and straightness of fortune ever withstood such temptations to have been a villain.' S. Pepys to W. Hewer of Atkins, Nov. 7th, 1680. *Rawl. MSS. A.* 194, f. 224.

By the last day of October Pepys was becoming aware of the net that was closing round him. He wrote sadly to his friend James Houblon of the public troubles and the shackles which they placed on him: 'I should be mighty glad of an opportunity of an hour's chat with you upon the common subject of our present griefs and fears, as a matter that calls no less now for the deliberations of all good men than it appears to have been for a long time the meditation of bad.' He begged him, therefore, to meet him at the Court to be held next evening at Christ's Hospital, 'we will thence step and talk and grieve together'. It was the day of Sir Edmund Berry Godfrey's funeral, when the London mob – 'so heated that anything called Papist, were it cat or dog, had probably gone to pieces in a moment' – escorted the corpse through crowded streets to St Martin-in-the-Fields.[1]

While Pepys was walking with Houblon on the gloomy evening of Friday, November 1st, and discussing how he could best dispose of Morelli, his beloved musician, in order to conform with the proclamation banishing all Catholics from London, his enemies struck. That night Samuel Atkins, one of his clerks, failed to return to Derby House. Once or twice before the young man had stayed out beyond his proper hour, and he had been warned that it must never occur again.* At nine o'clock, his nerves on edge after the trials of the past few days, Pepys gave peremptory orders to the porter to shut the doors and tell the truant that he should never be allowed within them again.[2]

Next morning Pepys learnt that the unhappy lad had been

---

* On April 26th, 1677, young Atkins had written a penitential letter to Pepys, promising that – 'upon my first ill comportment on being (on any occasion) found a minute out of your house without your leave, I willingly lay this at your feet as my own act to banish me for ever your service, favour or countenance'. *Rawl. MSS. A.* 181, f. 188.

arrested on a warrant from the Secretary of State and carried to Newgate on the evidence of a namesake, Captain Charles Atkins, a young officer of good birth but depraved character, who two years before had been deprived of his command for surrendering an English ship of war to Algerian corsairs.* A few days before this bankrupt Captain had made a deposition that he had been approached by a seaman called Child, acting on behalf of some highly placed personage, to commit a murder. At the time of making this deposition the Captain told his acquaintances that he would soon have money again and the command of a frigate. He had now, apparently under inspiration, recalled that Atkins the clerk had subsequently asked him whether Child was a man that would be stout and secret, for Sir Edmund Berry Godfrey had very much injured his master, Secretary Pepys, and would ruin him if he lived. At this request he had sent Child to Pepys, and had later been approached to join in the murder. A curious circumstance of this new accusation about Pepys was that the Captain only made it after an interview with his uncle, Sir Philip Howard,† one of Shaftesbury's henchmen on the Committee for examining the Plot, though after his previous statement to the Secretary of State he had sworn that he had delivered all he knew.[3]

On his arrest on the evening of November 1st Atkins had been taken before this Committee, and saw before him the enemies of his master and the Duke – Shaftesbury, the Duke of Buckingham, Lord Essex, Lord Halifax, the Marquis of Winchester, Sir Philip Howard, and Compton the ambitious, ultra-Protestant Bishop of London. Shaftesbury wasted no time in getting to the point. 'Did you ever say', he asked the lad, 'that there was no kindness (or a want of friendship I think 'twas) betwixt Mr Pepys and Sir Edmund Berry Godfrey?' 'No, my Lord.' Essex then demanded if he knew Child, and, on Atkins innocently enquiring whether he meant the Victualler, added: 'No, no: this is another sort of man, and one whom you will be found to know very well.' But when Child came in, he turned

---

* See p. 121.

† 'Observe this being buoyed up by his uncle who . . . spoke several times at the Committee and vouched (as it were) what C. A. had said, assuring them he had so strictly examined him, that it was not possible he should lie, that he was Sir J. A.'s son, his nephew, and otherwise well allied, and would not want an estate' – a lie, as Howard must have known, as his father had cut him off without a penny. *Rawl. MSS.* A. 181, ff. 11–24.

out to be a plain seafaring man, whom Atkins had never seen in his life and who at once denied ever having seen him.

Captain Atkins was then introduced. Though the two knew each other well, the clerk, who was a kindly soul, having several times lent the broken dissolute Captain money, they had not met since the summer, and Samuel Atkins after hearing the charges against him said as much. 'Did you not ask', said Shaftesbury, 'whether this Child was a man of courage and secrecy, and bid Captain Atkins send him to Derby House and enquire for your master, but be sure not to ask for you?'

'No, my Lord, not in my life, one word like it.'

'You know,' said the Captain, 'Mr Atkins, this discourse was between us in your large room in the window.'

'Captain Atkins, God, your conscience and I know 'tis notoriously untrue,' the young man replied, and proceeded to give a description of their last meeting, which was on account of the Captain's desire to borrow half-a-crown.

Here Shaftesbury began to do, what his detractors called, wheedle. 'Come, Mr Samuel Atkins,' says he, 'you are an ingenious, hopeful young man, and truly for ought I can see a good and serious one. Captain Atkins has sworn this positively against you, to whom he bears no malice but has acknowledged several obligations; besides, to tell you truth, I don't think him to have wit enough to invent such a lie.' But again the prisoner denied it. 'What!' Shaftesbury said, 'we believe Captain Atkins to be a man that has loved wine and women, but would you have us think him a rascal!' But young Atkins was undaunted and told the story of his accuser's surrender to the Algerines, at which there was an awkward silence.

Lord Shaftesbury shifted the discussion to questions of theology.

'Pray, Samuel Atkins, what religion are you of?'

'My Lord, I am a Protestant, and my whole family before me.'

'Did you ever receive the Sacrament?' The lad, remembering his master's injunction, replied that he was under an obligation to do so next Sunday. At which the pious Lord Essex observed that it was time, and the jolly Earl of Shaftesbury that surely he would not do so now, for, he would warrant, he could not forgive his accuser.

After the prisoner had given an account of his lifelong Protestantism and of his upbringing under a Nonconformist schoolmaster, Shaftesbury supposed that now he frequented the Duke's Palace of

St James', it might be otherwise; 'for, Mr Atkins,' said he, 'we are apt to suspect people inclining to the sea'. But again Atkins asserted his Protestantism.

The great 'contrivers' were nothing if not masters of human nature. They now with good words and sorrow for his obstinacy told him what advantage his confession would be to him. 'Well, Samuel Atkins,' said the Duke of Buckingham, 'I never saw you before, but I'd swear you are an ingenious man. I see the working of your brain; pray declare what you know of this matter, whether you did say these words or no.' So, kindly, the great Lords tempted and flattered him. But he remained firm, and in the end they asked him to withdraw.

When he was called back into the room, Shaftesbury again addressed him. 'Mr Atkins,' he said, 'we are to be plain with you; here's a positive oath against you. We can't answer the Parliament by doing less than commit you to Newgate.'

'What your Lordships please,' replied the young man, 'if you send me to be hanged I could say no more nor otherwise.' Then each of the great ones spoke to him in turn, telling him that he would be very safe so long as he did not keep anything back and expressing their pity for the harm that must attend him otherwise.

'My Lords,' said Atkins, 'telling a lie will do me a great deal of hurt.'

'Mr Atkins,' Sir Philip Howard answered, 'you have not lived so long in an office but you know the laws of the nation to be such as will bring you under severe punishment if you be found to conceal anything of this nature.'

'Sir, I very well know it, and I know also that the laws of God will bring me into a worse guilt if I tell a lie.' After that there was nothing for it but to have the troublesome young man removed to Newgate, where he was left 'in a thinking condition, without pen, ink, paper or liberty to write or speak with any person'.*[4]

Outside Pepys hastily entrenched himself. To his clerks he gave orders to take the Sacrament on the next Sunday and to prepare

---

* Samuel Atkins' own account of these proceedings will be found in his 'Narrative' (*Rawl. MSS. A.* 173, ff. 113 *et seq.*), written a few weeks later with that meticulous love of detail which he shared (more than any of his other clerks) with his great employer, and in his written statement of November 25th, 1678 (*Rawl. MSS. A.* 181, ff. 11 *et seq.*). From them Roger North compiled his brief account of Atkins' trial in his *Examen*, 96, 243–51. See also *State Trials* VI, 1473.

themselves in the meantime 'towards that holy work', and begged that kindly Huguenot, James Houblon, to use all his powers to persuade Morelli to enter the Protestant fold. 'I beg you heartily', he wrote, 'to take this trouble in good part from me and doubt not your doing it, there being so much humanity and charity towards a helpless stranger concerned in it.' But Morelli refused to abandon the faith of his fathers, and on the next day the good merchant secured lodgings for him at Brentwood.

At that moment Pepys could ill spare his gentle musician, 'whose qualifications', he told Houblon, 'have rendered him the almost sole instrument of all the pleasure his Majesty's service leaves me any leisure . . . of enjoying, namely his music, languages and sobriety'.[5]

But there was no help for it, for the law must needs be obeyed. And on Sunday, November 4th, the Secretary of the Admiralty Office, with all his clerks, save poor Atkins, about him, was seen taking the Sacrament at St Margaret's, Westminster. He was careful to provide them all with certificates of their former Protestancy, particularly his French copyist, Paul Lorrain, who fortunately was a Huguenot and greatly addicted to piety.[6]

But everything he possessed, including his life, now rested on the constancy of the young clerk lying in solitude in Newgate. On November 6th the Lords' Committee received a message that Samuel Atkins wished to be brought before them again. The great men assembled in the Lord Privy Seal's Chamber in the Parliament House had no doubt of their triumph: Pepys would go down on Atkins' apostasy, and the Duke of York in his turn on Pepys'. 'Well,' said Lord Halifax, 'we hope you have considered of this business and are ready to give the Committee some light in it.'

Samuel Atkins then raised everyone's hopes by asking what would happen to him if 'out of the pure invention of a lie', he was to admit the truth of the Captain's story. 'What then?'

'Nay,' said Lord Shaftesbury, 'leave us to make the use; do you but confess it, you shall be safe and we will apply it.'

But this was just what the lad, defenceless and alone, was not prepared to let them do; for, as luck would have it, they had struck at a rock stronger even than their own tumultuous power, the inner rigidity of the boy's early Puritanism. At this critical juncture of his own and his master's life nothing would induce him to tell a lie.

His accusers repeated their charges and examined him closely about Pepys. Once the young clerk broke out almost violently: 'My Lords, I avow to you Mr Pepys never in his life committed any secret to me of any kind, nor ever mentioned to me upon any occasion one word about Sir Edmund Berry Godfrey. And this you'd believe if you knew how totteringly I stand in his opinion, having been turned away from him, and am this minute in his very ill apprehensions.'

'Why!' said the Bishop of London, 'are you given to drink and debauchery?'

'No, my Lord, I thank God, not, but Mr Pepys is the severest man in his house in the world, and whoever serves him laudably for seven years, for an hour's absence from his business without his knowledge shall lose his favour.'

'Why, you talk,' Shaftesbury interposed; "twill be made to appear you are the greatest favourite he has, that you read all his letters, read to him o'nights, and it will be proved you are reputed a Catholic in the house.'* But all that Atkins would admit was that in his earlier days with Pepys, before he had fallen into disgrace, he had sometimes read to him. Asked what, he replied the Bible and other good books, history at some times and at others divinity; no, never any Popish book, but once a work showing the error of Transubstantiation. This reply was so profoundly unsatisfactory, that the Committee felt they could do no more for the moment and sent him back to Newgate.[7]

But they had another card in their hand, though a soiled one. A few days before a low-down, international swindler, 'of base birth and worse manners'†, smelling an opportunity, had written from Bristol offering the authorities new discoveries about the Plot. This rascal, whose name was Bedloe, arrived in London on November 7th and was at once brought before the Lords' Committee. In him they had no Puritan prejudices to overcome. Early next morning

---

* S. Atkins' Statement of Nov. 25th, 1678. *Rawl. MSS. A.* 181, ff. 11 *et seq.*

† Archdeacon Echard, *History of England* (3rd ed., 1720), Book II, p. 951. 'He was skilful in all the arts and methods of cheating; but his masterpiece was his personating men of quality, getting credit for watches, coaches, horses, borrowing money upon recommendations, bilking of vintners and tradesmen; lying and romancing to the degree of imposing upon any man that had any remainders of humanity and good nature. He lived like a wild Arab, upon the prey and ramble; and wherever he was, in Flanders, France, Spain or England, he never failed of leaving the name of a notorious cheat and imposter.'

Captain Atkins, who knew Bedloe of old, called at Newgate and found his namesake in bed. The latter left a spirited description of the scene. '"Oh, good morrow," says he, so I leapt out of bed. "Good morrow," says I, and as Captain Richardson' (the prison governor who had brought the Captain up) 'was going down stairs again: "Hold, Captain," says I, "a word with you." So I took him into the next room. "For God's sake", says I, "don't leave me with this man alone; he'll positively go and swear God knows what against me!"'

But the Governor, a discreet man, knew his duty. When he was gone, Captain Atkins, wringing his hands, cried out, '"Oh! Samuel Atkins, we are all undone." "How undone?" says I. "Oh Lord!" says he, "there's a man came last night and has sworn positively against you that you were at the murder or was to have been there."' The Captain, who incidentally pretended that this new informer was a stranger to him, went on to say that his uncle Howard had ordered him to tell him of it at once that he might repent before it was too late.

Warming to his task the Captain then related an imaginary conversation in which Samuel Atkins had told him that Pepys had a secret house at Rouen and was ready to take the guilt of the murder in order to shelter the Duke of York.

'Oh God,' the prisoner exclaimed, 'when have you sworn to that lie?'* But the Captain merely became confidential and said that he had been sent by the Committee to warn him to confess and to promise him rewards for doing so. 'Come,' he added, 'we are both young men, and we ought to lay hold on this fair occasion of making our fortunes.'†[8]

Later that day the prisoner was carried again before the Committee to find, standing on the other side of the table, a stranger in a black periwig and campaign coat, who saluted him as though he knew him. It was Bedloe, 'the man out of the country'. That very morning he had told the House of Lords that the murder had been committed on the Saturday night in the Queen's Palace, Somerset House, by a gang of desperadoes hired by Jesuits, and that Atkins had been seen there two nights later standing over the corpse by the light of a dark lanthorn. But the new informer, who was of a cautious

---

* S. Atkins' Statement of Nov. 25th, 1678. *Rawl. MSS A*. 181, ff. 11–24.
† S. Atkins' Narrative. *Rawl. MSS. A*. 173, ff. 113–32.

turn, lacked Oates' brazen courage, and scenting the danger of an *alibi* now refused to commit himself absolutely. All he would say for certain was that the man he had seen was called Atkins and had told him he was one of Mr Pepys' clerks, and looked very like the prisoner.

After Bedloe had withdrawn Shaftesbury made Samuel Atkins a direct offer. 'Mr Atkins, if you are innocent you are the most unfortunate creature alive. I'll tell thee what, here is good news for you; here's but one way to save thy life, and you may now have it. Confess all you know and make a discovery in this matter and your life will be saved.' But still Atkins begged him not to strain his conscience. 'Then, I'll tell thee what,' said the great Earl, 'you'll be hanged or knighted; if the Papists rise and cut our throats, you'll be knighted; if not you'll be hanged.'*[9]

This time Atkins returned to Newgate in irons. Here he remained in solitary confinement for over two weeks without news of the outer world and with no visitors but the Captain, who twice returned to promise him great rewards if he would join with him and a halter if he refused. Four gentlemen of the House of Commons, among whom he recognized as his master's old enemies, Birch and Sacheverell, also came and told him in how desperate a condition his life was and how there was no hope unless he would make a discovery. He would be pardoned, they told him, if he did so and hanged if he did not. And they examined him closely as to where he had been between Saturday, October 12th, and Monday the 14th. As they left, Sacheverell remarked that he was one of the most ingenious men to say nothing he had ever met.

After they had gone Atkins tried to recall exactly where he had been during those days; after a while he found himself able to recollect every hour. For the rest he cheered his confinement by praying, confessing his sins and selecting a text for his funeral sermon. 'I thank Almighty God', he wrote afterwards, 'I found great refreshing and was not without hope to find Mercy, through the merits of Christ, though the unworthiest of all mortals and the greatest sinner: I plainly see the hand of God in the judgment.'†For the young man had something of his own on his conscience.[10]

What it was his former employer, seeking feverishly but methodically for an *alibi* to rescue him, was now discovering. By November

* S. Atkins' Statement of Nov. 25th, 1678. *Rawl. MSS. A.* 181, ff. 11–24.
† S. Atkins' Statement of Nov. 25th, 1678. *Rawl. MSS. A.* 181, ff. 11–24.

14th Pepys had completed a long and circumstantial account of Atkins' birth, education and lifelong Protestancy: his one fault, he admitted, was 'an inclination sometimes of taking the advantage of his master's absence to spend his time out of doors'. Pepys' researches soon showed him how Atkins had indulged that inclination during the fatal weekend of his own absence at Newmarket. 'Now,' he wrote to Captain Lloyd, then about to embark on a long voyage,'* 'for as much as it becomes all of us equally to contribute what we can to discover the just truth of this matter, so that neither the guilt of so execrable a murder should be smothered . . . nor the guilt placed upon an innocent . . . I have made it my endeavour by the strictest and most impartial enquiries to find out how Atkins spent those three days in my absence, I being then at Newmarket, and find (if my informations be true) that he employed the opportunity . . . in entertaining himself more than, had I been present, he either could or durst to have attempted, which (for the present at least) I am contented to overlook his offence to me as his master and apply myself to the enquiring how far he stands chargeable or excusable in this much more detestable wickedness that is laid to him of having his hand in blood.' For it appeared that the yuoung man had visited the New Exchange in Lloyd's convivial company on the Saturday, drunk with him at the 'Rose' tavern on Sunday and seen him to the waterside when he took boat on Monday.[11]

On the morning of November 19th poor Atkins in Newgate was loaded with a great iron and told that he was to be tried that day. He had no witnesses, legal advice or sight of the depositions against him. 'I got up and dressed myself', he wrote, in the assured manner of his age, 'and prepared to go without the least fear or discord within, but with great quiet, expecting the sentence of death.' But there was no trial that day, and two days later his sister and Pepys' lawyer, Mr Hayes, who had been moving heaven and earth to reach him, were admitted to the prison. They told him that they were doing all they could to draw up his defence and showed him a paper that Pepys had prepared, revealing exactly how he had spent his time on October 12th, 13th and 14th. And they also gave him pen and paper with which to draw up his own account of those days.[12]

* By November 19th Pepys had obtained special permission from the King for Lloyd to postpone his voyage in order to give evidence. *Admiralty Letters* VIII, 293.

The great 'contrivers' were pressing home their attack both in Parliament and the Courts of Law, for in the panic-stricken state of public opinion, they knew that judges and juries were prepared to believe almost any tale. Atkins' trial was expected to come on at any moment. On the 21st Pepys despatched urgent orders to the Captain of the *Katherine* yacht to send up his boatswain and three seamen to give evidence, 'at the express command of his Majesty', by whom all their expenses would be paid – a singular circumstance since they were to appear for the defence against the official prosecution of the Crown.[13]

But not even the panic of that frantic time could enable the prosecution to get over the kind of evidence which Pepys had prepared for his clerk's defence. With the utmost method he had drawn up a list of witnesses to prove how every hour of Atkins' time was spent during the disputed three days. His clerk's education and religion, his actions and the lives and reputations of his accusers were all recorded and tabulated as neatly as the lists of the King's ships in the office at Derby House. For Friday night there was Mrs Bulstrode and her maid to prove that the young man lay at his lodgings till eight next morning. His fellow clerks, Lewis, Lawrence, Walbanke and Roberts, with Tom, the porter, would then prove him in the office till midday. Mrs Bulstrode and her maid would again testify how he dined at home, while his Saturday afternoon and evening up to one o'clock next morning would be shown by Captain Lloyd and others to have been spent mostly at the 'Blue Post' in the Haymarket. So the carefully planned Schedule continued, accounting for every minute till Tuesday. After that followed a wealth of illuminating detail about Captain Atkins' delivery of his ship to the Turks and his 'profane swearing and wicked loose life ever since', of Bedloe's notorious career both before and after his discoveries, and the correspondence which had existed between the two rogues before they became officially acquainted.[14]

Against this sort of thing even Shaftesbury was temporarily powerless. To bring on the trial against this formidable band of witnesses, marshalled and directed by the most industrious and methodical man in England, might end in shaking the credit of the whole plot. The Committee of the Lords proceeded therefore more cautiously. Atkins was allowed the free use of pen and paper and encouraged to write down exactly how he had spent his time and with whom he had conversed during the three fatal days. As soon as he had finished, his paper was taken away from him and examined by the Committee and the Counsel for the prosecution.[15]

There for the moment, with Atkins in prison and Pepys awaiting the assault with his marshalled witnesses, the matter was allowed to rest. Early in December the latter wrote to his sister and father in Huntingdonshire to tell them how one of his clerks had been charged 'by a most manifest contrivance' in the death of Sir Edmund Berry Godfrey, 'which,' he added, 'though most untrue, cannot be thought to pass in the world at so jealous a time as this without some reflections upon me as his master, and on that score does occasion me not a little disquiet'.*[16]

It was, as Pepys truly said, a jealous time. Everybody suspected everybody and good men and their wives went armed in the streets in expectation of a massacre. It was rumoured that there was gunpowder piled high beneath Parliament, cellars full of hatchets and cutlasses in every Papist house and an army of 40,000 French desperadoes hovering on the English coasts, now landed in the isle of Purbeck, now tunnelling under the Channel. In Parliament and Council, Oates, dressed like a Bishop in silk gown and cassock† and hailed by all as the Saviour of the Nation, made accusation after accusation; even the Queen was struck at. From his presence those who knew him drew back as from a stench from Hell.[17]

Though Pepys' enemies had been temporarily checked by his Newmarket *alibi* and again by his industry to save Atkins, they did not despair to bring him down. In Parliament he was charged by one of Shaftesbury's henchmen with granting passes to Jesuits to go overseas. But he was able to answer that the granting of such passes was wholly foreign to his employment. Another attempt was made on November 28th by Colonel Birch to cause him to reveal prematurely the evidence which he had prepared for the defence of

---

* 'In the meantime pray desire my Father to give no way to any fears concerning me, for that I bless God I have lived so carefully in the discharge of my duty to the King my Master and the laws I live under ... that I have not one unjust deed or thought to answer for ... it being of no use to any man in my place to think of supporting himself by any other means that has such an innocence as mine to rely on, and there, I bless God, lies my comfort, whatever befall me.' S. Pepys to Mrs Jackson, Dec. 5th, 1678. Tanner, *Further Correspondence*, 328–9.

† As one contemporary put it – 'leapt from an alms-basket into a coach and equipage'. *Observator*, No. 183, Aug. 2nd, 1682.

Atkins. But Pepys refused to be drawn. Atkins, he said, was formerly servant to his head clerk Hewer and was now one year out of his apprenticeship; where he was during the weekend of Godfrey's murder, he did not know, as he was then at Newmarket. If the House wished for information as to Atkins' general deportment, he could produce members of his household who would inform them of it.[18]

In fact Pepys was fully aware of the extent of his peril, and his conduct was a model of circumspection. The Navy, which thanks to his loyalty had been long under the influence of the Duke of York, was particularly liable to the charge of Popery: he now made it his business to deprive his foes of every ground for such an accusation. When in the middle of November Oates gave out that he had discovered a Catholic plot to seize the Fleet, Pepys issued orders to all commanders and dockyard officials to have a strict watch kept night and day, 'till', as he told Sir Richard Beach at Chatham, 'this consternation under which all now justly lie, be over, which I pray God of Heaven send, the whole government seeming at this day to remain in such a state of distraction and fear, as no History I believe can parallel'.* And as a liberty, as he termed it, was being taken of calling into question the Protestancy of naval officers, he ordered that all commanders should examine their officers as to their religion and the time of their last taking the Sacrament. The returns which he subsequently received were highly satisfactory. 'It is a matter of great joy to us all', he assured Sir John Kempthorne, 'to hear from you the opinion you have of the clearness of the Navy from people of that profession in Religion, it being what I have always from the best of my observation thought, and a blessing which I hope God Almighty will still preserve to the Navy.'†[19]

Pepys' circumspect integrity maddened his enemies, and they sought every opportunity to attack and irritate him. It is not improbable that they were responsible for the discharge from Bedlam that November of poor, demented James Carcasse, whom long ago he had had dismissed for fraud from the Ticket Office. But the libel which Carcasse soon afterwards published on Pepys in a

---

* S. Pepys to Sir R. Beach, Nov. 19th, 1678. *Pepysian MSS., Admiralty Letters* VIII, 296.

† S. Pepys to Sir J. Kempthorne, Nov. 23rd, 1678. *Pepysian MSS., Admiralty Letters* VIII, 319.

book of poems called *Lucida Intervalla* was so rambling and wild an affair that it was able to do him little damage. The Secretary of the Admiralty Office might be a middle-aged gentleman who loved comfort and had known pleasure, but he was singularly difficult to bring down.[20]

On December 13th his enemies therefore returned to the charge against Atkins. On that day the Lords Committee carefully examined the witnesses whom Pepys had assembled. The central figure of the proceedings was a jovial and loyal salt named Captain Vittles, who had at the time of the murder commanded the *Katherine* yacht then lying off Greenwich. After being sworn by the Bishop of London he gave an account of Atkins' proceedings from four o'clock till midnight on the fatal Monday. It appeared that on that morning the Captain had come up to Derby House to report to Secretary Pepys for orders: finding him away at Newmarket (one suspects much to his relief), he and young Atkins had had a leisurely yarn. In the course of it the jolly clerk mentioned that he had pledged himself for the afternoon to a couple of young gentlewomen; might he, he asked, bring them down that afternoon to see over his yacht. So Vittles had gone back to Greenwich, cleaned his ship and waited till half-past four, when Atkins and his two charmers arrived. They all went down to the cabin and drank a glass of wine, and 'the wine being good and just come from beyond seas', they drank some more. The long and short of it was that at seven o'clock, Captain Vittles refusing to let them go, Atkins discharged his boat. They continued drinking till nearly half-past ten when it became palpably necessary to put the young man and his lady friends into the ship's wherry. Here together with a thoughtful present of a Dutch cheese and half-a-dozen bottles of wine, they were placed in a state which Captain Vittles, long experienced in such matters, could only describe as 'very much fuddled'. As the tide was flowing strongly the four seamen who rowed the wherry were unable to make London Bridge, and finally set their passengers down by the iron gates at Billingsgate at half-past eleven, over two hours after Bedloe deposed to having seen Atkins standing solemnly over Godfrey's body in Somerset House. At that moment he was certainly not able to stand at all, being as one of the seamen put it 'much in drink' and fast asleep. With great difficulty he and his companions were finally got into a coach for Westminster. And as one of the young gentlewomen,

Sarah Williams, figured on Pepys' subsequent list of witnesses to prove that Atkins had spent the rest of the night in his own bed, it appeared that even there he had continued to enjoy her not very improving company. It was probably this that was on the young man's conscience.

After the Committee had finished with Captain Vittles, whose evidence proved as unshakable as it was unsatisfactory, William Tribbett, the bosun, and the four tars, Dickinson, Stephens, French and Holcroft, were called in. They also were unshaken by the great Lords' examination, though much was made of a piece of paper which the Captain had rather injudiciously got them to sign before the examination as to the evidence they were going to give. But, though the Committee sought hard for it, there was not the slightest proof that Pepys had suborned them.[21]

So once again Atkins was taken back to prison, and Pepys' enemies sought for other ways to come at him. One of his maids, it was said, had committed the unforgivable crime of casting doubt on the Plot and had whispered, doubtless on her master's suggestion, that the whole affair was a sham. Just then there were tales circulating in high quarters that the real plot was to bring in a Commonwealth again under the management of Shaftesbury and Buckingham, and the great Contrivers were seeking eagerly for the carriers of such stories to destroy them while they had power. That they were unable to proceed further in this instance was probably due to Mr Secretary Williamson, who as an old friend of Pepys' was ready to help him when he was able and allowed the complaint to go no further than his office.[22]

Amid growing panic and the trial of poor priests, the year closed with a violent parliamentary furore caused by the carefully premeditated and treacherous production* in the Commons by Ralph Mountagu, late English Ambassador in Paris, of secret correspondence between the English and French Crowns. All hope of obtaining money from Parliament for a vigorous naval policy, or even for the defrayment of the deficit caused by the mobilization of the previous spring, was at an end. When Pepys in the House tried to raise the state of the Fleet, he was merely answered by Shaftesbury's lieutenants that if he would give an account how Popery came to be

---

* News of Mountagu's action was rumoured in Paris two days before the English Embassy received the news from London. *H.M.C. Lindsey*, 398.

planted in the Fleet, he would be heard: other hearing there would
be none. On January 4th, 1679, at the first meeting of the Admiralty
Board held since the beginning of the Plot, Pepys drew attention to
the gravity of the financial situation. Everything was at a stand for
want of money: the Victuallers alone were owed £38,000. The
government accordingly recalled Narbrough from the Mediterranean, with instructions to make one last attempt to enforce peace on
the Algerines and in default to leave five frigates under Admiral
Herbert in the Straits.[23]

With the withdrawal of the Mediterranean squadron Louis had
achieved the principal purpose for which he had financed the
republican party. For the moment England was a cipher: it was all
her government could do even to hold Tangier. The attack which
Charles had now to face was not foreign but domestic, and its focal
point the 'King's Head' tavern in Fleet Street where the republican
party chiefs, assembled in their Green Ribbon Club, marked down
their victims, planned the secret tortuous courses by which they
were to perish, and directed, through their libel writers and rumour
mongers, public opinion and the London mob.* On January 24th,
abandoning all further hope of the existing House of Commons, he
threw down the gauntlet to his enemies and dissolved Parliament. A
new one was called to meet at the beginning of March, and for the
first time in eighteen years the country enjoyed the excitement of a
general election.[24]

Pepys wasted no time in securing his own return. On the day after
the dissolution he wrote to the Duke of Norfolk, to his cousin
Thomas Pepys of King's Lynn, and to the Mayor and Burgesses of
Castle Rising. He trusted, he told his cousin, that his past contributions towards the rebuilding of Castle Rising Church – 'a work a
man may have some satisfaction in the remembrance of when it is
done' – would not be forgotten, especially when it was remembered
how much his first election had cost him. But not feeling too certain
that such piety would secure his return he applied himself also to the
naval boroughs of Portsmouth and Harwich.

---

* For Pepys' copy made by him from the original lent him by King Charles II – of
'The Journal of the Green Ribbon Club at the King's Head Tavern over against the
Temple in Fleet Street from 14th November 1678 to 29th June 1681' see *Pepysian MSS.*
2875, *Miscellanies* VII, 265–91. 'In lieu of Saints', runs Pepys' endorsement, ''twas a
club of Devils.' Among its later members was John Scott.

Both towns expressed their readiness to elect him. He also received an offer of a borough in the Isle of Wight from his friend the governor, Sir Robert Holmes. It was as well, for he discovered that his old constituency was secretly proposing to elect another in his place – an act of ingratitude on which, he told his friends, he preferred not to comment, 'knowing the world too well to expect more than is to be found in it'. He needed such philosophy the more, for later he learnt that the two gentlemen whom he had left in possession of the Election, Sir Robert Howard and Sir John Baber, had repaid him by reviving the old charge of his being a Papist and the new one of his having had a hand in the Plot. So he chose Harwich, where his friend Sir Anthony Deane was also standing, and, going down there in person, was elected almost unanimously – meeting with 'all the satisfaction possible', in what he described 'a free, speedy and almost chargeless election'.[25]

Pepys got back to London just in time for Atkins' trial. That event had been postponed for as long as possible by its prosecutors, who had now little hopes of its success and considerable fears of the damage it might do to their informers. 'And now', as one contemporary put it, 'the business was to get well off with *salvo* to the credit of the Plot. So now, no more fish to be caught, all the hurry, hurry to trial came to nothing at all.' But they could not evade the issue altogether.[26]

On Saturday, February 8th, Atkins was brought to the Court of King's Bench in Westminster Hall and arraigned as an accessory to the murder of Sir Edmund Berry Godfrey. It was as an accessory only, for the murder had been hastily planted on three poor creatures associated with Somerset House. These were sentenced to death on Monday the 10th on evidence that ought not to have hung a cat. Atkins, who had been present in Court, was then brought to the Bar. The Chief Justice began by asking him if he had bail ready.

'No, my Lord, I am prepared for my trial, if your Lordship pleaseth, but not with bail.'

'Ay, but Mr Atkins, 'tis the latter end of term, and many people's livelihoods lie at stake. We can't lay aside all business for yours.'

'My Lord, my life lies at stake, and I have been under severe imprisonment a long time. I humbly pray I may be tried; besides I have many witnesses who have remained in town on purpose to give evidence for me ever since the last term.'

'Mr Atkins, we cannot do it. You must be content; you shall be tried at the Sessions.'

But here Captain Lloyd intervened to point out that, as Captain of one of the King's ships ordered to sea, it would be impossible for him to remain any longer. The Lord Chief Justice gave way: 'Well, I don't know; if it be so, you shall be tried to-morrow, and so bring him up very early.'[27]

Tried next morning Atkins was. His master Pepys stood by with his 'cloud of reputable witnesses'. The Attorney-General – the bullying Sir William Jones, himself deep in the Opposition's council – opened the prosecution by describing how Bedloe had seen Atkins shortly after nine on the evening of Monday, October 14th, standing over Godfrey's body and consulting with the murderers how to dispose of it.

Captain Charles Atkins then gave evidence of how the prisoner had approached him with a view to securing Child to commit a murder for his master. 'What', asked the Lord Chief Justice, 'is Mr Atkins' master's name?'

'Mr Pepys.'

'What, Mr Pepys of the Navy?'

'Yes, my Lord.'

At this point the Attorney-General intervened, to ask leave to introduce a new witness, found, it seemed, by Providence at that very moment. 'Now, my Lord,' he said, 'because it seems a strange thing that Mr Atkins, who says he is a Protestant, should be engaged in this business, we have a witness here to prove that he has been seen often at Somerset House at Mass, and so he is a party concerned, for those that are of that party it was their interest to cut him off.' On this, there stepped forward a ragged hooligan lad, whom he described as 'an angel from Heaven to deliver the truth'.

But before he could do so, Samuel Atkins, who was standing in the crowd below the Bar, with great presence of mind and in a loud voice asked him whether he knew him. The lad, taken aback and not realizing he was the prisoner, answered 'No', so that his evidence was wrecked even before he could be sworn.

After this abortive attempt, Bedloe was called; and a very halting witness the great man on this occasion turned out to be. For knowing that Atkins could prove an *alibi* as to his whereabouts at the hour he had formerly declared his having seen him standing over

Godfrey's body he would now do nothing but hedge: there was very little light, he could not swear to take away a man's life when he was not certain, now he came to think of it he recollected that the man he had seen beside the body had a more manly face and a beard.

The Attorney-General hurried on to the next witness, who was no other than Samuel Atkins' old schoolmaster and who had invited his former pupil to a dinner at 'Mount Horeb' in Pudding Lane on the very day of the charge. This appointment Atkins had unaccountably failed to keep. 'When I heard that this gentleman was in this unhappy affair', added the worthy pedant, 'I said, how much better it had been for him to have been in my company, that I might have vouched for him.'

But the graceless lad merely pleaded that he had completely forgotten the invitation, for it was soon to be proved that he had had livelier company that day. Here he wisely took advantage of his old schoolmaster's presence to ask him to testify as to his religion, which the honest man very willingly and satisfactorily did: Atkins had not only always been a good Protestant but a very zealous one. 'There is very much good in that', observed the Lord Chief Justice and then asked, after the manner of Judges, where 'Mount Horeb' was.

That ended the case for the prosecution. The accused opened his defence by starting to show that the conversation with his namesake about Pepys and Godfrey's murderer was a complete fabrication, but in this he was not permitted to proceed. For the Court, which had allowed it to be published by the prosecution, now resolved that Captain Atkins' narration was immaterial to the case. So after three months in gaol the prisoner had to content himself by calling witnesses to prove that he was elsewhere at the hour when Bedloe had charged him with being at Somerset House.

This Captain Vittles very effectively did. After a ready admission that his name was Vittles, he repeated his story of the visit to the yacht at Greenwich and the subsequent *partie carrée* in the cabin. 'And so about 8 or 9 o'clock, we had drunk till we were a little warm, and the wine drinking pretty fresh, and being with our friends, we did drink freely till it was indeed unseasonable; I must beg your Lordship's pardon, but so it was.'

But the Lord Chief Justice did not mind at all, for he himself was a notable hand at the bottle. Indeed afterwards, while the bosun

Tribbett was being fetched, he was pleased to be facetious and even a little bawdy with the jolly commander.

'Did the women pledge you, Captain?' he asked.

'Pledge me, my Lord?'

'Aye, did they drink with you?'

'Aye, and drink to us, too, my Lord.'

After this the Attorney-General threw in his hand, for the thing was plainly hopeless.

There was a little farce at the end. It was the Attorney-General's business to make certain that the sacred testimony of the informers was not called in question, and with Bedloe there had been some awkward moments. 'I would desire,' he said, 'because some perhaps will make an ill use of it, that they will please to note here is no disproving the King's evidence: For Mr Bedloe did not at first, nor doth he now, charge him directly to be the man. So likewise for the first man, all that he says may be true, and yet Mr Atkins be innocent.' The Lord Chief Justice politely agreed.

'I desire the company may not go away with a mistake as if the King's evidence were disproved.'

'Not in a title.'

After that the Jury returned a verdict of Not Guilty. Atkins, with the weight of his long suspense suddenly lifted, knelt down and cried out three times, 'God bless the King and this honourable Bench'. But he did not, as he might well have done, cry 'God bless Mr Pepys', who had had in his turn even more cause to bless him. For Samuel Atkins, as Roger North justly wrote, had saved his master and more than his master 'when it was scarce thought possible that human nature could bear such trials'; he had seen 'the Death's head brought to his very nose' and had given the plot-makers their first check.

But Captain Vittles, good soul, turned all to laughter. For when the Lord Chief Justice, voicing the acceptable sentiment of the moment, expressed his relief at Atkins' innocency and declared that if any Protestant had been guilty of the charges brought against him it would have grieved him to the very heart, the Captain could not restrain his little joke: 'My Lord, here is his schoolmaster will give your Lordship an account of how he was bred and brought up, and what a good conditioned young man he was'. Nor was the Lord Chief Justice displeased: 'Well, well, Captain, go you and drink a bottle with him.' Then Mr Atkins went from the Bar.[28]

10

The Traitor's Gate

'Whether I will or noe, a Papist I must be.' S. Pepys to the Duke of York, May 6th, 1679.

But if Atkins had escaped, Pepys had still to do so. The general election went by in a full stream of republican victories; in all but close boroughs like the Cinque Ports, where the Crown still ruled, the Courtiers who were without cohesion or organization went down before a Party which had both. It was close on forty years since the great Pym had evolved the art of swaying a small, corrupt and ill-educated electorate; but it had not been forgotten in the interim, and Shaftesbury and his henchmen of the Green Ribbon Club now revived it on the brave old model of '40 and '41. A flood of insinuations and libels swept the country; Popery was the cry that brought all the King's men toppling down.

Pepys, though he gained his seat, did not escape libel. In '*A List of one unanimous Club of Voters in His Majesty's Long Parliament dissolved in '78 and very fit to be thought on at the next new choice*', he figured as '*Samuel Peipys. Plot, Popery, Piracy*', the last being an insinuation now busily circulated in the City that he had been concerned in the depredations committed against English shipping by a privateer called the *Hunter* during the last Dutch War. In the same pamphlet one of his parliamentary friends, Robert Wright, the shipowner, was branded: '*by his interest in Coleman and Pepys hath* 40s. *a day –* '. The implication was that Pepys, as the Duke's other chief lieutenant, would be the next to follow Coleman to the gallows. In his old and new constituency alike every art was used to make him a Papist and a participator in the Plot. Even his colleague at Harwich, the grave Sir Anthony Deane, though it was impossible to fasten a charge of Popery on so solemn a Protestant, was attacked as an atheist – an absurd suggestion, which moved Pepys to observe 'he has too much wit to be an Atheist, it being the fool only that Solomon tells us says in his heart, There is no God'.

As for his own pretended Popery, Pepys told his new constituents, let them examine the entries in the Parliament books 'upon occasion of a controversy some time since happening between a great Lord and myself upon that subject, and they shall find such a trial and proof of my Protestancy as I doubt no private man in England can show but myself upon record in Parliament'. Both he and Deane, he concluded, were ready to come down to Harwich and give the Corporation full proof of their 'devotion towards God Almighty'.

Some slight compensation for all this Pepys obtained by withhold-ing from his ungrateful traducers at Castle Rising the £50 which he had long ago promised them for rebuilding their church. For years they had procrastinated over putting the work in hand; now they suddenly dunned him for his subscription. 'To find them arraigning me afresh of being a Papist and I know not what', he wrote to his cousin of Lynn, 'is a usage which I cannot but resent ... Pray therefore let them go to work as soon as they will upon the contributions given them by their new Burgesses, and leave me to the choice of my own time for the ordering out of mine'.[1]

Yet chosen for both Harwich and Portsmouth, Pepys was more fortunate than many of his colleagues who could secure no seat at all. His own expectations at Portsmouth he tried to dispose of to Lord Brouncker, until he learnt from the King that the seat was urgently needed for the Chancellor of the Exchequer, Sir John Ernle. Pepys at once wrote to the Governor of Portsmouth, Colonel Legge, asking him to secure Ernle's election. But Legge, who had already committed himself to the return of another, resented Pepys' pretence to dispose of the seat. In an injured and angry letter Pepys enclosed the Lord Treasurer's commands, adding majestically, 'whatever inequality you may fashion yourself between your interest and mine in Portsmouth, I think we owe them both equally to the credit derived to us from his Majesty'. On receipt of this characteristic Pepysian sentiment, Legge lost his temper and wrote a reply which bluff Sir Henry Coventry, the Secretary of State, who did not love his colleague of the Admiralty, described as 'too witty for a Governor and too plain dealing for a courtier'. It was far too much for Pepys. 'I doubt not', he wrote back, 'but we are each of us sufficiently cautioned against giving ourselves the disquiet of any like unnecessary conversations for the time to come, my friendship being (I must confess) of too simple and uninterested a breed to receive any content from a mixture with one so uneasy and suspicious as yours.' It was a good illustration of the lack of understanding that prevailed between the supporters of the Crown.[2]

One tiny triumph Pepys enjoyed in the election which swept so many of the Court's pieces from the Board. In the middle of February he went down to Rochester to assist in the return of his friend, Sir John Bankes, on whose behalf he had used his influence with the dockyard officials at Chatham. He described it all in a letter to his dear Lady Bankes; how they had been ridden into the town at the head of two hundred mounted supporters amid the cheers of the populace, and after 'a long strict (yet quiet) poll' placed her husband 'firmly at the head of it'. But then Sir John had many links with the Opposition, which in its more moderate aims he often supported, and, not being a loyal public official, was in small danger of being accused of Popery.[3]

It was a troubled season. Even Pepys' own Admiralty Board rebelled against him. On the last day of January, with Prince Rupert in the chair, and Lord Anglesey, Lord Craven and Secretary Coventry, none of them friends to Pepys, at the table, complaints were raised of the way in which during the past year the King and their Secretary had monopolized their functions. They curtly ordered the latter to prepare detailed returns of the state of the Service calling for many months of needless labour. And though the King, to whom Pepys appealed, announced at the next Admiralty Board two days later that such enquiries would be inconvenient for the Service and must be respited, the tension between the 'Admirals' and their Secretary remained.[4]

With the general election fell the Duke of York, on whose favour Pepys had risen to power. In March, on his brother's command, he went into exile as the only means of averting civil war. Pepys, who never faltered in his perilous allegiance, continued to write to him in Flanders about the affairs of the Navy and the rumours of French preparations at sea; 'God grant I may soon be enabled to tell your Royal Highness of such proceedings in our Parliament as may best answer them.'[5]

For, even on the verge of revolution and civil war, Pepys' enduring interest remained with the Navy. Here was his ruling passion; and he could never quite credit his countrymen with the indifference which for ninety-nine days out of a hundred they felt for that organization on which, under Providence, their safety and well-being chiefly depended. The hectic politics of the moment were to him only a fevered dream that must pass; that the King's ships should be at sea was his business and the eternal need of every Englishman.*

So in the quiet of Derby House Pepys turned his eyes from the angry strife between Whitehall and Westminster to the grey frontiers of England which he seldom saw but never forgot. To rule and guard them he was forging rules which would be honoured and obeyed when the catchwords of 'Exclusion' and 'No Popery' were remembered only in school text-books. Regardless of the folly at such a moment of making new enemies, he returned to his task of enforcing on a rough and turbulent generation, who could not even conceive its necessity, a discipline that should stand the test of time and grow into a habit and an inspired creed of service. It was not to be hoped, he wrote, during the revolutionary days of early 1679 to a flag-officer who had refused to account for the misdemeanours of his favourite captain, 'that sobriety and good discipline should ever be supported in a fleet where those in chiefest trust are either unwilling or afraid of detecting even their inferiors in their misdoings'. Pepys was never so afraid.[6]

He reaped the inevitable consequence of his courage. 'I have of late come to understand (now all mouths as well as ears are open)', he told his friend Sir John Holmes, 'how much Mr Legge, Captain Russell, Captain Priestman and some others of their intimacy, do take a liberty not only of censuring me but uttering no small menaces against me as an enemy to gentlemen-captains, from my endeavours by ... restraining that neglect and contempt of the necessary discipline of the Navy which I find them prone to, in absenting themselves without leave or limitation from their charges.' 'I will discharge my part towards his Majesty and Lords of the Admiralty', he wrote to another, 'in the preservation of the good discipline of the Navy as long as I shall have the honour of serving them in it, by making due representations of any violences I see offered to it, whereof (God knows) few days together escape without some fresh instances, and as few of them without giving me fresh

---

* Compare Winston Churchill's noble chapter on the mobilization of the Grand Fleet in *The World Crisis*. He also during his tenure of the Admiralty found the impassioned battles of party politics a little unreal compared with the needs of the Service by which England in her last resort lives.

censure and disquiet from my non-compliance with them, even to the rendering my employment as truly burdensome to me as others (who know not this) make it the subject of their envy.'[7]

In those last weeks, before the blow which his enemies had been preparing for him fell, Pepys, undaunted by discouragements, never relaxed his administrative vigilance. The new ships continued to be built as fast as he could press them forward; that year two of the 2nd and twelve of the 3rd rates were completed and launched. All his schemes for the betterment of the sea-service he continued to pursue; even his resolution to prevent naval chaplains from holding pluralities and the collection of materials for the noble history he was planning of the Navy: in March he wrote to his friend, Dr Gale of St Paul's School, to thank him for the dimensions of a vessel given by Lucian. Round the walls of his office were stacked the monuments of his labour: the rules and precedents he had laid down, the bound volumes of the letters he had sent out, the registers which he and his clerks had prepared of all things belonging to the English Marine. And now he was preparing a new system of General Instructions for officers, a work he had long intended and proposed to complete as soon as he should have time and vacancy of thought for it.[8]

But the ultimate disposal of his time was in the hands of his enemies. Their renewed attack on the great Secretary began in Parliament on April 14th, when Bennet, Shaftesbury's jackal, demanded an enquiry on the state of the Navy. Its extravagances, he declared, would beggar the nation; as things were managed, they were paying 12*d.* for every 6*d.* received. And 'under these villainies' the ships were riddled with Popery for every officer in it had been made by the Duke of York; recently a Captain had even been dismissed for calling his Lieutenant 'Papist'. 'I will prove Popery in your Fleet at the Bar,' he shouted.

As angrily Pepys answered that he was at liberty to do so. In a breathless and indignant House he stood up to defend the Duke of York; he was an unfortunate Prince, he admitted, and would give his life to rescue him from his religious error, but there had never been a greater Lord High Admiral or one better fitted to name naval officers. And, so far as sleepless care could secure, there was not a single Catholic in the Fleet. 'In the name of God', he said, 'go on in your inspection.'[9]

They went on. But while Pepys was collecting papers to refute them, the earth opened beneath his feet. All the good fortune he enjoyed, he had written a little before, was due to the opportunities which the envy or ignorance of others had given him of recommending himself to the just opinion and favour of his royal master. Now, he felt sure, it would be so again; 'such is my case at this day as that I think no man capable of doing me a better office than he that would charge me deepest'.

But on April 20th an extraordinary thing happened: the Government fell. There was no civil war, no revolution, but the King, feeling himself unable to withstand the strength of a parliamentary majority backed by a populace maddened by the fear of Popery, dismissed his principal Ministers and Privy Councillors and invited the leaders of the Opposition to take their places. It was a constitutional innovation which in time was to become an essential part of the governance of Britain. But at the moment it seemed to Pepys and his friends as if the King, in choosing a Council of 'Mutineers', had merely opened the gates of the fort and allowed his enemies to make its faithful defenders prisoners.[10]

The King's logic was inexorable. On the day after Shaftesbury became President of the Council and the 'Mutineer' chiefs took their places at that stately board, the Admiralty also was delivered into new hands. On Monday, April 21st, 1679, a fresh Commission were appointed for executing the office of Lord High Admiral of England. To it were called Sir Henry Capel, Lord Essex's brother, Sir Thomas Lee, Sir Humphrey Winch, Sir Thomas Meres, Edward Vaughan, Edward Hales and a young politician called Daniel Finch, later as Earl of Nottingham to play a leading part in two revolutions. All but one were members of the Opposition and three of them were among Pepys' bitterest enemies. Yet the King retained him as Secretary of the new Board. Here also he showed his grasp of the new political principle which his mind had conceived; for while elasticity was secured by giving the symbols of power to the men of the hour, continuity of control was to be achieved by a permanent Secretariat.[11]

But it was a principle which neither Pepys nor the Opposition chiefs understood. Pepys' own view was that the holy places had been given to the heathen and that he had best depart quickly before worse desolation befell. Two days before the change he had written mournfully to Sir John Holmes of the penniless plight of the Service and the persecution he suffered from its creditors, so much 'that, were the encouragements of my employment tenfold what they are or what the world takes them to be, they should not invite me to hold it one year more upon the terms I have now done it for several unless his Majesty's express commands require it from me, which with bread and water shall render everything sufferable'.

Now nothing but those commands could keep him at Derby House a day longer. For, as he confided in a long letter to the Duke of York, he was charged with the duty of informing those who should inform and were to command him, though accountable for all the failures that might follow his obedience to their commands, however contrary these to his own advice. 'Besides,' he went on, 'however fairly some of these gentlemen seemed disposed towards my continuance in this Secretaryship, yet that compliance of theirs I well know to be grounded upon some opinion they have of the necessariness of my service to them till they had obtained a stock knowledge of their own, and then, Farewell.' With the rest of the new Commissioners he had lived for years in a constant state of war, they censuring and he defending the state of the Navy. How could he work under such men? He therefore begged the Duke to intercede with the King to admit him to the Admiralty Commission or make some other provision for him, as one superannuated in his service and almost blind after twenty years' continuous drudgery.[12]

His triumphant enemies were even less willing that Pepys should continue at his post. One of them, William Harbord, had marked down its emoluments for his own, while Shaftesbury, though Pepys was no longer the means by which he could destroy the Duke, had some old scores to pay. On Monday, April 28th, a Parliamentary Committee was appointed to enquire into the Miscarriages of the Navy.* On the same day, Colonel John Scott, acting on Shaftesbury's secret orders, landed at Folkestone under the name of John Johnson.[13]

On the Committee were gathered Pepys' greatest enemies – Harbord and Bennet, Meres and Sacheverell, and the republican merchants, Player, Papillon, and Peyton. They met for the first time at four o'clock on the same afternoon in the Speaker's Chamber. From such a body Pepys could look for neither mercy nor justice.[14]

---

* . . . 'And Mr Pepys, however prepared, must certainly be destroyed.' Sir R. Southwell to the Duke of Ormonde, April 28th, 1679. *H.M.C. Ormonde* IV, 506.

Next day he received a letter from its chairman, William Harbord, demanding a list of all serving officers and the names of those who had recommended them, an account of all passes issued and a copy of the instructions for the court martial of Captain Roydon, who, it was alleged, had been dismissed for calling his Lieutenant a Papist. Pepys answered by return that there was not an officer in the Navy who had been appointed on his sole recommendation or who had paid him directly or indirectly so much as sixpence, though the fees that he might legitimately have taken for the commissions that had passed through his hands amounted to no less than £15,000. But the Committee cared little what he replied. Already its members were secretly inviting his servants and clerks to visit them.[15]

Meanwhile Colonel Scott was fighting his way past the port authorities. On landing at Folkestone he had been recognized and arrested on a warrant which had been outstanding for his apprehension since the previous autumn. Sent to Dover for examination by the Commissioners of the Passage, he explained that he had been surveying lands in Picardy and Burgundy for the Prince of Condé and that the only reason for his return was a wish to visit his native country. Why he had come secretly in a fishing boat and avoided the ordinary passage he did not explain. But in his trunks were suits of rich apparel worth several hundreds of pounds and a number of maps of English coasts and harbours beautifully fringed with blue silk. And what the Dover authorities did not know, but his tavern acquaintances in Paris did, was that for weeks past he had been preparing these maps and in communication with England through his mysterious friend Benson, alias Wilson, alias Harrington, Lord Shaftesbury's Paris agent, and that he had frequently declared in his cups his hatred of the House of Stuart, his sense of its impending downfall and his determination to be revenged on Pepys for his attempt to get him arrested.[16]

Scott did not remain in Dover gaol. As soon as he was lodged there, he asked with great confidence for pen and paper and wrote a letter to the Earl of Shaftesbury, who as President of the new Council was now virtually head of the Government. Shortly afterwards a mysterious horseman, named Cavendish, arrived to enquire for him, and on learning of his imprisonment, showed signs of uneasiness and rode hastily away. Meanwhile he was visited by the leading Quakers and Nonconformists of the town, one of whom supplied him with money and sat up drinking with him all night. Four days later he was released on an order from the Secretary of State, Henry Coventry. He at once set out for London.[17]

On May 1st Pepys delivered in his reply to William Harbord's letter, answering in full the questions asked by the Committee. At the end of his letter that accompanied it, he announced his intention of resigning. To many he seemed to have no option in the matter: 'Mr Pepys', wrote his friend, Sir Robert Southwell, 'is to be pulled to pieces.' But for nearly three more weeks he fought manfully against the Committee on the one side and his own Admiralty Board on the other. Only when the latter procured from the King a revision of their powers which virtually made them the arbiters of all his work, did he feel he could bear no more and laid down his office.[18]

But his enemies had not finished with him. On May 20th the Committee made its report to the House. The Secretary of the Admiralty Office, Harbord stated, was guilty of Piracy, Popery and Treachery. During the Dutch War he had fraudulently procured a royal grant of the sloop *Hunter* to his friend Anthony Deane and his brother-in-law, Balty St Michel, who had furnished her as a privateer out of government stores and caused her to prey on English shipping and to seize a London ship called the *Catherine* as a prize. He was either a Papist or a most remarkable lover of that religion, for he had not only filled the Navy with the Duke of York's Catholic nominees but kept a tame Jesuit of his own named Morelli. Worst of all, four years before, he had sent to France by Sir Anthony Deane a number of confidential maps of English coasts and harbours with other naval secrets which he had sold to the French King for a vast sum. He was sorry, Harbord added, to say all this of a man with whom he had once lived on terms of friendship.[19]

The benches of the House before which Pepys was thus arraigned were packed with republicans and men who followed the orders of Shaftesbury and the Green Ribbon Club. Outside in the crowded lobby, the professional informers, who had sent Coleman to the gallows, swaggered and whispered to the members who passed in and out of the Chamber. Among them, resplendent in lace and silver, could be seen the tall form and dark, leering countenance of Colonel Scott. An old acquaintance of his, a seal-graver named John Browne, who had known him in his shadier days in Paris, was surprised to see him there and to be greeted by him with a hearty

'Welcome, friend!' A few minutes later Scott was begging him to do his King and country a service by testifying how, in the autumn of 1675, looking through a window, he had seen Sir Anthony Deane give Monsieur Pellissary, the late Treasurer-General of the French Navy, a packet of confidential naval charts and plans. To do so, Scott explained, would not only provide the requisite corroboration to prove Pepys a traitor but make both their fortunes. This, however, Browne refused.[20]

  With an oath that it was all as true as light shined, Scott left his old acquaintance and, shepherded by the great Mr Harbord, swaggered up to the Bar of the House of Commons to tell, as one gentleman to his fellows, what he had seen through the late Monsieur Pellissary's window four years before. Nor was it only through the window. For Monsieur Pellissary, he told his new friends, like all the great men of France, had treated him with the utmost respect and trust, showed him the incriminating papers Deane had brought (each with the Secretary of the Admiralty Office's signature upon it) and told him how the latter was asking £40,000 for these treasures, armed with which the French King could now at any time burn the English Fleet as it lay in harbour. Pepys was a betrayer of his country – an arch-traitor. The House gasped.[21]

  After the Colonel had retired, Harbord rose to introduce a new witness to prove that Pepys was also a concealed Papist – John James the ex-butler, who a year before had been dismissed after being caught by Morelli in bed with his employer's housekeeper. This hopeful young man described to the House how Pepys kept a Portuguese Jesuit in his family called Morelli, with whom every Sunday morning he used to sing psalms after the Romish manner. The pair of them, he said, would often whine out Masses of Morelli's composition in the most mournful manner, and sometimes go away together for a devotional weekend at Pepys' Chelsea villa. At St James' chapel this Morelli was treated with the greatest respect; and when he walked in the Park he always carried a dagger and a pistol in his pocket. His closet, which had a secret door to it in the wall, was full of crucifixes, beads and daggers. As for Pepys, James had often heard him say that there was no chance of naval employment for any man unless he could get himself on the Duke of York's list. And when his Majesty gave anyone a post without his knowledge, this Mr Pepys would puff out his cheeks indignantly and say the King did not know what he did. The last touch was so characteristic, that the House, even in that tense and heated moment, may well have smiled.[22]

These revelations were followed by an angry buzz. One member rose to say that he had just spoken with Mr Oates in the lobby, who had told him that he knew Morelli, who was indeed a Jesuit and deeply concerned in the Plot. Garroway declared that there had been a land-plot and that now they had found a sea-plot, and old Serjeant Maynard, the republican veteran of the Bar, swore that the charge was on a par with that against the Papist Lords in the Tower.[23]

Pepys rose to defend himself. It was a misfortune, he observed, that he had been charged with so many accumulative ills at once, and all by surprise. He would not complain, but he was bound to say that it was strange that no word of this had been spoken before him in Committee. As a member of the Commons and as an Englishman he should have been acquainted with the charges beforehand: he was not aware that the House had intended to set up a secret Committee. As for the accusations themselves, he had never been concerned, directly or indirectly, in the *Hunter*, and he referred the House to his books. Of Colonel Scott, he could only say that he was a complete stranger whom he had never seen before. All he knew of him was that six months before he had had occasion to attempt his arrest at Gravesend under another name, and had subsequently presented the House with his papers, which showed him to be guilty of the very crimes of which he himself was now charged. Since there was no corroboration of his evidence about the sale of the charts, it was a case of this Scott's *Yea by report* against his own *No, before God Almighty.*

As for James' information, he continued, it was of a servant against his master, and that master a member of the House, who had never even been called before the Committee to hear his accusation. The man had been his butler, recommended to him by Sir W. Coventry and Sir R. Mason, and had had the ill-fortune to fall into an amour with his housekeeper. Morelli had caught them together at an unseasonable hour of the night; to be precise three o'clock on a Sunday morning: 'the better the day, the better the deed'. For this he had turned him away; later, having reason to suspect him of robbing his house, he had procured a warrant from Sir Edmund Berry Godfrey for his arrest. The Morelli of whom James had spoken was a harmless musician and a man of learning, whom he had taken into his household because his own business never permitted him to go abroad for diversion. He was a close scholar and perhaps the greatest master of music in England; he had come to him through a Protestant merchant from Lisbon, where he was thought so mild a Catholic that he had fallen under suspicion of the Inquisition. And it was a lie that he had ever spent a night with him at his Chelsea villa; if he was proved to have done so, and if he was not the most harmless and virtuous of creatures, he prayed the House never to believe him again.

Deane's defence was equally a denial of all that had been charged against him. He admitted that he had had an eighth share of the *Hunter* privateer, but had never received a penny profit from it, having been swindled by its Captain who brought the accusation. And if any act of piracy had been committed by the ship, it was entirely on account of the Captain; in any case the matter had been before the King and Council and had been discharged there. As to Scott's accusations, he had never conversed directly with a single Frenchman during his whole visit to France, for he could not speak one word of the language.[24]

All this availed Pepys and Deane nothing, for it had been decreed that they should fall, and the Party discipline of their enemies was rigid. Sacheverell and Harbord were inexorable: Pepys was an ill man and they would prove him so. A few like Sir William Coventry, who got up to say that James had been none too trustworthy while in his service, did their best to break the fall, but the republicans were like a pack of hounds in cry.

Poor Pepys was driven to his feet again by Sir Francis Rolle, one of Scott's correspondents, who sneered – one can hear the mocking laughter – at his domestic mischances; 'very unfortunate in his servants; one accused to be in the Plot, another, his best maid found in bed with his butler, another accused to be a Jesuit: very unfortunate'. Pepys admitted he had been unlucky in his domestics: but that surely was no crime. But Harbord and Garroway and Sacheverell rose in turn to assert that it was and to tell the House how fine a witness this Colonel Scott was – the ablest man in all England for a West India voyage and one who had been the intimate friend of the great De Witt and had commanded eight regiments in Holland. It was moved that Pepys and Deane should be taken into the custody of the Serjeant-at-arms until the matter could be examined.[25]

On May 22nd, the very day that the Bill to exclude the Duke of York from the succession passed the House, the two unhappy men were brought back to hear the charges against them repeated. There was little sympathy for them in the House, though a minority of moderate members, true to the enduring habit of England, felt ashamed at the kind of witnesses procured to bring them down.* They were committed to the Tower under the Speaker's Warrant and Mr Harbord was requested to acquaint the Attorney-General with the evidence against them that they might be prosecuted. There was no cause of commitment expressed in the Warrant.[26]

On the same day the Duke of York, responding to Pepys' letter of May 6th, wrote from Brussels to the King on behalf of his old servant of the Admiralty. 'Give me leave to say, your Majesty is bound to do something for him that has spent so many years in your service to your satisfaction.' But for the moment neither the King nor any other man could help Samuel Pepys, for he was held by a power greater than that of any prince – the 'mighty terrible Parliament' which in his proud integrity he had dared to defy. Yet though the iron gates of the mournful old fortress clanged behind him and though his former clerk, the humble, time-serving Tom Hayter – for the King would have none of Harbord – took possession of his office, Pepys' achievement of five years remained. He left at sea seventy-six English ships of war and twelve thousand men in pay, and a finer Fleet than any England had ever yet possessed in peace-time. It was to be left to his successors to bring it once more to the verge of ruin. That night the roadway beneath the windows of the Green Ribbon Club was lit by a triumphant bonfire.[27]

---

* 'They are neither my favourites, and I believe them not wholly innocent, but yet in these particulars they will fare the better rather than the worse from the warmth of the prosecution, and that their offences are magnified beyond a due proportion.' Sir John Hobart, MP, to William Windham, May 20th, 1679. *H.M.C. Ketton*, 184. A few days before the Secretary of the English Embassy at Paris had written to Henry Coventry of the indignation with which Scott's visit to England was spoken of there. *H.M.C.* Rep. 4 (Bath, 244).

Prisoner of State

'Cases in those days were carried by huzzahs instead of votes, and bear-garden law was all many an honest man had to trust to for the liberty of the subject.' Sir R. L'Estrange, *Brief History*, Part III, 110.

Four days of silence elapsed. Then the old fighting spirit awoke, and Samuel Pepys from his cell in the Tower addressed himself to the task of re-establishing himself in the eyes of mankind. On the very day that the King, declaring that he would no longer endure the House of Commons, prorogued Parliament, Pepys addressed himself to two old acquaintances at Paris, fat Harry Savile, the English Ambassador, and John Brisbane, the Secretary of the Embassy, for particulars of Scott's past life. 'It is with as much unwillingness as surprise that I find myself driven to give you this trouble,' he wrote, 'but without any apprehension of your begrudging me the pain of it when I tell you that they who occasion it aim at no lower mischief than what concerns my life.'*[1]

That was the beginning of Pepys' long campaign to discover and publish the truth about his accuser, begun at a time when he was a prisoner awaiting trial for his life and when Judges and Juries were still reflecting the national terror of Popery and his enemies felt certain of him. Dining on the King's birthday at Lord Grey's in Essex a company of republicans laid bets that he and Deane would be dead before the year's end. But the gentle Morelli, writing from his rustic lodging at Brentwood, to give thanks for a gift of five guineas, expressed his belief that his innocence would speak for him and that the storm raised by those who wished his destruction would be dispersed to their own confusion. He was ready, he said, to give his life to save him. A few days later he sent him some music for the flute and guitar.[2]

* S. Pepys to H. Savile, May 26th, 1679. *Rawl. MSS. A.* 194, ff. 1–2. This large volume containing many hundreds of Pepys' private letters sent out between 1679 and 1683 has been curiously little used, though it is probably the most important of his letter-books extant.

With a method and industry that was now automatic, Pepys did what he could to put his broken affairs in order. He surrendered the lease of his little summer-house at Parson's Green to Colonel Norwood, that he might 'be at ease to bestow it upon somebody more fortunate in his liberty of enjoying it', and borrowed £100 to meet his legal and prison fees. Then he sent out letters to all his friends and took the advice of his solicitor, Mr Hayes, and stout, jovial Mr Saunders, the great royalist barrister, the honestest and best-natured fellow in England.[3]

On the last two days of May Pepys and Deane appeared under custody of the Lieutenant of the Tower in the Court of King's Bench to desire their discharge on their own Writ of Habeas Corpus. The Act that gave them that right had been the one achievement of that otherwise most barren of Parliaments. No cause had been assigned in the Speaker's Warrant for their commitment, and the House that had imprisoned them was prorogued. In the Attorney-General's absence, the Solicitor-General stated that he had as yet received no information from Harbord against the prisoners and demanded that they should be sent back to the Tower. This the Court, contrary to law, but in obedience to the party that had passed the Bill, ordered. For the Habeas Corpus Act was not intended to apply to Tories, and the first two men to demand its protection were promptly denied it.

On Monday, June 2nd, the last day of term, Pepys and Deane were again brought into Court to hear the evidence of Scott, James and Captain Moone of the *Hunter*. Once again, when they asked for immediate trial or bail they were refused, the Attorney-General confessing that, though he had two witnesses to prove Sir Anthony's felony and piracy, he had only one for the major charge of Treason – enough, he argued, for a further commitment, but not enough to prove the crime. He would endeavour to get further evidence before the next term began on June 20th. On such grounds Pepys was taken back to the Tower.[4]

But Sir John Bankes waited in Westminster Hall to bid him God Speed as his gaolers led him away, and kind Mr Houblon and Mr Evelyn visited him among the lions and Popish Lords who shared his captivity, and the King himself sent him a fat buck out of his forest of Enfield Chase. For Pepys, though the mob might howl for his blood, had friends who knew his worth. Even the timorous Hayter came to see him. And no one who really knew him doubted his innocence for a moment. 'I hope 'ere this comes to your hands', wrote Colonel Norwood, 'you will have weathered that storm which Satan Scott has so unskilfully conjured to alarm you, and I make no doubt but your virtues will improve this affliction to your spiritual as well as your secular advantage.'[5]

To find the chink in Satan Scott's armour, letter after letter now passed out of the Tower through James Houblon's trusty hands to Pepys' friends. In Paris the Ambassador and his Secretary were driven half frantic by the long stream of correspondence, usually duplicated to defeat the vagaries of the post, which came to them asking for particulars about Scott and demanding, in the name of justice, that the Marquis de Seignelay and the heirs of Monsieur Pellissary should be asked to make a public denial of their ever receiving State documents at his hands. The Duke of York and his Secretary, Sir John Werden, in Brussels, Sir Robert Southwell's and James Houblon's acquaintances in Holland and Sir John Copplestone's in France were all bombarded with enquiring letters. Even Sir Ellis Leighton was indirectly approached and, though unwilling to appear publicly against Scott, gave Pepys' friends to understand that he would help him to proofs of his infamy. Possibly the Colonel's flight of the previous autumn after Godfrey's murder still rankled with some of his old associates.

To lay bare 'any part of the legend of this fellow's life', and obtain 'pregnant witnesses' to prove his villainies before the Courts, became for a time Pepys' whole existence. Even his eyes were forgotten in his eager search, till the strain on them became too severe to ignore any longer and he was forced to employ another's hand. And of all the letters that he now wrote or dictated on his own behalf, Pepys took copies and had them entered in a vast letter-book. Thus the methods of the Admiralty were carried into civil life.[6]

Within a few weeks of Pepys' first imprisonment, the outlines of Scott's career and past character began to take shape. 'A fellow who I thank God is not of my acquaintance', Harry Savile reported him, 'but is of so despicable a vile reputation in all places where he has lived that a real criminal would be very unfortunate to suffer by his means.' Mr Brisbane was able to report that he had manufactured maps and sold them fraudulently, and a Mr James Puckle wrote obligingly from Flanders with lurid particulars of his career in that country. But there was some difficulty about the Marquis de

Seignelay, whom the Paris Embassy seemed reluctant to approach for that flat denial of all knowledge of the matter which Pepys desired of him; in any case, Brisbane pointed out, it could do no good, since, the Marquis being a Frenchman and a Catholic, no one in England would believe him. But Pepys was insistent and continued to urge that a direct approach should be made to the old aristocrat.[7]

The chief agent in Pepys' attempt to track down Scott's villainies and his intrigues in France was Balty. A short while before his resignation from the Admiralty Pepys had procured for his brother-in-law the post of Agent General for the Affairs of the Navy at Tangier. Now he obtained from the King special leave for him to postpone his departure for the Mediterranean in order to conduct enquiries into Scott's past at Paris. Thither Balty set out in the middle of June, while Samuel still lay in the Tower, with strict injunctions to obtain written depositions from as many of the Colonel's old associates as possible, to avoid hearsay and to take the advice of Mr Brisbane in all things. Above all he was to be careful to keep down expenses – 'knowing how many ways of charge a business of this kind, which relates to so many countries must lead a man into' – and to be wary of making any offers that might give his opponents a chance of accusing him of subornation.[8]

Of his ability to vindicate his own innocence, Pepys did not doubt, for God would surely help him who helped himself. His conscience was clear. He had been accused, he wrote to the Duke of York, of Popery, Felony, Piracy and Treason, 'but so grounded as to render it hard for me to tell your Highness which of the two enjoys the greater pleasure, whether Mr Harbord in public from the contemplation of the conquest his malice has obtained over me, or I in private from what my innocence tells me I shall some time or other (if any justice may be hoped for) obtain against him'. The spirit in which he now faced the world was a proud one, too proud almost had it not been so loyal and staunch. Even that Protestantism, he told the exiled Duke, of which the world thought so doubtfully, only increased his gratitude to his old patron, who should have it, he assured him, to the last point of his life and fortune.[9]

On Friday, June 20th, the first day of Trinity Term, on the Attorney-General's declaring that he was not yet ready with the evidence against them, Pepys and Deane were at their own desire discharged from the Tower and re-committed to the Marshalsea in Southwark. Thus they were removed out of the power of an irresponsible Parliamentary Party into that of the Common Law. Though the Marshalsea was a far less comfortable place than the aristocratic Tower, the change was lightened for Pepys by his old acquaintance Mr Cooling, the Lord Chamberlain's Secretary, who wrote to his cousin, the Marshal of the prison, to do whatever he could to make him easy in his situation. And good Mr Houblon was as regular in his charitable pilgrimages across the Bridge to Southwark as he had been to the Tower.[10]

But though Pepys worked hard for a trial, sparing no expense to procure witnesses and attestations in Paris, The Hague, and Brussels, such as proved his accuser 'a very rogue', no trial came. For Harbord and his friends had over-reached themselves; and the blustering Attorney-General took fright as he realized how vulnerable was the reputation of such a witness as Scott in the hands of anyone as energetic and courageous as the late Secretary of the Admiralty Office.

For Pepys showed not the least fear of his accuser. When one of the witnesses he was bringing over from Holland expressed her terror of being assassinated, he wrote to Sir Robert Southwell: 'you may please to let her know that Mr Scott's way of doing mischief has been as little famous for his execution by deeds as it is truly notorious for the numberless injuries he has done by the falseness of his words and oaths'.* In this, as the sequel was to show, he was underestimating his villainy. But for the moment, thoroughly alarmed by the enquiries Pepys was making, Scott had little wish to come into the open. He had just tried on the Government a cock-and-bull story of a confession about the Popish Plot, which he swore had been made to him by the Catholic Earl of Berkshire on his deathbed in Paris,† but its reception had not been a success, and his nerve was badly shaken.[11]

---

* S. Pepys to Sir R. Southwell, June 24th, 1679. *Rawl. MSS. A.* 194, f. 17.

† Mr Pollock, in his brilliant classic on the Popish Plot, solemnly supports his thesis of the existence of a real Catholic Plot on the apparent honesty and disinterestedness of Scott as a witness. (See Pollock, *Popish Plot*, pp. 61–4.) Thus has the history of England in the later seventeenth century been written. For Colonel Roper's indignation and repudiation of Scott's lie about Lord Berkshire, see *Pepysian MSS., Mornamont* I, 26–8.

Yet as Wednesday, July 9th, the last day of Trinity Term, drew near, Scott, urged by his paymasters, made one final attempt to secure the additional witnesses needed to prove his charge of treason against Pepys. Approaching a London tradesman named John Harrison, who had been one of his gun-casting gang in France in 1675, he asked him to join him in swearing that he had seen Deane deliver Pepys' packet of plans to the French naval authorities: a taking thing, he called it, and one that would prove greatly to both their advantages. But Harrison, knowing the tempter of old, refused to believe his promises, and Scott was forced to content himself with the affidavit of a Houndsditch ironfounder who swore that two years before he had heard him declare that he had been invited by Coniers, the Jesuit, to carry over naval secrets on behalf of Pepys to France.

This ridiculous piece of hearsay was sprung on the defence in Court on July 9th, the Attorney-General endeavouring to make it a ground for defeating the prisoners' plea for bail. But on Pepys' demanding to have the matter tried, the prosecution was at a stand, despite Scott's assertion that he had been solicited by at least twenty persons (whose names he had forgotten) to be friends with Pepys. After a vain attempt had been made to prove Pepys guilty of breaking custody, because some days before he had been taken on a royal warrant to Whitehall to speak with the King, the Court yielded to the prisoners' demand for bail. Although the Attorney-General muttered angrily that Mr Pepys' eloquence would be more seasonable at his trial, Lord Chief Justice Scroggs observed boldly that Pepys and Deane should have the right of Englishmen. Indeed, when Sir William Jones' back was turned, he remarked to his colleagues that let the cause come whence it would, he would see right done, adding with rising indignation, 'They think to impose any story upon us and would fox us with Informations; for my part I am ashamed of it'.[12]

So Pepys escaped spending the hot days of the Long Vacation in confinement and was admitted to bail in £30,000, £10,000 on his own surety and £5000 apiece on that of four generous friends, Sir Richard Dutton, James Houblon, Sir Thomas Beckford the slop-seller and Mr Pallavicini. Deane was also released in the same bail. The republicans were furious and retaliated by setting the mob singing a ballad which ran:

Since Scroggs for Pepys and Deane took bail,
And on the Good Cause did turn his tail –
For £2000 to buy beef and ale,
    Which nobody can deny.
Our Juries and Judges to shame the Plot
Have traitors freed to prove it not,
But England shall stand when they go to pot,
    Which nobody can deny.

And when the Lord Chief Justice ventured to drive through the City a dead dog with a halter round its neck was thrown through the window of his coach.[13]

Pepys was now free to pursue his enquiries about Scott's past in the comfortable seclusion of Will Hewer's fine new house in York Buildings. Here, at the south-west end of Buckingham Street, overlooking the river and Inigo Jones' beautiful water-gate, he took up his residence at the entreaty of his devoted clerk and friend. From him, the fallen Secretary of the Admiralty Office, driven from his paradise at Derby House, received, as he told Balty, 'all the care, kindness and faithfulness of a son . . . for which God reward him if I cannot'. And here, save for a fleeting August visit to Sir Timothy Tyrrell at Shotover Park in Oxfordshire to secure further evidence against Scott, he spent the remaining summer months in seclusion, withdrawn from the long pressure of public affairs. Even an invitation from his faithful constituents at Harwich to stand again for the new Parliament he refused, though he so far interested himself in the election as to use his influence again on behalf of Sir John Bankes at Rochester. To Henry Shere in Tangier he wrote of the uninterrupted torrent of 'business and oppression' to which he had been for so many months subjected, and of 'the common errors of this depraved age wherein faithfulness and uninterested diligence in office are virtues so rarely found and little esteemed as to expose the professors of them to the censure of their friends for folly . . . and to be ranked by their enemies in the common list of knaves. Happy therefore', he added, 'he whose philosophy has strength enough to digest such usage. And such, I thank God, is in some degree mine'.[14]

He was to need it. For his foes, after an abortive attempt to kidnap Will Hewer at Hyde Park Corner, struck at Pepys in his most sensitive spot – that honourable outward appearance which he so loved to display to the world. At the end of August, following a serious illness of the King's, Pepys hurried down to Windsor to wait on him and subsequently attended the Duke of York, who had also hastened to his brother's bedside, during his brief return to England. This show of loyalty his enemies were quick to use against him. In the second week of September a scurrilous news-sheet which Lord Shaftesbury had set up that summer on the lapsing of the Printing Act contained a notice that he had been publicly rebuked by the Lord Chamberlain for trying to enter the Presence while still uncleared of an impeachment for High Treason, and that subsequently on worming his way into the King's bedchamber he had been met with an angry frown and a view of the royal back. This Pepys refused to take lying down and, obtaining a warrant for the arrest of the editor and printer for a scandalous and infamous libel, forced them to eat their words in the next issue.[15]

But the republican leaders had other shafts tipped with venom with which to pierce Pepys' armour. From his ex-butler, John James, retained at ten shillings a week by Harbord and deluded and flattered by the Duke of Buckingham and other great men with offers of public employment, they obtained a scurrilous account of Pepys' personal and financial activities. James was ready enough to supply it, for, besides having a personal grievance against his old master, he was faced by the unpleasant fact that Pepys was telling everyone how perjured his evidence had been and how it had been suborned by Harbord – 'bespattering and spitting out his venom against me', as the aggrieved butler put it, 'and basely reflecting upon that worthy gentleman as if he had been a person that had hired me to testify against him'. He therefore poured out his soul in a long hysterical document about his former master and his clerk 'Dark Lanthorn Hewer' (a confused but effective suggestion of the lantern by which the inspired vision of Bedloe had beheld Samuel Atkins standing over Godfrey's body) and made much, after the manner of his kind, of Pepys' lowly origin. 'I hope', he wrote, 'this tailor-like person with his hypocritical design and his Judas-like face may be a warning not to trust one of so poor a descent, so puffed up with pride through the advantages of his preferment, which swells him more than the wind colic with which he is sometimes troubled.'*[16]

* *Rawl. MSS. A*. 173, f. 178.

This rather puerile document of poor James' was handed over by Colonel Mansell, the most infamous of all Shaftesbury's secret agents, to 'Elephant' Smith. In the hands of the first pamphleteer of the age its infantile malice was transmuted into an imaginary and highly damaging dialogue between Pepys and his head clerk. Named by Mansell himself *Plain Truth or Closet Discourse Betwixt P. and H.* it was published by the republican Benjamin Harris, a few days before the opening of the Michaelmas Term, and was nicely calculated to prejudice any trial its victim might secure.[17]

This sprightly little dialogue opened with Pepys and Hewer discussing the financial advantages that would accrue to them if they procured an Order of Council for an embargo on all ships under pretence of a threatened war with France and by then issuing passes of exemption at exorbitant fees to merchants. Throughout its eight pages Pepys appears as a self-righteous pundit accepting with nicely-veiled astonishment and delight the worldly and corrupt suggestions of his clerk.

P. But H., which way shall we go to work upon this to get an Order of Council for an Embargo upon all ships?
H. O God, Sir, easily.
P. But how?
H. Sir, you know that in anything that you will propose to the Commissioners of the Navy for their assistance they will be ready to serve you; and you joining together may find reasons to the Council of the necessity there is for it.
P. The Commissioners of the Navy shall dine with me tomorrow; and then we'll agree together how we shall do it, and of our reasons for the necessity of it.
H. That's very well, and gad, Sir, I am very glad of it, for if it holds but two months, we shall get six or seven thousand pounds by it.
P. But how, H.?
H. I'll tell you, Sir. There is not one ship or coaster whatsoever to stir out but what must come hither for a Permission and Protection and must pay what rates we please . . .

Having introduced the entranced reader to Pepys' and Hewer's secret councils, the pamphlet went on to show their peculiar and villainous methods of collaboration:

P. . . . But now, as to the business, how to make the best advantage to ourselves of all sea-employs and that the world may not take any notice of me.

H. I'll tell you; leave it to me to take money for any employ, and you shall not need to take any notice of it that it comes within your knowledge.

P. But what if I should be charged with the doing of it?

H. Sir, that cannot be; because you do not do it, but I do it for you: therefore you may easily clear yourself from all such scandals, and for myself I'll handle them so that it shall never be found out, I'll warrant you.

P. Well, H., I'll trust to thy management of it.

H. Sir, you know I have never failed hitherto in my management of your affairs . . .

P. I thank thee, good H. It was strangely our good fortune that we ever met together. (Then they hug and kiss one another.)

One by one, and with exquisite malicious wit, every one of Pepys' cherished administrative virtues was misrepresented and turned to wickedness: his integrity, his care for English mercantile interests, his zeal for established routine. Thus the rule he had tried to establish for regular promotion by seniority instead of favour, was shown to be merely a clever devise for making money:

H. Sir, there is a Boatswain of a First-rate ship is dead.

P. Is there so? Of what ship?

H. The *Royal* – . Now, Sir, as to this vacancy; if you please to give me leave, we will put a Boatswain of a Second-rate into her; into that a Boatswain of a Third; and into that Third a Boatswain of the Fourth-rate; into the Fourth-rate a Boatswain of the Fifth-rate; so that all these shall be advanced; and the Fifth-rate shall be a clear vacancy. So that none of them but will be willing for preferment to give me five or ten guineas, and as much to put a new Boatswain into the Fifth-rate. And this amounts to money and makes no notice at all.

P. I thank thee, good H., I protest so it does; and thus we may run through all the Boatswains' and Gunners,' Carpenters' and Cooks' employs; which will be considerable in the year, and much more if there comes a rot amongst them. But for the Pursers I hope you intend to manage them at a better rate than this.

H. O God, Sir, yes, yes.

The sale of Dockyard appointments, the fraudulent purchase of foreign timber, the misappropriation by Pepys and Deane of the balances of the parliamentary grants for the new ships, all were alleged. Even Pepys' care for the Chatham Chest was vilified:

H. Sir, there is one thing more. You do not imagine what the twelve pences amount to in a year that we squeeze out of the cripples for their orders for renewing their pensions.

P. No, prithee, what may they come to?

H. Sir, there is about 6000 of them, which at 12*d*. an Order for each man amounts to above three hundred pounds a year.

P. Poor men! who would think there were so much to be gotten out of them. But it is very well, dear H.; nothing shall ever part us but death.

At the close the two friends are seen taking a social glass together:

H. Sir, I will take my leave of you till to-morrow morning.

P. No, prithee, H., stay, and let's drink a glass of sherry.

H. Thank you, Sir.

P. Give me thy hand, honest H.; here's to all our friends.

H. Sir, Your most humble servant.*[18]

This appetizing morsel was served up to the public on October 13th. Next day James Houblon wrote sorrowfully to its victim to condole with him: 'I see the malice of your enemies increases. God forgive them for that villainous paper published yesterday. If they call the master Beelzebub, they will not spare them of the household. You will make that religious use, no doubt, you ought to make of such kind of dispensation, which must be borne with Christian and manlike patience and submission.'† Pepys did so, though he admitted that his philosophy had never been under such a strain, for the cruel, mocking slander pierced deep. He comforted himself with the thought that he would not suffer in the esteem of the few whose opinion he valued most and went round to Mr Houblon's to hear what one of his Antwerp correspondents had to report about the past life of that 'villain' Scott. For the new Term was due to open on October 23rd and from four countries Pepys was still receiving almost daily accounts of his accuser's misdeeds.[19]

It was a strange and bewildering miscellany of information that for the past three months had poured in on him. For instance at the end of July a young clergyman whom he had befriended – with 'favours so undeserved that the thought of them might almost make my ink to blush' – informed him of a chance meeting in a Thames Street coffee-house with a certain Colonel Thornbury, a well-known citizen who had formerly resided in the West Indies. On being asked if while there he had known Scott, Thornbury had replied that he

* J. R. Tanner's MSS. Notes. Its publication is dated by James Houblon's letter to S. Pepys of Oct. 14th, 1679 (*Rawl. MSS. A.* 173, f. 18), and Pepys' reply of the same date (*Rawl. MSS. A.* 194, ff. 86v.–7).

† J. Houblon to S. Pepys, Oct. 14th, 1679. *Rawl. MSS. A.* 173, f. 18.

had and as 'an arrant coward and a great knave' and one who had been reprieved from the gallows with a rope round his neck.

It was all valuable. 'Such is the credulity of this unhappy age', Pepys wrote to Balty, 'that no accumulation of evidence can be too much to support the most obvious truth.' He therefore treasured a paper that his old neighbour of Derby House, Colonel Edward Sackville, sent him about Scott's American career, and the curious information supplied by Captain Dyer, a naval captain then about to sail for the Plantations, about Scott's deserted wife, in Long Island.* From Holland other correspondents produced tales of his accuser's diverse ill-doings – his interception of Ambassador Downing's letters, his infamous desertion of the States' service, his bigamous marriage, his theft of plates from Carr's *Map of English Roads* and subsequent sale of them as his own to Sir William Temple.[20]

The greater part of Pepys' evidence came from France, collected by Balty and canvassed in his own unceasing correspondence. His attempts to obtain a denial from the Marquis de Seignelay that he had corresponded with him were at first hampered by the old gentleman's memory, which confused him hazily with his predecessor Wren. In the end, after much hesitation, caused by deference to the Marquis' aristocratic quality,† and a great deal of consultation with Brisbane, who was plainly becoming rather bored by the whole affair, Pepys wrote direct to the Marquis, not so much in any hope that the word of a French Catholic Minister of State would in any way aid his defence in an English Court of Law as with the desire to clear himself of any doubts of his loyalty that might remain in King Charles' mind, 'whose good thoughts of me', he told Balty, 'I had rather die under than live to have the good opinion of the rabble purchased by one ill deed or thought'. The letter, which was in his best French, brought a courteous and entirely satisfactory answer.[21]

Meanwhile, through a little group of Parisian merchants to whom James Houblon had given him introductions, Pepys obtained attestations, formally witnessed by French magistrates, from all those

---

* It appeared that the lady, whose maiden name was Reyner, was living at Southampton, Long Island, with another man, having had neither news nor support from Scott for many years, while his old mother, miserably poor, lived upon the support of the people of Cornbury, New York. *Rawl. MSS. A*. 175, ff. 77–9.

† '. . . his Quality being such as requires his being treated with all respect.' S. Pepys to B. St Michel, Aug. 7th, 1679. *Rawl. MSS. A*. 194, ff. 35–6.

with whom Scott had accused him of being concerned. From these it
appeared that the Sieur de Pellissary and De La Priogery, the two
deceased officers of the French Navy who according to Scott had
been most intimately associated with Pepys and Deane in their
treacherous anti-Protestant designs, were both Protestants and were
never engaged in the particular branches of the naval service in
which Scott's story had placed them. And Pellissary's widow and his
servants gave their testimony that it was a lie that Scott had been
present on the day in August 1675 when Deane dined with him.[22]

Yet there were many difficulties in the way of proving all this in an
English Court of Law. For one thing, as his Counsel warned Pepys,
the Law would not admit written evidence, however carefully
attested, from living witnesses, but required them to appear in
person and be subjected to cross-examination. For another the
testimony of a Catholic, of whatever integrity and reputation, was
likely to do more harm than good. 'A Popish witness', Pepys told
Balty, 'were enough to prejudice the justest cause in the world.'
Most of the French witnesses whom Houblon's friend, good Monsieur Trenchepain, the merchant, collected, were Catholics, while
some of the English were Benedictines from whom Scott had tried to
borrow £500 on the security of his charts of the English coast. Their
very presence in Court would have been fatal.[23]

All this was proving terribly expensive, at a time when Pepys'
affairs were already dangerously embarrassed. His enemies, who
still had a partial control of the Government, were now questioning
his past Tangier accounts. He was even for a time, till he could see
where he stood, reduced to doing without an amanuensis. His
friends and relations, he warned Balty, must be prepared to share
with him the change in his own fortune, though he hoped the King's
justice and goodness would enable him in some way or other to
make a modest provision for him and his family. And he again
warned him to be a careful husband of the money allowed him for
his researches; 'those infinite expenses which this fellow's villainy
puts me to, in my enquiries through so many nations after him,
makes me earnest in my caution to you about it'.* Pepys' confidence
in his brother-in-law's economy was not increased by the reckless
way in which that optimistic being was conducting his own private

---

* S. Pepys to B. St Michel, July 17th, 1679. *Rawl. MSS. A.* 194, f. 31.

affairs. At this moment Balty announced his intention of bringing back to England a French tutor for his small son – 'the uttermost circumstance of greatness', Pepys commented, 'that Sir John Bankes or any man of £5000 or 6000 p.a. can enter upon'.[24]

Yet Balty paid for his keep. For once his optimism was an asset, for in tracking down his benefactor's accuser he was ready to follow any and every clue with the utmost enthusiasm. And within little over a month of his reaching Paris he had lighted on a very happy one – an English watchmaker named John Joyne at whose house Scott had lodged. It appeared that the Colonel had left owing forty pistoles, and Joyne was therefore only too delighted to tell Pepys' friends all he knew about him. As he had begun his association with Scott four years before in his gun-casting and copper-blanching operations this was a good deal. Through his help Balty became acquainted with a whole nest of scoundrels, all of whom the Colonel appeared to have left, in a greater or lesser measure, the worse off for his acquaintance.[25]

The first of Scott's friends thus brought to Balty's notice was a gentleman of the name of Sherwin, who like Joyne was full of lively recollections of the old days when they had worked in the same gang. It was from him that Pepys learnt that, in the month when Deane was accused of being seen by Scott delivering the charts to Monsieur Pellissary, the Colonel was at Nevers attempting to cast cannon. He had also more recent memories, for during the past winter he had heard him say that 'the King and all his family came from nothing but whoredom and witchcraft with many other base expressions'. Another of his acquaintances, a debauched young English exile of good family of the name of Foster, had not only seen Scott packing up his maps of England in the spring of 1679 but had heard him announce in his cups that he was going over to accuse Pepys and Deane on behalf of some great Lord or Duke, with an oath that he was heartily glad of a chance to revenge himself on the rogue who had tried to have him arrested as a Jesuit.

It turned out there was a drawback to both those witnesses, Sherwin because he expected to be paid for his revelations and Foster because, though willing enough to talk in private, he showed an inexplicable distaste to giving any sort of public testimony. Pepys tried to overcome this reluctance by approaching the young man's relations in England, Lady Pratt and Sir Timothy Tyrrell, but it was soon clear that behind, and in some way threatening, Foster were far more influential folk than these. Vaguely Pepys began to be made aware of their presence behind the world of needy adventurers he was exploring and to realize that he might stumble inadvertently on something he would be exceedingly unwise to discover. It was becoming necessary to proceed very carefully.[26]

Pepys warned Balty. It was good, he told him, that he had found so many witnesses, and he must not suppose him 'wholly without reflections of the Providence of God Almighty in my meeting with so large and easy a concurrence of testimonies of all sorts towards evincing the truth'. Certainly every word that could be obtained of Scott's past conversations was valuable, 'for against a liar the best defence in the world is to obtain the most you can of his discourse because, let his memory be never so good, if he gives himself the liberty of talking much he cannot avoid discovering himself'.* But, in view of the strictness of the law, the perfidy of his adversary and the public prejudice he lay under, he must be careful to avoid hearsay and exceedingly slow to believe what he wished to be true.† For his cause, if it were not to miscarry, must be supported in every tiny particular by first-hand evidence that would bear the test of cross-examination. As for Sherwin's demand for money, however reasonable it might seem, it was almost certain to be misconstrued, and might prove a trap, 'it being', Pepys wrote, 'not enough in this age and the company I am fallen into, to have the innocency of a Dove without some mixture of the serpent's prudence'.[27]

Doubting Balty's discretion, Pepys took into his confidence a worthy French merchant living in Long Acre named Denise who was both a Protestant and well acquainted with the leading figures in the French Court and Navy. In the middle of September he sent him to Paris to take attestations from the witnesses whom Balty had collected. Balty was greatly hurt at this want of confidence and complained that his brother-in-law did not even read his letters. 'As to your desiring me to read your letters all over,' Pepys replied, 'as long as they are for the most part and so ill as the condition of my eyes is, I have not spared to read every one of them myself over and

---

* S. Pepys to B. St Michel, Aug. 18th, 1679. *Rawl. MSS. A.* 194, ff. 42v.–44.

† 'And therefore, by the way, pray learn of me this one lesson . . . to be most slow to believe what we most wish should be true.' S. Pepys to B. St Michel, Oct 9th, 1679. *Rawl. MSS. A.* 194, ff. 80–1.

over, and with extraordinary content (I assure you), every one of them but this, which I wish with all my heart you had forborne.' For in the game of mutual reproach neither Balty nor anyone else living was a match for Samuel Pepys.[28]

Yet on the whole he was pleased with Balty, and particularly in his discovery of John Joyne, the watchmaker. 'Cherish your acquaintanceship with Mr Joyne,'* he told him, ' . . . I cannot express the content I have in the fullness of his report and the ingenuity of his giving it, upon the only consideration of doing right to the innocence of one man against the wrong done it by another whom he knows to be a villain.' Here, he pointed out, was a humble man who without private interest or temptation, but merely out of a love of justice, was ready to come into England to witness the truth. And in his enthusiasm at the spectacle of disinterestedness so singular and so providential Pepys overlooked the fact that Joyne, on his own admission, had shared in Scott's crimes. He wrote to him in his own hand to acknowledge his obligations.[29]

To Joyne also he sent a long list of the points on which he would be informed: the date on which Scott had left Nevers for Paris in 1675, whether he had revisited England between his flight from Gravesend in the October of 1678 and his return to accuse Pepys in the spring of 1679, and the links in the mysterious chain which bound Scott to Sir Ellis Leighton and Sir Robert Welsh, and them to the Duke of Buckingham. His accuser's association with the great men who rode the storms of revolution was every day becoming clearer.[30]

Yet Pepys remained serenely confident. 'I thank God', he told his father, 'I have always carried with me such a watchfulness and integrity as will support me against anything that the Malice of Mankind can offer to my prejudice.' Those who look powers in the face may be destroyed but they cannot be discouraged. And though Pepys was kept almost as busy by his vast correspondence as he had been in former days at the Admiralty, he still contrived to enjoy his friends and take an interest in their affairs. When Sir John Bankes' son was ill he was ready with a remedy, and when an acquaintance of Sir George Carteret's wanted to buy a barge, he entered into the

---

* Many years later Pepys was to deny this (see *P.R.O. Chancery Proceedings, Mitford* C.8, 376, No. 69), but at the time, as his correspondence in *Rawl. MSS. A.* 194 shows, he was delighted at the help Joyne offered him.

details of its purchase with as much enthusiasm as if it had been for himself. He had found, he wrote, at Mr Graves', the King's Bargemaster, one of six oars, 'a brave bold boat, which he had made for my Lord Treasurer before his late difficulties' (he was now in the Tower) 'and so now lies upon his hands finished in every respect but painting. She is very neatly furnished, as to carving, but not gaudy'. Under the circumstances Mr Graves would probably knock ten or twenty pounds off the price.

There was even a little time for music, and perhaps in that sad and anxious season it was the best thing life had to offer: 'for the little knowledge in music which I have never was of more use to me than it is now, under the molestations of mind which I have at this time more than ordinary to contend with'. So the fallen magnate wrote to Morelli, who constantly corresponded with him from his rustic habitation at Brentwood and sent him a table he had made for the guitar. Pepys got his musician to transcribe a sheaf of pieces that he might play, giving him many elaborate directions as to size and margins – that each page should end with a quatrain so that the singer should not need to turn the leaf in the middle of the passage and that it should be writ large in letter and note for the ease of his eyes. He asked for *The World's a bubble, No, no, 'tis in vain, Laudate Dominum* and a new English anthem by Dr Blow, the Master of the King's Music; he would have Morelli be as quick as possible, for he had nothing left to practise on but the Lamentations of Jeremiah.[31]

The new Term was due to begin on October 23rd. For some weeks before, Pepys' witnesses poured into England. Sherwin came uninvited, but made up for it by introducing Pepys to two of Scott's old gun-casting gang now living in London, Browne the seal-graver and Harrison the clerk. Pepys' hopes rose: 'though upon the whole', he told Balty, 'I do discover that in their dealings one with another there was none of the best correspondence ... nor too much honesty, yet I find them all agree that, whatever the rest were to one another, Scott was a villain to them all and to all the world, and are most ready to give their honest assistance towards the evidencing his being so to me ... so that when Mr Joyne is here (which I now much wish for and so do these poor men too) I make no doubt of having this whole fellow's wickedness made clear'.[32]

On the day before Term began Pepys and Deane waited with their solicitor on the Attorney-General to apply for copies of the affidavits against them and beg for a speedy trial. But Sir William Jones, like Lord Shaftesbury, had just recived his *quietus* from the King, who was secretly set on transforming the administration of republicans forced upon him in the spring into one more in keeping with his views. There was nothing to be done but to await the appointment of his successor. Next day, being the first of the Michaelmas Term, Pepys and Deane surrendered to their bail and had their appearance duly entered. But, as there was no one to prosecute, they were merely ordered to attend again on the last day of Term.[33]

All this time Pepys was expecting almost hourly the arrival of Monsieur Denise with the Paris watchmaker whose past knowledge of Scott, he believed, would reveal many secrets at present hidden both from himself and the Government.* The Colonel, he heard, had fled from London and was at present with the Duke of Buckingham in Paris. It was the month of the King's first counter-attack against the plot-makers; Shaftesbury had been dismissed, Monmouth banished and the Duke of York recalled from his Flemish exile to take over the government of Scotland.

On Monday, October 27th, four days after Term began, Pepys with many other loyal lords and gentlemen accompanied his Royal Highness as far as Hatfield. On that very same day the 'discovery' of a new 'sham plot' showed how dangerous it was for any private individual to attempt to penetrate the secrets of the great Contrivers. Through the agency of Colonel Mansell a packet of forged letters full of accusations of treason against Shaftesbury and his friends was almost miraculously discovered in a meal tub, and a number of foolish members of the Catholic Party who had been decoyed into the business by an informer found themselves arraigned for attempt-ing 'to scandalize Dr Oates and Mr Bedloe and render them persons of no credit'. There was a howl of execration, for Oates was still a national hero and the Green Ribbon Club with its rumour-mongers and bonfire pageantries controlled the mob of the capital.[34]

At this moment Joyne arrived in London with Monsieur Denise. Next day Pepys had the pleasure of entertaining him with the London members of Scott's old gang to dinner at the 'Crown' tavern

* 'For I am of opinion some further discoveries of his Roguery may be found out that might be of use to his Majesty as well as to me.' S. Pepys to Mr Bastinck of Dover, Nov. 1st, 1679. *Rawl. MSS. A*. 194, ff. 96–7.

behind the Royal Exchange. Though a little alarmed at the tale of roguery which they unfolded, he was much taken with Joyne, whom he boarded at Monsieur Denise's house and supplied with forty crowns for the support of his family in Paris. Pepys' hopes began to rise.[35]

Yet with every day of Term the chance of a trial grew more remote, though the King himself urged the new Attorney-General, Sir Creswel Levinz, to hasten it. But in the absence of Scott and Harbord the prosecution was unable to move. By November 13th Pepys had learnt that no trial was possible that Term. He continued however to correspond with those who could throw light on Scott's activities, and asked those who had promised to be his witnesses to be ready again to serve him in the new year.[36]

On the night of November 17th, the anniversary of Elizabeth's accession day, 100,000 Protestant fanatics marched through London in uproarious excitement behind a dummy Pope. This they burnt at Smithfield with live cats in his belly to make him squall realistically. The men of the Green Ribbon Club may not have been squeamish but they knew their London. On the same day Pepys heard that Scott, encouraged by the revival of the republican fortunes, had reappeared in town.[37]

Thanks to John Joyne, Pepys was not left long in ignorance of his movements. For Joyne, who found the pursuit more remunerative and congenial than the mending of watches, of which indeed he was no great practitioner, constituted himself his patron's secret service agent and sought out his old companion in evil to learn his secrets. His motive, he claimed, was solely to do an injured man justice, and Pepys was charitable enough to believe him. But, in view of the unfortunate fate of the victims of the 'Meal Tub' Plot, and his old foe Mansell's sinister association with it, he insisted that Joyne should keep a diary of his doings, which, under the supervision of his own clerk and copyist, Paul Lorrain, he was to write up whenever he visited York Buildings.[38]

This diary, which Joyne entitled 'A Journal of all that hath passed between myself and Colonel Scott from my first waiting on him in England',* and which is preserved among Pepys' personal manuscript collections at Cambridge, is a remarkable document. Over the

* *Pepysian MS.* 2881, *Mornamont* I, 285–328. Till now its existence has not been recorded.

brief period it covers, it constitutes what is probably a unique record of a rogue's own view of the London underworld of the time. It is almost as though Lockit or Filch had kept a diary. It opens on Monday, November 24th, on which day Joyne, going out from his lodgings at Monsieur Denise's in Long Acre, ran into Scott in Drury Lane. After 'mutual salutation and shaking of hands', during which Joyne explained that he was visiting London to recover some debts, Scott took him to a house in Queen's Street, where he had left his sword overnight. Here he introduced him as 'a very honest man and the best watchmaker in the world' to the son of Major Wildman, the great republican. Considering the circumstances under which the two rogues had last parted, the renewal of their old acquaintance-ship had begun surprisingly well, so much so that Scott entrusted Joyne with a letter to Lady Vane, whom he was still wooing. It was, he explained, an anonymous letter, supporting a false charge brought against him by the old Lady's daughter, who disliked him profoundly and had told her mother that he was the Colonel Scott who had commanded the Duke of Monmouth's regiment and fallen over in front of his men from a fit of the pox. This he would subsequently prove to be false and so discredit her.

Later the same afternoon Joyne visited Scott's lodgings and spent the evening drinking with him. Here he met several of the young republican rips including Lord Wharton. When they had gone Scott explained how he preserved his interest both with the sober men of the Party by pretending to espouse the interest of the People and with the young mad fellows by drinking with them, adding with his hand on his mouth in a drinking posture, 'And so I have all the Parliament to espouse my interest'. The two friends then adjourned to the bar of the 'Dog and Dripping Pan' below, where they drank with an old Cromwellian captain and whence the Colonel was called by a summons from Mr Penn – the King of the Quakers, he explained, adding jovially that the Presbyterians had Kings and the Anabaptists had Kings and that altogether there were a great many Kings in the country. After which, late as it was, Joyne hurried off to Pepys to tell him all about it.[39]

Next day Joyne spent closeted with Pepys at York Buildings, dining there with Sir Anthony Deane, Denise and Browne the seal-graver. On Wednesday 26th he returned to Scott's lodgings and breakfasted with him on purl and small red herrings at Newman's

coffee-house.* Here they met a lean-faced man 'in a campaign coat
faced on the sleeves with blue', who proved to be the Chief Searcher
at Gravesend – a rogue, Scott explained confidently, but useful at
times – and whom at present he was using to recover a horse which
he had left at Gravesend a year before.†

Later, walking in the street, Scott kept stopping people and telling
them that Parliament would sit shortly and that it would be the
'salve of the nation'. At that time Shaftesbury was concentrating his
efforts on forcing an early meeting of the Houses on the King. But
politics never monopolized Scott's activities and he dropped in on a
furrier to leave an otter skin to be made into a muff, for he was a man
of fashion, and gave Joyne another letter to take to Lady Vane.
When he was married to her, he said, and had an estate, he would go
into Parliament, 'where he was sure he would be able to do more
than ever was done by any man'.

Again that evening Joyne drank with Scott, meeting Harrington,
whom he had often seen in Paris in parson's habit passing under the
name of Benson.‡ Afterwards Joyne called on Pepys but, finding
him out, spent the rest of the evening dodging the Colonel about and
slept rather unaccountably, and one suspects drunk, at Southwark.
He was back at York Buildings early next day to report to Pepys.
That fastidious gentleman somewhat ungraciously pointed out that
he was very dirty and suggested that he should go home to shave
and shift. But the invincible Joyne was on the trail again by
nightfall, encountering Scott at Appleby's, 'and faining myself a
little in drink, I went to his lodging with him and lay with him all
night'. Dissimulation of this kind came easily to him.⁴⁰

Friday, November 28th, was the last day of the Michaelmas
Term. Again Pepys and Deane appeared in Westminster Hall to
press for a trial or a discharge. But the Lord Chief Justice replied
that he could do nothing without the Attorney-General and added
that he was sure that their bail would think it no hardship to

   * An old haunt of the Colonel's in Talbot Court, Gracechurch Street. *Pepysian MS.*
2882, *Mornamont* II, 1089.
   † See p. 169.
   ‡ See p. 158. Joyne's details of the associates of Scott whom he encountered are
largely confirmed by the accounts of them to be found in entirely different sources
among the *Rawl. MSS.* See also *H.M.C. Lindsey*, 403–4, for John Brisbane's letter of
March 19th, 1679, from the English Embassy at Paris, describing Benson as Lord
Shaftesbury's Paris agent and Colonel Scott as the Duke of Buckingham's.

continue bound for them till the beginning of the new Term. 'Such is the law of England', Pepys wrote to Balty, who was still awaiting instructions as to what he should do with the French witnesses.[41]

When, accompanied by Deane, Pepys got back that day to dinner at York Buildings, he found Joyne waiting for him with important news. That morning Scott had pulled out of his pocket a crumpled letter bearing a September postmark which he said was from one Dailly, a broken-down Paris writing master, telling him that Balty St Michel had offered him £2000 to testify that Scott had been with the Duke of Buckingham at St Maures and had spoken of the King as the Protector of the Whore of Babylon. With this letter, Scott swore with a great oath, he would claw off those dogs as soon as Parliament met. Actually Pepys had written to Balty on this very subject early in September, when he had first heard of Dailly's readiness to make discoveries: he was to be careful, he had warned him, to offer him nothing but his expenses and to have creditable witnesses of all conversations held with him, though for the rest, he added – 'what is allowed for good in our proceedings upon the public plot, cannot (I conceive) be excepted against in the case of a private one, namely to make an honest use of one villain to discover the iniquity of another'. But this accomplishment, it seemed, was more easily said than performed.[42]

During the next fortnight Joyne saw little of Scott, beyond a picturesque encounter one morning at his lodgings when he found him talking with a young wench at the foot of the stairs and blacking his eyebrows and beard with a little brush which he explained he always carried for purposes of disguise.* But he was able to transmit to Pepys various secondhand rumours of the Colonel's activities; that he had given out in coffee-houses that he could produce the original papers delivered by Deane to the Secretary of the French Admiralty, that he could prove attempts to suborn Dailly and Foster, and that he had eleven new witnesses whom he was going to bring over from France as soon as Parliament was allowed to meet. Fortunately for Pepys' peace of mind, this was just what the King

* For this, he told Joyne, he also set great store on his black periwig. In matters of costume it always paid to attend to details; for instance he had intended to change the black ribbon on his muff for a red one, but as he was now going among the French masters of ships to secure Joyne a passage for France, he would not do so, as in such company it would be a mistake to be too 'gaudy'. *Pepysian MS.* 2881, *Mornamont* I, 303; *Joyne's Journal*, Friday, Dec. 5th, 1679.

was determined not to allow; on December 11th, despite his own poverty and the monster petitions from every quarter of England which the Whig leaders were showering on Whitehall, he again prorogued the expected meeting of the Houses. His action gave Pepys breathing space.[43]

On the same day Joyne re-established direct contact with Scott, catching him in bed at the 'Dog and Dripping Pan'. Later they shared three bottles of sack and one of cider in the kitchen of Newman's coffee-house, where they were joined by Harrington and Captain Newman, with whom after handshakes and kisses they fell to telling stories of the brave old days at Paris. Newman spoke much of Pepys and of what a great man he had been before all this happened and how he had made everybody stoop to him and how humble he was now, on which Scott observed that he was a rogue and that he would claw him off as soon as Parliament met. 'Said I to Newman', wrote Joyne, 'there is nobody knoweth the Colonel better than I do, to which he replied that the Colonel was a very honest gentleman and loved his country'. After this tribute, Joyne invited Scott to sup with him next day before he returned to France. The company then broke up, Scott and Harrington taking coach with a couple of women whom they met in Fish Street, while Joyne stopped to buy a lobster.[44]

Scott did not keep his appointment next day. Nor did Joyne return to France as Pepys had intended. For on the latter expressing some doubts of the wellnigh incredible stories of Scott's villainous talk which Joyne kept bringing him, the latter offered to invite the Colonel to a farewell meal at his sister's public house, where Pepys, concealed behind a curtain, might overhear their conversation. And when on Sunday, December 14th, Joyne learnt that the reason of Scott's failure to keep his appointment was the unexpected death on the previous day of Lady Vane, he went to the barber's shop in Bishopsgate Street where places for the Dover coach were reserved and cancelled his seat.[45]

Two days later Joyne, after a long wait at Newman's coffee-house, ran Scott to earth again. For just as he was about to leave, 'Scott came in in a very melancholy humour, . . . so', Joyne recorded, 'we fell to call for coffee, and I told him that I was sorry for his great loss, he answering that it was the greatest loss in the world, he using this very expression, that it was a Devil for a loss. And so I comforted him as well as I could and gave him a Portugal orange, he telling me that the palate of his mouth was down'.*

Before the evening ended, Joyne had obtained from Scott a promise to dine with him and Harrington next day on a calf's head and bacon at his sister's public house at St Clement's in the Strand. Then he made his way triumphantly to his sister's and sent a note to Mr Pepys to join him there. 'And so by and by . . . Mr Pepys came according to my note, and after a small stay drinking a tankard of warm ale went home.' The bar parlour of a little Strand tavern was a strange place to find the great and cultured Mr Pepys.[46]

Yet next day saw him in a stranger, hidden in a dark closet on the first floor of the same house and listening to Scott over his thirty-shilling treat in the next room giving 'such a narrative of his own villainies as even exceeded all he had before been told of him'.† It was well worth the money. Scott began by bemoaning his loss of Lady Vane, 'saying that no man had ever such a loss, sometimes magnifying the excellency of her wit and spirit and sometimes her extraordinary love to him, saying that when he came in, though there were never such company there, she would tell him that the very sight of him fed her soul (that was his expression) and so ran on from one thing to another impossible to be set down in order . . .'.

From this melancholy topic, the Colonel turned awhile to speak of 'a well-turned whore' whom he had seen and fallen in love with and whom he hoped would take away his melancholy. Joyne heartily agreed with him and said that if anything could cure melancholy, that would. But the honest Colonel soon reverted to the subject of his lost mistress, whom he plainly could not drive from his thoughts; how she would have settled £3000 a year on him and how she had been wont to say that could she but see him once a week it would be content enough for her. God damn him, he said suddenly, he would go on in the line and marry Lady Vane's sister, for he had now got the affections of the people of England and only needed to marry himself into Parliament to be one of the greatest men in the world. But first, he said, he would make love to Lady Vane's unmarried

---

* *Joyne's Journal, Pepysian MS.* 2881, *Mornamont* I, 310.

† The details of this extraordinary conversation will be found in *Joyne's Journal* for Wednesday, Dec. 17th, 1679, in *Pepysian MS.* 2881, *Mornamont* I, 311–20. Of its substantial truth there can be no doubt, for Joyne wrote it at Pepys' command, and Pepys, as Joyne knew, had heard every word of it.

daughter, whom he hated, and if he could but marry her, would imprison her, for she was a bitch that looked as if she would give crooked pins in bread and butter to children, and if ever any of her children should die, he would bring witnesses out of France to swear that she had poisoned it. Joyne must have glowed with pride as he heard all this and thought of the crouching listener in the adjoining room.

All afternoon as he sat over the wine cups and the remains of the thirty-shilling treat the Colonel's talk ranged gloriously between love and politics. Once he commended the Whig merchant, Sir Thomas Player: 'a very worthy and honest man', he thought him. Some time soon, he said, he might visit France again: in fact whenever the people of England should desire him to do so for their service. He lacked nothing now but to be thrown into the pool Bethesda, for he had got an interest in the people and moreover knew the affairs of every sovereign Prince in Europe better than any man living. Then he spoke of the Petition from the City which he had helped to draw up to force an early meeting of Parliament on the King; originally he said it had opened with the words, 'Damned confounded Plot', but, knowing the feelings of Princes, he had had it softened. Soon the Royal Government would fall. The Duke of York, he admitted, had some friends but not so many as he thought. When Joyne asked who, he replied – that rogue Pepys and the officers of the Navy.

But soon Venus and Bacchus banished politics from the Colonel's mind. 'He said', Joyne noted in his journal, 'that he never valued himself among the women upon the account of his being a Beau Garçon, but upon his knowing himself to have some good humour and some sense above the common, and that therefore it was no fault in him, whatever it was that they liked in him if he hath the good fortune of prevailing upon them more than other men. He said he never came into the Coffee House if there were a hundred in the room but they all came and flocked about him to hear him discourse and that he could impose anything upon them . . . As he grew more and more in drink, which he called very freely for, both wine and tankards of ale, he grew in his swearing and cursing till it came to an excessive degree.'

Now and then in the midst of his talk the Colonel would break into a French song. Once he spoke of the speech he had just made in the Guildhall on behalf of his friend Harrington, who had been prosecuted for a libel. At last, 'having drunk himself to a high pitch', he became very loving and fell to kissing Joyne's sister and her maid.[47]

All this and much more the astonished Pepys heard from his darkened room. In after years he declared that the way in which Joyne had concurred in all that the scoundrel proposed against him, as well as his association in his past villainies, had made him very nervous as to the kind of company into which he had fallen and deeply suspicious that he was being betrayed. Yet at the time he found it expedient to retain Joyne in England for some months further and to correspond with him in grateful and even affectionate terms.[48]

About the time of this interview Pepys was again attacked in a malicious libel entitled 'A Hue and Cry after P. and H.', which was printed and hawked about the streets of London. It was even more personal than its predecessor and, to everyone but its unhappy victims, cruelly amusing. Years afterwards Pepys believed it to have been written by his clerk, Donluis, with whom his enemies had long been tampering. At the time he suspected Scott.*[49]

It began with the familiar charge of a conspiracy between Pepys and Hewer to cheat their country under the outward forms of virtue. 'These are to give notice', it ran, 'to P. and H. that if they will forthwith come forth with an humble submission and refund all the money they have unjustly taken by Permissions and Protections, to the merchants or owners of all such ships as were fitted out for the last Embargo, and also give satisfaction for the extraordinary gain made to yourselves, P. and H., in buying of timber for building the new ships of war . . .'

You must also refund those before-hand guineas or bread-pieces, and also the jars of oil and boxes of chocolate and chests of Greek wines and chests of Saracusa wines, and pots of anchovies and quarter-casks of old Malaga and butts of Sherry, and Westphalia hams and Bolonia sausages, and barrels of pickled oysters and jars of olives and jars of tent, and Parmesan cheeses and chests of Florence wine and boxes of orange flower

---

* That the ex-butler James was concerned in its preparation, though not in its writing, and that it passed into the skilled hands of 'Elephant' Smith and Benjamin Harris we now know, though this also at the time was hidden from Pepys.

water; and all those dried cods and lings, and hogsheads of claret, white wines and champagnes, and dozens of cider; and also all those mocos, parrots and parrakeets, Virginia nightingales and turtle-doves, and those fat turkies and pigs; and all those Turkish sheep, Barbary horses and lions and tigers and bears; and all those fine Spanish mats; all which were received from Sea-Captains, Consuls, Lieutenants, Masters, Boatswains, Gunners, Carpenters and Pursers, or from their wives or sons or daughters . . .

This scandalous document contained all the familiar charges: dockyard bribery, the robbing of the Chatham Chest and the widows and orphans of poor seamen, the vast sums raised by the sale of passes and the issue of warrants. 'Also, P. and H.,' the unhappy victims were enjoined, 'that you take a more vigilant care the next time you are called into any business depending upon state affairs, and to be so prudent to yourselves as to deal honestly, justly and uprightly and never more trust to, or make use of any Dark Lanthorns, but take the most transparent crystal lights you can purchase with all the honesty you both have or ever had; and that you may foresee things with that brightness, that you need never come within the reach of the Printing-Press, for at this time it squeezes you both very hard with the matter of truth.' For a new power had arisen in England, and it was not altogether a power for righteousness.

But the climax of the libel was its description of Pepys' former coach and barge, familiar as they must have been to every Londoner. Here the anonymous author surpassed himself:

P., there is one thing more you must be mightily sorry for with all speed – your Presumption in your coach in which you daily ride as if you had been son and heir to the great Emperor, Neptune; or, as if you had been infallibly to have succeeded in his Government of the Ocean. All which was Presumption in the highest degree.

First, you had upon the forepart of your chariot tempestuous waves and wracks of ships; on your left-hand forts and great guns and ships a'fighting; on your right-hand was a fair harbour and town, with ships and galleys riding with their flags and pennants spread, kindly saluting each other, just like P. and H. Behind it were high curled waves and ships a'sinking, and here and there an appearance of some bits of land.

In place of all this, the author suggested a more appropriate symbolism, well knowing that in doing so he would awake the inveterate snobbery of the English people. 'And now really consider with yourself that you are but the son of a tailor, and wipe out all this presumptuous painting, and new paint it with those things agreeable to your quality. In the first place, paint upon the fore-part as handsome a tailor's shop-board as you please, with the Old Gentleman, your father, upon it at work and his journeymen sitting about him, each man with his pint of ale and halfpenny loaf before him, and the good old Matron your mother and yourself and the rest of your brothers and sisters standing by: this will be agreeable to your qualities. Then behind your coach, paint all the evil deeds of P. and H. in particulars; also on your right hand, paint your Jesuit, M., playing upon his lute and singing a Holy Song: on your left hand paint two or three poor cripples, which P. reformed, and giving them his charity which he never was wont to do. All this will show P.'s great humility and reformation and reducement to his right station.'

Poor Pepys' Admiralty barge provided even better sport. 'You must also, P., correct your barge and take out all those damask curtains and cushions, and put in good shalloon ones and some of your shop-board cushions; and wipe out those little seas that are painted, and paint it anew with an honest green, and here and there a pair of great shears with open mouths: the ignorant sort of people may take them for some strange and monstrous fishes. All this will do very well.'

The paper ended with a cut at Pepys in a still more intimate particular. Lady Bankes, who lived in Lincoln's Inn Fields, and Lady Mordaunt, who had a villa at Chelsea, and the young Houblon ladies were all coupled by allusion with his name, and perhaps also Mary Skinner who was then residing in the Haymarket.* 'For the better enabling this Hue and Cry, this is therefore to give notice to all persons whatsoever, that if they can apprehend P. and H., or either of them, or give notice of them to a Lady in Lincoln's-Inn-Fields, or to a Lady at her country-house in Chelsea; or to another at her house near the Exchequer, or to two merchants' daughters in London, they being both well-known to these two persons, especially P.; or to any of the Officers of Bridewell in Whitefriars' (the reformatory for prostitutes) 'or to M.'s coffee-house in Westminster or to C.'s coffee-house by the Royal Exchange; before, or at, the next Session of Parliament, they shall have a great Reward.'[50]

* *Pepysian MS.* 2881, *Mornamont* I, 209–13.

Pepys pretended that all this did not touch him. 'As to the malicious paper you speak on,' he wrote gallantly to a friend, 'it is like the rest of Scott's villainies, and whatever he may do abroad does neither me nor my clerk any injury here.'* But the stab must have struck deep, for he told his friends that he was looked upon as a criminal, yet denied the right of proving his innocence. Therefore, though he had small hope of a trial, he redoubled his efforts to have every proof of Scott's villainy ready against the next Term, cost him what it might to procure it. Balty, he directed, was to bring over the remaining French witnesses at his expense and lodge them in his house, where Pepys already had had a Dutch lady staying for the past two months; Monsieur Denise's was already full. He kept Joyne by his side to watch Scott's actions.

Charles II remarked about this time how strange it was that all his friends kept a tame rogue. John Joyne was Pepys'. From him he heard reports of the Colonel's political conversations with obscure conventicle preachers, of the poached eggs he ate and the small beer he drank. Meanwhile, from America, Holland, France and Flanders the tale of Scott's life-long crimes continued to accumulate, till Pepys was master of almost his whole history. Nor was he without light on the doings of other rogues: one of his informants remarked that if only Scott, Charles Foster and Sir Robert Welsh would write one another's lives, there would be nothing like it. And behind these Pepys was made aware of the shadows of far greater men, for Lord Shaftesbury's and the Duke of Buckingham's names began to reappear in the informations that kept reaching him with an ominous reiteration.[51]

* S. Pepys to Mr Carr, Dec. 16th, 1679. *Rawl. MSS. A.* 194, ff. 118–20.

Rehabilitation

'As the world goes, Justice ought to be welcome at any time, and so I receive it with thanks to God Almighty.' S. Pepys to Mrs Skinner, July 1st, 1680. *Howarth*, 96.

Three weeks before the opening of Hilary Term, late at night on the second day of the new year, Pepys' coach stopped at the house of an obscure tradesman named Spackman in Foster Lane to desire him to call at York Buildings next morning. Thither Spackman came, to be asked whether he knew anything of Hill, a founder, who lived in Gutter Lane. On his replying 'No', Pepys asked him if he would make enquiries in the trade as to his reputation for honesty. This Spackman promised to do and soon afterwards was able to report that it was none of the best.[1]

Some days later Spackman at Pepys' request met Hill by appointment at an ale-house in Gutter Lane and asked him if he would tell the truth of certain passages which Colonel Scott had alleged had passed between him and Coniers, the Jesuit, relating to himself. This Hill did with great frankness. Two or three years before, he said, when Scott was lodging at his house in Houndsditch, he had returned home one day in a great rage saying he had been dogged by a stranger who had accosted him in Henrietta Street. Later, while making water in Lincoln's Inn Fields, Scott had again seen the stranger watching him and believed that he had followed him home. And on going out Hill had thereupon seen the very man making enquiries about Scott of the woman over the way.

Hill went on to describe how a conversation had ensued between Scott and the stranger, in which the latter asked Scott if during his residence in France he had ever heard of Mr Pepys. This Pepys, he explained, was anxious to see him and could do a kindness for him with the Duke of York. Afterwards a neighbour, a tobacconist named Major Gladman, who had joined in the conversation, told them that the stranger was Coniers, the Jesuit.

All this, Hill said, he had almost forgotten till reminded of it a short while before by Scott, who had caused him to be examined by a magistrate as to the truth of it. Asked whether he was prepared to repeat what he had said to Pepys, Hill replied 'Yes', for this Pepys had behaved like an honest man in sending a neighbour to him first. Accordingly a few days later Pepys met Hill by appointment at Spackman's house and heard his story. Afterwards he asked him if the man called Coniers had said he had been sent by him. Hill paused and rubbing his head replied he was only a tradesman, but after a while said that now he recalled it he had done so. Pepys thanked him and, pressing him to nothing, left him to go his way.[2]

The story illustrates the kind of subterranean existence to which Scott's villainy had condemned Pepys. Across the Channel he was having to move with similar caution in the perilous Paris underworld where Dailly and Foster were alternatively offering him discoveries, which from other sources he knew to be true, and then declaring that his agent Balty had offered them vast sums for perjured evidence. Between the two capitals moved the mysterious Harrington or Benson, linking alike the great Duke of Buckingham in Paris with the republican lords in London and the humble Dailly with Scott. Behind everything, as Pepys knew, lay the threat of any change in the political situation. As long as the King held his precarious control of affairs he was safe, provided he could keep the letter of the Law between himself and his unjust accusers. But, if once the King was forced by his penury to yield to the petitions for an early meeting of Parliament, his case, however just, was doomed.[3]

Knowing this, Pepys made every effort as Term approached to bring on his trial and so secure an acquittal while the rules of the Common Law were still untrammelled by a higher and more arbitrary power. A fortnight before Term began he and Deane visited the Attorney-General in his chambers in Gray's Inn. From him they learnt that during the vacation Harbord had announced that he had obtained a new witness against them, though nothing further had been heard from him since. There the matter rested till January 23rd, when, with all their far-called witnesses about them, Pepys and Deane heard their four Counsel, led by fat, jovial Mr Saunders, move the Court of King's Bench for a trial or an immediate discharge under the rules of the Habeas Corpus Act. After a good deal of legal argument as to whether they came within the terms of the Act – the Whig Judge Pemberton maintaining obstinately that they did not – Pepys took the matter out of his Counsel's hands by observing that they were not asking for a discharge but a trial. They had been nearly a year in the hands of the Court and, their adversary having laid the scene of his charge in France, were at the incalculable cost of maintaining witnesses from overseas; they would, therefore, like to know as soon as possible when they were going to be tried. The upshot was that the Attorney-General was asked to give the Court an account of what he proposed to do in the matter by the following Tuesday.[4]

But when Tuesday came, it brought only disappointment, for the Attorney-General was forced to admit that having only one witness he could not prosecute the charge for treason, and Mr Harbord, who was in Court, when called upon for further witnesses, replied that he could only produce them when Parliament was sitting, since they flatly refused to give evidence at any other time. After this statement, the Court was for some time silent; then, the Judges having conferred, the Lord Chief Justice remarked to the Attorney-General that he and his brethren were of opinion that he must either tell the Court by the last day of Term exactly how he proposed to proceed to trial or give full and satisfactory reasons why the prisoners should not be discharged. It was the most Pepys could obtain. 'Taking in all circumstances of scandal, expense, trouble and hazard,' he wrote to Balty, 'no innocent man was ever more embarrassed than I have been, from the villainy of one man of no acquaintance with myself or credit with any honest man else that knows him. The thoughts of which,' he added, 'should I give much way to them, would distract me.'* They would have done so still more could he have heard Harbord coming out of the Court of King's Bench into Westminster Hall – still filled with scaffolds for the trial of the Popish Lords – telling his friends amid hearty laughter how he had got Pepys and Deane by the legs for another Term.[5]

But in the meantime a very extraordinary thing had happened. On January 12th, 1680, one of Pepys' former clerks at Derby House, Phelix Donluis or Lewis, made a written statement in the presence of Will Hewer and Paul Lorrain about John James, the ex-butler who had accused Pepys before Parliament. From this it appeared that in the previous autumn James had visited the goldsmith at the sign of

* 'But God is above all.' S. Pepys to B. St Michel, Jan. 26th, 1680. *Rawl. MSS. A.* 194, ff. 132v.–3.

the 'Black Boy' in Fleet Street, who was Harbord's banker, and there in Donluis' company had drawn out monies which he stated at the time he was receiving each week from Harbord. James had also shown him letters from the Duke of Buckingham, Mr Vaughan, Sir Henry Capel and other Whig leaders recommending him for naval employment.

But two months later, James, who previously had been full of praise for these great men, had had a very different tale to tell of them. Their promises of employment had all proved worthless. 'The Devil take me', he had told Donluis, 'if I believe any one of them any more, for they are my arse all over.' And he had added that he was heartily sorry for what at their bidding he had testified against Pepys, unkindly as the latter had used him; and if it were to do again, he would see them damned first, for he would meddle no more with such rascally fellows. 'How now, James!' Donluis had replied, 'no more *Pater-nosters*, no more pence!' But James had been most emphatic: Harbord had taken away his allowance, and he would therefore take the first employment he could get and never trust a son of a whore of them any longer, for, God damn them all, they had got what they could out of him and now merely slighted him.*

Donluis then proceeded to make some revelations on his own account, of how at the time of Pepys' accusation before Parliament he had been secretly employed by Harbord and Sir Henry Capel to prepare from the Admiralty records a list of all his Majesty's ships with their dimensions, guns and crews and how he had been closely examined by Harbord as to Pepys' private life. He also deposed to having recently seen in a lawyer's chambers a bundle of forged letters in his name to the French Queen's confessor, which he understood were shortly going to be used against him.[6]

Donluis was a shifty fellow and it was difficult to know how far to believe him and still more difficult to know how to make use of his evidence. But about the same time Pepys and Deane began to receive a number of mysterious communications from the former porter at Derby House, one John Harris, to the effect that he could, if he chose, do them a great piece of justice. Harris had been

---

* I have followed as near as possible the downright and picturesque phrasing which Donluis puts into James' mouth in *Pepysian MS.* 2881, *Mornamont* II, 1237–44. For gross as it may be, it is the authentic speech of the seventeenth century.

dismissed from his post by Pepys for some misdemeanour, and had subsequently befriended James. Pepys was therefore apt to regard him with considerable suspicion. But on coming home late on the night of Saturday, January 24th, the day after the opening of Hilary Term, he had found Sir Anthony Deane waiting for him with news that Harris and his brother, Alexander Harris, the Admiralty messenger, were begging an interview.

That night Pepys spoke with Alexander Harris in the great parlour below stairs. Harris began by mentioning the long unkindness that he and his brother had received from Pepys; how he had been mulcted of his fees at the time of the parliamentary clamour against Passes, and deprived of the arrears of pay owed him by the King. 'To which', Pepys recorded, 'I answered that the first and only thing I took ill of him was the untruth that he told the Lords of the Committee touching words of mine upon the business of Atkins. Whereto he replied that others of my servants, naming Thomas Beckwith, had been with the Lords before he was, and he believed had said things as little to my advantage as he. For the other particulars I shortly and calmly told him that he had no reason to expect kindnesses from me and that for doing of him wrong I never did, nor nothing should provoke me to do it towards him or any man.'*

For again, under the necessity of keeping a check on his slightest words and actions, while moving in a world of perilous intrigue, Pepys had reverted to his old habit of keeping a diary. Of this day's interview with the Harrises and of all the other interviews to which it led during the next two months he kept a long-hand record, noting carefully where in the interim he went and whom he saw. Once more for a brief period we see Samuel moving about the London of the seventeenth century by looking, as it were, over his own shoulder.

Harris went on to say how troubled he was in his conscience for the wrongs Pepys had suffered and the new ones still designed him. He now desired to do him all the justice he could, and, though he trusted that Pepys would help him and his brother to obtain satisfaction for their debts from the Crown, he made no condition

---

* *Pepysian MS.* 2881, *Mornamont* II, 1189–1235, entitled 'Journal commencing upon Saturday the 24th of January 1679/80 containing an Account of all Passages relating to the Information given me by Harris and James'. The last entry was made on March 29th.

but one. But that, he added, was an indispensable one, for he could not perform the service he wished unless Pepys promised on his honour to forgive one man whom he should name, however great the injury that man might have done. At which Pepys, fearing it might be James, tried to except him. But Harris repeated so firmly that he could do nothing without this unconditional promise, that at last he gave it.[7]

There the matter rested till the following Tuesday, when coming home at night after taking his cousin, Wynne Houblon's wife, to the play *She would if she could,* Pepys found Alexander Harris waiting to tell him that the person he had spoken of was in a coffee-house hard by. It was James. Before he would speak with him, Pepys insisted that Hewer should be present as a witness. Harris, Hewer, James and he then sat down together in the inner parlour.

'I begun', Pepys wrote, 'with observing to James what had passed lately between A. H. and me. To which J. replied with beginning (as A. H. at first did) with a repetition of the injury I had done him, saying that the only fault for which I put him away (meaning as I suppose about my woman) was indeed true, but a slight thing not worth naming, and that therefore it was the more hard that I should deny him a certificate of my having discharged him my service, and should accuse him in the House of Commons with robbing my house.' Of this, James protested, he had been entirely guiltless, having been in Holland at the time serving the Prince of Orange. 'He complained, too, that I had lately made it my business to bespatter him in my discourse everywhere and to hinder his having any employment by speaking to Sir Thomas Lee and Sir Humphrey Winch against him . . . To all which, I studiously giving him very sparing answers and on the other hand taking notice, though gently, of the great wrongs that I had sustained . . . he proceeded and told me that it was more in his power to do me right than in any man's in England, for that everything that had been done had passed through his hand, he having been the man that first got the merchants together to complain of the Piracy and that it had never been done but for him.'*

Of this and much more James now spoke: that he had been employed by Pepys' enemies, 'and those men of the greatest quality',

---

* *Pepysian MS., Mornamont* II, 1192–6.

to collect evidence against him, that Garroway was one of the fiercest enemies Pepys had, and that new and worse mischief was now brewing against him in which both Scott and the politicians had a part. Yet, James asserted, he could prevent it all, for he knew enough to stop Scott's mouth and that of others too. If he did so, however, he expected that Pepys would get the Harris' arrears paid and himself preferred to some employment in the Navy. 'To which I told him that it was not for me to make nor him to expect promises of that or any other kind from me, especially since I asked nothing of him. But if of his own accord he thinks fit to do me this great justice which he tells me (and I believe) he is so well able to do, I was very confident he had no reason to doubt my being ready to do him and them all the just offices of kindness I can.' For Pepys refused to put it into his enemies' power to say that he had made use of promises to obtain that bare truth which was all he asked.*[8]

Both parties feeling the need of caution and wanting time to think matters over, nothing of consequence happened till the evening of Friday, February 6th, when in Hewer's inward parlour in York Buildings, the same four sat down again before a coal fire. James, Pepys recorded, 'began with saying that he was come to give me an account of things relating to myself, and which had passed of late to my great prejudice, and that he would begin with a question or two; of which the first was, whether it was a due method of proceeding for a Committee of Parliament to adjourn themselves from one day to another, and in the interval that that Committee should have private meetings in other places, it having been so in my case, Mr Harbord together with Sir Hugh Bethel with a patch on one eye, and I think Mr Rich and others having private meetings at the "Mitre" in Fenchurch Street where the merchants were conferred with and satisfaction promised some of them out of our estates. That to that purpose our estates were enquired after and mine not found.'

'His other question was whether it was a due method of proceeding for Parliament men to give money to witnesses.' James then gave particulars of the sums he and Captain Moone had received from Harbord. He also spoke of Garroway's and Colonel Mansell's part in these proceedings, and about some new ones which were now

---

* '. . . all that we are desirous of knowing being only the Truth and consequently what in conscience every good man is bound in our case to tell to another.' *Pepys' Journal,* Jan. 30th, 1680, *Pepysian MS.* 2882, *Mornamont* II, 1198.

planning against Morelli, who was to be accused of receiving letters from abroad brought to Derby House by a priest now lying in Newgate on Oates' charges. All that Pepys had before suspected was at last clear.[9]

Before the matter could be pursued further, the Term had ended. On February 10th Pepys and Deane spent the afternoon closeted with their Counsel. Next day the King himself at Pepys' desire spoke to the Attorney-General in the Council Chamber to do his best on the morrow to bring matters to an issue. The Attorney's reply, which was to the effect that up to six o'clock that evening he had received no further information from Harbord, his Majesty was graciously pleased to repeat to Pepys the same night. He also asked Colonel Phelips of his Bedchamber to mention the matter to Mr Justice Dolben before he went to Westminster Hall in the morning, though, as Pepys carefully noted in another journal which he was keeping of his proceedings at law, 'without the least intimation of any partiality to be desired from them but only to bring our case to some issue'.[10]

Once again he was disappointed. When the Court met on the morning of Thursday, February 12th, the Lord Chief Justice asked the Attorney-General what he had to say. To which he answered nothing, save that last night an attorney named Goodenough* had brought to him on behalf of Colonel Scott extracts from several treasonable letters written from beyond seas. But when Scott was called, Goodenough rose to explain that he had refused to come. Hayes, who caught a glimpse of the letters, noticed that they were in Goodenough's writing.

With some indignation the Lord Chief Justice forbade the reading of them, and turning to Pepys said, 'Why, Mr Pepys, would it be much inconvenient to you to appear again here the next Term?' In this he was seconded with a 'great deal of respect and gentleness' by his brothers Dolben and Jones, Pemberton alone remaining silent. 'I replied', Pepys noted in his diary of the proceedings, 'that it would be very inconvenient, first in regard of the greatness of our bail and the keeping of our friends so much the longer in bond for us, which we above all things desired they might be eased of. And next, that being now wholly unconcerned in public business, my affairs did call

* Later to be concerned in the Rye House Plot and Monmouth's Rebellion. See *D.N.B.*

me very earnestly into the country, where I had not of many years been to look after them. To the former of which the Court answered they would wholly discharge our bail and take our single obligation for our appearance, and to the other that if the next Term were too soon we should take the first or the last day of the Term following. Upon which I asked my Lord's leave to demand what assurance we should have then more than now of being fully discharged. Whereto he replied, with some fresh expressions of respect, that as to any assurance, the Court could give us none, but from their present proceedings, we might very well judge what the inclinations of the Court would be.'*

At this, knowing the construction that would be put on any too strong insistence on a discharge and hearing Deane whispering urgently at his side, 'Take it, take it, take it!' Pepys gave way and agreed to their reappearance in Court on the first day of Trinity Term. They were thereupon released from their bail, while recognizances of a bare £1000 each were taken from them to appear on the given date. 'For which, thanking the Court, we departed.'[11]

The foreign witnesses departed also. For the next ten days Pepys was busy packing them off, taking full depositions from them first. On Wednesday, March 3rd, he gave his last dinner to the 'Frenchmen' and next day saw them off under Balty's escort to Dover. Even Joyne went, though most reluctantly, for in five months he had made over £300 from his new employment. Pepys' guests left behind in his hands a vast accumulation of papers, which amounted to nothing less than a full and detailed story of Scott's life.[12]

Before the witnesses departed, Pepys was again in communication with James. On Ash Wednesday, the day after his last appearance in Court, he received a note from Hewer, who was paying the Chest at Chatham, that James was dangerously ill. On the same evening Alexander Harris reported that he could not live forty hours, and that he was anxious to communicate something before he died to Hewer. Hewer being out of town, Harris had in turn suggested Atkins, Walbanke and Gibson, the three among Pepys' former clerks who were most in his confidence, but James had turned them all down, saying that he must have someone who understood the law. Harris had therefore come to Pepys for his advice. After suggesting

* *Pepysian MS.* 2881, *Mornamont* I, 72–7.

Justice Warcup, whom James also rejected, probably on account of his earlier association with the Green Ribbon Club and Colonel Mansell, Pepys proposed Mr Povey. As Povey was also a friend of Harbord, this was a bold suggestion, but Pepys knew he could rely on Povey's absolute impartiality. He therefore sat down and wrote to him a note which Harris delivered to him at six next morning.

But before Povey, hastening from his bed, had arrived, James had taken a turn for the better and had sent word that he soon hoped to be in a condition to put the whole matter himself into writing. He begged therefore that he might be spared the embarrassment of a visit from Povey or any other gentleman of quality in his present plight, for his poverty was so great that he, his mother and his sister were all sharing the same bed. So Pepys forbore to send anyone, and Harris promised to be watchful and to bring him word from day to day how he fared.[13]

Pepys' entry in his Journal for one or two of the ensuing days contains the disappointing word 'Nothing'. But on March 2nd, feeling death to be near, James in the presence of his mother and sister, Povey, Will Hewer and John Hayes, the solicitor, made a full statement which was committed to writing and signed by him.* In it he described in detail how, in the previous April, Colonel Mansell had promised him preferment if he would relinquish the employment of a gentleman with whom he was about to sail for Spain and remain in England to give testimony against Pepys. On agreeing he had been given board at Alexander Harris' house, where Mansell was also lodging, and was taken by the latter to Harbord's home in Covent Garden. Harbord examined him closely about Pepys' private life, gave him money and promises of preferment, and promised him protection in case the business on foot against Pepys should fail. From Harbord he had carried letters to various City merchants, inviting them to dine with him and Colonel Scott and promising them satisfaction for all their past losses out of Pepys' and Deane's estates.

On other occasions James had attended private meetings of the Parliamentary Committee on the affairs of the Navy at the 'Mitre' in Fenchurch Street, at which the members, Harbord, Sir John Hotham, Sir Hugh Bethel, Captain Rich and Mr Papillon had laid

---

* *Pepysian MS.* 2882, *Mornamont* II, 1245–9. Also *Rawl. MSS. A.* 175, f. 215.

their plans and consulted with Mansell, Scott, Captain Moone and the injured merchants. At these meetings written informations against Pepys were drawn up by Harbord without even the formality of debate.

James spoke also of the sums paid him and the promises made to him by Harbord and other Whig leaders. He described how he had supplied Mansell and Benjamin Harris with the material to write the libel, *Plain Truth*. He was ready, he said, to place on record that what he had said before Parliament as to Pepys being a Papist and Morelli a Jesuit was a lie. And thus John James the butler discharged his conscience.[14]

During the next two days James sank fast. In this dire moment he became to his former master, who was a man of his century and a believer, no longer a means to defeat his enemies, but a fellow Christian in need of aid. Pepys sent him money, at his request sought out Dr Curle, who advertised in his bills that he could cure consumption, and visited his friend Dr Littleton, the saintly Rector of Chelsea, at his lodgings in the Cloisters, to beg him to give him the last services of the Church. These the good Doctor administered on March 6th, James' mother, a dissenter, receiving the Sacrament in tears by his side. During his visit, James unasked poured out his heart to Littleton, declaring how troubled he was for what he had testified against Pepys, and telling him all that had passed. Afterwards Littleton told Pepys that what he had heard that day made him doubt the truth of the whole Plot.[15]

All this made a great noise about the more fashionable quarters of the town, which was just then beginning to rally to the King's side. It was the moment when the Tory Party was first taking shape, the violence of the Whig Petitioners everywhere provoking associations of Abhorrers or Tories as they were contemptuously called, who combined to express their detestation of republican principles. The methods employed against Pepys became a seven days' wonder; by the middle of March they were being discussed at Newmarket.[16]

Harbord and Mansell were naturally perturbed by this. But they were not the men to lie down under a reverse of fortune. True to the tried tactics of their Party they began their counter-attack by an attempt to lull their enemy into a false sense of security. They were well aware of Pepys' intense desire to be at peace, and to free himself from the stigma which they had laid on him, and they knew how to play on it.

Their first overtures to represent Mansell as an honest man who was seeking a reconciliation failed through Pepys' flat refusal to have anything to do with him. They then tried a stronger line, by falling on Alexander Harris, a weak well-meaning creature, whom they understood how to intimidate and to bribe. On March 10th Harris, under pressure, began to retract what he had said as to Harbord's having bribed James to give false evidence. Shaken by Harris' surrender Pepys was lured to a meeting with Harbord in the dying man's room where he was confronted with three Justices of the Peace, including the notorious Sir William Waller, several clerks, Dr Spratt, the Dean of Westminster and another divine, and Harbord's brother-in-law, Captain Russell of the Navy. Pepys came with Hewer, the long-suffering Povey and his solicitor, Hayes. As all these important people crowded into the poor squalid room where James lay, they could hear the Abbey bell outside chiming the hours.

After Povey had read out the correspondence between himself and Pepys and the depositions which he had taken from James, who from his dying pallet acknowledged their truth, Harbord publicly asked to be cleared from the imputation that he had given money for false evidence. All the rest he acknowledged, including the payments to James. But he insisted that they were merely to support evidence which at the time he believed to be true. He then presented to James a paper denying that he had given him money to accuse Pepys falsely.

But when the paper was examined, Pepys found that the word 'falsely' had been omitted. When it had been inserted, as Pepys in his Diary put it, 'the standers-by concluded and declared that in what J. J. now did, he did both clear Mr Harbord of the Bribery and me of Popery and what he had alleged concerning Morelli'. After all he had been through even this seemed a great thing to Pepys.[17]

Before the end of the meeting, Harbord acknowledged quite frankly that he had never believed Pepys to be a Papist. 'When the meeting was broken up and the company parted, Colonel Mansell walked with me as far as Westminster Abbey, professing all the integrity that he could, and declaring that he was able to do me a great deal of right in this matter . . . and said he would meet me at any time to discourse with me, for that he had long observed this J. J. to be a rogue, and had advised Mr Harris and his wife to put him out of their house.'* But Harbord had no intention of letting the matter rest there. With James' paper in his hand, he could now protect himself from the fatal truth which his confessions made to Povey and Littleton had laid bare. He would now once more carry the war into the enemy's country. He would brand Pepys with the same stigma as Mrs Cellier, Blood and those other rash fools who had tried to discredit the Plot. Then, when Parliament at last was allowed to meet, he would show Pepys exactly where he stood.

Four times during his last delirious hours James was visited by Harbord, Captain Russell and Sir John Hotham, with papers which they tried in vain to make him sign that he had been suborned by Pepys to charge them falsely. All the while, as his mother afterwards testified, they roared and blustered about the room like lions. Meanwhile they filled the republican press with paragraphs stating that James had freely acquitted those whom he was thought to have reflected upon of any attempt to suborn him. Pepys preserved a dignified silence, broken only by a denial which at the special request of the dying man he had inserted in Hartford's *Mercurius Anglicus* to the effect that James had never actually sworn to the statements which he had made against him in the House of Commons and so had not technically perjured himself. The thought of this seemed to give James comfort.[18]

Early on Saturday, March 20th, James died, leaving Harbord's counter-attack in the air. During his last hours he struggled repeatedly to clear his mind of something, but the effort was too much for him. What others might say of his words and actions concerned him no longer. But to those who survived him they had become of vital importance, and Pepys was careful to draw up statements which he got Dr Littleton, the Harrises and James' mother and sister to sign as to exactly what had happened during those tumultuous last weeks. His own view of the whole strange affair he expressed in a letter which he wrote to Morelli a week after James' death:

... it having pleased God to lay his affliction by sickness upon my man James, and thereby to bring him to the ... confession of the wrongs he has

* *Pepysian MS.* 2882, *Mornamont* II, 1215.

been tempted to do towards me and you, which he has largely, solemnly and publicly done upon receiving the Holy Sacrament; not without making some such discoveries of practises used against me, in the seducing him to the doing me those wrongs, as (to my grief) will, I believe, charge some eminent pretending Protestants with dealings as unbecoming Christians as the worst of those we generally reproach Papists with.

'And now', he continued, 'as to music, which I hope in a little time to find myself better composed for the taking the pleasure thereof...'[19]

Some concerned were unable to take so detached a view. Thomas Povey, always temperamentally nervous, confessed to Pepys as he walked with him in St James' Park that he was worried at the charges which Harbord was bringing against him for having been concerned in the dead man's confession and would gladly effect an accommodation between him and his foes. But Pepys replied with an absolute refusal, 'and so' (in the curt style of his later Diary) 'home'. Nor would he have anything to do with the proposals of Donluis, who came to him one morning with a tale of some momentous discovery he wished to make about Shaftesbury and Mansell; the 'Meal Tub' Plot had proved how easy it was to get trepanned that way, and though Donluis unquestionably knew a great deal about the activities of both, he was not to be trusted. Besides, Pepys reflected, he had enough to do to defend himself without concerning himself gratuitously in high politics.[20]

For of the struggle between the enigmatic King and his furious opponents Pepys had now become a mere spectator. He would speak the truth, give his accusers the lie and for the rest mind his own business; it was for him the only safe way. So that Good Friday, when Shaftesbury, counter-attacking once more, was filling the town with Irish witnesses primed with new and unbelievable informations against the chief supporters of the Crown, Pepys wrote placidly to Mary Skinner's mother, now living with her brother-in-law and sister, Sir Francis and Lady Boteler, at Wood Hall in Hertfordshire:

Pray let Sir Francis know (as to his demand) that there is hardly a day passes without some new Plot discovered or old one laughed at, and, of the latter, none more than that wherein my noble Lord of Ossory is named; I having lately had the honour of... waiting on him, where it administered mirth in abundance, more, I believe, that the little Great Lord you mention ever intended either him or me. But by the present appearance of things he may live to make us yet a great deal more, the Knavery designed against my Lord of Ormond in Ireland being likely to prove ten times more contemptible than against his son in England.*

He added that the Duke of Buckingham† had just come out of France 'in expectation . . . upon the success of his agitators here in the business of their Counter-Plot. But his disappointment therein is such . . . as he thinks fit to keep close; little Justice Overdoe (Sir W. W.)‡ being no longer able to serve him or yourself'.[21]

Yet though Pepys' part had become that of a spectator, there was no question of his sympathies. He paid his loyal court to the Duke of York now back from Scotland, attended him at Whitehall and St James' and at the end of March waited on him at Newmarket. Thither he journeyed by way of Brampton and Ellington to look after his country affairs and catch a glimpse – it was no more – of his father. It was a long time since he had expressed his duty in this way to the old gentleman. He found him in good health. A few weeks later another visitor to Ellington, reporting its continuance, mentioned that Mr Pepys senior had made 'fewer complaints than I have been accustomed to hear. I heartily wish', he added, 'that you also may have less trouble in that kind'. The casual sentence reveals another of Pepys' crosses.[22]

The diary that Pepys kept to record the battle that raged round James' last days tells us also something of his personal doings during the February and March of 1680. In the three weeks between March 5th and 26th he dined no less than ten times with Lady Mordaunt in Portugal Row. Once it was on lobster pie. Sometimes her sister, Mrs Stewart, shared their company, though more often she was ill; sometimes Mrs Higgins was there also. On Saturday, the 20th, Pepys accompanied Lady Mordaunt by water to Vauxhall, and on the following Friday took all three ladies to that place of pleasure and thence by barge to Putney in order to pay a call at Wimbledon. After Lady Mordaunt and her sprightly sister, the Houblons

---

* S. Pepys to Madam (Skinner). Good Friday night, April 9th, 1680. *Rawl. MSS.* A. 194, ff. 146v.–7.

† The name is left blank in Pepys' letter book *(Rawl. MSS. A. 194)*, but the presence of the 'the' before the blank and a reference of Pepys' in a letter of March 29th makes this assumption fairly certain. In another letter of April 15th Pepys writes of the Duke as 'him that lives like an owl'.

‡ Sir William Waller, the Whig magistrate.

stood first in the list of Mr Pepys' loves. In the same period he visited Winchester Street six times and twice took his cousin, Sarah Houblon, to the play; on another occasion he drove her and her children in his coach to Chelsea. Sir John Bankes is mentioned once and his wife with whom Pepys supped one Sunday evening; so also is Lord Berkeley, at whose house he dined with Lady Mordaunt. Another friend was Sir John Holmes, the Admiral, with whom Pepys dined and who in turn supped at his house. There are also references to Mary Skinner* whom he carried on March 10th to Knightsbridge, and to her uncle, Sir Francis Boteler.

On Sundays Pepys appears to have been in the habit of attending morning and afternoon services at Covent Garden Church – a short stroll up the hill from York Buildings and across the Strand – followed by a jaunt abroad in his coach; on March 14th it was to Hyde Park, 'the first time this year, taking two bottles of champagne in my way'. One afternoon he spent on the water, visiting the Neat Houses. Four times during March he went to the theatre: of the plays seen *The Orphan* and *She would if she could* are the only ones mentioned by name.[23]

All this while Pepys was living with Will Hewer and his mother at their house overlooking the river in York Buildings. Here he kept his own books and belongings and his own servants – his maid, Katherine, David the coachman and Paul Lorrain, his amanuensis and copyist. Three times in the Diary for March there is a reference to a morning or evening spent with Richard the joiner shifting and arranging the things in his bedchamber and study: probably, one suspects, the inevitable book-presses and their attendant gilded mirrors. For as he grew used to retirement and the pressure of his enquiries to clear his name diminished, the relative importance of the golden volumes behind their glazed doors increased, till they became more and more the chief factor in life.[24]

Yet the summer of 1680 brought Pepys little respite from labour or anxiety. The meeting of a vengeful and threatening Parliament had, it is true, been again postponed, but his enemies were still busy and there was talk of new witnesses against him and of a trial at last in the summer Term. From Paris Joyne maintained an interminable correspondence about Scott's past villainies, present movements

---

* If the initials M. S. may be taken as indicating her. We know from *Joyne's Diary* that Pepys was still a close friend of hers.

and future intentions, and was supported by the varying but doubtful testimonies of four unfathomable scoundrels, De La Tour, Dailly, Moreau and a shady Portuguese of the name of Moralles, who had all at one time or another enjoyed the privilege of the Colonel's friendship and who now for a consideration were ready to bear witness against him.

Pepys was often at a loss what to make of it all. There were times when he felt lost without Joyne and urged him to penetrate the mist that concealed the sinister shadows threatening him. On such occasions he thanked him profusely for his almost daily letters and spoke gratefully of his friendship, diligence and prudence. At others he was filled with distrust for the importunate watchmaker, who instead of returning to the exercise of his trade seemed to be making it his whole study to create employment for himself at his expense.[25]

With the necessity of surrendering to his bail on the first day of Term and the renewed hope of a trial – 'all I have now left to ask', as he told Joyne, 'as being fully prepared, I thank God, to show the impiety of the age we live in'* – Pepys again collected attestations abroad and witnesses at home. Whatever charges Scott might bring, the long course of his past villainy and consistent treason to his King and country could be published. Yet Pepys' thoroughness defeated the object he was pursuing, for faced by such a superfluity of damning evidence against them, Scott and his backers did not dare to bring matters to a public issue.

On June 11th, the first day of Term, Pepys and Deane appeared in Court, only to be told that their Motion for a discharge must be respited till the last day of Term. For two weeks Pepys despaired of either trial or liberty.† But on June 28th the latter came with almost startling suddenness. For when the Lord Chief Justice asked the Attorney-General what he had to say against the prisoners' Motion, he answered 'Nothing'. On which the Court without any further words told them they were discharged and directed them to depart.[26]

---

* S. Pepys to J. Joyne, June 10th, 1680. *Rawl. MSS A.* 194, ff. 162–3.
† . . . 'my adversary continues his old practice of keeping out of my way and giving no evidence at present, but saying that his purpose is to respite it for the Parliament. So I am likely to remain in the same condition till the Parliament sits, which is a very great hardship.' S. Pepys to J. Joyne, June 28th, 1680. *Rawl. MSS. A.* 194, ff. 167–8.

13

The King's Turn

'The lies of this age will be the history of the next. And so will the false principles be the poison of it.' *Observator*, Vol. II, No. 21, Feb. 25th, 1684.

After fourteen months of unbroken persecution and suspense Pepys was a free man. Very naturally the first thing he did was to tell his friends. As soon as he reached home he sat down and wrote to James Houblon, who more than any other had cherished and befriended him during that dark year:

I could not but give you the earliest notice I could of my being at last, what I had long since been had others been as just as you were charitable and myself blameless: I mean a free man, viz.: in every circumstance but that of obligations to you and your family, which nothing but the grave shall, or can, or ought, to put an end to.*

Next day he wrote in the same vein to Mrs Skinner to inform her that at last he was discharged from a bondage which but for one villain's practice would have ended a year before: 'however (as the world goes), justice ought to be welcome at any time, and so I receive it with thanks to God Almighty'. He had learnt his lesson at last.[1]

Pepys did not make the mistake of supposing that he was in no further danger. His enquiries had made him fully aware of the secret causes that had brought him so close to the scaffold; and at any moment the political situation might cause them to operate again. For the necessities of Tangier and the ambitions of France were making it impossible for the King to live any longer on his standing revenue, and additional supply could only be obtained from Parliament. And when it met anything might happen to Pepys. Writing on behalf of Mary Skinner's brother to his old friend, William Howe, in Barbados, he expressed his sense of the purpose of his enemies, 'whose designs being levelled at the King my master, they thought no surer aim could be taken at him than through his servants who stood nearest to him, among whom their malice having done me the

* S. Pepys to J. Houblon, June 30th, 1680. *Rawl. MSS. A*. 194, f. 168 v.

honour of reckoning me one, they deemed me worthy to be first
removed, though at the price of perjury'.[2]

At one moment Pepys even spoke of taking the offensive against
his enemies by an appeal to Parliament for some satisfaction for the
wrongs done him. But this was in a letter to Joyne, who was trying to
scare him into renewed expenditure by hinting at horrible projects
that were being prepared against him by his enemies; and it was not
in his interest that Joyne should think him frightened. None the less
he asked him to continue his enquiries and supplied him with a
cipher. And he asked that Moralles, the Portuguese blackguard
who appeared so frequently in Joyne's letters, should put his
revelations on paper so that he might show them to the King; 'I
should esteem it a very extraordinary kindness from him if he would
give himself the trouble of letting me have it under his own hand
before a Notary'.* He enclosed a letter of compliment to him,
though he would not, he told Joyne, be so discourteous as to ask a
stranger directly for this favour. Pepys' ceremony in addressing
these rogues was quite touching. Yet, as they themselves were to
discover, his caution in his dealings with them was to prove even
more striking than his good manners.[3]

All that Pepys collected about Scott from his friends of the
underworld, he had copied out in Lorrain's exquisite hand in two
vast folio volumes. Their contents constituted a detailed record not
only of the proceedings against himself but of the Colonel's whole
life. He called them his book of Mornamont, after a fabulous castle
of that name to whose hereditary possession Scott in his pot-house
hours was wont to lay claim.[4]

One who had played a notable part in the formation of that
collection was now no longer at Pepys' service, for Balty after some
difficulty had been restored to the King's. It had not been easy to get
him back into the Navy, for the present Commissioners of the
Admiralty, though their anti-Court sympathies had been tempered
by their year of office, had no wish to befriend Pepys or his
dependants. But Pepys had been insistent, writing repeatedly to
their new secretary and his old acquaintance, John Brisbane, and
bombarding the Lords Commissioners with letters and visits until
they at last yielded and posted Balty to the office of Agent for the

---

* S. Pepys to J. Joyne, June 28th, 1680. *Rawl. MSS. A.* 194, ff. 167–8.

affairs of the Navy at Tangier to which the King had appointed him a year before. Yet there was a further difficulty to be overcome for the Navy Office was proposing a salary of only £200, no more than Balty had been getting at Deal, whereas Pepys argued the King had intended the appointment as a promotion and that it ought to be remunerated at not less than £250 per annum. It was not asking much, he said, after his own twenty years' service, for his brother-in-law was the only relation he had left to appear for in the Navy.[5]

Though it was not strictly true to suggest that this was the only occasion on which the late Secretary of the Admiralty Office had asked, and even obtained a favour for a protégé since his retirement, those in the Navy who had been connected with Pepys came in for a good deal of victimization. Samuel Atkins after nine years' service was summarily dismissed, though this did not stop him from boldly petitioning for the post of Judge Advocate. Even Child, the humble seaman who had denied the accusation of having procured God-frey's murder at Pepys' direction, had been ruined and left 'a distracted creature, forced to see his wife and children starve for bread'. Pepys himself was victimized in various minor ways familiar to administrators; harried for papers left in his possession and dunned for long-forgotten sums by the Public Auditors and Navy Board, 'they being resolved', he wrote, 'never to leave me in quiet, but to torment me and my friends to the very last'.* The continued favour of the King alone saved him from worse. That autumn when he began to bank with Richard Hoare at the 'Golden Bottle' in Cheapside, his account was overdrawn to the tune of £16. 9s. 8d.[6]

All these circumstances made Pepys thankful to see Balty depart for Tangier. He proved a reluctant traveller, and wrote the most pathetic letters about being torn from the bowels of his 'pretty sweet family and five small babes (perhaps never more to return)' and of his having now, after many years of faithful and honourable service 'no other recompense but to be sent to the Devil for a New Year's gift'. His very departure was attended by unmerited disaster, for taking a cheap boat down the river,

By the time we were got as far as the lower end of the Hope, such a fog and storm arose . . . that our cockleshell took every sea over and we like to perish, not seeing one inch before us, not knowing whither to steer, so that

* S. Pepys to B. St Michel, Oct. 2nd, 1680. *Rawl. MSS. A*. 183, f. 283.

my good husbandry had like to have made at once a poor widow and five miserable orphans, but God had mercy of them and would not have it so.

But it had been borne with courage, he assured his brother-in-law, 'sufferings (though innocent) having been my meat and drink for some years past'. The gist of it all was that Pepys, as 'the dear lord and chief-half of my never-to-be-forgotten dear sister', should exert himself to get him a better post at home, 'that so I may not . . . die in employments full of danger, great trouble and no gain, such as none but I could be singled out to have (Lord why was I born!)'. 'Shall I never', he ended, 'have ease from fightings and storms, but continue when my youth likewise and greatest vigour is past.'* From anyone who knew him there could be only one answer.[7]

In the September that saw Balty's departure, Pepys lost another relation by death. Early in the month John Jackson, yeoman of Ellington, died. His affairs had long been ailing, and Pepys, who had frequently advanced him money, had been corresponding with an old friend of Lord Sandwich's household, Dr John Turner, now Rector of Eynesbury, about settling the Ellington land on Pall and her two little sons as a mortgage for his advances. This Pepys did more to give his father quiet than from any opinion he had of the estate, for he knew from experience that every loan made to the Jacksons was throwing good money after bad. The whole subject was so painful to him that he could hardly bring himself to write about it.† His brother-in-law's sudden death came, therefore, rather in the nature of a providence, even though it meant liquidating his debts and clearing up his derelict estate in order to provide a livelihood for his sister and her children.[8]

For himself Pepys resolved, if only the politicians would give him leave, to settle down to that 'less encumbered state of life, whereto my (ill-meant) good fortune has conducted me'. So at least he told Admiral Herbert, the Commander-in-Chief in the Straits, when he wrote to him in September to recommend Balty to his care. He was no longer a housekeeper now; even his black boy had been sold for

* B. St Michel to S. Pepys, Sept. 24th, 1680. *Rawl. MSS. A.* 183, ff. 47 *et seq.*

† . . .'The truth is the occasion of your trouble . . . is so unpleasant to me in the very contemplation, that for my own quiet I suppress what I can the memory of it, and so am with much difficulty able to bring myself to admit the care of it into my own thoughts.' S. Pepys to Dr J. Turner, Aug. 14th, 1680. *Rawl. MSS. A.* 194, ff. 182v.–3.

him by kind Captain Wyborne, who had taken him off to the
Mediterranean in the previous autumn and brought back instead
twenty-five pistoles, transmuted at Cadiz into chocolate and sherry
for Pepys' drinking. He therefore spent a lazier August and September than any he had known since boyhood – for it was 'Paradisian
weather' – visited Morelli at Brentwood in company with young Mr
and Mrs Houblon and their children and corresponded at placid
length with the learned Mr Evelyn and Dr Gale about the early
history of shipbuilding and the sea, propounding to them such
conundrums as who was the Genebelli who built the block-houses at
Gravesend in '88, and what instances were there in the past of
nations overvaluing their own naval strength and underestimating
that of their enemies.

A gentleman of leisure for the nonce, Pepys visited his cousins at
Impington and his old red-nosed friend, Dr Peachell,* now Master
of Magdalene, at Cambridge. And though he still dared not have
Morelli back in London he freely indulged his taste for music.
Evelyn spent a happy evening at one of his Wednesday chamber
concerts, and then hastened home to pay his dear Mr Pepys 'some
tribute for the loss of his time in diverting me this afternoon, and
whenever I wait upon him and interrupt his more serious affairs'.
Indeed to that good but prolix man, Pepys' freedom from public
affairs was an estimable blessing: all the rest of mankind might be
bored by his passion for disseminating information, but Pepys could
never be. He sat up all that night writing him a letter of sixteen folio
pages in answer to his historical enquiries, and ranging happily over
the Greeks, Egyptians, Parthians and Old Britons, Herodotus,
Thucydides and Plutarch. A desultory and unmethodical trifle, he
called it. 'But now', he ended, ''tis now near three in the morning; I
will sleep a little and finish what I have more to say before I wait on
you to the Philosophers this day, for wide day it is, Thursday 8th of
July.' For during the summer Evelyn had persuaded Pepys to
resume his attendances at the meetings of the Royal Society, which
had been on the verge of dissolution, begging him, and not in vain,
for 'one half-hour of your presence and assistance toward the most
material concern of a Society which ought not to be dissolved for
want of a redress . . . I do assure you', he wrote, 'we shall want one

* 'My old acquaintance, Mr Peachell, whose red nose makes me ashamed to be
seen with him, though otherwise a good-natured man.' *Diary*, May 3rd, 1667.

of your courage and address to encourage and carry on this affair. You know we do not usually fall on business till pretty late in expectation of a fuller company, and therefore if you decently could fall in amongst us by 6 or 7, it would, I am sure, infinitely oblige . . . the whole Society'.*[9]

With Parliament meeting before the end of October, the political atmosphere grew more sultry as the autumn advanced. While Pepys made the best of the London sunshine in Lady Mordaunt's company or helped to promote the marriage of two of his young cousins at the request of good Mrs Ursula Pepys,† the rich widow of Thomas of Merton Abbey, Colonel Scott went into the West of England with Monmouth, whose mother he told all and sundry had been to his certain knowledge the King's wife. Thence he slipped away from Lyme Regis to France to brew new enchantments against the coming feast at Westminster. At the end of September Pepys himself accompanied his sovereign to Newmarket, hoping to get his accounts settled and the arrears he was claiming paid before it was too late.

Here amid dogs and hawks and horses, he took down in short-hand from the King's own lips the tale of the royal flight from Worcester. He began it on Sunday, October 3rd, and finished it on the Tuesday. From its sharp incisive opening – 'After that the battle was so absolutely lost as to be beyond recovery, I began to think of the best way of saving myself . . .' to its dispassionate but triumphant close, 'I was met by my mother by coaches short of Paris and by her conducted thither, where I safely arrived.' – its magnificent narrative, half Charles' and half his own, never flagged. On what seemed to most men the verge of a new revolution, it served to recall to a short-memoried people the heroic loyalty that had redeemed the errors of an earlier and more awful one. It remains to this day the best and most authentic account of the most romantic incident in the history of the English throne.‡[10]

It had been Pepys' intention to set out from Newmarket on

---

* J. Evelyn to S. Pepys, June 25th, 1680. *H.M.C. Hodgkin,* 177 and *Pepysian Miscellanies* V, 54–5.

† His cousin Alcocke to Miss Hutton, the niece of rich Mrs Ursula Pepys of Merton, Surrey. See *Howarth,* 97–8 and *Rawl. MSS. A.* 194, f. 173v.

‡ It was first printed from Pepys' longhand transcription of his own shorthand notes in *An Account of the Preservation of King Charles after the Battle of Worcester* in 1766. The original is in the Pepys Library, No. 2141.

October 4th and spend a day with his father in Huntingdonshire on his way back to town. But on that very day, while he was waiting at Newmarket to complete the royal narrative, his father, unbeknown to him, was laid in earth at St Mary's, Brampton. There Pepys, pursued by ill news, hastened to find a distracted household with his sister lying dangerously ill of the same ague that had slain both her husband and father. After seeing her safely settled in the charge of her cousin Mrs Hollingshead, he went on to London to round up his own affairs before the opening of the session and to take out letters of administration for his father. Then, taking Lorrain and his volumes of Mornamont with him and driven by Hewer's coachman (his own had fallen sick of the prevailing ague) he returned down rain-soaked, mud-foundered roads to Brampton, leaving Parliament to look after itself.[11]

There he remained from October 25th to November 19th, administering his father's will and disposing of his affairs in the rustic Courts of Brampton and Buckden.* It was a wretched, tumble-down little estate that he was called upon to put in order, with its deeds mislaid and lost, its rents unpaid and its buildings in ruin,† but his passion for order and his wonderful energy were thrown into its Lilliputian affairs with as much zeal as though they were the concern of kingdoms. He disliked it heartily, the dull, heavy country life in the gloom of falling winter, and the distracted household with his sister lying sick and helpless in the midst of it, but it was in the day's work and must needs be borne with. 'Here I am,' he wrote to James Houblon, 'as full of land matters as ever you knew me of sea; with this difference, that whereas practice rendered the utmost of the first supportable, ignorance makes a little of the latter ten times more than it is, I go so awkwardly about it. However my comfort is I can't miscarry in this work more than, with all my knowledge, I have made shift to do in the other.'‡[12]

While he was absent, Pepys corresponded almost daily with Will Hewer. To him it was that he wrote when he found he had left

* The old gentleman had left his lands to Samuel and his personal estate to be divided between himself and Pall, with small legacies for his Jackson grandchildren and the poor of Brampton and Ellington.

† '. . . through my father's incapacity by age to look after them himself and the very ill conduct of my brother Jackson.' S. Pepys to W. Hewer, Oct. 28th, 1680. *Rawl. MSS. A.* 194, f. 218.

‡ S. Pepys to J. Houblon, Oct. 28th, 1680. *Rawl. MSS. A.* 194, f. 217.

behind some of the papers he needed to complete his volumes of Mornamont; they were in one of the drawers on the right hand of his scriptor, with his flute and music books. In the same drawer, he found it necessary to explain, was a volume of Lord Rochester's poems, 'written before his penitence, in a style I thought unfit to mix with my other books'. But Hewer, who could recall Deb, probably needed no explanation. 'However, pray let it remain there,' Pepys added, 'for as he is past writing any more so bad in one sense, so I despair of any man surviving him to write so good in another.'

Hewer told him of the illness of his maid Katherine, of the slow recovery of David the coachman, and of the tender thoughts that he and his mother constantly had of him: 'I pray you to believe', the faithful fellow wrote, 'that nothing relating to you can ever be thought a trouble either by my mother or self.'* It was from Hewer that Pepys was sent a remittance of £50 when the £60 he had brought with him had been exhausted by his father's funeral expenses and 'several dribbling scores', and from Hewer that he learnt of a fire that, kindling all day under a wooden hearth next door to Pepys' own sacred closet, had all but burnt down York Buildings: the very thought of it put the friends into such a fright that they could scarcely contain themselves; 'I hope', Pepys wrote, 'it will conduce to the awakening in your neighbours and self a great caution in that particular'. And to Hewer Pepys confided the trouble he was having with his coachman who, falling under the influence of one of the idle young servants of Brampton, became one day hopelessly intoxicated. Pepys' first intention was to send him straight back to London, and Hewer, furious that his master should be made uneasy, offered to dismiss him – 'a fault of such a nature being impossible for any sober family to bear'.† But when the poor man expressed his penitence and made promises of amendment, Pepys did not pursue his resolution.[13]

Yet the heart of the correspondence between the two friends was not domestic but political. It was Hewer who sent Pepys news of the world of Whitehall and Westminster, once more, after the opening of Parliament on October 21st, the focus of all eyes. Pepys, far from well himself, with a host of petty vexations and his sister lying sick and helpless, could not face the resort of small country squires round

---

* W. Hewer to S. Pepys, Nov. 4th, 1680. *Rawl. MSS. A.* 183, f. 144.

† W. Hewer to S. Pepys, Nov. 2nd, 1680. *Rawl. MSS. A.* 183, f. 146.

the thumbed papers in the Huntingdon drinking houses where the news of the great world was retailed and discussed, and relied on Hewer and his old clerk Gibson to send him a regular supply of Gazettes and news-sheets. The more secret and perilous items Hewer wrote in cipher.*

At first the news seemed reassuring and Pepys wrote back with relief of 'the happy beginning of the King's concurrence with Parliament', but this unexpected calm did not last. Hewer's next letter told how other servants of the King were receiving the same treatment from the new Parliament as he and Deane had from its predecessor of eighteen months before; one of them, confronted with a false oath made by three strangers that he had been seen at Mass, had not waited for the sequel but left a note at his lodgings that he did not think fit to expose his person to such unreasonable men but was withdrawing himself till the times were better and truth was restored. And as before the full cry of Parliament and rabble was joined that 'York must be taken off without more ado'.†[14]

In these proceedings Pepys' old enemies bore their wonted part, particularly Harbord, Capel and Bennet, who were unwearied in speaking in the Commons against those in authority, while in a lowlier sphere Colonel Mansell and the ubiquitous Harrington served on the Committee of the Green Ribbon Club which organized the great Pope-burning orgies of Queen Elizabeth's accession day. For the moment they had so much quarry to pursue that they had no time for Pepys, beyond putting out a rumour that he had fled with the Duke of York to Edinburgh. Meanwhile Scott, newly returned from France, had been seen at Newman's coffee-house by one of Pepys' former clerks, whose poverty and rather dubious honesty Hewer wisely fortified against the parliamentary chieftains by a little timely pecuniary aid. To make all as secure as could be, the same wise steward sent Pepys' chests and hampers of papers from York Buildings down to his country house at Clapham.[15]

Between the interstices of his rustic business, Pepys, with the virtuous Lorrain writing all in his copperplate hand, completed his volumes of Mornamont. From them he prepared a memorandum of his case, which Deane, who joined to his genius and integrity an incorrigible fretfulness, was anxious should immediately be made

* *Rawl. MSS. A.* 183, ff. 124 *et seq.*
† W. Hewer to S. Pepys, Nov. 2nd, 1680. *Rawl. MSS. A.* 183, f. 146.

public both in press and Parliament and had promised to one or two
of the more moderate members of the House for that purpose. Under
the assumed name of P. Bayly, Deane entreated his fellow victim to
hasten its despatch: 'I pray to send it or let me know what to do to
make good my word,' he scrawled in urgent, staccato sentences, 'for
will it not look ill for us to neglect to enable a friend to serve us in the
just truth . . . Pray excuse my zeal . . . Really, I fear we are very
unfortunate if you do not send it, and if it had been in my power it
should have been done.'*

But Pepys was wiser, and the shrewd faithful confidant whose
advice he took even more so. For Hewer pointed out how dangerous
it would be at such a juncture to force his adversaries to fight and to
place in their hands facts which with their host of paid informers
they could easily pervert to his ruin. The best thing he could do, he
advised, was to put copies of his paper in the hands of a few
trustworthy friends, who could be relied upon to use it wisely when
need arose and in the meantime to keep it out of the reach of his
enemies. These, Hewer wrote, were at present in Committee,
'swinging Sir George Jeffreys off', as they will do anybody else that
comes in their way. Pray God keep you out of their hand'.† Pepys
concurred and warned Deane that little good was like to come of
exposing Scott's crimes; 'were this villain's character yet worse than
it is', he continued, 'it would not at all prevent their purpose who
had use of his testimony. Nor is he at this day to learn how to digest
the name of villain. Nay, it seems more probable that he will
endeavour to recommend himself the more by confessing it, and
perhaps make the advantage by getting a general pardon by it, as
others have done, and then we shall have little to thank ourselves for
it, as bereaving ourselves as well as the King of an opportunity of
calling him to account for the wrongs he is guilty of to both'.‡ It was
surprising how much worldly wisdom Pepys had of late acquired.[16]

Hewer's present advice was that Pepys should return to London
as soon as he could dispose of his business and so defeat the ends of
those who were saying that he had hidden himself for fear of
Parliament. To this Pepys' own tastes** and the entreaties of his

* P. Bayly (Sir A. Deane) to S. Pepys, Nov. 9th, 1680. *Rawl. MSS. A.* 183, f. 138.
† W. Hewer to S. Pepys, Nov. 11th, 1680. *Rawl. MSS. A.* 183, f. 132.
‡ S. Pepys to Sir A. Deane, Nov. 11th, 1680. *Rawl. MSS. A.* 194, ff. 229–30.
** '. . . besides the little pleasure to be had at this time of year in the country. . . .'
S. Pepys to W. Hewer, Nov. 9th, 1680. *Rawl. MSS. A.* 194, f. 228v.

friends alike inclined him. Even the King was asking for him, a dispute having arisen at the Council Board about the salutes due to foreign flags in the Mediterranean, which to the disgust of the Admiralty Commissioners his Majesty had promptly directed should be referred to Pepys, 'as being best able to give satisfaction on that point'. It was good to know that one was still wanted.[17]

How much, James Houblon told him. 'From sea we have news except that we are (God help us) totally without guard in the Mediterranean, not one man-of-war there. The *Antelope* was sent several months since but not got beyond Cadiz, as we can hear of. That cursed money's being so much coveted by our Sea Captains robs us poor merchants of half the protection the King intends us and his treasure pays for.' For under the inept rule of the politicians who since Pepys' fall had lorded it at the Admiralty Board, the discipline he had built up with such pains and labour had vanished from the Service, and 'good voyages' and all the old abuses had broken out with redoubled force. 'I wish I had some pleasanter matters to entertain you with,' Houblon added, 'but in these times we must not expect them.'[18]

Yet the very thought of James Houblon's affectionate care – his letter was full of anxious directions for Pepys' health* – was cheering. To this unassuming friend, who had stood by him in the day of trouble, Pepys felt drawn ever closer. Before he left the quiet of Brampton he sent him his portrait, with presents for all his family and children, heralding them in a letter of great tenderness: 'My last said I should be in town the beginning of this week; but . . . though there be no place (I thank God) where I dare not show my head, yet there is one where I am ashamed to show my face again till I have done something (that ought long since to have been done) for securing the remembrance of what I am owing there, though I can never hope to discharge it, and that is at a namesake's of yours in Winchester Street.

'But don't mistake me, that his forgetfulness I am jealous of, and not my own . . . He is one of so tender a memory that there is no good deed of his own that will stick in it, for he shall do you twenty good offices before he will think them one . . .

---

* 'I hope as you say we shall soon have you here again; in the meantime, Sir, save yourself as much as you can from a fenny ague by eating a good breakfast and not being out late, nor without a good fire in the evening.' J. Houblon to S. Pepys, Oct. 30th, 1680. *Howarth*, 103–4.

'To supply which, I have bethought myself of fastening my picture (as a present) upon him, in hopes that, when he sees that, it will be out of his power not to recollect his errands on my score to Westminster Hall, his visit to the lions, his passings over the Bridge to the Patten in Southwark, and a thousand other things which, by his good will, he would never come within the hearing of. Nay, in my conscience, if he knew this were the design of my present, he would turn his head a' one side every time he comes in sight on't.

'And even, lest he should do so, I have been fain to think of an assistant device; and that is, to send a small bribe to everyone of his family to get them, in such a case, to be putting in some word or other as he passes by, to make him look at it, as thus – "Was Mr Pepys in these clothes, father, when you used to go to the Tower to him?", or thus – "Lord cousin, how hath this business of Scott altered my poor cousin Pepys since this was done!" Or thus – "What would I give for a plot, Jemmy, to get you laid by the heels that I might see what this Mr Pepys would do for you." '* It was Pepys' occasional capacity to write like this that made his friends – among whom posterity counts itself – so love him.[19]

Another friend who had stood by him in adversity Pepys remembered in this brief interval of country quiet, among the white mists and autumnal silences of the Ouse water meadows. To Samuel Atkins, who after a long illness brought on by his sufferings, was about to sail for Tangier in the hope of there mending his broken fortunes, he sent a parting loan of £20. 'His case', Pepys wrote to Hewer, 'deserves all manner of compassion, and above all from me, for certainly no youth of his wit and straightness of fortune ever withstood such temptations to have been a villain as that poor creature has done, and I hope God will bless him accordingly.'† Hewer also, as Treasurer of Tangier – a post he had held since Pepys' final retirement from it earlier in the year – did his best to succour Atkins and give him a new start on the Mediterranean station: early in the new year as a result of his intervention, the young man was given an ensign's commission in the Earl of Inchiquin's company in Tangier.[20]

On November 17th (the day that the London mob burnt the Duke

* S. Pepys to J. Houblon, Nov. 14th, 1680. *Rawl. MSS. A.* 194, f. 231. Printed in *Howarth*, 106–7.
† S. Pepys to W. Hewer, Nov. 7th, 1680. *Rawl. MSS. A.* 194, ff. 224v.–5.

of York's effigy surmounted by the word Ninny writ in great letters), Pepys left behind a Brampton 'in the homeliest and unhealthiest dress it has at any time of the year',* and set out for town where he knew that whatever perils the future might hold a warm welcome would be waiting in Hewer's house. 'I know nothing can make my life more uneasy to me than your making any other place your home,' the faithful fellow had written. His matter-of-fact, sensible optimism was a constant reassurance: 'though', he went on, 'the integrity and faithfulness wherewith his Majesty and the public have for so many years been served by us may not at present protect us from malicious reports, yet I am satisfied that God Almighty, who is always just, will make it up to us some other way to the shame of those who now triumph over us . . .' For the moment, however, the Almighty had a further small test in store, for half-way between Highgate and the town's end Pepys suffered 'the misfortune of being robbed by six highwaymen. But my loss not great', he noted laconically.† After eighteen months of Colonel Scott's attentions, six highwaymen may well have seemed a little thing.[21]

Yet, though Morelli greeted him with a couple of young ducklings from Brentwood, hoping his old employer would eat them with gusto,‡ and Hewer with the news that the Bill to exclude the Duke of York from the throne had been dramatically defeated at the eleventh hour in the Lords, Pepys' troubles were not over. At any moment the King's gossamer defences against the republican majority in the Commons might collapse and every friend of the Duke of York's fall like a hunted beast to the merciless pack. And even if the King, defying public clamour and his own poverty, still stood fast, civil war seemed the inevitable alternative. As with the approach of Christmas that terrifying contingency became more imminent, men of all views drew closer to each other till the country presented the spectacle of two camps ready to spring to arms under the King and the Earl of Shaftesbury. Lord Halifax, now in the royal camp, remarked to a Tory neighbour that if it came to war, they must go together, while in the City Colonel John Scott, now on the proposal of the Taunton republican, John Trenchard, admitted into the Green Ribbon Club, was reported, in conclave with the Duke of

* R. Gibson to S. Pepys, Nov. 16th, 1680. *Rawl. MSS. A.* 188, f. 123.
† S. Pepys to P. Lorrain, Nov. 20th, 1680. *Rawl. MSS. A.* 194, f. 234v.
‡ C. Morelli to S. Pepys, Nov. 1680. *Rawl. MSS. A.* 183, f. 70.

Buckingham, Colonel Mansell and Mr Jenks, to be supervising the secret manufacture of halberds with which to arm the mob of Wapping and Southwark. About this time Shaftesbury confided to Justice Warcup that he would shortly draw a line round Whitehall, and that the King would suffer on the scaffold as his father had done. And in such a case there can be small doubt that Samuel Pepys would have suffered likewise.[22]

In such troubled waters John Joyne, the watchmaker, engaged in a little fishing on his own account. For some time past his behaviour had been growing more and more mysterious. During the autumn Pepys had continued to correspond with him and to consult him about Scott's movements, and even to send him an occasional roll of tobacco and other small gifts. Joyne in return had made presents to Pepys, though it transpired later that he expected him to pay for them – thirteen indifferent crayons and a very ill-conditioned print of Michael Angelo's Day of Judgement, 'too mean', according to their recipient, 'to have been thought furniture fit for the vilest office in the house'.* He had also continued to offer new revelations from Moralles, Dailly and De La Tour. But when, without the slightest authority, Joyne announced that he was about to obtain additional secrets out of the Portuguese Moralles by pretending to comply with a plan to swindle Pepys out of three or four hundred pounds, the latter began to take alarm. This was followed up, while Pepys was still at Brampton, with the news that by a miraculous chance he and Moralles had lighted on two new French informers who, at Scott's request, were about to set out for England to testify against him and Deane. After that letters from Paris came almost daily describing the heroic efforts that the altruistic watchmaker was making to prevent these dangerous scoundrels from crossing the Channel; in the end, and only at the eleventh hour was he able to obtain from them a written promise of abstention in return for an offer of 6000 livres, a sum which he begged Pepys for his own safety to despatch at once to the 'White Lion' at Calais.

But Pepys' reply, when at last it came, proved to the last degree discouraging: 'Pray see that they . . . be left at liberty to come over with as much knavery and folly as they can bring along with them,

---

* Pepys' Answer to Joyne's Complaint, March 6th, 1702. *P.R.O. Chancery Proceedings, Mitford* C. 8. 376, No. 69.

for I promise you they shall have the reward of it.'* And to Moralles, a stranger to him, he wrote in more formal terms that he would not promise sixpence to anyone for the greatest advantage that could happen to his cause, and that in any case he could think of none greater than that of suffering these new witnesses to come into England and deliver what they could: 'for the evidences of my innocence, are, I thank God, above all human practice to shake'.† It was this maddening epistle that caused Moralles to observe to his friend Joyne: 'By God, this Mr Pepys is so devilish cunning that in his letters to me there is nothing but my extraordinary justice and to that purpose . . . so that by God I would have burnt them, for there was nothing to be taken of them', and to propose, as the only way to get saleable evidence against him, a little discreet forgery of his hand.[23]

But the state of public affairs in England was so encouraging, with a furious Parliament seeking for fresh informers, that Joyne and Moralles before proceeding further with Pepys hit on the plan of inventing a new Popish Plot, of which they should accuse the Queen and the Portuguese Ambassador before the politicians at Westminster. The fact that Moralles was himself a Portuguese would of course inspire the credulous English with an immediate belief in its truth. And the presence of the Whig Lord Cavendish in Paris, who as Moralles observed could not have come there for nothing, offered them just the channel to a pension and free quarters at Whitehall that they needed. 'For', he said, 'my Lord – and my Lord – are my very good friends, and we shall not want for more as soon as we get to London.'‡

This 'impious and detestable machination', as Pepys called it, was happily averted by a sudden panic on the part of the conspirators, who each nursing with considerable reason a profound distrust of the other, appeared separately at the English Embassy and proceeded to arraign one another of having concocted the whole affair. Each of them also, unbeknown to the other, wrote to Pepys to reveal the other's wicked proposal. Astonished, indignant, and not a little bewildered Pepys made no reply. Meanwhile Scott was bragging in

---

* S. Pepys to J. Joyne, Nov. 14th, 1680. *Rawl. MSS. A.* 194, f. 233.
† S. Pepys to Moralles, Nov. 7th, 1680. *Rawl. MSS. A.* 194, f. 227.
‡ The names are left blank on the roll in the Public Record Office, which being compiled in the reign of William III probably did not admit of their safe inclusion.

Newman's coffee-house that his old foe had been betrayed by his pretended friends and that he would soon make all he had declared before Parliament as plain as the sun.[24]

But by mid-January, that body no longer existed. Moreover its successor, which the King had summoned for March, was called to meet not in London, where the mob could stimulate or support its decisions as required, but at Oxford, the high stronghold of the loyal Church of England. Unknown to Pepys and almost everyone about him, the King was in almost nightly conference with men who knew the counsels of the armed revolution which Lord Shaftesbury was planning in the recesses of the City; the cloaked figures who passed up and down the secret stairs of Whitehall were the shuttles on which the loom of all England in that mysterious hour worked. In country manor-houses men were gazing on the rusty pikes and breastplates that their fathers had used in the legendary, tragic days of '42: soon, they believed, they would have cause to use them again.* But the King thought otherwise, for he knew men and women to a hair and how to rule them with a sheathed sword. And in this he was one inch taller in stature than his great adversary.[25]

The last weeks of the winter of 1680–1 saw ancient foes girding on their armour against a decisive battle. From the close electoral corporations and the printing-presses, the mutineers poured defiance on the gathering forces of the Crown. The elections were as auspicious to the republicans as those of 1679. But the voice of the Rotten Boroughs was not yet the voice of England. In rustic parsonage and manor, in village ale-house and city tavern, a mighty flood of loyal feeling was silently rising. Nor could the clamour of a thousand republican libels stem it.†[26]

The lying tongues did not spare Pepys. On January 15th he wrote to Morelli to warn him to postpone a visit he was proposing to London and to tell him that his amanuensis, Lorrain, was now being accused of Papistry. 'But I hope God Almighty', he added, 'will in his due time deliver us from the "lying tongues" mentioned in your

* 'Although it be counted even Popery, yet I cannot but pray God to preserve us from the tumults, confusions and rebellions of 1641 and '42, which seem to threaten us on one hand as much as Popery on the other; I fear God hath a controversy still with the land.' Dr J. Peachell to S. Pepys, Jan. 11th, 1681. *Howarth*, 110.

† Even that staunch and irascible Protestant, Sir Geoffrey Shakerley, the old Cavalier Governor of Chester, was accused of having 'a Pope in his belly'. Sir G. Shakerley to Sir L. Jenkins, Feb. 1st, 1681. *C.S.P.D.* 1680/1: 152.

last anthem.' Among these Colonel Scott was still to be numbered. In February he was practising his old trade by making depositions before a London magistrate against the reputation of Lord Stafford, the Catholic nobleman, who still protesting his innocency had perished on the scaffold at the beginning of the year.[27]

But the King had taken the measure of his opponents. When the remaining 'Mutineers' on the Council, alarmed by the determined steps he was taking to meet the threat of armed rebellion, desired leave to withdraw, he replied that they could not make any request he could more easily and cheerfully grant. The Government was rapidly changing its complexion. On February 19th Capel, Lee and Vaughan departed from the Admiralty Commission which they had done so much to degrade and were succeeded by Lord Brouncker and Sir Thomas Littleton. On the next day Pepys plucked up confidence to write to Sir Thomas Meres to beg a post in the Navy for an old servant.[28]

It was an extraordinarily sharp cold spring, with not a leaf on the trees and frost and snow lying everywhere. But Pepys, with his sister Pall sick on his hands in town, whither he had brought her to consult the London physicians, was all impatience to be in the country. With this intention he had opened negotiations with Colonel Norwood for a new lease of his old villa at Parson's Green. Norwood was actually living there, but so determined was Pepys to effect the move at once that he offered to transport himself to an adjoining garden house and allow his friend immediate occupation. But it turned out that the garden house was still 'furnished with onions . . . you must therefore have patience till over Lady Day,' Norwood wrote, 'and whenever you please to bring your friends here to survey the quarters, you may perhaps be convinced by the aguishness of the country that a little more sun will do no hurt'.*[29]

Before Pepys, an eager boy as ever, could obtain his desired pleasance, the Parliament had met at Oxford. The guns of the Tower were trained on the City and soldiers patrolled the road to the Chilterns. As the King drove through the Oxford streets, an old man called out to him from the cheering crowd: 'Remember your royal father and keep the staff in your own hands.' 'Aye,' replied the King, 'by God I will, and the sword too!' Others who passed that

* Col. H. Norwood to S. Pepys, Feb. 12th, 1681. *Rawl. MSS. A.* 183, f. 76.

way thought also of the sword – the Parliament men who rode over Magdalen Bridge with the picked blades of Shaftesbury's brisk Wapping boys roaring behind them, a blue cockade in every ragged hat and a leaden flail in every Protestant hand.[30]

Pepys who was not well did not go to Oxford. The news of that dramatic week's battle was sent him by his old clerk, Walbanke, who had gone there to defeat a scandalous petition against himself which his ex-colleague Donluis was presenting to Parliament. That erratic being, though he was still protesting to Pepys his desire to betray Lord Shaftesbury's plans to the King, had all unbeknown to his former employer gone to Oxford in the strangest company – with College, the Protestant joiner, designer of the warlike flail and author of the lewdest of the republican ballads against the King, 'and several others of that gang'. His activities of the week, during which he shared College's bed at the 'Chequers' inn, were to bring him within an ace of the gallows.[31]

For the week ended in a triumph for the King, as unexpected as it was dramatic. Unknown to all but a few, he had concluded an agreement with Louis which in the last resort would enable him to pay the Fleet and the Guards and govern without a Parliament whose demands were now incompatible with the very existence of monarchy. He offered his enemies all, and more than all, they could reasonably demand: the perpetual banishment of the Duke of York and the vesting of the Crown on his own death in the regency of Mary of Orange. These expedients were refused without even a debate, the republicans seizing the rope the King had proffered them and furiously twisting it round their own necks. On March 28th he gave the noose a jerk and dissolved Parliament.[32]

14

New Courses

'When the ill-offices which were levelled through me at our Royal Masters shall be found terminating to their honour and the advantage of their service, I may haply resume my tongue and pen again.' S. Pepys to Vice-Admiral Herbert, Sept. 20th, 1682. *Rawl. MSS. A*. 194, f. 207.

By the time the news of the King's dramatic victory reached the capital, Pepys was seriously ill of the ague that had been threatening him all the winter. On Easter Sunday for the first time in many years he was unable to take the sacrament from Doctor Milles' hands beneath his wife's memorial at St Olave's Church. Morelli, who was still at Brentwood ruling psalms and songs for him to sing with pretty Sarah Houblon, hearing of his fever, told him of a local healer possessed of miraculous sympathetical powers and asked for the parings of his toe nails and three locks of hair for the magician to work upon. Another friend sent a recipe for China ale:

Take ½ lb. of China Root. Slice it in thin pieces and put in a pipkin of 6 quarts, then put the cover on the pipkin and 'lute it with meal and water. Put it in a copper of water up to the neck, and set the copper a'boiling for 24 hours continually, and as the water in the copper diminishes, replenish it. And take two or three spoonfuls in a morning fasting and rest half an hour.

'It quenches drought', he added, 'and cools mightily, and withal cleanses the stomach of phlegm and creates an appetite.'*[1]

By the beginning of May Pepys was well enough to take his part in the great demonstration of monarchical feeling that followed the King's victory at Oxford. He procured a loyal Address to the Throne from Trinity House and wrote to the Duke in Scotland enclosing a copy of it and offering to procure another from the officers of the Fleet. The Duke replied promptly that it would not be Mr Pepys' fault if all about him did not do what became them, but expressed his doubt of the propriety of those in the King's pay expressing loyalty in any other way than by service. Instead he

* *Rawl. MSS. A*. 183, f. 57.

asked – it was the second time he had done so – for a copy of Pepys' Relation of His Majesty's Escape from Worcester.[2]

Pepys apologized for what he modestly described as 'the presumption of mentioning to your Royal Highness about sea commanders, etc.: it was barely mentioned, and shall have no further place with me'. He enclosed a longhand transcript of his 'Royal Relation', with an account he had procured from Colonel Phelips, who had taken a chief part in the latter stages of the escape, but explained that he had not yet had time to put together the full history he intended; 'my covetousness of rendering it as perfect as the memory of any of the survivors (interested in any part of that memorable story) can enable me to make it, has led me into so many and distant enquiries'.[*] As happened consistently throughout his life, Pepys' very thoroughness in collecting historical material tended to defeat his own object. Yet it was no small achievement for a busy and harrowed man to have secured and placed on record the four best and most authentic accounts of the royal flight – those of the King, Father Huddlestone, Mr Whitgreave and Colonel Phelips. It was a work that occupied part of his time, on and off, for the next year.[3]

It was, perhaps, the same devotion to the Muse of History that caused him that Whitsuntide to obtain from Doctor Milles and a score of fellow-parishioners a certificate of his regular attendance at divine service at St Olave's, Hart Street, 'this being the very time', he told the Rector, 'of my 21 years being expired since my good fortune of coming within your knowledge and friendship'.[†] Among those who obliged their old acquaintance by signing it were Sir Robert Knightly, Lady Richard, John Lethieulier, that 'pretty, civil, understanding merchant' and husband to 'our noble, fat, brave lady in our parish' of Diary days, John Buckworth, the Deputy Governor of the Turkey Company, old Daniel Skinner and Will Hewer.[4]

Pepys was never entirely free to devote himself to the study of the past, for even at the quietest moments of his life the history of the present always claimed him. While the King pursued his ding-dong battle for the throne with Shaftesbury and Monmouth, now entrenched in their City fastness behind the protection of packed *Ignoramus* Juries, Pepys continued to be plagued by Joyne. By repeated letters

* S. Pepys to the Duke of York, June 4th, 1681. *Tanner, Correspondence* 1, 13–14. Also in *Rawl. MSS. A.* 194, f. 253.

† S. Pepys to Dr Milles, May 21st, 1672. *Rawl. MSS. A.* 194, ff. 248v.–50.

and explanations that persistent craftsman had managed to pass off his unholy alliance with Moralles as a well-meant, if ill-received, attempt to fasten a plot on Lord Shaftesbury. 'An accountable, hazardous and impious undertaking', Pepys termed it, such as might give the world 'a most reasonable suspicion of my having been interested, if not the very author of the whole contrivance, which had they done me ten times more injury than they have . . . I would rather choose to be swallowed quick than entertain so much as a thought of'.* But, for the moment at any rate, he found it best to forgive him.[5]

For a while, therefore, Joyne continued to supply information about Scott, whose prosecution had now become one of the chief ends of Pepys' existence. Only by bringing him to book in a court of law for the injuries he had done him, he felt, would he be able to re-establish his own credit in the eyes of the world. But soon it became clear that so long as Shaftesbury controlled the Sheriffs who appointed the London Juries there was no hope of any loyalist obtaining his legal rights against a republican. Thereafter Pepys' enquiries of Joyne ceased. But Joyne's own letters continued and took on a more mercenary tone. After a while they became threatening. Pepys wrote to him no more.[6]

The summer of 1681 saw Pepys finally released from his long persecution at Shaftesbury's and Harbord's hands, and free to devote himself at last to his own business. For the moment his affairs at Brampton and Ellington had chief claim to his attention. As his sister was still too ill to return to Brampton, he had thoughts for a time of disposing of it to his cousin, Roger of Impington. But the possibility that he might one day, and perhaps no distant one, wish to retire there, restrained him, and he gave orders for reflooring the hall, though with old timber, and had the chimney-piece re-whitened. Meanwhile he busied himself about his sister's derelict little estate at Ellington, disposed of her pasture grounds in Bladon Meadow at 9*d.* a pole, and corresponded in his grandest manner with the Bursar of Peterhouse about the failure of poor Jackson and his tenants to pay their rents to the College.[7]

On June 21st Pepys set out on a personal visit to Brampton. Thence he went on to Cambridge to interview his Peterhouse

---

* S. Pepys to J. Joyne, March 7th, 1681. *Rawl. MSS. A.* 194, ff. 236v.–40. Also in *P.R.O. Chancery Proceedings, Mitford* C. 8. 376, No. 69.

landlords and pay his respects to old friends. While there he told a young cousin, Joseph Maryon of Clare Hall, how content he would be to retire out of the world and live for ever in that delightful place. It was the kind of wish which an old Cambridge man might make during a July visit. It had an unexpected sequel. For on his return to London at the beginning of August he received a letter from his cousin telling him that Sir Thomas Page, the Provost of King's, was dead and assuring him that if he could obtain the King's mandate for the preferment, he would certainly be accepted in his place.[8]

Pepys thought it over. The more he thought of it, the more the idea appealed to him: it would give him leisure, the society of learned men, a near neighbourhood to his small Huntingdonshire estates and an opportunity which nothing else was ever likely to give him of putting together his collections of naval and Admiralty papers and of writing the great sea history he intended. He therefore approached Lord Hyde, the King's principal adviser, and Colonel Legge, the Duke of York's agent in London. But Legge had already promised his influence to his old tutor, Doctor Copplestone. Pepys therefore withdrew with elaborate protestations of his own unworthiness. It was perhaps well, for Fate had a still greater work for him to perform.[9]

He consoled himself by visiting Morelli* at Brentwood with Lady Mordaunt and her sister and by spending the autumn with the Houblons in the little pleasance at Parson's Green which he and they had rented from Colonel Norwood – 'a relaxe of two or three months which I have lately allowed myself in the country', he told a friend. His amanuensis, Lorrain, was on a visit to his relations in Holland, so he could more readily allow himself a holiday. He enjoyed it so much that Colonel Norwood was forced to enquire sadly but politely whether those worthy persons who designed to honour his poor cottage intended to return to London at all, as if so he would like some time to occupy it himself. It was not till the middle of November that Pepys was back in town.[10]

It must not be supposed that in these halcyon days he cast off all

---

* Since his enforced departure from London in November 1678 Pepys had paid Morelli £85. 17s. 6d., the equivalent of a retaining fee of over £200 per annum in our present money. As Morelli was disabled from serving him and Pepys at that time was faced with many heavy claims on his purse, this was not ungenerous. *Rawl. MSS. A.* 183, f. 247. Printed in *Smith* 1, 270–1, and *Howarth*, 118–19.

responsibility. There was one burden, voluntarily shouldered, which he could never lay down – the needy relations whom Elizabeth had left behind. Balty himself was far away – at least so Pepys supposed – victualling Tangier from Gibraltar and writing home by every post about his wrongs. But there was still his 'weeping wife and desolate babes', to whom he had referred so touchingly on his departure and for whose maintenance he had made, it appeared, so little provision. After his retirement from Deal Balty had established them with some pomp in a new house of Will Hewer's at York Buildings, where they lived, in the tradition of the St Michels, well above their means. But as Balty left England £700 in Hewer's debt, and the rent was never paid, this arrangement could not be continued indefinitely. Pepys therefore offered his sister-in-law the empty house at Brampton. To this he added an allowance of £1 a week.

Esther St Michel described her acceptance of this provision as laying down her children's and her own life to Samuel's mercies. She then proceeded to live beyond her means at Brampton as she had done in London. When Pepys wrote to protest, she covered half-a-dozen sheets of paper with lamentations and complaints of Balty's neglect – 'I being a stranger as well to my husband's estate as actions, always in a worse condition than the meanest servant he kept, not having the liberty of asking for my necessaries without the fear of a rude denial, his private ways known only to himself till by their great expenses brought forth . . .'*[11]

But Pepys was not the man to be brow-beaten by a tearful woman. He wrote back sternly, called attention to the ill-manners of her children and explained in minute detail, supported by illustrations of his own Elizabeth's frugal housekeeping in the good old days, how she could live on 20*s*. a week. 'This being as much', he wrote, 'as I and my wife had for several years to spend, and yet lived so as never to be ashamed of our manner of living, though we had house, rent and tax to pay which you have not, and this in London too, and yet free from ruin on that score, the truth and assurity of which do appear in the daily paid account she kept of every issuing of her family expense, even to the bunch of carrots and a ball of whiting, which I have under her hand to show you at this day.'†[12]

Esther admitted the ill-manners of her children – 'their age tells

* Mrs Esther St Michel to S. Pepys, Aug. 28th, 1681. *Rawl. MSS. A*. 183, f. 177.
† S. Pepys to Mrs Esther St Michel, Oct. 1st, 1681. *Rawl. MSS. A*. 183, f. 165.

me they have enough, too much, and shall endeavour to correct that fault'. But she continued to maintain that £1 a week was inadequate to support house and home. 'Sir, you do not consider that although I am in the country all things are as dear here as at London, and some dearer, except chickens or pigeons, which are not for me and therefore of no profit. As for butcher's meat, bread, beer etc., roots, as turnips, carrots, onions, in fine all gardenage, is dearer near a penny in two pence.' The same, she said, was true of soap, starch, oatmeal, salt, pepper, candles, thread, tape, shoes, stockings, gloves, cloth, mending tubes 'and a great many more things too many to trouble you with or ever before sent in a letter by me'.[13]

Pepys did not flinch. Good housekeeping and frugality, he was resolved, should reign at Brampton as he had once made them reign in the King's ships and dockyards. But in Esther St Michel he met a foe worthy of his steel. At the end of November he was confronted by a letter, confused in grammar but unequivocal in purpose, 'to advise you that you and family are now reduced to the last and wait your further directions and orders, assuring you that to the uttermost of my power I have managed every mite with the best housewifery as possible'.* Pepys was all but forced to surrender, for he could not leave his sister-in-law to her obstinate resolve to starve herself and her children to death in his own country house, especially when his Majesty had just graciously put him into the Commission of the Peace for the shire.[14]

In the midst of these encounters Balty reappeared in England to lay his wrongs before the Admiralty. To Pepys his unexpected appearance can have brought little comfort. He sent him down to enjoy the domestic bliss awaiting him at Brampton, noting a few weeks later that he was glad to hear from Mr Hewer 'the account you give him of the considerations you are under towards the better settlement of your family, wherein I wish you all good success'.†[15]

The St Michels were not Pepys' only family responsibility. There was Pall to be nursed and her children, Samuel and John Jackson, to be educated. He placed them with John Matthews, a young Huntingdon schoolmaster and a distant cousin, supplied them (a

* Mrs Esther St Michel to S. Pepys, Nov. 29th, 1681. *Rawl MSS. A.* 178, f. 73.
† S. Pepys to B. St Michel, Jan. 7th, 1682. *Rawl. MSS. A.* 194, f. 262.

trifle reluctantly)* with clothes and linen and watched over their learning. The youngest boy John, their tutor reported, would infallibly make a scholar, the elder 'an honest and well-tempered man'. As the latter showed a modest talent for writing and arithmetic, his uncle resolved to send him to sea as soon as possible.[16]

For retirement had robbed Pepys of none of his passion for dedicating the youth of his country to the sea. In the spring of 1681, after an enforced retirement of two years, he had returned to his old duty on the Governing Body and Mathematical Committee of Christ's Hospital. He was far from pleased with the way things were going there. In a volume of rough notes which he was keeping on matters maritime, he jotted down his reflections on the inadequacy of the City Fathers who controlled the Charity:

... the ignorance and supineness of its Governors (though men of trade) of keeping the King's new Mathematical Foundation, notwithstanding the ample maintenance provided for it, and particularly their frequent objecting to the children's learning Latin, or even more mathematics, or better writing than they say boys abroad do set out commonly with and yet make good seamen; neither considering the ill effects of that general want of literature in our best sea-commanders and masters, nor the charge his Majesty has been pleased to put himself to for this Foundation to remedy it.†[17]

In the autumn of 1681 therefore Pepys tore himself from his riverside pleasure house to attend the examination of the Mathematical boys by Trinity House which he had so wisely inaugurated eight years before. The results were far from satisfactory; in nine months, it seemed, the boys had only learnt 'what an indifferently diligent man might have made them learn in one'. Their new master, Doctor Wood, an over-learned man of the study whose appointment Pepys had opposed in vain a year before, had neglected them shockingly and covered his own idleness by farming them out

---

* '... I am forced (by your kinsmen's great want of clothes) to write this second time ... Those clothes which they have indeed are so bad as that they are both dangerous (by reason of their thinness) and almost disgraceful.' J. Matthews to S. Pepys, Nov. 6th, 1681. *Rawl. MSS. A.* 178, f. 97. For Pepys' frugal reply of Nov. 12th – 'Nor will you (I suppose) think it of any use to make them over fine ... provided what you buy be such as will keep them warm and clean and last well' – see *Rawl. MSS. A.* 194, f. 259.

† *Naval Minutes*, 102. (Printed from *Pepysian MS.* 2866.)

to one Hudson, 'a kind of mathematical curate to look after in his frequent absences'.* Hudson was 'an idle drunken fellow ... a person who by the meanness of his conversation, indecencies in habit, looseness of manners and public exposing of his intemperance to the children' had forfeited all respect.† Pepys was so perturbed that he told Mr Parrey, the Clerk of the Hospital, that if things were allowed to remain as they were a further year, the whole design of the Foundation would be lost. 'I would loath', he added, 'the thing should fail, if any reasonable pains of mine can save it.'‡[18]

Those pains were not wanting. They took the form of an exhaustive report prepared by Pepys after a conference with his Brethren of Trinity House on January 4th, 1682. The Mathematical boys, he wrote, were without exception unfitted for their future work, and mostly apprenticed to masters whom Trinity House would not trust with a footman and who took them only for their money. A month later, presiding over a Sub-Committee appointed to investigate the conduct of Doctor Wood, he drew up a damning indictment of that gentleman and his tipsy usher and of the deplorable discipline of their scholars, 'even to the playing of football . . . idling away their time by the fireside, while others have been lying all along upon their backs on the table'.** The Doctor himself, it seemed, never so much as appeared in school, constantly sat in his private closet, where he refused to see the boys, and had even 'assumed a liberty of absenting himself at his own pleasure from his attendance on his duty, frequently repairing into the country . . . upon his private occasions'.†† It was the unanimous report of the Sub-Committee that he should be dismissed.[19]

While Pepys was grappling with the scandals that had dishonoured his beloved Mathematical School, he was also exerting himself to do honour to its founder. At the end of 1681, he used the rising tide of royalist feeling to revive his old project for commemorating King Charles' benevolence by a painting in the Great Hall. The Mathematical Committee agreed, and on January 12th Esquire Pepys and Mr Hewer were desired to interview Signor Verrio, the

---

* J. Flamsteed to Sir J. Frederick, Sept. 27th, 1681. *Pepysian MS.* 2612.
† *Pepysian MS.* 2612, f. 413. Misquoted by the late E. H. Pearce in *Annals of Christ's Hospital*, p. 111.
‡ S. Pepys to Mr Parrey, Oct. 3rd, 1681. *Rawl. MSS. A.* 194, f. 258v.
** *Pepysian MS.* 2612, f. 409.
†† *Pepysian MS.* 2612, f. 413.

painter, and procure a draft design from him as soon as possible. A month later he was borrowing the scarlet Aldermanic gown of his old acquaintance, Sir Thomas Beckford, the slopseller, for inclusion in the picture.[20]

It was never Pepys' way to neglect his own affairs in his attendance on those of others. Free at last from the expense of legal proceedings and the menaces of the republican caucus, he sat down in the autumn of 1681 to put his worldly estate in that perfect order in which he loved to see everything about him. His old Tangier accounts had long been outstanding with the Treasury, and in November he was given an awkward reminder of the necessity of settling them by a notification from the Exchequer Office that he would be charged for an unaccountable imprest of £5000 made to him nine years before out of French subsidies received by Mr Chiffinch, unless he could immediately get the account passed by the Treasury. Pepys put in a counter-claim against the Crown for three times that sum for naval services and explained that the £5000 paid to him by Chiffinch in 1672 was a special grant made to him by the King, 'my receiving and giving an acquittance for it . . . under the name of Tangier serving only to supply the want of a present and formal adjustment of the said arrears'.* And as correspondence on these lines was still continuing with the Exchequer a year later, here as in other matters, Pepys' tenacity proved an asset.†[21]

The winter saw Pepys adjusting belongings of a more intimate kind. On his return to York Buildings he made a careful inventory of the papers in his 'office'. In his great chest he placed his Admiralty Journal, his two volumes of Mornamont and a loose volume of papers about Scott, two letter books, two old catalogues of his library, his 'great book of Commission Officers' and the Journals of Sir John Narbrough and Captain Jenifer. To these he added a collection of valuable historical manuscripts which he had been lent by the Duke of York, including a history of Mary Stuart and a

---

* S. Pepys to Mr Auditor Done, Nov. 29th, 1682. *Rawl. MSS. A.* 194, f. 281.

† A minor claim which he was called upon to settle about the same time was for £147 which his brother John had before his death made himself liable for by standing bond for a fraudulent Collector. This Pepys as his executor had to pay. He was also involved in an unmerited loss through the failure of the tenant, to whom at the time of his misfortunes he had sub-leased the stables and coachhouse he rented in Cannon Row, Westminster, a deficiency which he was forced to make good to his landlord. *Rawl. MSS. A.* 178, ff. 16, 81; *A.* 183, f. 158.

number of maps of 1588. Other documents he disposed of in the drawers of his secretaire and his great Chatham chest box. To his inventory he added a note of papers lying loose on his table and to be overlooked at the first opportunity, a parliamentary Journal of business relating to the Navy, and Colonel Scott's bogus volume of maps.[22]

For as 1681 drew to a close Pepys' energies, released from more urgent cares, turned more and more to the great historical and naval work he had so long ago envisaged: the time had come to clear the deck of his study. It was more than eighteen years since he had risen early on a June morning to gather all the more important letters and papers of his office into a single volume and seventeen since Coventry had shown him his ancient naval manuscripts and suggested that he should devote his talents to writing a history of the First Dutch War – 'A thing', he had written that day, 'I much desire, and sorts mightily with my genius and, if well done, may recommend me much.' It had never been done. But the idea of it, and of something greater,* had long occupied his leisure thoughts.[23]

For many years past Pepys had been assiduously collecting and copying every naval manuscript he could. Now he would deal with them. His friend Mr Evelyn was at hand to tell him how. Pepys wrote to him at the beginning of December to ask for his advice and beg the loan of his manuscript on the Third Dutch War, his account of Trajan's Pillar and the Battle of Lepanto and Walter Raleigh's notes on the defences of England, and a great deal more. With this extensive request Evelyn did his best to comply, and the more valuable of the papers he sent remain in Pepys' library to this day.†[24]

With Evelyn's bundles of manuscripts came some sobering counsel. 'As to the compiler's province,' he wrote, "tis not easily to be imagined the sea and ocean of papers, treatises, declarations, relations, letters and other pieces that I have been fain to sail through,

---

* 'My work this night with my clerks till midnight at the office was to examine my list of ships I am making for myself and their dimensions, and to see how it agrees or differs from other lists, and I do find so great a difference between them all that I am at a loss which to take, and therefore think mine to be as much depended upon as any I can make out of them all. So little care there has been to this day to know or keep any history of the Navy.' *Diary*, Jan. 16th, 1668.

† Notably Drake's pocket-book. At the end of Evelyn's accompanying letter was a pathetic postscript: 'These . . . when you have done with you may please to take your own time in returning.' *Tanner, Correspondence* 1, 20.

read over, note and digest before I set pen to paper. I confess to you the fatigue was insufferable and . . . did rather oppress and confound me than enlighten, so much trash there was to sift and lay by . . . And this, Sir, I dare pronounce you will find before you have prepared all your *materiam substratam* for the noble and useful work you are meditating.'[25]

But Pepys embarked on these labours with boundless confidence. There was no limit to what he told himself he could accomplish: he even proposed to add a life of Lord Sandwich to his other tasks. Since the previous year he had been keeping a folio in which to enter miscellaneous notes for his guidance in matters historical. December 1681 saw an outburst of entries. There were notes of books to be bought or borrowed – Matthew Paris and Sir Thomas Browne's *Pseudodoxia Epidemica* – manuscripts and rare volumes to be consulted in libraries like the King's at St James', naval allusions to be pursued and dug out of vast tomes. His researches went into the most remote periods and places, and he eagerly sought out Josephus' account of the port and mole of Caesarea and the precedents for the privileges of the Cinque Ports in the Laws of Jutland. Yet sometimes they had a more direct bearing on modern times: 'observe', he wrote, 'the character of Sir Walter Raleigh in Coke's Book of Lives, and remember that he was a gentleman, and the first great seaman of England that ever was so, unless it was the Earl of Nottingham; and therefore what he observes concerning the debauchery of our young gentlemen then sent to sea is the more observable in one of his little tracts.'[26]

Every passing event became fraught with matter for his labours, even the Lord Mayor's Show which inspired a scornful note about the ridiculous pageants of ships and trade exposed in it. All his friends who could contribute to his knowledge were conscripted to aid his labours: particularly Evelyn, and his cousin Doctor Gale of St Paul's School, who was consulted about the antiquity, title and office of steersman and the true construction of the word 'versonia' in Plautus. 'I conjecture', the learned Headmaster replied, 'that Plautus meant thereby that part of the stem of a ship upon which the stern turneth as a door upon the hinge.' Even Esther St Michel added her mite: 'My sister St Michel living long in Holland and at Deal has observed to me that the Dutch seamen are ever better clad than ours, and either are soberer or can bear drink better.'

Another who aided the varied chase was the former clerk of the Council, Sir Robert Southwell, now enjoying a blissful retirement at King's Weston. He sent Pepys naval rarities and much curious information, as well as the occasional speculations of that volcano of learned ingenuity, the great Sir William Petty, who was a particular confidant of Sir Robert's and whom the two friends called their Irish Apollo. 'I am here among my children,' Southwell wrote, 'which is at least an innocent scene of life, and I endeavour to explain to them the difference between right and wrong. My next care is to contend for the health which I lost by sitting many years at the ink bottle.' But the industrious Pepys had no such care.[27]

Sometimes the King himself aided his late Admiralty Secretary's labours. Pepys was often with him that winter and was careful to enshrine in his notes any sea aphorisms that fell from the royal lips. On the last day of the year he listened to him talking to Sir Leoline Jenkins, the learned Welsh Secretary of State, about a tradition of a great ship called the *Rose* built by Henry VII which had been wrecked in the Thames. His Majesty then showed Pepys a very neat case that had belonged to the Earl of Warwick, furnished with drawings and plans of every ship of every rate. On several other occasions he presented him with rare naval manuscripts, including the famous and lovely Anthony Roll of Henry VIII's Navy still preserved at Magdalene College, Cambridge.[28]

On matters connected with navigation and shipbuilding the King was a really great authority and Pepys often applied to him for information. Early in the new year he sought his advice about a decision of the Navy Board's to remove the lead-sheathing from all ships to prevent the consequent rusting of rudder-irons and bolt-heads. Charles, questioned by Pepys, agreed as to the propriety of the Board's decision, but confessed himself at an entire loss to account for the cause, 'unless it be the nails', Pepys noted, 'whose composition he knows not but will enquire after, not apprehending that the lead has anything of corrosive in it'.

Of the King's naval advisers Pepys had the lowest possible opinion. As Charles shared it and frequently said as much in his private discourse, Pepys, sore to see all he had wrought for falling into ruin, was apt, during these embittered years, to blame him. 'No King', he once scribbled in his notebook, 'ever did so unaccountable a thing to oblige his people by, as to dissolve a Commission of the

Admiralty then in his own hand, who best understands the business of the sea of any prince the world ever had, and things never better done, and put it into hands he knew were wholly ignorant thereof, sporting himself with their ignorance, and was pleased to declare to me his dependence was upon my service to keep them right.' But in this Pepys was hardly just, for it had not been in the King's power to do otherwise.[29]

Nor was it yet. For, though the flood of loyalty was now running strongly in his favour, the King was still in deep waters. At home the corrupt Corporations, with their stranglehold on the whole legal and parliamentary system, were in the hands of the republicans, while abroad the ally, to whom his poverty and his past kept Charles fettered, was arousing ever deeper feelings of hatred and suspicion by a bigoted ultra-Catholic and militarist policy. Pepys' old Puritan tutor, Joseph Hill, wrote sadly from Holland that unless England intervened, Europe and the Protestant interest must be ruined. If Charles gave his people their head and broke with Louis, he would have to choose between a republican parliament and bankruptcy, yet so long as he kept them on the leash he was subject to their constantly recurring suspicion. He had still therefore to move with the greatest caution. Even as late as 1682 Pepys was still to the public branded with the taint of Popery and treachery, and his restoration to his old place might have proved fatal to the cause he supported.[30]

None the less the tide had definitely turned. In January 1682 there were further changes at the Admiralty which gave the Commission a more Tory complexion, and already Pepys' recommendation had ceased to be a handicap to applicants for naval appointments. He was able to do a good turn to Doctor Milles of St Olave's by bespeaking a place for his son-in-law at the Navy Office, and even to befriend Bagwell, the carpenter, who was looking for a better post. 'What I pretend to know of him', he told Lord Brouncker, 'is shortly this; that being born in the King's service (son of Owen Bagwell, that has been for near 30 years ... and is at this day Foreman at Deptford) he has from a boy served the King through sundry ships as Master Carpenter till by due degrees he rose to his present charge in a Ship Royal wherein he has been now about four years ... Nor will his Diligence, Sobriety and Fidelity (I believe) want full testimony from the Officers of the Navy, nor his ... experience in war as well as in peace, I having always looked upon him as one giving exemplary proofs of all, during the whole time of my service both in the Navy and Admiralty.'* He did not add that Bagwell had shown himself an obliging cuckold. Possibly he had forgotten.[31]

At the beginning of March 1682 Pepys had the satisfaction of seeing Balty sail again for his post at Tangier. But the Admiralty made the reluctant traveller depart at seven hours' notice, and he poured out his heart to his generous benefactor:

I hope still (with a great faith) in God and your dear goodness to me-wards, that when you next see the Duke it will not be long now 'ere I shall be eased from these so many thraldoms and miseries I groan under (only cut out for poor me), and removed according to justice to some other employment at home of more honour and profit, but particularly of more capacity of service to you-wards, where I may with my dear, poor family pass the remnant of my days in comfort, for otherwise I fear me, for their sakes (God is my Judge) and not for my own, and am almost sure that in this I shall worry my life and days out . . . in an employment which will not hardly give me bread now, much less gain for my support in my age hereafter . . .†

'Pray', he said, 'give my drooping spirits the cordial of a line from you.' He plucked them up sufficiently however, even without this stimulus, to enclose a long list of articles which he desired of 'that most worthy gentleman, Mr Hewer'. They included four Holland shirts, a ream of the best paper, a hundred pens, two pairs of sand coloured kid gloves and a white beaver hat. A week later he was seen in passing at Plymouth by an acquaintance, who reported him depressing company, – 'the thoughtfullest and melancholiest man I ever saw'.‡[32]

Esther remained behind. She was still at Brampton with the children when Pall returned there in April. Though she made no trouble and piously hoped that Madam Jackson would not mind her lodgings crowded with people who had not the honour of her acquaintance, it took another six months to get her out of the house. In the meantime Pepys tried to secure her a Rocker's place in the household of the Duchess of York, who was just then expecting a baby.[33]

For Pepys' long and painful loyalty to the Heir Presumptive was

---

* S. Pepys to Lord Brouncker, Dec. 17th, 1681. *Rawl. MSS. A.* 194, f. 261.

† B. St Michel to S. Pepys, March 9th, 1682. *Rawl. MSS. A.* 183, f. 302.

‡ H. Fielding to S. Pepys, March 17th, 1682. *Rawl. MSS. A.* 178, f. 45.

beginning to bear fruit. That March the King gave his brother permission to come south to join him at Newmarket. The visit was a great success. Pepys, who went there expressly to greet him, wrote triumphantly to James Houblon, to tell his 'Whigship' – for the kindly merchant had a mild Whiggish tendency – of his old patron's good health – 'plumper, fatter and all over in better liking than ever I knew him'. 'A thing that I cannot answer for,' Pepys went on merrily, 'but so it is and worse, by how much with his natural, his political state of body seems to be much mended too, since his nearer partakings of his brother's sunshine. Yet all this you will do well to bear with, if the King will have it so. Nor do I despair but you will when I have told you that the King (God be blessed) seems in no point less fortified against mortality than the Duke, but in one particular more, namely, that (as much as that signifies) he hath the prayers of the very Whigs for his health, while we Tories are fain to pray by ourselves for his brother's. Under which odds I leave you with great content . . . I kiss all the fair hands with and about you', he ended, 'and hope to do it nearer in three days.' After which the Duke's loyal adherent went off to pay his respects at Mistress Nelly's.*[34]

The success of Pepys' Newmarket visit gave him new confidence. He felt himself no longer the persecuted victim of injustice, but a man of weight and influence, whom the world, whether it would or no, could not do without. Certainly the Navy of England ('which nothing can extinguish my solicitude for') could not. On his return he sat down and penned a mighty letter to the Lords of the Admiralty ('uncalled for') on an 'extravagant proposition' of theirs for building an unnecessary and expensive wet dock at Chatham in which to lay up the new ships of the line. Such a project, Pepys declared, would be a standing invitation 'to a known enemy from abroad or a false friend (of whatever principles) at home', of destroying the Fleet at a single blow. To put so 'essential a share of the strength and security of England within the power of any one villain' or the carelessness of an idle workman† was folly beyond contempt.[35]

* Pepys appears to have retained his early admiration for Nell Gwynn. After Charles II's death he still did her small favours connected with the sea and preserved among his prints an engraving of the greater part of her person, unexpectedly clad in nothing but a pair of angel's wings.

† 'The incorrigible liberty found among workmen or watchmen taking tobacco.' S. Pepys to Commissioners of Admiralty, March 21st, 1682. *Rawl. MSS. A.* 194, ff. 267 v.–70.

With equal pugnacity and zest Pepys threw himself once more into the unsatisfactory affairs of Christ's Hospital. On March 25th he fired off an ultimatum at the head of Mr Parrey, 'being unable to suffer the business of the Mathematical School to remain any longer in its present condition without bringing it either to an immediate reformation or finally washing my hands of it'. He proposed, he said, to make 'a thorough motion at the next Court'* – Dr Wood, the Mathematical Master, must go. And go he did, with many indignant mutterings.[36]

That done, the business was to find a successor. Pepys, who received innumerable applications,† was at pains to prepare a report on the necessary qualifications for the post. To it he added an elaborate Latin curriculum for each form in the school and a list of disciplinary rules: for instance, henceforward there must be weekly Monitors appointed by the Master to 'observe the behaviour and decent apparel of the children, and that they presume not to come before him with dirty hands etc., to the disgrace of the government of the Foundation'.‡[37]

Pepys' views, or 'humble thoughts' as he called them, on the qualifications of a Mathematical Master he embodied in a letter to Sir John Frederick the President of the Hospital, on May 2nd. The Governors, he said, must be careful to avoid appointing anyone 'to whom it will not be a benefit and promotion, late experience having shown you that he who neither needs it not or thinks his merit superior to it . . . can never be expected to submit . . . to the lowness and drudgery of it'. This had been the trouble with Doctor Wood. They must also decline 'a person knowing only the theory of navigation – a bare land navigator'. Rather they should take a bold step and appoint a man with practical experience of the sea. For such a one even ignorance of the classics should be no bar. And he suggested that Trinity House should be made the final judge.[38]

Before the letter was despatched, Pepys was called from his

---

* *Pepysian MS.* 2612, ff. 447 *et seq.*

† Thus the Lord Chief Justice of the Common Pleas, the great Francis North, asked to do an office of civility for a friend, wrote to Pepys to recommend Samuel Mountford the schoolmaster of Sturbridge – 'a man of learning and good life; . . . you are a Governor and by your merit have great influence beyond your own suffrage'. *Rawl. MSS.* A. 183, f. 310. Mountford was duly chosen as Master of the Grammar School from a short list of five. *Pepysian MS.* 2612, f. 467.

‡ Pepys' Report, April 27th, 1682. *Pepysian MS.* 2612, f. 494.

attendance on Christ's Hospital by the rising fortunes of his master the Duke. Soon after Easter it became known that the Heir Presumptive was to return to Scotland only in order to make an end of his affairs in that country before resuming his ancient place at his brother's Court. The 'Yorkists', who three years before had seemed at the mercy of their enemies, had triumphed. Pepys who had suffered with them in the days of their adversity and had all but been numbered in the roll of their martyrs, was entitled to a place in the rising sun of their fortunes. He resolved therefore to accompany the Duke to Edinburgh.

On April 29th he informed Captain Wyborne of the *Happy Return*, who with his wife had continued to correspond with him through all his troubles, that a sudden propose had come into his head to wait upon his Royal Highness to Scotland and that he hoped to have an opportunity of taking his passage with him. 'I mean', he wrote, 'to be very sick. Therefore pray let me have a little room with you if I come . . . and wherever your Lady is (if she be with you) I kiss her hands and should laugh to see her in Scotland.'*[39]

But there was no room in Wyborne's ship when on the morning of Thursday, May 4th, Pepys accompanied the Duke of York aboard the *Gloucester* in Margate Roads. He therefore moved from the crowded flagship to the comfort and seclusion of the little *Catherine* yacht, where he had only Sir Christopher Musgrave, the Lieutenant-General of the Ordnance, to keep him company. At eleven o'clock the little flotilla of frigates and yachts sailed from Margate Roads with a southerly wind. After a three years' exile Pepys had returned to the sea. He went so suddenly that he could not even take leave of his friends.[40]

Yet Shaftesbury all but triumphed over the Duke and his servant Pepys. That evening the wind shifted into the north, and the weather changed. At night the squadron was fogbound, and all next day battled off the East Anglian coast in a fresh easterly gale. At midday Dunwich steeple could be seen three leagues off, and at nightfall Lowestoft town to the north-westward. Then, to avoid the Yarmouth Sands, the fleet stood out to sea.

While the ships were battling with the waves of the North Sea in the early hours of darkness, a furious argument was waging on

---

* S. Pepys to Capt. Wyborne, April 29th, 1682. *Rawl. MSS. A.* 194, ff. 271v.–2.

board the *Gloucester* between its officers and the pilot as to the course which the latter was holding. For the pilot, confident alike in his experience and the favour of the Duke, was bent on making the voyage quickly and refused to tack to the south in order to weather the sands, as Sir John Berry, the Captain and his Master and Mates, Colonel Legge and even the Duke himself urged him to do. All night the controversy continued, but the pilot was quite firm. At half-past five on Saturday morning the *Gloucester* struck the Lemon and Oare. For a moment or two she beat on the sands: then a terrible blow tore off her rudder and knocked her side open.[41]

Pepys, wakened from troubled slumbers, watched from the deck of the *Catherine* the tragedy in which he had so nearly participated. The dawn was already on the waters, otherwise the whole company of the doomed ship must have perished. The Duke himself, with the future victor of Blenheim by his side, escaped by boat, the poor seamen even in that panic-stricken moment clearing a way that the King's successor might be preserved. Fat Sir John Berry, the last to leave the sinking vessel, swam to the *Happy Return*, which had only been saved from a similar fate by the speed with which her captain had dropped anchor. Pepys' yacht took up several, including his old friend and rival, Colonel Legge, the Master of the Ordnance, and the famous physician, Sir Charles Scarborough, who was almost dead after long exposure in the cold water and a homeric struggle for a plank with the Duke's dog, Mumper. Some two hundred, including many noblemen and great persons, were drowned. 'Nor ought I', Pepys wrote to Hewer, 'to be less sensible of God's immediate mercy to myself in directing me (contrary to my purpose at my first coming out) . . . to keep to the yacht. For many will, I doubt, be found lost as well or better qualified for saving themselves by swimming and otherwise than I might have been.'[42]

For by the time the royal party had reached Edinburgh on Monday the 8th, Pepys had recovered enough from his shock to write long letters to Will Hewer and James Houblon describing the calamity. He was fully alive to its dramatic and historical significance. 'Mr Hewer,' he began, 'after having told you that the Duke is well and then myself, I may safely take notice to you of what will I know soon be the talk of the town.' It was, and gave all his friends in England a rare fright. But the thought did not much worry him, and, his royal master being busied about State affairs at Edinburgh,

Pepys spent a happy week touring Scotland with Colonel Legge. The pair, between whom a common loyalty in suffering had bred confidence and friendship where before had been misunderstanding and dislike, visited all 'that was most considerable within reach', including Stirling, Linlithgow and Glasgow. The last impressed Pepys particularly – 'a very extraordinary town for beauty and trade, much superior to anything to be seen in Scotland. But the truth is,' he added, 'there is so universal a rooted nastiness hangs about the person of every Scot (man and woman) that renders the finest show they can make nauseous, even among those of the first quality'.* For abroad as at home Pepys remained an Englishman.[43]

But if the Scots were dirty in their persons they were tidy in their government. Pepys who attended two debates in Council with the Duke was much impressed, after three years of England under the Whigs. For the Duke had shown an unusual facility in managing Scotland; his authority, Pepys reported, 'being maintained with so much absoluteness and yet gentleness, to the rendering it morally impossible for any disquiet to arise in his Majesty's affairs. And truly as', he went on, 'their government seems to be founded upon some principles much more steady than those of ours, so their method of managing it in Council (his Royal Highness having been pleased to give me opportunity of being personally present at it with him two Council-days) appears no less to exceed ours in the order, gravity and unanimity of their debates'.[44]

As though to emphasize the contrast a letter arrived from Will Hewer in London, posted on the day of the shipwreck, complaining of the anarchical management of the Navy, where the Admiralty, who were spending £28,500 on a totally unnecessary wet dock at Chatham, refused to allow Sir Phineas Pett more than a single clerk at £50 per annum to keep a check on the Stores. 'The King's service goes to wrack', Hewer ended, 'and is at this day in such a pickle as it never was . . . every day plainly showing the different management in the Duke's time and now.' The only consolation was that Sir William Jones, the republican Attorney-General of the old days of Pepys' prosecution, was dead – 'not much lamented . . . but by those who are factiously inclined'. 'I thank you', Pepys replied, 'for the news of that insolent and mutinous lawyer.'[45]

* S. Pepys to W. Hewer, May 19th, 1682. *Rawl. MSS. A.* 194, ff. 276–7. Printed in *Smith* 1, 294–8, and *Howarth,* 139–41.

Pepys did not return to England with the Duke and Duchess by sea, for the eternal tourist was as alive in him as ever. Never having been farther north before than Castle Rising, the opportunity of travelling through the North was not to be lost. The roads, however, were in a shocking state after the abnormal spring rains, and he therefore joined Colonel Legge, who as Master of the Ordnance had business at several of the northern towns and had the use of a yacht for the purpose. On Wednesday, May 17th, Legge and Pepys were at Berwick, where they saw the sails of the Duke's returning ships. Calling at Holy Island, they arrived at Newcastle on the 23rd, where they were met in state at Clifford's Fort by the Mayor and Aldermen in their barges and escorted up the river by a fleet of boats. Next morning Colonel Legge, Sir Christopher Musgrave, Sir George Fletcher and Pepys were made free Burghers of Newcastle and feasted by the Mayor. In the afternoon they rode on to Durham, dining there on Thursday with Archdeacon Musgrave. 'Our business was so much to eat, drink and be merry', wrote one of the company, 'that we had not much time to talk of business.'* 'A step to Durham', Pepys called it, 'where the Bishop seems to live more like a prince of this than a preacher of the other world.' On Friday the 26th they were back at Newcastle, only to be bidden to dine with a local magnate, Sir Ralph Delaval, the great iron master, at Seaton Delaval a few miles away.[46]

At Newcastle, before he sailed for Scarborough, Pepys had received news from his friends in London that made his homecoming a matter of some importance. John Scott had once more appeared in the public eye. On the day that the *Gloucester* struck the Lemon and Oare, a Coroner's Jury sitting at the 'Horseshoe' tavern on Little Tower Hill brought in a verdict against him for wilful murder. It appeared that while drinking at the 'Horseshoe' a few days before the Colonel had had occasion to send for a hackney coach to take him to Temple Bar. Unable to agree as to the fare, for which the coachman demanded one and sixpence, Scott had dismissed him, only to be asked for something for his pains in coming so far. The Colonel replied that he would give him something for his pains, walked out with him into the street and then and there ran his sword through his belly.[47]

* Sir G. Fletcher to Sir D. Fleming, May 29th, 1682. *H.M.C. Fleming*, 185–6.

A warrant was out for Scott's arrest and the news-sheets were full of his crime. One advertisement for his apprehension described him as 'a very great vindicator of the Salamanca Doctor. He is a lusty tall man, squint-eyed, thin-faced, wears a perruque sometimes, and has a very h ... look. All good people would do well, if they can, to apprehend him, that he may be brought to justice'. Another account described him as the Scott that cheated the States of Holland of £7000 and was hanged in effigy at the Hague. 'He had played a thousand pranks more, and hath been of Sheriff Bethel's club lately, and great with all the Popish evidences, plot-drivers and discoverers.' For the Colonel's membership of the Green Ribbon Club was not unnoticed by his contemporaries.*[48]

After the murder Scott's papers had been seized and examined by the Secretary of State, Sir Leoline Jenkins. Pepys, guessing how much he could tell if he chose to confess, wrote from Newcastle to Hewer to urge him to put in a caveat against his receiving any pardon from Court until his own case against him had been heard, for 'confessions ... I am confident he is able to make relating to the State as well as us, that might well enough atone for this, his last villainy; nor do I doubt but to save his own life, he will forget his trade and tell truth, though to the hazard of the best friends he has'. But Scott preferred not to risk it. There was no trace of him anywhere. God, Pepys observed, had been 'pleased to take him out of our hands into his own for justice'.[49]

His London mail also told Pepys of the consternation into which his friends had been thrown by the wreck of the *Gloucester*. The tale of disaster had reached town in a garbled form on the morning of Wednesday, May 10th. The ladies of Crutched Friars, Winchester Street and Portugal Row, Hewer reported, had been in a rare taking, and nothing would convince them that their beloved Samuel was not drowned. 'They have been so disordered in Winchester Street that I am commanded to tell you they shall not be themselves till they see you.' James Houblon wrote that the news of his safety was the welcomest thing in the world, for before its arrival on the night of the 12th, 'as you were numbered among the dead by almost all the City except myself ... so no arguments could work upon my women and girls to believe otherwise, and though I assured them from Sir J.

* He had been elected on Dec. 16th, 1680, on the motion of Mr J. Trenchard. 'The Journal of the Green Ribbon Club', *Pepysian MSS., Miscellanies* vii, 487.

Narbrough, Sir R. Haddock, Mr Petts and others that you were embarked in the *Catherine* yacht, they had no faith and would have you with the Duke, for they were sure you loved him so well you could not be from him. You see, and are like to be told so when you come home, what your *Iter Boreale* hath cost us, and what it is to leave us on that sudden as you did without either asking, or for all that I know having, our prayers, we were all so angry at your going'. But soon, and the good merchant took joy in the thought, their Mr Pepys would be home again, though he was afraid it would be ill-travelling with wet roads after the stormy weather – the very streets of London were flooded that spring – and there would be little opportunity for taking the evening walks after each day's journey which his friend so loved. If his cold permitted, he added, he would meet him and dine with him at the end of his last night's stage.[50]

Betty Mordaunt wrote for herself – an anxious, tremulous, reproaching letter. 'You can't imagine the trouble we have been in for you, and being you remember my dream, I must put you in mind of what you said to me that same day, that you had forgiven me a hundred faults and hoped I would forgive you seven, but I think this going into Scotland by sea is worse than a thousand.' For the element over which their Mr Pepys had once reigned seemed very uncertain and treacherous to his fair friends: it was quite a consolation that he had been so sick. 'My sister gives you her humble service and bids me tell you she perceives water does not agree with you so well as with her. 'Twas the kindest thing you ever did', Lady Mordaunt concluded in a postscript, 'in not letting me know you went . . . I will assure you I had not my senses till I saw your hand. My prayers are heard. Adieu. God of his mercy preserve you.'*[51]

But the ladies had their revenge on Samuel in the end. For when landing at Hull on Saturday, May 27th, he resolved that afternoon to take a step to York ('being within a little distance of that place'), he walked into a trap that only one who knew him well could have set for him. There at the posthouse he found two letters from Will Hewer. The first, posted from London on Thursday the 27th, gave news of his affairs and his London friends: that Scott had absconded and was not to be found, that the guardship at Chatham had been

* Lady Mordaunt to S. Pepys, May 13th, 1682. *Rawl. MSS. A.* 178, f. 155.

burnt to the water under the very noses of the Admiralty Commissioners who were yet still proceeding with their ridiculous project for a wet dock, that the Houblons had laughed a great deal at his description of the Scots, and that Lady Mordaunt had been kept to her chamber for several days by a shrewd fit of the stone.[52]

The other letter was of a different sort. It was brief but infinitely disturbing. Dated the 25th past midnight, it ran:

> Sir, There has something happened since my letter went to the Posthouse of great consequence, and very ill both to you and myself and some other of our friends, which I dare not communicate to you with pen and paper, and therefore wish for your speedy return, which I hope in God you will defer no longer than bare necessity requires.
>
> Your humble servant, W. HEWER.

In an agony of apprehension, Pepys sat down to reply. Knowing women so well, he yet did not for a moment recognize the sharp talons of those who both most easily are hurt and best can hurt. The letter, he told Hewer, had put him 'into an inexpressible pain to aim at the ground of it, a thousand things running in my head, but without knowing what to pitch upon or what kind of misfortune it is that could so suddenly surprise you. But be it what it would, God's will be done and submitted to . . . All the ease I can give myself is by applying myself to all means of hastening home, which I would have done directly from this place if I could have got any means of doing it. But the nearest I can hear of will not bring me to you before Tuesday come sevennight, and I trust in God I shall be with you before that by sea. I have made shift', he added, 'for decency's sake to write to Portugal Row and Winchester Street . . . but with a great deal of regret, as not knowing almost what it is I have writ.'* And he at once set out for Hull to rejoin the yacht.[53]

When he got back to London Pepys discovered that the letter that had so disturbed him had come, not from York Buildings, but Portugal Row. He had the offending missive copied down in his great letter book, and added an explanation at the foot of the page:

> This letter above written was founded upon one sent to me dated 25 May, . . . who in a sportful revenge for my taking this journey without their knowledge designed to interrupt the pleasure of it and hasten me

* S. Pepys to W. Hewer, May 28th, 1682. *Rawl. MSS. A.* 194, f. 278.

back before my time by a feigned letter from Mr Hewer, wherein his hand was so well counterfeited that I was easily imposed upon.*

There were times when women palled. How much more satisfactory, he must have reflected, was Mr Evelyn's belated letter telling him in decorous phrase of the 'mixture of passions not really to be expressed' into which the wreck of the *Gloucester*, that 'dismal and astonishing accident', had put him. ''Tis sadly true there were a great many poor creatures lost, and some gallant persons with them, but there are others worth hundreds saved, and Mr Pepys was to me the second of those same.'[54]

It is possible that some of the Governors of Christ's Hospital did not share this sentiment. The battle around the Mathematical School was rejoined soon after his return, when Pepys suffered a crushing defeat. On June 14th the Court began its proceedings by adopting a unanimous report of the Mathematical Committee in favour of his Instructions for the new master: it also listened politely to a long speech of his about the qualifications needed by the successful applicant. It then proceeded to his election.

Of the five candidates on the short list, only two had had any practical experience of the sea. Neither was chosen, though Pepys had expressly laid down such experience as a *sine qua non* for the post. Instead the Court chose Edward Paget, a distinguished Mathematician and a Fellow of Trinity, Cambridge, with a whole army of eminent backers including Isaac Newton behind him. What particularly appealed to the Governors was that he was a first-class Latinist and would, so they argued, following the age-long fallacy of amateur educationists, 'by his great learning lead the boys to converse with one another here familiarly in that language . . . to enable them to converse with strangers abroad'. This was just the kind of appointment that had proved so disastrous in the case of Wood. Pepys' indignant protest at Paget's utter ignorance of the sea was met by the bland suggestion that Mr Paget 'could acquire something of practice in navigation by spending now and then a few days at sea in some of the yachts . . . in the Channel'.[55]

Pepys gave up the unequal contest. He wrote down his despairing opinion of the whole business in his book of Naval Minutes and withdrew from further attendance at the Committee. Instead he

* S. Pepys to W. Hewer, May 28th, 1682. *Rawl. MSS. A.* 194, f. 278.

applied himself to more tranquil tasks, such as he could complete to his own satisfaction undisturbed by the folly and knavery of other men. He wrote a Latin epitaph for Houblon's ninety-year-old father, the progenitor of many worthy merchants and gave his eager mind to the consideration of Mr Evelyn's essay on 'the martial perform-ances of dogs'. These could be contemplated with so much more composure than those of humans. And in this quiet he found himself able to correspond with content even with his enemies, at least when they proved themselves to be such learned and enquiring gentlemen as Doctor Robert Wood. For the latter, freed from his uncongenial duties at the Mathematical School, gave Pepys his 'very hearty, though perhaps unexpected thanks' and sent him a manuscript copy of their friend, Sir William Petty's 'Physico-Mathematical Discourse of Ships and Sailing, of Naval Policy, of Naval Economy or Husbandry'. This was just the kind of present Pepys liked to receive, especially when accompanied by such a letter as Wood enclosed with it. 'No indisposition', the Doctor wrote, 'can render me incapable of being a lover of navigation, I had almost said a naval philosopher, if you will pardon the pride of the expression. I reckon that naval excels land architecture, in the same proportion as a living moving animal a dull plant. Palaces themselves are only like better sorts of trees, which, how beautiful or stately soever, remain but as prisoners, chained during life to the spot they stand on; whereas the very spirits that inform and move ships are of the highest degree of animals, viz. rational creatures; I mean seamen.' Pepys may have reflected that it was a pity that one who so well understood the poetry of navigation should have been so unsuccess-ful in explaining its science.[56]

It was becoming a pleasant custom for learned men interested in matters relating to the sea to send their manuscripts and dedicate their labours to Samuel Pepys. Among those who did in 1682 was Doctor Nathaniel Vincent of Clare Hall, whom he had often met at the Houblons' house in Winchester Street. This sage, who had always had a leaning for the world of affairs – he had once shocked King Charles by preaching before him in holland sleeves and a long periwig – and was now seeking to leave Cambridge and settle in London, sent Pepys a copy of his *Conjectura Nautica* and shortly afterwards placed at his feet a most remarkable invention. The fruit of many years of leisure and 'brought to that degree of perfection that it is, it may be, the best treasure I am master of', it was a secret method of writing that could never be deciphered, since its characters vanished a few minutes after being read – 'so that no letter written by it can ever be a witness against its author . . . by which means the writer is secured as well against curiosity and sauciness or accidental discoveries'. Vincent called it 'Cryptocoiranicon', on account of its transcendent value to princes, and suggested that Pepys should sell it for him to the Crown for £1000. 'I will stay', the learned patriot added, 'for your answer hereunto a week or ten days, before I prepare any despatches to a foreign Court upon the same enquiry, but upon higher demands. I wish that another New World may not be lost from England for want of faith to believe the discoverer.'

Pepys waited a fortnight before answering this Columbus of the cipher world. It was, he agreed, a wonderful invention, and seemed to out-do all that he had ever heard of in that sort and to merit a suitable reward. There was, however, one defect. For 'if he who so reads it be the person that is to answer it, that person must either understand how to write it, or you must want his answer. And if that be so, then the secret cannot be made use of as such above once'. Besides, he added, unfortunately 'it is very rare that either our own or any other princes give themselves the care or labour of any correspondences about the affairs of their states with their own hands . . . that work being universally lodged by princes in the hands of their Secretaries of State, who I find, too, are so practised and satisfied in the security of their ordinary methods of ciphering . . . that they do not seem to be under any solicitude or search for better'. Three days later Vincent wrote back with unimpaired optimism.[57]

For Pepys was again become the kind of personage to whom the learned turn when in need of patronage or worldly counsel. Once more he stood high in the public eye. He was much at Whitehall and Windsor, where he stayed with his old friends of Axe Yard days, the Pearses (though Madam was twenty years older than when he had so much admired her), was frequently seen at the Duke's side, and was spoken of as the friend of that rising man, Colonel Legge, who that year was promoted to the peerage as Lord Dartmouth. To him he wrote in July on the sudden death of Sir Jonas Moore through a fall from his horse, to urge the appointment to the vacant Surveyor

Generalship of the Ordnance of his friend Henry Shere, engineer of the great Mole at Tangier, 'of whose uprightness of mind, universality of knowledge in all useful learning particularly mathematics, and of them those parts especially which relate to gunnery and fortifications, and lastly of whose vigour, assiduity and sobriety I dare bind myself'.[58]

For Pepys did not forget his old friends. When poor Tom Edwards died, who had once been his singing-boy, who had worked in his office and over whose naval career he had watched even in the darkest hours of his own fortunes, he placed the eldest of his two small children as a scholar of Christ's Hospital and took his widow, Jane, back into his service after an interval of thirteen years. He secured his cousin, Thomas Alcocke, the ship's carpenter – a modest, industrious man whose only fault was that he would never speak for himself – a favour at Chatham Dockyard, and wrote gratefully to the Master Shipwright who had done him that service to thank him for doing it at a time when he was not in a way of making him 'any present return of kindness for it'.* And all who had claims on him, and many who had not, like the poor Huguenots whom Louis was busy expelling from his dominions, found that with returning fortunes Sam Pepys was as ready as ever to befriend the unfortunate.[59]

Pepys was not well in the winter of 1682–3 and for a time was unable to pay his wonted visits to the great library at St James'. But this did not prevent him throwing himself with all his strength into his naval and historical studies. Captain Alford of Lyme Regis, who had been concerned in the royal escape from Worcester, came to visit him at York Buildings, bringing his account of that romantic transaction, while all his learned acquaintances called bearing with them the usual toll of marine manuscripts and anecdotes. 'Solicit Sir William Petty to make an end of his scheme of Naval Philosophy', ran his assiduous Minutes; 'consider the old saying among the divines, *Qui nescit orare discat navigare*'; 'Consult Mr Shere for his notes upon Noah's Ark'. And there was a great deal of reading from old books, out of which much curious information was extracted regarding England's sea history – Holinshed, Stow and Knighton.[60]

As he pursued these studies, what struck Pepys most forcibly was

* S. Pepys to Mr Lee, Feb. 18th, 1683. *Rawl. MSS. A.* 194, ff. 285v.–6.

the little regard, considering its manifest importance, in which the sea and all that belonged to it was held by his fellow-countrymen. Again the child puppetry of the Lord Mayor's Show gave rise to serious reflections: 'Observe the low place of the Shipwrights among the Companies of London.' Everywhere it seemed that the English scorned the service of the sea; attorneys made fortunes but shipwrights were poor, good seamen were despised, the parents of the very paupers in the charity schools refused to allow their children to be trained as sailors. Our law merchant was an inchoate jumble. The very ale-conner's was an office more provided for in the law of England than a ship.[61]

Yet the sea, his researches showed him, was the very life-blood of a country which had blindly taken as its patron-saint, St George, a mere knight-errant. It might, he reflected, have had instead a fishing Apostle. How few, he noted as he conned the Custom-House books, were the manufactures and commodities which England could properly boast of as her own! How great a part of the King's revenue was derived from his subjects' overseas trade! And yet how defenceless would the merchant marine of England be if unprotected by a strong and efficient Navy! In time past – in that of Elizabeth for instance a hundred years back – merchantmen had been able to defend themselves; now with the specialization in fighting ships and the growth in the sea-power of our neighbours, France and Holland, the whole situation had changed. To be saved England must look to her moat.[62]

So with every day Mr Pepys' naval studies took a more practical bent. He could not keep his eyes from Derby House, where ignorant Commissioners were making hay of the good rules and precedents he had so laboriously established, or from the new Navy Office in Crutched Friars where men who had once been good public servants were now sunk in supine ease and corruption. 'Run through the particular qualifications of our whole list of Admirals', he wrote impatiently, 'as to their being men either of pleasure or at least generally men of quite another education than that of the sea.' The muddle they had made of things was appalling. £100,000 had been wasted in a year on a foolish project of theirs in Ireland, merchantmen had been captured because they had withdrawn their convoys before the peace terms with Sallee had been ratified, and the stores through their neglect were practically empty. Tales of corruption came from every hand: the Chatham Chest was three years in arrears with its disbursements and £10,000 in debt. Nor was it any use protesting. One of his former clerks told him how the Commissioners of the Admiralty, urged to follow one of his old regulations, had answered roundly that they would not be obliged by Mr Pepys' rules.[63]

On April 17th, 1683, Deane, Hewer and Pepys visited Woolwich and Deptford to see the launching of the *Neptune*, the last but one of the thirty ships. There to their confusion and sorrow they were eyewitnesses of the state of the Yards, the workmen standing idle in hundreds for lack of materials on which to employ them. A few weeks later came the news of an English captain who had lowered his flag to the Spanish Fleet at Cadiz sooner than risk the loss of the merchandise he was carrying.[64]

But the times were changing fast. The summer of 1683 that saw Pepys busied in academic discussions with his learned friends at Gresham College about Sir William Petty's double-bottomed boat or discussing his shopping commissions with Sarah Houblon, witnessed the last despairing attempt of his enemies to overthrow King Charles II. Shaftesbury, like Scott, had fled abroad in the previous autumn after the election of a loyal Lord Mayor and Sheriffs, and had died an exile's death in Holland. But several of Pepys' old foes were concerned in the conspiracy of the republican lords to raise an armed rebellion against the Crown and in the darker one to murder the royal brothers as they drove past the Rye House on the Newmarket road. The plot was discovered and several of the plotters paid the penalty with their lives. Others fled overseas.[65]

Confronted by these events the Government felt itself strong enough to take a long-contemplated step. For twenty-one years the North African station of Tangier had proved a constant strain on the royal finances, seldom absorbing less than £70,000 a year, for which Parliament had made scarcely any provision. A gold-mine to many of his servants, who like Pepys and Hewer founded their fortunes upon its crazy finances, Tangier had come to present itself to the King chiefly as a hole in his pocket.

But Charles, who had learnt at last that he could only be a real king at the price of that repugnant thing economy, had made up his mind. In the utmost secrecy, Lord Dartmouth was given command of a fleet, and entrusted with orders to demolish the city, its walls, forts and Mole, remove the inhabitants and assess rates for their compensation. At the last moment the King suggested that the expedition should be strengthened by the presence of the most just and industrious man in his dominions, Samuel Pepys.[66]

Pepys went at two days' notice. He made lists of his debts on his tablets, crossing each off as it was paid, and of his requirements. There were clothes and linen to be packed, shoes, periwigs, combs and powder, plasters, teeth water and wash balls, a tooth-pick case and a perspective glass. For work he took his spectacles, a silver pen, instruments, mathematical paper and tablets. He also took a white hat and a velvet cap, three pairs of worsted stockings and three of thread, eight cravats and thirteen handkerchiefs, four shirts and bosoms, four pairs of linsey drawers and two flannel stomachers to keep away the wind colic. Galoshes, a new sea gown, and two laced and quilted indoor caps complete the picture.

He did not forget his books. These he divided under the heads of Marine, Musical and Fortification. He added the *Holy War,* Thomas à Kempis, a few classics and some Spanish works. He also arranged for money and credit, procured recommendatory letters to merchants in Spain, Portugal and Africa, disposed of his plate and papers and wrote to Brampton. In addition to these manifold tasks he was asked to find a chaplain for Lord Dartmouth. He consulted his cousin Gale and was recommended to the saintliest churchman of his day, little Dr Ken, one of the prebends of Winchester, whose voice was 'like to a nightingale for the sweetness of it'.[67]

Then he bade farewell. Among his papers is a brief list of them – his 'adieus'. The names are headed, as one might expect, by the Houblons, Lady Mordaunt and the Skinner kinship at Wood Hall. They include Dr Gale and the learned Sir Peter Pett, Deane, Lord Brouncker, pretty Lady Wyborne, John Evelyn and Lady Tuke, and the faithful Gibson. On Monday, July 30th, after two days of swift, methodical preparation, Pepys crossed to Lambeth and with Dr William Trumbull, a rising civilian who had also been requisitioned for the expedition, took coach on a familiar road. He did not even know for what purpose he was going. It was enough that he had been called back to the King's service and pay,* and was to sail once more – as long ago on a spring day in 1660 – with his Fleet.[68]

---

* He received pay at the rate of £4 a day throughout the expedition. *H.M.C. Dartmouth* III, 39–40.

That night he lay at Godalming. Next day he dined at Petersfield, and afterwards drove across the lonely Hampshire downs to summon Dr Ken from Winchester. There he slept the night, dining on the Wednesday at the College. On the evening of the same day he came to Portsmouth.[69]

After a week of waiting, while Lord Dartmouth was at Windsor receiving final instructions, Pepys boarded the *Grafton* at Spithead. He was happy. He had pleasant companions – his valued acquaintance, Lord Dartmouth, Dr Trumbull, with whom he had often corresponded on learned subjects, and two of his oldest and dearest friends, Will Hewer, the Tangier Treasurer, and Henry Shere, the great engineer who had completed its Mole. What his task might be, he told Evelyn, he was not solicitous to learn; 'this only I am sure of that over and above the satisfaction of being thought fit for some use or other ('tis no matter what) I shall go in a good ship, with a good fleet, under a very worthy leader, in a conversation as delightful as companions of the very first form in divinity, law, physic and the usefullest parts of mathematics can render it . . . with the additional pleasure of concerts (much above the ordinary) of voices, flutes, and violins; and to fill up all (if anything can do't where Mr Evelyn is wanting) good humour, good cheer, some good books, the company of my nearest friend Mr Hewer and a reasonable prospect of being home again in less than two months'. 'You leave us so naked', Evelyn replied, 'that till your return from Barbary we are in danger of becoming barbarians: the Heroes are all embarked with my Lord Dartmouth and Mr Pepys.' But he added how overjoyed he was that his friend had been recalled to the service of the Public and that he was not to resign himself wholly to speculation nor to withdraw his industrious and steady hand from the helm of the State. 'Methinks I respire again and (tired as I am) hope to see the good effects of God Almighty's late providences.'[70]

While Pepys lay aboard the *Grafton* at St Helen's, Lord Dartmouth in the privacy of his cabin broke to him the real reason for the voyage and told him that the King had appointed him to be his sole counsellor in the affair. Later, sitting alone upon the poop, Pepys read over the Admiral's Commission and secret Instructions. He realized that it was likely to be a perilous business, for the loss of Tangier was certain to raise an outcry and those concerned in its execution might be called to account for what they had done. It was perhaps to guard against such charges that Pepys once again began to keep a diary – the fullest and longest of any since he had closed the greatest of all in 1669. He wrote it in shorthand, and after his enforced rest from official business, his eyes once more proved equal to the strain.*[71]

On Sunday, August 19th, the Fleet weighed from St Helen's and stood out to sea. That night in his cabin poor Pepys was 'sick so as to vomit'. But next day the weather was fine and the wind moderate, and he and his friends had a pleasant day of it, 'walking, talking, reading and music, and a fine moonshine evening'. Tuesday saw them off Portland and the Start. On the afternoon of the 22nd they came to anchor in Plymouth Sound, where Pepys landed to see the Citadel and have his linen washed. That done he crossed by barge to Mount Edgecumbe and was there made much of by Lady Edgecumbe who had once been Anne Mountagu, recrossing again in the evening light to visit St Nicholas Island† and its great historic figure, 'my Lord Lambert', who had lain there in an easy captivity for a generation. It was almost like shaking hands with the Great Rebellion.

Here Pepys received the last farewell letters from his friends – from James Houblon and his 'little congregation in the Forest',‡ whose prayers he told him he valued more than a whole convocation of mercenary priests, from Lady Wyborne, tremulous at his departure and, like a woman, begging him either to remove her husband from the command of his bitterest enemy, Admiral Herbert, or reconcile them, and from Tom Miller of Brampton wishing him and Will Hewer 'healthful bodies, merciful seas, successful enterprises and safe and honourable returns'.**[72]

---

* *Rawl. MSS. C.* 859. Transcribed by the Rev. John Smith and first printed (in a garbled and incomplete form) in his *Life, Journals and Correspondence of Samuel Pepys*, 1841. Reprinted by R. G. Howarth in the *Letters and Second Diary of Samuel Pepys*, 1932. Re-transcribed from photostats in possession of the Huntington Library of San Marino, California, by Mr Edwin Chappell and published with the omission of certain passages by the Navy Records Society in *The Tangier Papers of Samuel Pepys*, 1935. A full transcript from the original in the Bodleian Library was made for me for the purpose of this work by Mr W. Matthews, to whom I am much indebted.

† Which Mr Edwin Chappell, the latest and most accurate editor of Pepys' Journal towards Tangier presents in human guise as 'Sir Nicholas (Acland?)'. *Tangier Papers*, 7.

‡ Epping Forest, where the Houblons had taken a summer retreat.

** Tho. Miller to S. Pepys, Aug. 12th, 1683. *Rawl. MSS. A.* 190, f. 29.

There was another letter that awaited Pepys at Plymouth. It concerned Scott. Ten days before Deane had written to inform him that he had received a mysterious communication from an old acquaintance in Norway, one John Gelson, who had formerly been employed in Lord Arlington's office.* It appeared that Gelson in the course of his business at Christiania had met Scott and received from him a surprising confession. It was about this that he had written to Deane.

Pepys had written accordingly to Gelson to thank him and to ask him for further information of Scott. 'I have not (I thank God)', he said, 'any further propensions of revenge towards him for what concerns my own particular than what should easily give way to his making atonement for it by his discharging his duty . . . to the King in a full and ingenious confession of what he has so amply declared to you his knowledge of, touching the designs laid against his Majesty and the Government by the Party under which he was (as he says) so employed . . . This only I shall say that if the declaration he has made to you be with the sincerity that becomes a true penitent . . . I do as little doubt of the benefit he might receive from his Majesty's goodness and mercy upon his dutiful and faithful confessions of the whole truth of his knowledge touching things and persons relating to the evils he has opened to you.'† For himself, he had added, he wished for nothing but to be informed upon whom to place the guilt of the devilish practices against his life to which Scott had owned being put against him for his destruction.[73]

A further document now came to Pepys' hands. It was addressed to himself and written by Gelson from Skeen in Norway. It was dated July 12th, 1683.

Sir,

I cannot think of the civilities I received from you at Newcastle without a great sense of my obligation, and am very glad of any occasion to express my gratitude as well as duty, and do therefore give you the trouble of an adventure I met with. –

The other day at Christiania I saw the infamous Colonel Scott who I believe was not well pleased to see me, because that he might be conscious that I knew him to be otherwise than he had insinuated in these parts, an

---

* There is a reference to Gelson in *C.S.P.D.* XIII, 1672, 30, which shows that as far back as June 1672 he was acquainted with Scott.

† S. Pepys to Mr Gelson, Aug. 11th, 1683. *Rawl. MSS. A.* 190, ff. 49–52.

opinion among the most Eminent, and falling upon him with a great deal of freedom about the villainous practices that has of late years been in our nation, he as freely acknowledge himself a tool much used, as well as a Cabinet Councillor about the business, and told me many things about the same.

That one that hoped to be your successor in the Secretary's employment put him upon contriving your destruction, and that what he did was merely upon that account, and that they designed to take away your life, but that the said person found he was not like to succeed in case they had proceeded.

That their design was to destroy the Government and make themselves Kings, or rather Tyrants, and for that end did all they could to bring an odium and hatred upon his Majesty and family, and by their fictions to delude a giddy and unthinking people.

That their party was of three sorts. Those that wanted offices and were disappointed, those that were enemies to the government of church and state, and tools that the other two brought over to be of their side.

He told me many particulars of their cabals and debates.

That Oates did acknowledge to him he swore that the King was to be killed merely to get a party of such as were dear lovers of the King, and to make the Papists more odious that they might the better serve their ends by them, and in a fit time would have brought in his Majesty to have given Commissions for the destroying his Protestant subjects.

That they set up the Duke of Monmouth for no other end than the dividing his Majesty's friends.

That the Protestant cause was used only to make a party of the zealously blind.

That they struck the government through the side of the Romanists. That they had no other way to destroy or wound it.

That my Lord Shaftesbury promised great settlement to him to make parties in the West and elsewhere, and that he had spent much time, speeches etc. for that purpose.

That the said Ld S. did appoint him to order and manage the Irish Witnesses etc.

That he particularly knows those that were the principal actors in the brave Protestant cause (as they called it), the authors and spreaders of the infamous treasonable libels, particularly the History of the Black Box, and many other discourses which possibly might be thought troublesome, which I the rather waive with other matters at this time, because I hope in September to wait upon you in London. In the meantime, if to make any particular enquiry of him be desired, upon the least notice I will endeavour my utmost to procure a satisfaction.

Mr Margerum, an Ipswich Master of a ship, hath engaged to give this into your own hand, and saith he is suddenly to return into these parts, and if he comes not into this place will carefully send anything to me, and by an expresse if desired. If you please to honour me with a line, please to direct for me at Mr Cornishe's in Skeen, being

> Sir, Your most faithful and most humble servt.
> JOHN GELSON.*[74]

The Fleet was due to sail next day. Pepys rose at dawn, copied out Gelson's letter and wrote a line of advice to Anthony Deane, advising him to consult James Houblon and Mr Pallavicini. 'All the caution that I would propose to be used in it is that it should not be too much known till we have done what is to be done towards the bringing him over, for fear of the other party, and particularly Harbord's making some provision (by pension for his life) for the keeping him abroad. For it concerns him and the Party enough to be at that charge to prevent his coming over. Which consideration alone has made me . . . forbear the immediate sending of Mr Gelson's letter to Mr Secretary Jenkins, which my Lord Dartmouth seems inclined to, out of a certain apprehension that by the interest Harbord (among other rogues) has still in some persons about the King, he will come to hear of it and find means to prevent it . . . And so once more, Adieu.'†[75]

Then he got Lord Dartmouth and others of his friends to attest the copy and sent it to the shore. After dinner, the boats having returned with the laundry, the Fleet weighed anchor.[76]

---

* *Rawl. MSS. A.* 190, f. 56.
† S. Pepys to Sir A. Deane, Aug. 23rd, 1683. *Rawl. MSS. A.* 190, f. 58.

APPENDIX

AN UNPUBLISHED MS. OF

SAMUEL PEPYS

from the Pepysian Papers in the Bodleian Rawlinson MSS. A. 185, ff. 206–13

THE PRESENT ILL STATE OF MY HEALTH
(Spelling modernized)

Survey

Besides shortness of breath:

Pain increasing from two or three months backwards in the joints of my hip and knees upon any motion till it is now fallen down to the calves of my legs, joints of my ankles and feet upon motion, and a constant weariness in my legs even when abed. As also risen up to my back, shoulders, elbows, wrists and fingers, and particularly a constant pain in my wrist.

Moistures of my head and body, swellings and fullness in my lips before wet weather, and risings with great bladders all over my body and thighs about three years ago, being a very wet year and continued during the whole wet season. But were it any time in a quarter of an hour taken quite away by sweating, and within a few days up again, and as I sweated was laid again.

Never free at this day from spitting and spawling in wet weather, falling down from my head (as I infer) from its makings its way through the nostrils as well as through the mouth by retching it up through my throat.

As also by the falling down of the palate of my mouth, so as in wet weather to be greatly subject to the frequent losing of my voice for days together.

But very little of this during a dry season be it summer or winter, but always under some degree of retching and spitting every morning as soon as I am out of my bed, and at all other times upon my coming out of a warm place into a cold, as out of any throng whether in a church, playhouse or (as this evening) out of the Council Chamber, out of a cabin when I go up upon the deck, or upon my first entrance on the road in the morning at my first coming out of an inn.

Pain in my Eyes

Which seizeth me in a minute upon applying my eyes not only to any book, small character or other lesser object, but to any object great or small that I am obliged to look upon as near (or nearer) than the ordinary distance at which a man reads from the object, while on the contrary I see as small an object as I ever did in my life at the distance that other men can see it and without the least pain let me look as long as I will at objects that are farther distant. That this has risen from my over labouring them as long as I was able to work with my own eyes by daylight and candlelight for little less than 18 or 20 hours a day for several years together, and therein very much using shorthand and doing this in a constant smoke of candles till I have wrought my eyes to such a weariness as at last hardly to be able to see my way out of my office by candlelight, I infer. From this pain seizing of me in the height of this my labour and to such a degree that till I did entirely leave off working with my own eyes I was never free from paining them night nor day, with a constant redness and issuing of a waterish humour though I never was subject to an issue or defluxion in my eyes all my life before.

But when I came to leave off working with my own eyes and fell to the employing clerks, my eyes shortly grew well, and from that time to this never knew any of that pain till [by] the necessity of my employment, which is often indispensable, I am driven often to write and read with my own hand and eyes when pain immediately ensues (as I have already said) and continues longer or shorter as I continue working with them.

Here only I would note what I can in no wise comprehend, that be it at a public audience before the King, Council-table, etc., when the nature of the affair and company fills my mind so as I cannot consider the labours of my eyes (which the pain will not suffer me to do where I am at liberty to think of it) there I can neither read nor write for half an hour together without much pain following it.

Memorandum that I have not omitted trying of spectacles and the mathematical tube used by the ancient man about Salisbury, but all without success, it appearing from my experience from the beginning of this my misfortune to this day that the posture of my eyes as it is required to be in reading and writing will of itself bring the pain, be the object great or small.

I have sometimes thought that it might be barely weakness of sight and been induced thereto partly from my remembrance that the first time that I took particular notice of the suddenness of my pain upon reading or writing it was immediately upon my having been at the glasshouse showing some friends the works there and gazing much upon the flame within the furnaces, and never before and always since. Partly from my being conscious of my having for many years together employed my eyes constantly against a bright window by day and candles by night, and my observing from thence to this day looking against the light or any near bright object doth presently bring my pain, redness and water in my eyes. Even the brightness of a white paper will do it after my eyes begin once to ache.

But however this may imply, my eyes being become more weak than heretofore, I conceive most evident that it is not nevertheless from that kind of weakness that this pain is brought upon my eyes in reading, partly from my meeting with no success in the use of the mathematical tube before mentioned and partly from their being liable to the same pain upon my turning my eyes into a reading posture even when I am in the dark.

But there is another cause to which I am able to impute at least a great part of this pain of my eyes, namely from the moisture of my head and that upon these observations.

First, that before and during wet weather I shall have a heaviness in the forepart of my head and a pain in my eyes, and very troublesome too, though not attended with that pricking heat, redness and wateriness that follow reading and writing.

Secondly, that I have in some degree more or less the same pain at my rising every morning till I have drained my head by spitting, and at my nose, and as that is voided my pain goes gradually away.

Thirdly, that upon my drinking more liberally at one time more than another, especially thin French wine (though never to excess), I have the same pain, and, till I have soundly drained my head as before, the pain continues. And that in all these cases, the discharging my head of this moisture removes the pain.

But though this (as the other) may contribute much to the disposing my eyes to pain in their exercise of reading, and the more probably so because I find the pain of reading to seize me quicker, afflict me more and continue longer in rainy weather than in dry and upon my head being troubled with this moisture than at other times. Yet at all times, let the weather or my head be how they will, the reading posture of my eyes brings me a pain, so much as not only to render my life much less comfortable than it would otherwise be, but to oblige me to the loss of the whole use of my own eyes in reading and writing, saving on the occasions of utmost importance which I dare not either impart to, or cannot be executed by others.

Wind Colic

From the furthermost of my memory backward (both before I must cut out the stone and since) to this day I have been subject upon all cold, especially taken in my feet on an empty stomach, to have the same pains in my bowel and bladder and stoppage of urine, and almost in the same degree as what the stone itself gave me. And this so certain and orderly that I never have a fit thereof but I can assign the time and occasions of it, as also of its cure, namely so soon (and not before) as I can break wind behind in a plentiful degree. For from my fullest agony of pain and after my longest and most entire suppression of urine, so as I have not been able to let go one drap or a few drap by drap, one eruption of wind backwards shall in the same moment ease me of pain and give me freedom of urine more or less as that eruption shall be weaker or strong and more or less forward by the like issues of wind. And to show a little more particularly my natural aptness to wind upon cold, as the cold shall be greater or less, it shall not (as for the most part it does) confine its effects only within my bowels and bladder, but transmit pain over my whole body by running from one part to another in that very part that is at that time uppermost as my desire of ease in my bed shall occasion the changing my posture there, sensibly carrying its pain upon every such variation of posture through the mediate parts of my body which therewith shall then become uppermost.

The preventions which I use, and always successfully as long as my ease or the accident of my employment will let me use them, are the keeping of my feet warm and my stomach full. Which later the trouble of eating without any pleasure from it as having very little taste occasions my very frequent failure in.

The method to my cure is principally if not wholly the opening of my body by glisters or some other physic; I being by a constant excess of natural heat for the most part bound and more especially upon cold, more sensibly drawing together the mouth of the anus so as hardly without pain to admit the pipe of the suppository. But as the cold is stronger or weaker and the frequency and strength of these applications, passage is made for the wind sooner or later, and with it away goes the pain.

I am at this time in the 45th year of my age.

Further notes towards the judging of the true state of my health, good and bad.

I have during my whole life been in a constant heat of body little below a fever. My life has been wholly sedentary, without any opportunity for seasonable exercises, the pains of the stone preventing me therein before I was cut and business constantly since, as it doth at this day.

I remember not my life without the pain of the stone in the kidneys (even to the making of bloody water upon any extraordinary motion) till I was about 20 years of age, when upon drinking an extraordinary quantity of conduit-water out of Aristotle's well near Cambridge (where some scholars of us were for refreshment in a hot summer's day walked), the weight of the said water carried after some days' pain the stone out of the kidneys more sensibly through the urater into the my bladder, from which moment I lived under a constant succession of fits of stone in the bladder till I was about 26 years of age when the pain growing insupportable I was delivered both of it and the stone by cutting and continued free from both (by God's blessing) to this day, more than what may be imputed to it of the aptness which I still retain to cold and wind and the pain attending the same in those parts. I make to this day very foul water with a viscous sediment, but without any pain or stoppage, saving in fits of the aforesaid colic. Which to prevent, besides what I have mentioned of keeping my stomach warm and full, I have been forced sometimes to wear something extraordinary for warmth before my belly and am now driven to do it constantly by both summer and winter. One certain warning of the fit of the colic approaching is my sudden falling to the breaking of wind backward and continuing by frequent eruptions so to do until that passage be (as I have noted before) drawn up and the wind thereby confined within.

I have been for the most part, and now more than ever, subject to a mighty drought, so as upon intent speaking to be rendered unable to speak articulately till I take time to moisten it.

In the morning also my mouth is very foul, dry and furred.

My employment for about 10 years together preventing the regularity of my meals by day, I was necessitated to make my last meal about or after midnight and thence immediately to bed, and continued the said practice until being seized upon by an aptness to be dizzy in my head, and mostly upon my laying myself down upon my bed and rising, I was led to an apprehension that my irregular eating might be the occasion thereof, since which for about four years backward I have by little and little (the nature of my present employment admitting it) laid aside that practice of eating late and with it (I know not whether from it) that dizziness has by little and little also left me and seems at this day totally gone as my eating of suppers also is.

As to my eyes I never was subject in my life to the least dimness, weakness, defluxions or any other infelicity appertaining thereto, nor am now, more than the pains here before mentioned arising from about eight years since upon occasion of reading and writing, or being applied to over-bright objects, or this excessive moisture of my head. From which three occasions when I happen to be a little time free (as upon a journey when I am less liable to reading and writing and in dry weather I sometimes am) I am under as constant a health and ease in my eyes as myself ever was or any man is. At meals I make no distinction of meats but affect the salt most and for the prevention of the colic only can be tempted by company and long sitting to fill my belly. But can never do so when alone. Nor am I under any regularity in my drinks saving that I never drink to excess and seldom or at all but at meals and thereto at dinner principally now, but then I drink liberally (with a temperance still) and for the most part of the wines that are reckoned strong, viz. Greek, Italian, Spanish and Portuguese and at the small Bordeaux claret.

The thin French wine, flying presently into my head, occasioning a moisture and with it the same in my eyes (which I have already observed), does ordinarily attend it and therefore I rarely meddle with any of these sorts where any other coarser or stronger wine can be had.

I bleed in my arm about once or twice a year, but that not

certainly nor at any stated time. As a proof of that excess of natural heat which I take myself to have, I find that in all hot summer weather I am subject to the breaking out of heat in my arms, wrists, breast, thighs and legs, and continued prickings and itchings when the weather grows colder.

Courses or seasons of taking of physic I never knew, nor my employment since my manhood ever allowed me time for more than sometimes on my occasions of crossing the sea between this and France or the like short trip has given me occasion of being seasick, which I am to the utmost extremity and (I have fancied) to my health's for some time after.

Other evils than these with reference to my bodily health (either chronical or other) I thank God I never knew and those according to the respective following:

viz. the stone from my cradle till 'twas cut out,

the wind colic from same time,

the pain of my eyes from about eight years backward.

And that is I take to be the survey from about six months backward which last three I labour to and at this day under in the manner and degree before mentioned.

Abbreviations

Manuscript Sources

Pepysian MSS. In the Pepys Library, Magdalene College, Cambridge.
   Adm. Letters. Admiralty Letters.
   Miscellanies.
   Mornamont. 'My Two Volumes of Mornamont', Pepysian MSS.
      Nos. 2881–2.
Bodl. Bodleian Library, Oxford.
Rawl. MSS. Rawlinson Manuscripts, Bodleian Library.
B.M. British Museum, London.
Addit. MSS. Additional Manuscripts, British Museum.
P.R.O. Public Record Office, London.
S.P. State Papers, Public Record Office.
Greenwich MS. Volume of S. Pepys' Official Correspondence,
      1662–1679, in possession of the National Maritime Museum,
      Greenwich.
Hinchingbroke MSS. Manuscripts in the possession of the Earl of
      Sandwich at Hinchingbroke.
Tanner and Wheatley MSS. Manuscript notes collected by the late Mr
      H. B. Wheatley and the late Dr J. R. Tanner, in the possession of
      the author.

Printed Sources

Braybrooke IV. Vol. IV of Diary and Correspondence of Samuel Pepys.
      Ed. Lord Braybrooke. 1898.
C.J. Commons' Journals.
C.P. MSS. A Descriptive Catalogue of the Naval Manuscripts in the
      Pepysian Library. Ed. J. R. Tanner. 1903–23.
C.S.P.D. Calendar of State Papers, Domestic series. 1860–1921.
Clowes. W. L. Clowes, The Royal Navy. 1897.
Colenbrander. H. T. Colenbrander, Bescheiden uit vreemde archieven
      omtrent de groote Nederlandsche Zeeoorlogen. 1919.
Corbett. J. S. Corbett, England in the Mediterranean. 1904.

Dalrymple. J. Dalrymple, Memoirs of Great Britain and Ireland (4th ed.). 1773.

Davey. S. J. Davey, Catalogue. 1889.

D. Diary of Samuel Pepys. Ed. H. B. Wheatley. 1893–6.

Duckett. Sir G. Jackson and Sir G. F. Duckett, Naval Commissioners 1660–1760. 1889.

Echard. L. Echard, History of England (3rd ed.). 1720.

E.H.R. English Historical Review.

Evelyn. J. Evelyn, The Diary of. Ed. A. Dobson. 1908.

Examen. R. North, Examen. 1740.

Grey. A. Grey, Debates of the House of Commons. 1769.

Harris. F. R. Harris, The Life of Edward Mountagu, First Earl of Sandwich. 1912.

Hatton. Correspondence of the Family of Hatton. Camden Society. 1878.

H.M.C. Historical Manuscripts Commission Reports.

Hooke, Diary. Diary of Robert Hooke. 1935.

Howarth. Letters and the Second Diary of Samuel Pepys. Ed. R. G. Howarth.

L'Estrange, Brief History. Sir R. L'Estrange, A Brief History of the Times. 1687–8.

L.J. Lords' Journals.

Muddiman. J. G. Muddiman, The King's Journalist. 1923.

Naval Minutes. Samuel Pepys's Naval Minutes. Ed. J. R. Tanner. 1926.

Ogg. D. Ogg, England in the Reign of Charles II. 1934.

Parlt. Hist. The Parliamentary History of England. Ed. W. Cobbett. 1806–20.

Pearce. E. H. Pearce, Annals of Christ's Hospital. 1908.

Penn. G. Penn, Memorials of Sir William Penn. 1833.

Pepysiana. H. B. Wheatley, Pepysiana. 1899.

Pollock. J. Pollock, The Popish Plot. 1903.

Ranke. L. von Ranke, A History of England principally in the seventeenth century. 1875.

Sitwell. Sir G. Sitwell, The First Whig. 1894.

Smith. The Life, Journals and Correspondence of Samuel Pepys. Ed. Rev. J. Smith. 1841.

State Trials. Complete Collection of State Trials. Ed. W. Cobbett. 1809–28.

Tangier Papers. The Tangier Papers of Samuel Pepys. Ed. E. Chappell. Navy Records Society. 1935.

Tanner, Corr. Private Correspondence and Miscellaneous Papers of Samuel Pepys, 1679–1703. Ed. J. R. Tanner. 1926.

Tanner, Further Corr. Further Correspondence of Samuel Pepys, 1662–1679. Ed. J. R. Tanner. 1929.

Whitear. W. H. Whitear, More Pepysiana. 1927.

Williamson. Letters addressed from London to Sir Joseph Williamson. Ed. W. D. Christie. 1874.

Bibliographical Notes

CHAPTER I. THE SECOND DIARY

[1] Monument in St Olave's Church, Hart Street; *D*. I, XXX–XXXI; *Pepysian MSS., Miscellanies* VI, 387.

[2] *Harris* II, 198; *Hinchingbroke MSS., Sandwich Journal* X, 38–56, 86–97; *Naval Minutes* 152; *Pepysian MS*. No. 2554; *D*. 30 Jan., 8 July 68.

[3] *H.M.C. Rep*. 8 (*House of Lords* 131); *C.P. MSS*. I, 33; *Harris* II, 198; *Pepysian MS*. No. 2554; *Miscellanies* VI, 387.

[4] *Pepysian MSS., Miscellanies* VI, 387; *Tanner, Further Corr*. 261; *C.J*. IX, 99; *Howarth* 37–8.

[5] *Tanner, Further Corr*. 261; *B.M. Harleian MS*. No. 2751; *Penn* II, 543–6; *C.P. MSS*. I, 33–5; *Rawl. MSS. A*. 457; *Pepysian MS*. No. 2554.

[6] *Pepysian MS*. No. 2554; *D*. 31 Oct. 60; 10 Feb., 16 July, 10 Sept. 63; 1 May 69.

[7] *Pepysian MS*. No. 2554; *Miscellanies* VI, 387; *Tanner, Further Corr*. 261; *D*. 9, 19, 23 Jan., 2, 20 Feb., 6 Dec. 60.

[8] *Tanner, Further Corr*. 261–2; *D*. 12 April 62; *Miscellanies* VI, 388.

[9] *Sandwich Journal* X, 38–56, 86–98; *C.J*. IX; *Pepysian MSS., Miscellanies* VI, 388; *D*. 24 May 69.

[10] *D*. 31 May 69; *Pepysian MSS., Miscellanies* VI, 385–504.

[11] *Pepysian MSS., Miscellanies* VI, 389–93.

[12] *Pepysian MS*. No. 2554; *C.P. MSS*. I, 33; *Penn* II, 551–7; *H.M.C. Rep*. (*House of Lords* 133).

[13] *Pepysian MSS., Miscellanies* VI, 393–4.

[14] *Smith* I, 124–6; *Pepysian MS*. No. 2554.

[15] *Pepysian MSS., Miscellanies* VI, 393–9.

[16] *Pepysian MSS., Miscellanies* VI, 399–406.

[17] *Pepysian MSS., Miscellanies* VI, 406–28.

[18] *Pepysian MSS., Miscellanies* VI, 428–35.

[19] *Pepysian MSS., Miscellanies* VI, 435–52.

[20] *Pepysian MSS., Miscellanies* VI, 452–65.

[21] *Pepysian MSS., Miscellanies* VI, 465–83.

[22] *Pepysian MSS., Miscellanies* VI, 483–504.

[23] *Harris* II, 198; *Tanner, Further Corr.* 263–4; *D.* 3 July 60.

[24] *Naval Minutes* 152; *Howarth* 37–8.

CHAPTER II. THE MAN MADE

[1] *Pepysian MSS., Mornamont* I, 38–44; *Rawl. MSS. A.* 174, ff. 255, 291, 466; *Edward Hoare, 'Mr Pepys and his Bank', Daily Telegraph,* 7 Sept. 1928; *D.* 1 Oct. 65; 7 April 69 et passim.

[2] *D.* 18 Sept. 61; 17 Aprıl 66; 19 April, 1 June 67 et passim.

[3] *D.* 16 Dec. 60; 6, 15 June 63; 24 Feb.; 24 June 64; 28 March 65; 14 July 67; *Tangier Papers* 42–3.

[4] *D.* 10 Aug. 63; 28 Nov. 66; 11 Sept. 67; 9, 23 Jan., 20 April 69; *Howarth* 139; *Pepysian MS.* No. 2612, f. 494.

[5] *Davey,* Item 2874; *D.* 30 July 66 et passim; *Tanner, Corr.* II, 109; *Sir Frederick Bridge, Samuel Pepys, Lover of Musique* 75–94.

[6] *D.* 16 Dec. 62; 24 Nov. 65; *Naval Minutes* 197–8; *Rawl. MSS. A.* 172, ff. 93, 107, 135; *A.* 194, f. 234; *Pepysian MS.* No. 2554; *C.P. MSS.* 1, 33–5; IV, 607–8.

[7] *Tanner, Corr.* 1, 38; *Further Corr.* 263–4; *Rawl. MSS. A.* 194, ff. 47, 278; *Pepysian MS.* No. 2612, f. 447; *Greenwich MS.* 884.

[8] *Rawl. MSS. A.* 173, ff. 178–9; *A.* 181, f. 62; *A.* 183, f. 258; *A.* 190, f. 29; *A.* 194, ff. 117, 231, 271–2; *Smith* I, 316–18; *H.M.C. Dartmouth* 1, 187–9; *Braybrooke* IV, 210–11; *Tangier Papers* 48, 51–2; *Howarth* 83, 106–7, 144, 198.

[9] *Rawl. MSS. A.* 170, ff. 28–9; *A.* 194, f. 251; *D.* 5 Sept. 64; 5 Jan. 68; *Howarth* 128; *Tanner, Corr.* I, 37; *Further Corr.* 299–300, 305; *Pepysian MSS.,* Adm. Letters XIV, 370.

[10] *Rawl. MSS. A.* 174, ff. 189, 191; *A.* 179, f. 32; *A.* 183, f. 66; *A.* 189, f. 33; *A.* 194, f. 285; *C.S.P.D.* 1671; 185; *Pepysian MSS.,* Adm. Letters X, 114; XIII, 128–9; *Howarth* 183–4, 187; *D.* 25 May 63; *Pepysian MSS., Mornamont* II, 1235.

[11] *D.* 9 Sept. 62; 17 Jan. 63; *Howarth* 48–9; *Pepysian MS.* No. 2612, f. 238.

[12] *Howarth* 170–1, 181–2; *C.P. MSS.* II, 29, 394; *Tangier Papers* 93–4, 152, 212; *Rawl. MSS. A.* 172, f. 87; *A.* 194, ff. 156, 233; *Pepysian MSS.,* Adm. Letters VIII, 313, 432, X, 299–300, XII, 32; *Smith* II, 218–19; *Pepysian MS.* No. 2612, ff. 429, 719; *D.* 17 Sept., 19 Oct. 63; 29 Jan., 26 July, 1, 9 Nov. 65; 26 Feb. 66; 5 March 67;

26 March, 14 July 68; 6 March 69; *Howarth* 170; *H.M.C. Dartmouth* 1, 241, 245.

[13] *Examen* 243; *Pepysian MSS., Miscellanies* VI, 390–1, 465–83; *D.* 20 Oct. 63; *Rawl. MSS. A.* 194, f. 227; *Tanner, Further Corr.* 328–9; *Howarth* 68–9; *C.P. MSS.* III, 145.

[14] *Rawl. MSS. A.* 174, f. 249; *D.* 21 Jan. 66; 5 Nov. 68; *Howarth* 39; *Pepysian MS.* No. 2836.

[15] *D.* 1 Nov. 65; *Pepysian MSS., Miscellanies* VI, 393–4; *Tanner, Further Corr.* 268–9, 293–5; *Howarth* 165; *Rawl. MSS. A.* 189, ff. 293, 302–3; *A.* 194, f. 121.

[16] *D.* 9 July, 5 Oct. 62; 5, 19 April 63; *Tangier Papers* 30; *Naval Minutes* 76; *Howarth* 78–82, 101, 160–2; *Smith* II, 91–5; *Grey* VII, 111–12; *Rawl. MSS. A.* 171, f. 217; *A.* 174, f. 396; *A.* 185, f. 32; *Tanner, Further Corr.* 317–18, 350–1; *S. Pepys, Memories touching the Royal Navy* 131.

[17] *D.* 26 Oct. 63 et passim.

[18] *C.S.P.D.* XV, 1673: 565; 1676/7: 551; *Rawl. MSS. A.* 170, ff. 20, 42; *A.* 178, f. 209; *A.* 183, f. 207; *A.* 185, f. 133; *A.* 194, ff. 179, 248–50; *Howarth* 53–5, 57–66, 89, 96–7, 171–2, 201–2; *Notes and Queries*, 13th Series, CXLVI, 291; *H.M.C. Rep.* 4 (*Bath* 231); *Smith* I, 170; *Tanner, Further Corr.* 292–3; *Whitear* 93; *Pepysian MSS., Mornamont* I, 209–13; *Pepys Club, Occasional Papers* II, 65.

[19] *C.S.P.D.* 1671: 32; *Rawl. MSS. A.* 174, f. 235; *A.* 184, ff. 235, 237–8; *Tanner, Further Corr.* 271–2.

[20] *Rawl. MSS. A.* 180, ff. 175, 293; *A.* 182, ff. 410, 413, 457; *Howarth* 38–9; *H.M.C. Rep.* 8 (*Trinity House* 254).

[21] *Rawl. MSS. A.* 185, ff. 206 et seq.; *D.* 31 July, 12 Aug. 68; *Pepysian MSS., Mornamont* I, 47–56; *Sir D'Arcy Power, Why Pepys discontinued his Diary*.

[22] *C.S.P.D.* Addenda, 1660/70: 205; 1671: 267; *Rawl. MSS. A.* 174, f. 181, f. 409; *Tanner, Further Corr.* 266–7; *Hinchingbroke MSS., Sandwich Journal* X, 270–4; *Harris* II, 206–7.

[23] *Rawl. MSS. A.* 174, ff. 179, 409–10; *Tanner, Further Corr.* 264–5, 267–8.

[24] *Rawl. MSS. A.* 174, ff. 409–10; *Evelyn* 22 July, 28 Aug. 1670.

[25] *Rawl. MSS. A.* 174, ff. 255, 291, 437, 446; *Edward Hoare, 'Mr Pepys and his Bank', Daily Telegraph*, 7 Sept. 1928; *C.S.PD.* 1671: 463.

[26] *Tanner, Further Corr.* 268–9; *D.* 2 April 64; *Duckett* 30; *C.P. MSS.* I, 12; *Corbett* II, 70.

[27] *Evelyn* 18 Jan., 19 Feb. 1671.

[28] *Rawl. MSS. A.* 174, ff. 345, 372–84; *C.S.P.D.* 1671: 243; *Tanner, Further Corr.* 269, 280; *Corbett* II, 70–1.

[29] *D.* 19 Feb. 64; *C.S.P.D.* 1671: 191, 201, 490; *Rawl. MSS. A.* 172, f. 133; *C.P. MSS.* III, 172; *Evelyn* 25 Aug. 76; *Tanner, Further Corr.* 305–8.

[30] *Rawl. MSS. A.* 174, f. 189; *D.* 27 Feb. 67; 9, 22, 24 April 68; *C.S.P.D.* 1667/8: 308; 1671: 185, 243; 1671/2: 15; *Davey,* Items 2893–4.

[31] *D.* 3 July, 13 Nov. 62 et passim; *C.S.P.D.* XI, 1671: 358–9, 364, 366; XII, 1672: 59; *Rawl. MSS. A.* 172, ff. 73, 75; *Smith* I, 133–7.

[32] *Rawl. MSS. A.* 174, ff. 197–200.

[33] *Rawl. MSS. A.* 174, ff. 183, 390, 392; *C.S.P.D.* XI, 1671: 185, 213–14, 267, 276, 317, 427.

[34] *Evelyn* 28 Aug. 1670; 21 Oct. 1671; *Hatton* I, 63, 66, 68; *Rawl. MSS. A.* 174, ff. 195, 407; *Tanner, Further Corr.* 270; *C.S.P.D.* 1671: 514.

[35] *Rawl. MSS. A.* 174, ff. 402–7; *H.M.C. Fleming* 81; *D.* 4, 5 May 61; *Hatton* I, 62; *Pepysian MSS.* No. 2265, Paper 36; *Verney Memoirs* (1925 ed.) II, 274–313.

[36] *C.S.P.D.* XI, 1671: 579; XII, 1671/2: 3, 41–3, 63, 66, 87, 102, 194, 215; *Négociations relatives à la succession d'Espagne sous Louis XIV,* ed. F.A.M. Mignet (1835–42) III, 694; *H.M.C. Fleming 82; Edward Hoare, 'Mr Pepys and his Bank', Daily Telegraph,* 7 Sept. 1928; *Hatton* I, 74; *H.M.C. Rep.* 6 (*Ingilby 368–9*).

CHAPTER III. THE THIRD DUTCH WAR

[1] *Rawl. MSS. A.* 187, ff. 361–2; *H.M.C. Fleming* 87; *Evelyn* 3 Feb. 1672; *C.S.P.D.* XII, 1671/2: 121.

[2] *Hatton* I, 75, 81–2; *H.M.C. Fleming* 87, 90; *C.S.P.D.* XII, 1671/2: 131, 133–4, 136, 141, 145, 175, 180, 189–90, 197–9, 200, 205, 210–11, 214, 220, 251; *Evelyn* 12, 21, 24 March 1672.

[3] *Rawl. MSS. A.* 182, ff. 410, 413; *H.M.C. Rep.* 8 (*Trinity House* 254).

[4] *C.S.P.D.* XII, 1671/2: 203, 272; *H.M.C. Fleming 90; Evelyn* 4 April 1672.

[5] *C.S.P.D.* XII, 1671/2: 209, 396, 563; *Tanner, Further Corr.* 270–

1; *Greenwich MS.* 674; *Duckett* 30; *C.P. MSS.* I, 13, 16; *C.S.P.D.* XII, 1671/2: 130.

[6] *C.S.P.D.* XIV, 1672/3: 338, 353, 407; *Hatton* I, 82; *Bibliotheca Pindesiana* (1910) No. V; *Rawl. MSS. A.* 184, ff. 237–8; *H.M.C. Hastings* II, 157; *H.T. Colenbrander* II, 77 et seq.

[7] *Colenbrander* II, 77 et seq.; *Ogg* 357–8; *C.S.P.D.* XII, 1671/2: 246, 356, 466; *Rawl. MSS. A.* 189, ff. 253–4; *Verney Memoirs* (1925 ed.) II, 355; *H.M.C. Fleming* 90–3.

[8] *C.S.P.D.* XII, 1671/2: 465–6, 541, 556–7; XIV, 1672/3: 358; *P.R.O., Foreign Entry Book* 177: 9 May 1672.

[9] *C.S.P.D.* XII, 1671/2: 541, 556, 592; XIII, 1672: 23; XIV, 1672/3: 358.

[10] *Evelyn* 10, 14 May 1672; *Hatton* I, 84; *C.S.P.D.* XII, 1671/2: 592; XIII, 1672: 4, 8, 19, 27, 57, 74.

[11] *Ogg* 359; *H.M.C. Dartmouth* III, 6–23; *C.S.P.D.* XIII, 1672: 83; *Clowes* II, 303.

[12] *Rawl. MSS. A.* 184, f. 270; *C.S.P.D.* XIII, 1672: 85, 102.

[13] *Evelyn* 31 May 1672; *Pepysian MS.* No. 138; *Harris* II, 249.

[14] *H.M.C. Hastings II, 159; H.M.C. Fleming 93–4; Hatton I, 86;* *C.S.P.D.* XIII, 1672: 102, 109, 144.

[15] *H.M.C. Dartmouth* III, 6–23; *H.M.C. Fleming* 93; *Clowes* II, 308; *Ogg* 359–60; *Hatton* I, 87–8; *Blok, De Ruyter* 321; *Harris* II, 250; *Hinchingbroke MSS.* (Captain Richard Haddock's Account at end of Lord Sandwich's *Journal*) X, 576–7; *Rawl. MSS. A.* 173, f. 5; *C.S.P.D.* XIII, 1672: 74, 90; *S.P. Foreign (Holland* 189: 3 June 1672); *Pepysian MS.* No. 2873, f. 137; *A True Relation of the Engagement of His Majesty's Fleet . . . with the Dutch Fleet, May* 28, 1672 (London 1672).

[16] *C.S.P.D.* XIII, 1672: 191, 212, 256, 276; *H.M.C. Fleming* 94; *Hatton* I, 89–90.

[17] *London Gazette,* No. 691: 1–4 July 1672; *Evelyn* 3 July 1672; *D.* I, XXXIV; *Rawl. MSS. A.* 174, f. 417; *C.S.P.D.* XIII, 1672: 304.

[18] *Rawl. MSS. A.* 174, f. 239; *Braybrooke* (1825 ed.) 606–7; *Hatton* I, 68, 89.

[19] *C.S.P.D.* XIII, 1672: 272; *Pepysian MS.* No. 2866, 305; *C.P. MSS.* I, 40; *Hatton* I, 94; *Tanner, Further Corr.* 271–2; *Duckett* 13.

[20] *C.S.P.D.* XIII, 1672: 118, 156, 167, 191, 153; *Evelyn* 6 June 1672.

[21] *C.S.P.D.* XIII, 1672: 253; 684; *Tanner, Further Corr.* 271; *Hatton* I, 93.

[22] *C.S.P.D.* XIII, 1672: 221; *H.M.C. Rutland* II, 25; *Ranke* III, 523; *H.M.C. Hastings* II, 379; *Hatton* I, 90–1, 93.

[23] *C.S.P.D.* XIII, 1672: 304, 366–7, 370, 376, 413, 685; *H.M.C. Fleming* 96–7; *Hatton* I, 95–6; *Anthony Wood, Diary,* 19 Aug. 1672.

[24] *C.S.P.D.* XIII, 1672: 67, 484, 685; XIV, 1672/3: 370–1; *Hatton* I; *Rawl. MSS. A.* 187, f. 349.

[25] *Rawl. MSS. A.* 187, ff. 347–9; *A.* 191, ff. 209–10; *C.S.P.D.* XIII, 1672: 643; XIV, 1672/3: 368, 377.

[26] *Evelyn* 18 Aug., 1 Sept. 1672; *C.S.P.D.* XII, 1672: 525, 557.

[27] *Rawl. MSS. A.* 187, ff. 357–8.

[28] *Rawl. MSS. A.* 187, ff. 345–6.

[29] *C.S.P.D.* XIII, 1672: 493, 498, 540, 556, 660, 685; *H.M.C. Fleming* 98.

[30] *C.S.P.D.* XIII, 1672: 317; *Whitear* 161–5; *D.* 13 June 63; 11 Dec. 66; *Smith* I, 132–3, 144–5; *Rawl. MSS. A.* 174, f. 440; *B.M. Addit. MSS.: Papers of Charles Stuart, Duke of Richmond* II, f. 240; *Howarth* 41.

[31] *C.S.P.D.* XIII, 1672: 460; *H.M.C. Rep. 6 (Ingilby* passim); *Rawl. MSS. A.* 172, ff. 442, 444; *Evelyn* 9 June 1667; *Braybrooke* IV, 204–5; *D.N.B.*

[32] *C.S.P.D.* XIV, 1672/3: 14, 18, 39, 41–2, 92, 175, 183, 203; *Pepysian MS.* No. 2581: Navy White Book.

[33] *Rawl. MSS. A.* 173, f. 93; *D.* 17, 19 March 65.

[34] *C.S.P.D.* XIV, 1672/3: 17, 22, 127, 136, 160, 237–8, 482, 577.

[35] *C.S.P.D.* XIV. 1672/3: 189, 251, 257–8, 291–2, 451–2.

[36] *Hooke, Diary* 29 Jan. 1673; *Whitear* 103–4, 161–3; *D.* 24 Aug. 66; 15 Oct., 6 Dec. 68; 22, 25 Jan., 3 March 69; *Tanner, Further Corr.* 280.

[37] *C.S.P.D.* XIV, 1672/3: 498–9, 508, 517; *Rawl. MSS. A.* 174, f. 275; *H.M.C. Hodgkin* 172; *Davey,* Item 2897; MSS. Notes by W. G. Perrin in the author's possession, Admiralty Sec. Letters 3554; *Howarth* 163.

[38] *C.S.P.D.* XIV, 1672/3: 508, 553–4, 560, 589; XV, 1673: 227; *Rawl. MSS. A.* 185, ff. 384–5.

[39] *C.S.P.D.* XIV, 1672/3: 335; *Ogg* 364–71; *Evelyn* 30 March 1673; *A. Bryant, Charles II* 225–7.

[40] *C.S.P.D.* XV, 1673: 165, 167, 174–5, 184; 210–11, 221–2, 255; *Rawl. MSS. A.* 191, f. 211.

[41] *C.S.P.D.* XV, 1673: 197, 199, 309, 330, 333, 338; *Ogg* 372–4; *Hooke, Diary* 31 May 73; *Rawl. MSS. A.* 189, f. 251.

[42] *Rawl. MSS. A.* 172, ff. 81–2.

[43] *C.P. MSS.* I, 36–9; III, I; *Pepysian MSS., Miscellanies* II, 401, 405; XI, 221; No. 2867, *Naval Precedents* 35, 144, 149; *Duckett* 30; *C.S.P.D.* XV, 1673: 369, 371; *Rawl. MSS. A.* 180, f. 189; *H.M.C. Rep.* 6 (*F. B. Frank, Esq.* 454).

CHAPTER IV. CALLED TO THE ADMIRALTY

[1] *Pepysian MS.* No. 2265, Paper 47; *Hatton* I, 107–8; *Duckett* 13, 31; *C.P. MSS.* 1, 40.

[2] *C.P. MSS.* I, 107; II, 2–5, 7, 12, 14, 18, 70, 77; *C.S.P.D.* XV, 1673: 394.

[3] *Examen* 461; *Evelyn* 26 May 1671; *C.S.P.D.* XV, 1673: 385; *C.P. MSS. II,* VIII–IX, 10, 186–7.

[4] *Rawl. MSS. A.* 171, f. 137; *A.* 177, f. 121; *A.* 181, f. 217; *C.P. MSS.* IV, 340, 427–8; *Howarth* 43–4; *Smith* I, 144–5.

[5] *Pepysian MS.* No. 2612, ff. 6–7, 111, 121, 135; *C.S.P.D.* XV, 1673: 475; *E. H. Pearce, Annals of Christ's Hospital* (1908) 99–103; *Hooke, Diary* 6, 29 Dec. 1673; 21, 23 Jan. 1674.

[6] *C.S.P.D.* XV, 1673: 415, 417, 428, 432, 434, 448, 450, 459, 463, 490, 503, 509–10; *C.P. MSS.* I, 6; II, 10, 14, 24, 25, 27–9, 31; *Add. MSS.* No. 38, 849; *Colenbrander* II, 288, 293; *Ogg* 374–6; *Blok, De Ruyter* 349; *Hatton* I, 113–15.

[7] *C.S.P.D.* XV, 1673: 510, 537; *Colenbrander* II, 308–9; *C.P. MSS.* II, 36, 41, 45, 91; *Hatton* I, 113–15; *Corbett* II, 74–5.

[8] *Rawl. MSS. A.* 185, f. 364.

[9] *C.P. MSS.* II, 10, 17, 19, 54, 58, 64, 66, 89, 94, 123, 131.

[10] *C.P. MSS.* II, 89, 94, 121–2, 132, 136–7, 140–2, 144, 149, 152–4, 158, 161, 164–5, 168–70, 178, 187, 191, 196, 210–11, 222, 230, 238–41, 244, 246, 251, 304.

[11] *H.M.C. Rep.* 6 (*Ingilby*); *Tanner, Further Corr.* 273–7; *Smith* II, 140–2; *Rawl. MSS. A.* 172, f. 157.

[12] *D.* 21 Oct. 66.

[13] *Rawl. MSS. A.* 172, ff. 131, 141–6; *C.P. MSS.* II, 113, 118; *Smith* I, 142.

[14] *C.S.P.D.* XVI, 1673/4: 8; *P.R.O.: S.P. Dom. Car. II,* Case I, 5 Nov. 1673; *Grey* II, 222; *C.J.* IX, 284–5; *H.M.C. Rep. 4 (Bath* 231).

[15] *Rawl. MSS. A.* 172, ff. 30–72; *A.* 191, ff. 114–15; *C.P. MSS.* II, 100, 155, 203, 217, 229–30; *C.S.P.D.* XVI, 1673/4: 15; *Pepysian MSS.,* Adm. Letters II, 399; No. 2265, Paper 73.

[16] *Rawl. MSS. A.* 172, f. 131; *C.J.* IX.

[17] *Grey* II, 304; *C.P. MSS.* II, 91.

[18] *Grey* II, 329–33.

[19] *C.P. MSS.* II, 238; *Rawl. MSS. A.* 172, f. 131v.; *C.J.* IX, 304.

[20] *C.J.* IX, 306; *Rawl. MSS. A.* 185, f. 440; *Howarth* 44–7.

[21] *C.J.* IX, 306; *Rawl. MSS. A.* 172, f. 132; *Grey* II, 407–13.

[22] *C.J.* IX, 309; *Rawl. MSS. A.* 172, ff. 132v–3, 135, 137; *D.* I, xxxiii; *Grey* II, 420–1, 427–8, 432.

[23] *C.J.* IX; *Rawl. MSS. A.* 172, f. 133; *Grey* II, 425–33, 454; *C.S.P.D.* 1673/5: 149; *Pepysian MS.* No. 2265, Paper 63; *Tanner, Further Corr.* 285, 287.

[24] *Rawl. MSS. A.* 172, ff. 153–6; *Pepysian MS.* No. 2265, Paper 95.

[25] *Rawl. MSS. A.* 172, ff. 92–3, 100–1, 104–6; *A.* 183, f. 210; *A.* 194, f. 281; *D.* 17 March 65; *C.S.P.D.* 1671; 463; *H.M.C. (House of Lords,* 1690/1: 401–2).

[26] *Rawl. MSS. A.* 172, ff. 92–5, 107.

[27] *Rawl. MSS. A.* 191, ff. 201–8; *C.P. MSS.* II, 244, 246–7, 253, 258, 264, 268; *Hooke, Diary* 28 Feb. 1674.

CHAPTER V. THE SQUIRE OF DERBY HOUSE

[1] *C.P. MSS.* II, IX, 186–7, 313; *D.* 29 June 63.

[2] *Hargreaves, State Trials* I, 796; *C.P. MSS.* II, 313; III, 390; *Rawl. MSS. A.* 183, ff. 214, 239–40; *Greenwich MS.* 702.

[3] *C.P. MSS.* I passim; II, vii–ix; IV passim; *Pepysian MSS.,* Adm. Letters passim; *W. G. Perrin, The Lord High Admiral and the Board of Admiralty.*

[4] *C.P. MSS.* II, 6, 10, 11, 111, 162, 185; III, 42; *Rawl. MSS. A.* 185, ff. 392, 425; Letter in possession of Lady Gainsborough: Samuel Pepys to the Duke of York, 10 April 1676.

[5] *Naval Minutes* 194; *Tangier Papers* 229; *C.P. MSS.* II, 207–8; 232.

[6] *Naval Minutes* 256; *Tangier Papers* 158–9; Adm. Letters passim.

[7] *C.P. MSS.* II, 157–8; *M. Oppenheim, A History of the Administration of the Royal Navy,* 1509–1660 (1896).

[8] *C.P. MSS.* I, 195–6; II, 77, 81, 106; III, 85, 92–3.

[9] *Naval Minutes* 264; *Pepysian MSS., Mornamont* II, 1228; *H. Teonge, Diary* (ed. G. E. Mainwaring); *Tanner, Further Corr.* 356–7; *Howarth* 68–9; *C.P. MSS.* IV, 388, 398, 436–7.

[10] *Corbett* II passim; *C.P. MSS.* II, 337, 342, 383.

[11] *Rawl. MSS. A.* 172, f. 77; *C.P. MSS.* II, 366, 390, 421; III, 39.

[12] *C.P. MSS.* II, 342, 383, 386; III, 87, 107, 108, 111, 114; IV, 107–8, 114, 130.

[13] *C.P. MSS.* III, 139, 141, 251; IV, III, 268.

[14] *C.P. MSS.* III, 180; IV, 267, 279; *C.S.P.D.* 1675/6: 553.

[15] *C.P. MSS.* II, 303, 361; III, 180; IV, 267.

[16] *Pepysian MS.* No. 2876, Naval Precedents 416; *C.P. MSS.* I, 140–1; II, 240; IV, 218.

[17] *C.P. MSS.* IV, 438, 464, 520.

[18] *Pepysian MS.* No. 1608, *Miscellanies* XI passim; *E. Chappell, Shorthand Letters of Samuel Pepys* (1933) 94; *Rawl. MSS. A.* 174, f. I; *C.S.P.D.* 1673/4: 362; *C.P. MSS.* II, 361; IV, 204; *Henry Teonge, Diary* 3 June 1675.

[19] *Tanner, Further Corr.* 276; *C.S.P.D.* 1675/6: 133; 1678: 289; *C.P. MSS.* II, 418, 421; III, 2, 3, 4, 9; IV, 123–5, 449.

[20] *C.P. MSS.* II, 282, 300, 360.

[21] *Tanner, Further Corr.* 277; *D.* 27 Sept. 61; *C.P.MSS.* III, 311.

[22] S. Pepys to Duke of York, 10 April 1676 (in possession of Lady Gainsborough); *Pepysian MSS.*, Adm. Letters passim; *C.P. MSS.* I, 39.

[23] *C.P. MSS.* III, 255.

[24] *Rawl. MSS. A.* 185, ff. 51, 66, 80; *A.* 191, f. 7; *Tanner, Further Corr.* 282–329; *C.P. MSS.* II, 378; III, 47; *Greenwich MS.* f. 735; *C.S.P.D.* XII, 1671/2: 130.

[25] *C.S.P.D.* 1675/6: 208; *Rawl. MSS. A.* 133, 17 June 1678; *A.* 185, ff. 253, 398; *C.P. MSS.* II, 401; III, 101–2, 263, 271.

[26] *C.P. MSS.* II, 296, 299, 315–18, 371, 375; III, 98–100; IV, 163–4; *Evelyn* 21 Aug. 1674.

[27] *C.P. MSS.* II, 347–9, 357; *Howarth* 47–8, 156–7; *Rawl. MSS. A.* 172, f. 122; *A.* 190, f. 25.

[28] *Rawl. MSS. A.* 185, f. 30; *Howarth* 41–3, 49–51; *Greenwich MS.* f. 702; *J. Nichols, Literary Anecdotes* IV, 542n; *Hooke, Diary* 17 Aug. 1675.

[29] *Sir F. Bridge, Samuel Pepys, Lover of Musique; D.* 22 June 60; 11 Jan. 64; 15 April 66; *Howarth* 41–3, 47–50, 86–9; *Smith* I, 137, 157, 161; *Rawl. MSS. A.* 183, f. 53.

[30] *Rawl. MSS. A.* 173, ff. 178–9; *A.* 175, f. 255; *A.* 185, f. 157; *Smith* II, 293, *Tanner, Further Corr.* 326–7; *Howarth* 50, 73–4.

[31] *Rawl. MSS. A.* 175, f. 208; *A.* 181, f. 186; *A.* 183, ff. 130, 173; *A.* 185, ff. 4, 155, 157; *A.* 189, ff. 25, 27, 57; *A.* 194, f. 156; *Pepysiana* 258.

[32] *Tanner, Further Corr.* 279–81, 290–1; *C.P. MSS.* III, 20, 172; *Braybrooke* IV, 238; *Hooke, Diary* 10 Jan. 1673; *Rawl. MSS. A.* 171, f. 91; *A.* 181, f. 31; *A.* 183, ff. 239–40; *C.* 859, f. 39; *Pepysian MSS., Calligraphical Collections* III, f. 262; *C.S.P.D.* 1678: 187.

[33] *Rawl. MSS. A.* 173, ff. 189 et seq.; *A.* 181, f. 31; *A.* 194, f. 37; *C.* 859, ff. 39 et seq.; *Howarth* 49–50; *Tanner, Further Corr.* 296–7.

CHAPTER VI. THE THIRTY NEW SHIPS

[1] *C.P. MSS.* II, 254, 263–4, 270; *Rawl. MSS. A.* 185, f. 384.

[2] *C.P. MSS.* II, 270; *Rawl. MSS. A.* 181, f. 409; *Pepysian MS.* No. 2265, Paper 73.

[3] *C.P. MSS* II, 278, 292.

[4] *C.P. MSS.* II, 346, 350, 357, 360, 364, 379–80, 382, 385, 403–4; *C.S.P.D.* XII, 1672: 52–3; *Corbett* II, 88–9; *Charnock, Biographia Navalis* (1794) 1, 247.

[5] *Corbett* II, 98–9; *C.S.P.D.* 1675/6: 12, 28, 35; *Tanner, Further Corr.* 279–81; *C.P. MSS.* III, 15, 17–20, 24, 41, 48–9, 56; IV, 163–4, 174.

[6] *Rawl. MSS. A.* 185, f. 360; *Pepysian MSS., Miscellanies* V, 49, 663; *C.P. MSS.* I, 43–6; II, 407–8, 418; *Pepysian MS.* No. 2265, Papers 47, 68, 72–3; *Grey* III, I; *Essex Papers* 289.

[7] *Pepysian MS.* No. 2265, Papers 47, 68, 70, 72, 73, 90; *L.J.; B.M. Harleian MSS.* 6277, ff. 7–10; *Grey* III, 34; *E.H.R.* XII, 691; *Corbett* II, 101.

[8] *Grey* III, 34–40, 96–102; *Sitwell* 12–13.

[9] *Pepysian MS.* No. 2265 passim; *C.P. MSS.* III, 48–9, 56, 63–7, 70–1, 74, 76–81, 84, 104, 109–11; *H.M.C. Fleming; C.S.P.D.* 1675/6: 183, 188–91, 194–5, 197.

[10] *C.P. MSS.* III, 78–80; *C.S.P.D.* 1675/6: 185, 194–5, 197–8.

[11] *C.S.P.D.* 1675/6: 195, 197, 231, 252; *C.P. MSS.* III, 73, 78, 79; *Rawl. MSS. A.* 185, ff. 3–4, 11, 24, 58; *Howarth* 51–2; *Pepysian MS.* No. 2241.

[12] *Naval Minutes* 195; *Howarth* 51–2; *Rawl. MSS. A.* 185, ff. 11, 24; *Pepysian MS.* No. 2241.

[13] *L.J.; Grey* III, 317–20; *Pepysian MS.* No. 2265, Paper 70; *H.M.C. Hastings* II, 383.

[14] *Pepysian MS.* No. 2266, Paper 119; *Grey* III, 323–33; *C.P. MSS.* III, xliii; *Ranke* IV, 16–17; *H.M.C. Laing* I, 408; *Hastings* II, 383.

[15] *Grey* III. 323–38; *Pepysian MS.* No. 2266, Paper 119.

[16] *Grey* III, 333–49, 354–66.

[17] *Pepysian MSS.* No. 2265–6 passim; *Grey* III, 372–417.

[18] *C.J.; Parlt. Hist.* IV; *Grey* III, 448–59; IV, 54; *C.P. MSS.* IV, 257–60.

[19] *C.P. MSS.* III, 109–11; *Charnock, Biographia Navalis* I, 247–50; *H. Teonge, Diary* (ed. Mainwaring 67–70).

[20] *C.P. MSS.* III, 114–15, 176–82, 261; IV, 176–82, 333, 373, 389, 398.

[21] *Corbett* II, 98–9; *C.P. MSS.* III, 186, 230–1, 245, 266; IV, 339, 352–3.

[22] *Rawl. MSS. A.* 173, f. 133; *C.P. MSS.* III, 280, 284; IV, 356–7; *H.M.C. Fleming* 129, 149; *Corbett* II, 99–100.

[23] *C.P. MSS.* III, 276–7, 296, 298, 301, 305, 309, 319–20, 374; IV, 323, 334, 354–7, 377, 378, 382; *Essex Papers* 84.

[24] *C.P. MSS.* III, 346; IV, 382, 384; *Evelyn, Diary* Dec. 1676.

[25] *L.J.; A. Bryant, Charles II* 252–3; *L.F. Brown, The First Earl of Shaftesbury* (1933) 242–3; *Sitwell* 13–15; *Echard* 925–8; *Grey* IV, 63, 103–15.

[26] *Pepysian MS.* No. 2265 passim; *Miscellanies* II, 453–69; *Grey* IV, 115–18; *Ranke* IV, 29; *Naval Minutes* 283–4; *C.P. MSS.* I, 48–53.

[27] *Grey* IV, 118–30; *Rawl. MSS. C.* 859, ff. 8, 8 V; *Parlt. Hist.* IV; *C.P. MSS.* III, 380–2.

[28] *Grey* IV, 149–59, 173–7, 180–7; *Rawl. MSS. A.* 133, ff. 3–5; *C.* 859, ff. 9 v, 10 v, 15–16 v, 18 v, 21–4; *Howarth* 66; *Naval Minutes* 143.

[29] *Rawl. MSS. C.* 859, f. 38 v; *A.* 184, f. 7; *C.P. MSS.* III, xvii-xxiv, 203, 212; IV, 340, 427–8; *Tanner, Further Corr.* 287–90.

[30] *Grey* IV, 204–17; *Rawl. MSS. C.* 859, ff. 23, 24, 24 v, 38 v; *C.J.* IX, 405; *P.R.O. Paris Transcripts*, No. 135; Courtin to Louis XIV, 8/18 March 1677.

[31] *C.J.* IX, 405; *C.S.P.D.* 1677/8: 116, 128; *C.P. MSS.* IV, 427–8.

[32] *C.P. MSS.* III, 401–3, 406–9, 410, 412; *Rawl. MSS. A.* 185, ff. 149–50.

[33] *C.P. MSS.* III, 413–15; IV, 412–15, 422–4, 428–9; *Naval Minutes* 318.

CHAPTER VII. 'THE ENVIOUS NAME OF ADMIRAL'

[1] *H.M.C. Rep.* 8 *(Trinity House* 256*); Rawl. MSS. A.* 178, ff. 134, 136; *A.* 181, ff. 326–7; *A.* 191, f. 83; *C.P. MSS.* I, 41; *Tanner, Further Corr.* 313–14, 317.

[2] *Rawl. MSS. A.* 178, f. 195; *A.* 180, ff. 293, 302–3, 323, 347; *A.* 182, f. 410; *A.* 183, f. 51; *Tanner, Further Corr.* 305, 308–9.

[3] *Tanner, Further Corr.* 302–4; *C.S.P.D.* 1677/8: 317; *Naval Minutes* 57; *C.P. MSS.* III, 383.

[4] *Howarth* 67–9.

[5] *Pepysian MS.* No. 1476; *Miscellanies* II, 505–36; *The Petty –Southwell Correspondence* (ed. Marquis of Lansdowne 1928) 33, 54; *Howarth* 66; *Rawl. MSS. A.* 172, f. 17; *A.* 185, ff. 114, 116; *Tanner, Further Corr.* 317–18.

[6] *Rawl. MSS. A.* 172, f. 25; *A.* 190, ff. 99; *H. B. Wheatley, Samuel Pepys, Clothworker; Raikes, Honourable Artillery Company* I, 196; *Braybrooke* IV, 205–6; *Howarth* 90; *E.G. O'Donoghue, Bridewell Hospital* (1929) 162.

[7] *C.P. MSS.* II, 220, 232; *Evelyn,* 22 May 1676; *Rawl. MSS. A.* 172, f. 25; *A.* 174, f. 386; *A.* 180, ff. 287, 370; *A.* 185, f. 137; *C.S.P.D.* 1675/6: 251; 1676/7: 272; *Naval Minutes* 198–9, 233; *Tangier Papers* 300–1; *H.M.C. Rep.* 8 *(Trinity House* 257*); Rep.* 9 *(House of Lords,* Part II, 87).

[8] *Naval Minutes* 39; *C.S.P.D.* 1673/4: 467; 1675/6: 7, 173.

[9] *C.P. MSS.* III, 172, 178; IV, 343–4, 353–4, 390; *H.M.C. Fleming* 128; *Pepysian MS.* No. 2612, ff. 225, 227; *Rawl. MSS. A.* 467; *Charnock, Biographia Navalis* I, 378.

[10] *Evelyn* 26 Aug. 1776; *Naval Minutes* 7; *Rawl. MSS. A.* 185, f. 372; *A.* 191, ff. 50–1; *A.* 194, f. 79; *Pepysian MS.* No. 2350.

[11] *H.M.C. Rep.* 8 *(Trinity House* 255–6*); Greenwich MS.* 75; *C.P. MSS.* III, 127; IV, 220–1, 226–8, 230, 240, 243; *Pepysian MS.* No. 2612, f, 153; *Tanner, Further Corr.* 286.

[12] *Pepysian MS.* No. 2612, ff. 175, 232, 238–67; *Rawl. MSS. A.* 185, f. 103; *Christ's Hospital, Court Minutes,* Book 1661/77: 654–88; *Pearce* 106–7.

[13] *Pepysian MS.* No. 2612, ff. 238 et seq.; *Rawl. MSS. A.* 185, f. 109.

[14] *Pepysian MS.* No. 2612, f. 300.

[15] *Rawl. MSS. A.* 185, f. 202; *Smith* I, 189–97; *Pepysian MS.* No. 2612, ff. 232–4, 317.

[16] *Pepysian MS.* No. 2612, ff. 307, 313, *C.P. MSS.* IV, 565; *C.S.P.D.* 1677/8: 564.

[17] *Rawl. MSS. A.* 185, ff. 151, 159, 263, 265, 267; *Tanner, Further Corr.* 310–11.

[18] *Tanner, Further Corr.* 292–3, 311–15; *Smith* I, 169–82; *H.M.C. Rep.* 4 *(Bath* 231*); Howarth* 53–7, 64–6; *Rawl. MSS. A.* 185, f. 133; *C.S.P.D.* 1676/7: 551; *B.M. Addit. MSS.* No. 38, 849 (8 May 1677).

[19] *Howarth* 48; *C.S.P.D.* IX, 1675/6: 201–2; *Rawl. MSS. A.* 185, ff. 206 et seq., 337.

[20] *Rawl. MSS. A.* 185, ff. 206 et seq.

[21] *Rawl. MSS. A.* 173, ff. 178–9; *A.* 181, f. 120; *A.* 185, ff. 206 et seq.; *Howarth* 84.

[22] *C.P. MSS.* I, 233–41; *Pepysian MS.* No. 1340; Adm. Letters VI, 201–2; *Naval Minutes* 57, 182.

[23] *C.P. MSS.* II, 379; III, 314; IV, 382–3, 400–2; *Rawl. MSS. A.* 181, ff. 363–71; *A.* 185, f. 422; *Naval Minutes* 76.

[24] *C.P. MSS.* IV, 382–3; *Rawl. MSS. A.* 185, ff. 265–6.

[25] *C.P. MSS.* I, 206; IV, 400–2; *Pepysian MS.* No. 2876, Naval Precedents 161; *Naval Minutes* 76.

[26] *C.P. MSS.* I, 202–3; III, 29, 131; IV, 493–4, 535, 544–6; *Naval Minutes* 194; *Pepysian MSS.*, Adm. Letters IX, 202–3.

[27] *Pepysian MS.* No. 2867, Naval Precedents 241; *C.P. MSS.* I, 203–4.

[28] *C.P. MSS.* I, 204–5; IV, 569.

[29] *Howarth* 69–71; *Greenwich MS.* 810–13; *Braybrooke* IV, 206–7.

[30] *C.P. MSS.* I, 79; II, 21, 38; IV, 392–4, 399–400, 486, 491–6, 501, 505, 507–11, 513, 515–16, 528–31, 534, 540–3; *Naval Minutes* 57, 250; *Rawl. MSS. A.* 185, ff. 247, 370.

[31] *Pepysian MS.* No. 2866, Naval Precedents 61, 416; Adm. Letters VI, 228; *C.P. MSS.* I, 165–78.

[32] *Corbett* II, 101; *C.S.P.D.* 1677/8; *Pepysian MSS.*, Adm. Letters VII, 296, 361; *C.P. MSS.* I, 195, 197; III, 369; IV, 450, 454–6, 460–1, 501–22.

[33] *Howarth* 67–9.

[34] *C.P. MSS.* II, 327, 333, 366; III, 63–7; IV, 435, 467, 489; *State Tracts* (1693) 124–35; *Correspondence of Henry Hyde, 2nd Earl of Clarendon*, ed. Singer (1828) 1, 1–2; *S.J. Davey*, Item 2896.

[35] *C.P. MSS.* I, 55; IV, 550; *Tanner, Further Corr.* 309–10; *Pepysian MS.* No. 2266, Paper 129; *Miscellanies* V, 271–81.

[36] *C.P. MSS.* IV, 561, 563–4, 567–8, 584–5; *H.M.C. Egmont* II. 69; *Ranke* IV, 40; *H.M.C. Hodgkin* 189–93; *Pepysian MS.* No. 2266, Paper 165; *L.J.* 1675/81: 130; *Grey* V, 2–3.

[37] *Rawl. MSS. A.* 133, f. 9; *A.* 181, f. 413; *Grey* V, 77, 87–8.

[38] *Grey* V, 87–8, 107–9; *Rawl. MSS. A.* 133, f. 10; *A.* 181, f. 413; *H.M.C. Portland* III, 358; *Ranke* IV, 42.

[39] *H.M.C. Portland* III, 358; *Dalrymple* II, 160–5 167, 178–9; *Ranke* IV, 44–57; *H.M.C. Ormonde* IV (9 Feb. 1678); *W.A. Shaw, Calendar Treasury Books* V, lxxvii; *Naval Minutes* 142–3, 198, 264.

[40] *Rawl. MSS. A.* 133, ff. 10–16, 106; *Grey* V, 106, 110–11, 161–2; *C.S.P.D.* 1677/8; *Pepysian MS.* No. 2266, Paper 155; *Naval Minutes* 358–9.

[41] *Grey* V, 161–2, 170–2, 261–2; *C.P. MSS.* IV, 580; *C.S.P.D.* 1678: 55; *Dalrymple* II, 185; *Naval Minutes* 365.

[42] *Rawl. MSS. A.* 175, ff. 179–82, 208; *A.* 181, f. 11; *Dalrymple* II, 160, 165; *C.P. MSS.* IV, 570; *Sir John Reresby, Memoirs,* 16 March 1678; *Grey* V, 239–40, 248, 261–2; *Pepysian MSS., Mornamont* II, 1187.

[43] *C.S.P.D.* 1678; 121–3, 153, 155, 160–1, 177, 182–3; *Naval Minutes* 318.

[44] *Pepysian MSS.,* Adm. Letters VI, 471; *C.P. MSS.* I, 109; IV, 572–3, 578–9; *C.S.P.D.* 1678; 67; *H.M.C. Hodgkin* 194–5; *Rawl. MSS. C.* 859, ff. 49 et seq.

[45] *Corbett* II, 104; *C.P. MSS.* IV, 578–9; *Pepysian MS.* No. 1338; *Rawl. MSS. A.* 133 passim.

[46] *Parlt. Hist.* IV, 975–6; *Naval Minutes* 198; *Grey* VI, 32–5, 74–5; *H.M.C. Ormonde* IV, 431; *Pepysian MS.* No. 2266, Paper 187; *Rawl. MSS. A.* 133 passim.

[47] *Rawl. MSS. C.* 859, ff. 3–6.

[48] *Rawl. MSS. A.* 133, *Parliamentary Journal; C.P. MSS.* IV, 587–9, 591, 594–5; *Corbett* II, 104; *S. Pepys, Memories relating to the State of the Royal Navy of England,* ed. J. R. Tanner (1906) 3.

CHAPTER VIII. THE GREAT PLOT

[1] *C.P. MSS.* IV, 594–5, 597–8, 601–13; *Ranke* IV, 52–3; *C.S.P.D.* 1678: 372.

[2] *Tanner, Further Corr.* 304–8, 318.

[3] *Rawl. MSS. A.* 173, ff. 139–60; *A.* 174, ff. 101–7; *A.* 175, ff. 79–

80, 119–24, 157; *A.* 188, ff. 108, 112; *A.* 194, ff. I, 81–4; *Pepysian MSS., Mornamont* passim; *G. D. Scull, Dorothea Scott* (1882) 21–4.

⁴ *Hinchingbroke MSS., Sandwich Journal* X, 392; *Rawl. MSS. A.* 173, ff. 139–60; *A.* 175, ff. 1–15, 17–45, 62–9, 70–4; *A.* 194, ff. 4–6, 81–4, 109–11; *Pepysian MSS., Mornamont* passim; *C.S.P.D.* 1672: 30; *Naval Minutes* 237–8.

⁵ *Rawl. MSS. A.* 175, ff. 70–4; *A.* 188, ff. 147–50; *A.* 194, ff. 4–6, 81–4; *Pepysian MSS., Mornamont* I, 331–2, 463–82 passim.

⁶ *Pepysian MSS., Mornamont* I, 47–9, 296–301, 416–18; *Rawl. MSS. A.* 173, ff. 178–9; *A.* 175, ff. 163–5, 199; *A.* 188, f. 112; *A.* 194, ff. 10–11; *Sitwell* V; *J. Ferguson, Robert Ferguson the Plotter* (1887) 460; *H.M.C. Lindsey* 403–4; *Examen* 488.

⁷ *Rawl. MSS. A.* 173, ff. 178–9; *A.* 175, ff. 179–82; *A.* 176, ff. 105, 109; *A.* 188, f. 110; *Pollock* 378; *C.S.P.D.* 1678: 290; *Pepysian MSS., Mornamont* I, 35–6, 129–30, 285–301, 309–20; II, 1093; *Braybrooke* IV, 229.

⁸ *Rawl. MSS. A.* 175, f. 173; *C.S.P.D.* 1678: 290.

⁹ *H.M.C. Rep. 4 (Bath 245); C.S.P.D.* 1678: 282, 484; *H.M.C. Ormonde* IV, 462; *Pollock* 70–5; *Sitwell* 33–6; *Observator* II, 150–4; *Grey* IV, 163.

¹⁰ *C.P. MSS.* IV, 612–13; *Pollock* 1–12; *Burnet, History of My Own Time* II, 157; *A. Bryant, Charles II* 269–71; *Examen* 133–4, 157, 255; *R. L'Estrange, Narrative of the Plot* (1680).

¹¹ *Pollock* 76–80; *A. Bryant, Charles II* 271–6.

¹² *Tanner, Further Corr.* xxxiv, 325; *Pollock* passim; *C.S.P.D.* 1678: 472; *Pepysian MSS.,* Adm. Letters VIII, 231–3, 241.

¹³ *Echard* 947; *Sitwell* 38–41; *H.M.C. Ormonde* IV, 219; *Examen* 201–3; *L'Estrange, Brief History* III, 142; *National Review,* Vol. 84 (*J. G. Muddiman, The Mystery of Sir E. B. Godfrey* 140–2); *Pollock* 95–103; *B.M. Addit. MSS.* 32509, f. 54; *State Trials* VII, 295.

¹⁴ *H.M.C. Ormonde* IV. 458, 461–3; *H.M.C. Kenyon* 107; *Echard* 961; *Examen* 201–4; *Pollock* 84, 89–90.

¹⁵ *Examen* 198–9, 201; *Echard* 947, 961; *H.M.C. Rep. 6 (Ingilby* 388); *H.M.C. Ormonde* IV, 459; *National Review,* Vol. 84 (*J. G. Muddiman, The Mystery of Sir E. B. Godfrey* 139).

¹⁶ *H.M.C. House of Lords,* 1678–88: 46–8; *Pollock* 91, 151; *Sitwell* 35–6, 40; *H.M.C. Kenyon* 106–7; *Clarke, Life of James II* 1, 534; *Examen* 174, 199–200; *H.M.C. Ormonde* IV, 464.

¹⁷ *H.M.C. House of Lords,* 1678/88: 46–8; *Burnet, History of My Own*

Time; Pollock 148–51; *Sitwell* 40; *L'Estrange, Brief History* III, 187; *Examen* 174, 225; *A Sober Discourse of the Honest Cavalier with the Popish Covenanter* (1680) 7; *Echard* 947–8.

18 *Sitwell* 42–3; *Pollock* 149–66; *Sir J. Reresby, Memoirs* 325.

19 *Echard* 960–2; *Examen* 202; *L'Estrange, Brief History* III, 100.

20 *Echard* 961; *L'Estrange, Brief History* III, 101.

21 *Sitwell* 25; *Ranke* IV, 46; *H.M.C. Kenyon* 108.

22 *National Review*, Vol. 84 (*J. G. Muddiman, The Mystery of Sir E. B. Godfrey* 138–45).

23 *Rawl. MSS. A.* 188, ff. 112, 114–19; *Pepysian MSS., Mornamont* I, 113–17.

24 *Rawl. MSS. A.* 188, ff. 114–19; *Pepysian MSS., Mornamont* I, 113–17.

25 *Pepysian MSS.*, Adm. Letters VIII, 255–7, 261, 264–5; *E.H.R.* VII, 281–2; *C.S.P.D.* 1678: 484; *H.M.C. House of Lords*, 1678/88: 16.

26 *H.M.C. Rep.* 4 (*Bath* 246); *Pepysian MSS.*, Adm. Letters VIII, 264–5; *Mornamont* I, 121, 127–30; *Rawl. MSS. A.* 172, ff. 3–4; *A.* 188, ff. 125, 129; *H.M.C. Rep.*7 (*Verney* 470–1).

27 *Rawl. MSS. A.* 188, ff. 108–12, 125; *Pepysian MSS., Mornamont* 1, 105–9, 121; *C.S.P.D.* 1678: 509.

28 *C.S.P.D.* 1678: 494; *Grey* VI, 286–7; *Examen* 243–4.

CHAPTER IX. THE TRIAL OF ATKINS

1 *Tanner, Further Corr.* 326; *Examen* 204.

2 *Rawl. MSS. A.* 181, ff. 1, 11, 188.

3 *Rawl. MSS. A.* 173, ff. 113–32; *A.* 181, ff. 1, 11–24; *L.J.* 12 Nov. 1678; *State Trials* VI, 1473.

4 *Rawl. MSS. A.* 173, ff. 113–32; *A.* 181, ff. 11–24; *H.M.C.* Rep. 5 (*Sir A. Malet* 318); *Examen* 244–5; *State Trials* VI, 1473–8.

5 *Tanner, Further Corr.* 326–8; *Howarth* 71–4; *Smith* 1, 190.

6 *Rawl. MSS. A.* 181, ff. 1, 182, 184, 190–3.

7 *Rawl. MSS. A.* 181, ff. 11–24; *Examen* 264; *State Trials* VI, 1479.

8 *Rawl. MSS. A.* 173, ff. 113–32; *A.* 181, ff. 11–24; *Pollock* 109–13; *Echard*, 951; *B.M. Addit. MSS.* 11,058, f. 244.

9 *Rawl. MSS. A.* 181, ff. 11–24; *Examen* 246; *Cobbett, State Trials* VI, 1473–92.

10 *Rawl. MSS. A.* 181, ff. 11–24; *Examen* 248; *Sitwell* 51; *Cobbett, State Trials* VI, 1489–90.

[11] *Rawl. MSS. A.* 181, f.1; *Pepysian MSS.*, Adm. Letters VIII, 313; *E.H.R.* VII (*J. R. Tanner, Pepys and the Popish Plot* 288–9).

[12] *Rawl. MSS. A.* 181, ff. 11–24.

[13] *Pollock* 323–6; *Pepysian MSS.*, Adm. Letters VIII, 306; *E.H.R.* VII, 290.

[14] *Rawl. MSS. A.* 181. ff. 25–6.

[15] *Rawl. MSS. A.* 173, ff. 113–32.

[16] *Tanner, Further Corr.* 328–9.

[17] *A. Bryant, King Charles II* 274–6; *Naval Minutes* 209; *Grey* VI, 296–7.

[18] *Grey* VI, 286–7.

[19] *Pepysian MSS.*, Adm. Letters VIII, 284–6, 289–91, 294, 296, 300–1, 305, 319, 343, 350, 378; *E.H.R.* VII, 283–6; *Grey* VI, 207; *Rawl. MSS. A.* 181, ff. 139 et seq.; *Tanner, Further Corr.* 330.

[20] *Grey* VI, 207; *E. G. O'Donoghue, The History of Bethlehem Hospital* (1924); *Notes and Queries*, First Series, II, 87; *D.* 3, 7, 11, 12 March, 13–15 May, 14–15, 17 Aug., 16 Nov. 67; *Pepysian MSS.*, *Miscellanies* VI, 465–83.

[21] *H.M.C. House of Lords* 1678/88; 49–51; *Hargreaves, State Trials* I, 799–800; *Rawl. MSS. A.* 181, ff. 24–5.

[22] *C.S.P.D.* 1678; 589; 1679/80: 69, *Evelyn* 4 Dec. 1778.

[23] *Grey* VI, 207; *Pepysian MSS.*, Adm Letters VIII, 364–5, 370, 403; IX, 21, 108, 116; *C.P. MSS.* I, 109; VI, 613–15, 615–27, 630–2, 645; *C.S.P.D.* 1678: 228–9; 1679/80: 19, 48.

[24] *Examen* passim; *Pepysian MSS.*, *Miscellanies* VII, 465–91; *E.H.R.* LV (*Mrs George, Elections and Electioneering*, 1679–81, 552); *C.S.P.D.* 1679/80: 21; *Sitwell* passim.

[25] *Tanner, Further Corr.* 330–43; *Braybrooke* IV, 209.

[26] *Examen* 250.

[27] *Hargreaves, State Trials* I, 789, 792–3.

[28] *Hargreaves, State Trials* I, 795–800; *Rawl. MSS. A.* 171, f. 286; *A.* 173, ff. 113–32; *Examen* 250–1.

CHAPTER X. THE TRAITOR'S GATE

[1] *Tanner, Further Corr.* 341, 350–1, 353–4.

[2] *Tanner, Further Corr.* 337–8, 343–50; *H.M.C. Dartmouth* I, 29–30.

[3] *Greenwich MS.* 871–7.

[4] *C.P. MSS.* IV, 632–5; *C.S.P.D.* 1679/80: 59–60.

[5] *Greenwich MS.* 884.

[6] *Pepysian MSS.*, Adm. Letters IX, 44; *C.P. MSS.* 1, 200; IV, 664.

[7] *Tanner, Further Corr.* 356–7; *C.P. MSS.* I, 199; *Pepysian MSS.*, Adm. Letters IX, 203.

[8] *C.P. MSS.* I, 223; IV, 638–9, 641–2, 652; *Rawl. MSS. A.* 181, f. 404; *Tanner, Further Corr.* 352–3.

[9] *Grey* VII, 111–12; *H.M.C. Ormonde* IV, 506.

[10] *Rawl. MSS. A.* 181, f. 404; *Tanner, Further Corr.* 330.

[11] *C.P. MSS.* I, 57–81; IV, 664–5; *Naval Minutes* 71–2.

[12] *Tanner, Further Corr.* 357–8; *Howarth* 78–9.

[13] *H.M.C. Ormonde* IV, 506; *C.J.* IX, 60; *Pepysian MSS., Mornamont* I, 1–2; *Rawl. MSS. A.* 173, ff. 195,–201; *A.* 188, ff. 127, 133, 135, 139.

[14] *Pepysian MSS., Mornamont* I, 1–2; *Naval Minutes* 181.

[15] *Rawl. MSS. A.* 181, ff. 195, 217; *A.* 173, f. 175.

[16] *Naval Minutes* 181; *Rawl. MSS. A.* 173, ff. 195–201; *A.* 188, ff. 125, 127, 133, 137, 139.

[17] *Rawl. MSS. A.* 173, ff. 195–201; *A.* 188, ff. 135, 139; *C.S.P.D.* 1679/80: 134, 138–40.

[18] *H.M.C. Ormonde* IV, 508; *Rawl. MSS. A.* 181, f. 242; *A.* 193, ff. 234–40; *Pepysian MS.* No. 2867, Naval Precedents 236; *C.P. MSS.* I, 57–8; *H.M.C. Rep.* 7 (*Verney* 242).

[19] *Pepysian MSS., Mornamont* I, 3–10; Adm. Letters IX, 284; *C.J.* IX, 628–9; *Grey* VII, 303–12.

[20] *Pepysian MSS., Mornamont* I, 185–97.

[21] *Pepysian MSS., Mornamont* I, 17–20; *Grey* VII, 303–12; *Braybrooke* IV, 229; *Rawl. MSS. A.* 178, f. 149.

[22] *Rawl. MSS. A.* 173, ff. 178–9; *Grey* VII, 303–12; *Pepysian MSS., Mornamont* I, 121–8.

[23] *Grey* VII, 303–12.

[24] *Grey* VII, 303–12; *Rawl. MSS. A.* 173, f. 62.

[25] *Grey* VII, 303–12; *H.M.C. Ketton* 184; *C.J.* IX, 628.

[26] *H.M.C. Ketton* 184; *Grey* VII, 315; *C.P. MSS.* I, 75; *Pepysian MSS., Mornamont* I, 10–13, 78; *C.J.* IX, 629; *Rawl. MSS. A.* 173, f. 69.

[27] *Tanner, Corr.* I, 9–10; *Braybrooke* IV, 216; *S. Pepys, Memoires touching the Royal Navy* (ed. J. R. Tanner, 1906) 4–5.

CHAPTER XI. PRISONER OF STATE

[1] *Rawl. MSS. A.* 188, f. 143; *A.* 194, ff. 1–2; *Pepysian MSS., Mornamont* I, 141–3.

[2] *Naval Minutes* 376–7; *Rawl. MSS. A.* 181, ff. 62, 108; *Howarth* 83; *Smith* I, 192–3.

[3] *Rawl. MSS. A.* 173, f. 65; *A.* 181, f., 120; *A.* 194, f. 2 v; *Smith* I, 194–5; *Howarth* 84–5; *R. North, Lives* (Bohn ed.) I, 294–5.

[4] *Rawl. MSS. A.* 173, ff. 69, 85, 87; *Burnet* II, 870; *R. North, Lives* I, 247–8, 290–3; *Pepysian MSS., Mornamont* 1, 17–20, 45–7, 78–9, 84.

[5] *Howarth*, 84–6, 106–7; *Evelyn* 4 June, 3 July 1679; *Rawl. MSS. A.* 181, ff. 116, 120; *A.* 194, ff. 6–7; *Smith* I, 194–6.

[6] *Rawl. MSS. A.* 173, f. 177; *A.* 175, f. 199; *A.* 188, ff. 141, 143–4; *A.* 194, ff. 3–7, 10–13, 15–17; *Pepysian MSS., Mornamont* I, 145, 150–2.

[7] *Rawl. MSS. A.* 175, ff. 46–9, 51–2; *A.* 188, ff. 141, 147–51; *Pepysian MSS., Mornamont* I, 145, 152–4.

[8] *C.P. MSS.* IV, 603–4; *D.* I, lxxxix; *Pepysian MSS.,* Adm. Letters X, 155; *Rawl. MSS. A.* 173, f. 65; *A.* 194, ff. 12–14, 21–31, 33–4.

[9] *Howarth* 84–5.

[10] *Pepysian MSS., Mornamont* I, 148; *Rawl. MSS. A.* 173, f. 69; *A.* 181, ff. 83–4; *A.* 194, ff. 15–17; *Whitear* 105; *Howarth* 106–7.

[11] *Rawl. MSS. A.* 173, f. 69; *A.* 175, ff. 17–45, 70–4; *A.* 194, ff. 15–17, 19 v, 23–4; *Longleat MSS., Coventry Papers* XI, 397, cit. *Pollock* 61–4, 376–8; *Pepysian MSS., Mornamont* I, 26–8, 79.

[12] *Pepysian MSS., Mornamont* I, 33–6, 47–59, 79 passim; *Rawl. MSS. A.* 173, ff. 69, 85, 87.

[13] *Pepysian MSS., Mornamont* I, 59, 79, 89; *Rawl. MSS. A.* 173, ff. 69, 85, 87; *N. Luttrell, Brief Historical Relation* I, 79; *Hatton* I, 87.

[14] Rate Books of St Martin's in the Fields, cit. *J. R. Tanner, Mr Pepys* 244; *Wheatley MSS.; Rawl. MSS. A.* 194, ff. 32, 34–5, 37, 39–40.

[15] *Rawl. MSS. A.* 173, ff. 72–4; *A.* 188, ff. 93, 98,; *A.* 194, ff. 45, 55–7, 60; *Muddiman* 213–14; *Notes and Queries*, 1st Series, VI, 411.

[16] *Rawl. MSS. A.* 173, f. 178; *A.* 175, ff. 215, 218, 222, 236, 244, 279; *Pepysian MSS., Mornamont* I, 121–8.

[17] *Pepysian MSS., Mornamont* II, 1245–9; *Rawl. MSS. A.* 173, f. 180; *A.* 175, ff. 215, 218.

[18] *Rawl. MSS. A.* 173, f. 180.

[19] *Rawl. MSS. A.* 173, f. 18; *A.* 194, ff. 86 v–7, 89, 91; *Pepysian MSS., Mornamont* I, 79.

[20] *Rawl. MSS. A.* 175, ff. 77–9, 95, 157; *A.* 194, ff. 41, 58, 62, 81 v–4.

[21] *Rawl. MSS. A.* 188, f. 151; *A.* 194, ff. 30–2, 35–6, 45, 48–9, 51–2, 62–6; *C.S.P.D.* 1679/80: 197.

[22] *Rawl. MSS. A.* 194, ff. 31, 33–4, 42 v–5; *Pepysian MSS., Mornamont* I, 161–76.

[23] *Rawl. MSS. A.* 173, f. 65; *A.* 194, ff. 31, 33–8; *Pepysian MSS., Mornamont* I, 161–76.

[24] *Rawl. MSS. A.* 194, ff. 30–1, 33–6, 40, 48–9, 70–5.

[25] *Rawl. MSS. A.* 194, ff. 37 v–8; *Pepysian MSS., Mornamont* I, 169–280; *P.R.O. Chancery Proceedings: Mitford,* C. 8. 376, No. 69.

[26] *Rawl. MSS. A.* 194, ff. 37 v–8, 42 v–4, 45–7, 48 v–50, 85–6; *Pepysian MSS., Mornamont* I, 395.

[27] *Rawl. MSS. A.* 194, ff. 37 v–8, 42 v–4, 48 v–9, 51–2, 80–1.

[28] *Rawl. MSS. A.* 194, ff. 55 v–7, 59 v–75; *P.R.O. Chancery Proceedings: Mitford,* C. 8. 376, No. 69; *Pepysian MSS., Mornamont* I passim.

[29] *Rawl. MSS. A.* 194, ff. 55–7, 60–2, 67.

[30] *Rawl. MSS. A.* 173, ff. 195–201; *A.* 194, ff. 42–4; *P.R.O. Chancery Prooceedings: Mitford,* C. 8. 376, No. 69.

[31] *Howarth* 86–8; *Smith* I, 197–200; *Rawl. MSS. A.* 194, ff. 58–9.

[32] *Rawl. MSS. A.* 173, f. 69; *A.* 194, ff. 80–1, 85–8; *Pepysian MSS., Mornamont* I, 79.

[33] *Pepysian MSS., Mornamont* I, 59–60, 79; *Rawl. MSS. A.* 173, f. 69; *A.* 194, ff. 92, 94; *Howarth* 89.

[34] *Rawl. MSS. A.* 194, ff. 92, 94–7; *C.S.P.D.* 1679/80: 272; *Pollock* 204–13; *Sitwell* passim; *Pepysian MSS., Miscellanies* VII, 475.

[35] *P.R.O. Chancery Proceedings: Mitford,* C. 8. 376, No. 69; *Rawl. MSS. A.* 194, ff. 94–8.

[36] *Rawl. MSS. A.* 194, ff. 101–13, 115–16; *Pepysian MSS., Mornamont* I, 60–1.

[37] *Pepysian MSS.* VII, 475; *Sitwell; Rawl. MSS. A.* 194, ff. 111–12.

[38] *Pepysian MSS., Mornamont* I, 285–324.

[39] *Pepysian MSS., Mornamont* I, 285–91.

[40] *Pepysian MSS., Mornamont* I, 291–6.

[41] *Rawl. MSS. A.* 173, f. 69; *A.* 194, f. 114; *Pepysian MSS., Mornamont* I, 61, 79.

[42] *Pepysian MSS., Mornamont* I, 296–301; *Rawl. MSS. A.* 194, ff. 48–9.

[43] *Pepysian MSS., Mornamont* I, 301–3; *Rawl. MSS. A.* 194, ff. 116–17; *C.S.P.D.* 1679/80: 307.

[44] *Pepysian MSS., Mornamont* I, 303–5; II, 1089.

[45] *Pepysian MSS., Mornamont* I, 305–8; *P.R.O. Chancery Proceedings: Mitford,* C. 8. 376, No. 69.

[46] *Pepysian MSS., Mornamont* I, 309–11.

[47] *Pepysian MSS., Mornamont* I, 311–20; *P.R.O. Chancery Proceedings: Mitford,* C. 8. 376, No. 69.

[48] *Pepysian MSS., Mornamont* I, 209–13, 320–4; *Rawl. MSS. A.* 178, f. 105; *A.* 194, ff. 121–3.

[49] *Pepysian MSS., Mornamont* II, 1208, 1256; *Rawl. MSS. A.* 173, f. 180; *A.* 179, f. 48; *A.* 194, ff. 118–20; *Tanner and Wheatley MSS.*

[50] *Tanner and Wheatley MSS.*

[51] *Rawl. MSS. A.* 173, ff. 178–9; *A.* 175, ff. 79–80, 101–7, 145–8, 173; *A.* 194, ff. 118–20, 121–3, 124–7, 127–30, 132–3; *Pepysian MSS., Mornamont* I, 199–208, 209–13, 321–4, 535–8; *Howarth* 90–1; *Smith* I, 204–6; *G. D. Scull, Dorothea Scott* (1882) 21–4.

CHAPTER XII. REHABILITATION

[1] *Pepysian MSS., Mornamont* I, 37–8.

[2] *Pepysian MSS., Mornamont* I, 38–44.

[3] *Rawl. MSS. A.* 173, ff. 57, 178–9; *A.* 175, ff. 163–4; *A.* 194, ff. 124–5, 128; *Pepysian MSS., Mornamont* I, 535–8.

[4] *Rawl. MSS. A.* 173, ff. 69, 85, 87; *Pepysian MSS., Mornamont* I, 61–5, 80.

[5] *Pepysian MSS., Mornamont* I, 65–6, 80–1; II, 1170; *Rawl. MSS. A.* 173, f. 87; *A.* 194, f. 132.

[6] *Pepysian MSS., Mornamont* I, 121–8; II, 1237–44; *Rawl. MSS. A.* 175, f. 210.

[7] *Pepysian MSS., Mornamont* II, 1189–92.

[8] *Pepysian MSS., Mornamont* II, 1192–8.

[9] *Pepysian MSS., Mornamont* II, 1196–1202.

[10] *Rawl. MSS. A.* 194, f. 135; *Pepysian MSS., Mornamont* I, 72–7.

[11] *Pepysian MSS., Mornamont* I, 72–7, 81; *Rawl. MSS. A.* 173, f. 87.

[12] *Rawl. MSS. A.* 194, ff. 136–41; *A.* 173, f. 190; *Pepysian MSS., Mornamont* I, 217–33, 257–9, 324, 416–18, 463–82; II, 1206.

[13] *Pepysian MSS., Mornamont* II, 1203–5; *Rawl. MSS. A.* 194, f. 137 v; *Howarth* 91–2; *Smith* I, 206–7.

[14] *Pepysian MSS., Mornamont* II, 1025–6, 1245–9; *Rawl. MSS. A.* 175, f. 215.

[15] *Pepysian MSS., Mornamont* II, 1206–24, 1252–6, *Rawl. MSS. A.* 173, f. 220; *A.* 194, f. 138; *Howarth* 92; *Smith* I, 208.

[16] *Tanner and Wheatley MSS., Transcripts from Muddiman Newsletters in Bath MSS. from Longleat; Pepysian MSS., Mornamont* II, 1229; *H.M.C. Fleming* 166.

[17] *Pepysian MSS., Mornamont* II, 1206, 1209–16.

[18] *Pepysian MSS., Mornamont* II, 1217, 1219, 1223–4, 1228, 1230, 1232, 1251; *Rawl. MSS. A.* 175, f. 218; *Tanner and Wheatley MSS., Transcripts from Bath MSS. from Longleat.*

[19] *Rawl. MSS. A.* 175, ff. 222, 240, 244; *A.* 194, f. 145; *Pepysian MSS., Mornamont* II, 1226–9, 1252–6; *Smith* I, 208–10; *Howarth* 92–3.

[20] *Pepysian MSS., Mornamont* II, 1225–6, 1229.

[21] *Rawl. MSS. A.* 194, ff. 146–7.

[22] *Pepysian MSS., Mornamont* II, 1229–30,. 1234; *Howarth* 92–4; *Smith* I, 210–14; *Rawl. MSS. A.* 194, ff. 145–6.

[23] *Pepysian MSS., Mornamont* II, 1189–1235.

[24] *Pepysian MSS., Mornamont* II, 1226–9; *Rawl. MSS. A.* 181, ff. 310, 322; *A.* 183, f. 130; *Howarth* 95.

[25] *Rawl. MSS. A.* 194, ff. 147–53, 156 v–65; *P.R.O. Chancery Proceedings: Mitford*, C. 8. 376, No. 69; *Pepysian MSS., Mornamont* I, 507–10, 539–53.

[26] *Rawl. MSS. A.* 173, ff. 65, 69, 87; *A.* 194, ff. 162–5, 167–8; *G. D. Scull, Dorothea Scott* (1882) 15–28; *N. Luttrell, Brief Historical Relation* I, 50; *Pepysian MSS., Mornamont* I, 80–3, 331–2, 539–53.

CHAPTER XIII. THE KING'S TURN

[1] *Rawl. MSS. A.* 181, f. 320; *A.* 194, ff. 168–9; *Howarth* 96–8; *Smith* I, 216–21.

[2] *Rawl. MSS. A.* 194, f. 169; *Howarth* 96–7; *Smith* I, 217–18.

[3] *Pepysian MSS., Mornamont* I passim; *Rawl. MSS. A.* 194, ff. 167–8, 170–2, 174–9.

[4] *Rawl. MSS. A.* 173, ff. 139–60, 184 et seq.; *A.* 175, ff. 1–15, 62–9, 119–24; *A.* 183, f. 179; *A.* 194, ff. 174–81, 185–8, 191–2.

[5] *Rawl. MSS. A.* 194, ff. 105, 136 v–7, 155, 179, 188–90, 194, 203, 205–6, *A.* 181, f. 288; *Pepysian MSS., Mornamont* II, 1230.

[6] *Rawl. MSS. A.* 173, ff. 53, 57; *A.* 181, ff. 29. 102, 245, 247, 249,

250, 273; *A*. 183, ff. 242, 283; *A*. 194, ff. 57 v–8, 71, 89, 115, 180, 234; *Daily Telegraph* 7 Sept. 1928 (Article by Edward Hoare).

[7] *Rawl. MSS. A*. 183, ff. 47 et seq.

[8] *Howarth* 101; *Smith* I, 236; *Rawl. MSS. A*. 181, ff. 310, 315, 337; *A*. 183, ff. 33, 39–40, 45; *A*. 194, ff. 182 v–3, 194–5; *Whitear* 22.

[9] *Davey*, Item 2865; *Rawl. MSS. A*. 175, ff. 326, 328, 330; *A*. 181, ff. 317, 331, 333; *A*. 194, ff. 115, 166 v, 182, 190 v, 194–5, 207–11; *Howarth* 99–101, 118–19; *Smith* I, 224, 228–30, 236; *Pepysian MSS.*, *Miscellanies* V, 53–9, 63–89; *H.M.C. Hodgkin* 177.

[10] *Rawl. MSS. A*. 175, ff. 174–8; *A*. 181, f. 320; *A*. 194, ff. 173 v, 190, 202, 209–11; *Howarth* 97–8, 102; *Smith* I, 219–21; *Pepysian MS.* No. 2141.

[11] *Howarth* 102–3; *Whitear* 42; *Rawl. MSS. A*. 183, ff. 130, 141, *A*. 194, ff. 211–15.

[12] *Rawl. MSS. A*. 183, ff. 134, 157; *A*. 194, ff. 213 v–15, 217–18, 222–4, 227–8; *Braybrooke* IV, 357–8; *Whitear* 22.

[13] *Howarth* 104–5; *Rawl. MSS. A*. 183, ff. 144, 146, 151; *A*. 194, ff. 222–5.

[14] *Rawl. MSS. A*. 183, ff. 146, 150, 153, 155; *A*. 194, ff. 218, 222, 224 v–5; *Howarth* 102–3.

[15] *Howarth* 102–3; *Rawl. MSS. A*. 183, ff. 150, 153; *Pepysian MSS.*, *Miscellanies* VII, 484.

[16] *Rawl. MSS. A*. 183, ff. 130, 138, 144, 150–1, 153; *A*. 194, f. 220 v, 229–30; *Howarth* 102–3.

[17] *Rawl. MSS. A*. 183, ff. 124, 130, 144; *A*. 194, f. 228 v; *Howarth* 107–8.

[18] *Howarth* 103–4.

[19] *Howarth* 103–4, 106–7, *Rawl. MSS. A*. 194, f. 231.

[20] *Rawl. MSS. A*. 181, ff. 241, 250; *A*. 183, ff. 130, 142; *A*. 194, ff. 143 v–4, 224 v–5; *P.R.O. Great Wardrobe Books*, L.C. 3. 61; *C.S.P.D.* 1679/80: 603–4; 1680/1: 168.

[21] *Rawl. MSS. A*. 183, ff. 70, 124, 130; *A*. 188, f. 123; *A*. 194, f. 234 v; *C.S.P.D.* 1680/1; 86; *Howarth* 107–11.

[22] *Rawl. MSS. A*. 173, f. 189; *A*. 183, f. 70; *Pepysian MSS.*, *Miscellanies* VII, 487; *A. Bryant, Charles II* 306–9; *C.S.P.D.* 1680/1: 134, 665–6; *E.H.R.* XL (*Warcup Journal*).

[23] *Rawl. MSS. A*. 194, ff. 180 v–1, 191 v–2, 198–200, 202, 209–12, 215–17, 219–21, 225–7, 233; *P.R.O. Chancery Proceedings: Mitford*, C. 8. 376, No. 69.

²⁴ *Rawl. MSS. A.* 173, f. 189; *A.* 194, ff. 236–41; *E.H.R.* XL (*Warcup Journal*); *H.M.C. Fleming* 161; *Muddiman* 229–31.

²⁵ *E.H.R.* XLI (*Warcup Journal*); *Howarth* 110; *Braybrooke* IV, 218–19; *C.S.P.D.* 1680/1: 131, 137, 139, 146–7.

²⁶ *Luttrell* I passim; *Memoirs of Thomas Bruce, 2nd Earl of Ailesbury* (Roxburghe Club, 1890) I, 53; *C.S.P.D.* 1680/1: 139, 152–3, 675–8; *Muddiman* 229–35; *Prideaux Papers* (*Camden Soc.*) 83.

²⁷ *Rawl. MSS. A.* 183, ff. 31, 35–8, 288; *A.* 194, f. 235; *Howarth* III; *Smith* I, 261–2; Bodl. Tracts L. 5. 8. Th. *No Faith or Credit to be given to Papists*, by John Smith (1681), 26–7.

²⁸ *C.S.P.D.* 1680/1: 166; *H.M.C. Ormonde* v passim; *Pepysian MSS.*, *Miscellanies* XI, 224–5; *H.M.C. Rep.* VI (*Cooke of Owston* 425); *Ranke* IV, 126–9; *C.P. MSS.* I, 58; *Rawl. MSS. A.* 194, f. 265.

²⁹ *Evelyn*, 27 March 1681; *Howarth* 111–12; *Braybrooke* IV, 219; *Rawl. MSS. A.* 183, ff. 76, 245.

³⁰ *C.S.P.D.* 1680/1: 166, 216, 227–8; *Rawl. MSS. A.* 178, f. 69; *Ailesbury, Memoirs* 55.

³¹ *Rawl. MSS. A.* 183, f. 19; *A.* 189, ff. 433–8, 440, 442–4; *A.* 194, f. 19; *E.H.R.* XL (*Warcup Journal* 255); *Hargreaves, State Trials* II, 341–411.

³² *Ranke* IV, 125–32; *Ailesbury, Memoirs* 56–7; *H.M.C. Hodgkin* 321–2; *A. Bryant, Charles II* 314–15; *Diary of the Times of Charles II by Henry Sidney*, ed. R. W. Blencowe (1843) II, 177.

CHAPTER XIV. NEW COURSES

¹ *Rawl. MSS. A.* 183, ff. 11, 57; *A.* 194, ff. 248–52, 256; *D.* I, xlii; *Howarth* 112–13; *Smith* I, 263; *Braybrooke* IV, 220.

² *H.M.C. Rep.* 8 (*Trinity House* 257); *Tanner, Corr.* I, 11–13; *Rawl. MSS. A.* 194, f. 251; *Braybrooke* IV, 220; *H.M.C. Dartmouth* I, 49; *Sotheby's Catalogue*, II April 1919: J. W. Freshfield's Sale, Item 931.

³ *Tanner, Corr.* I, 13–14; *Rawl. MSS. A.* 171, f. 91; *A.* 194, ff. 253, 256 v.

⁴ *D.* I, xl-xlii; 13 Dec. 65; *Pepysian MS.* No 2141; *Rawl. MSS. A.* 194, ff. 248 v–50.

⁵ *C.S.P.D.* 1680/1: 270, 325; *H.M.C. Ormonde* VI passim; *Rawl. MSS. A.* 194, ff. 236V–40.

⁶ *Rawl. MSS. A.* 178, ff. 49, 52–4, 57; *A.* 183, ff. 168, 231, 253; *A.*

194, ff. 236 v–41, 246–7, 251–2; *P.R.O. Chancery Proceedings: Mitford,* C. 8. 376, No. 69.

⁷ *Howarth* 111–12; *Rawl. MSS. A.* 171, f. 91 v; *A.* 183, ff. 163, 273; *A.* 194, ff. 234–5, 245, 253 v; *Braybrooke* IV, 219.

⁸ *Rawl. MSS. A.* 178, f. 63; *A.* 183, ff. 214, 260; *A.* 194, ff. 253, 259 v–60; *Howarth* 115–16; *Smith* I, 265.

⁹ *Rawl. MSS. A.* 178, f. 61; *A.* 194, ff. 254–5; *Smith* I, 266–8, 271–2; *Howarth* 115–17.

¹⁰ *Rawl. MSS. A.* 183, ff. 258, 260, 268; *A.* 194, ff. 257, 259 v, 261.

¹¹ *Rawl. MSS. A.* 183, ff. 177, 184.

¹² *Rawl. MSS. A.* 178, f. 73; *A.* 183, ff. 165, 169, 177.

¹³ *Rawl. MSS. A.* 183, f. 169.

¹⁴ *Rawl. MSS. A.* 178, f. 73; *C.S.P.D.* 1680/1: 467.

¹⁵ *Rawl. MSS. A.* 183, f. 266; *A.* 194, ff. 257–8, 262; *C.* 384, f. 28.

¹⁶ *Rawl. MSS. A.* 178, ff. 97–9; *A.* 183, ff. 233, 235; *A.* 194, ff. 244–5, 259–60, 262 v–3.

¹⁷ *Rawl. MSS. A.* 194, f. 242; *Naval Minutes* 102.

¹⁸ *Pepysian MSS.* No. 2612, ff. 357, 381–7, 413; *Pearce* 110–11; *Smith* I, 260–1, 278–9; *Rawl. MSS. A.* 183, ff. 9, 272; *A.* 194, f. 258 v.

¹⁹ *Pepysian MS.* No. 2612, ff. 391, 409–13.

²⁰ *Pepysian MS.* No. 2612, ff. 390, 395, 403; *Howarth* 126; *Rawl. MSS. A.* 194, f. 265.

²¹ *Rawl. MSS. A.* 178, f. 14; *A.* 183, ff. 18, 31, 210; *A.* 194, f. 281.

²² *Rawl. MSS. A.* 183, ff. 239–40.

²³ *D.* 7 July 62; 4 March, 22 June, 4, 6, 7 July, 6 Aug. 63; 13 June 64; 24 Nov. 65; 16 Jan., 7 July 68; *Pepysiana* 184–8.

²⁴ *D.* 29 March 69; *Tanner, Further Corr.* 313–18; 1, 14–21; *Rawl. MSS. A.* 173, f. 12; *A.* 183, f. 90; *A.* 185, f. 93; *A.* 194, ff. 133 v, 184, 243; *Notes and Queries* VIII, 341, *Davey,* Items 2563, 2865, 2867–70; *Pepysian MSS., Mornamont* II, 1223; *Naval Minutes* 86, 95; *Howarth* 19–24.

²⁵ *Tanner, Corr.* I, 14–21; *Howarth* 119–24.

²⁶ *Naval Minutes* 1–211 passim.

²⁷ *Naval Minutes* 86, 103; *H.M.C. Hodgkin* 178; *Howarth* 125–6; *Smith* I, 280–2; *Rawl. MSS. A.* 173, f. 34; *A.* 194, f. 264.

²⁸ *Naval Minutes* 32–5, 101, 114–17; *Bibliotheca Pepysiana,* Part I, 70.

²⁹ *Naval Minutes* 71–2, 115–16.

³⁰ *Rawl. MSS. A.* 178, f. 88; *A.* 183, f. 245; *Smith* I, 273–7.

³¹ *Pepysian MSS., Miscellanies* XI, 224–5; *C.P. MSS.* I, 58; *Rawl. MSS. A.* 178, f. 84; 183, ff. 249, 257–8, 261, 264.

[32] *Rawl. MSS. A.* 178, ff. 9, 11, 13, 45, 141, *A.* 183, ff. 22, 302.

[33] *Smith* I, 283–4, 289–91; *Rawl. MSS. A.* 178, ff. 135, 150; *A.* 194, ff. 271, 276–7.

[34] *Pepysian MS.* No. 2612, f. 443; *Howarth* 126–8; *Rawl. MSS. A.* 194, ff. 266–7.

[35] *Rawl. MSS. A.* 178, f. 150; *A.* 194, ff. 267–70; *Howarth* 127–8, 132–3; *Smith* I, 289–91.

[36] *Pepysian MS.* No. 2612, ff. 443, 447, 453; *Christ's Hospital Minute Books* 1677/89; 28 March 1682.

[37] *Rawl. MSS. A.* 178, f. 7; *A.* 183, f. 310; *Pepysian MS.* No. 2612, ff. 467–505.

[38] *Rawl. MSS. A.* 194, ff. 272–3; *Howarth* 130–2; *Smith* I, 286–8.

[39] *Rawl. MSS. A.*178, f. 18; *A.* 194, ff. 271v–2.

[40] *Rawl. MSS. A.* 178, ff. 148, 155; *Howarth* 134, 137–9; *Correspondence of Henry Hyde, Earl of Clarendon,* ed. Singer 1828, Vol. I (*Narrative of Sir John Berry* I, 71).

[41] *Singer* I (*Narrative of Sir John Berry* 71–3).

[42] *Howarth* 133–6; *Singer* I (*Narrative of Sir John Berry* 71–3); *Rawl. MSS. A.* 194, ff. 274 v–6; *Naval Minutes* 150.

[43] *Howarth* 133–7, 139–41; *Rawl. MSS. A.* 178, f. 148; *A.* 194, ff. 274 v–6; *Smith* I, 294–8.

[44] *Howarth* 139–40; *Smith* I, 294–8.

[45] *Howarth* 139–41; *Smith* I, 294–8; *Rawl. MSS. A.* 178, f. 150; *A.* 194, ff. 276–8.

[46] *Rawl. MSS. A.* 194, ff. 276–8; *Howarth* 139–41, 141–3; *Smith* I, 294–8; *H.M.C. Fleming* 185–6.

[47] *Howarth* 136–7; *Braybrooke* IV, 229; *Rawl. MSS. A.* 178, ff. 112, 114, 145–6, 164.

[48] *Rawl. MSS. A.* 178, ff. 112, 114, 145–6; *Braybrooke* IV, 229; *Howarth* 137, 142; *Pepysian MSS., Miscellanies* VII, 487.

[49] *Howarth* 142–4; *Rawl. MSS. A.* 194, f. 277.

[50] *Rawl. MSS. A.* 178, ff. 146, 148; *Howarth* 136–9; *Smith* I, 291–4.

[51] *Rawl. MSS. A.* 178, f. 155.

[52] *Rawl. MSS. A.* 178, f. 151; *A.* 194, ff. 278–9; *Howarth* 141–2; *Smith* I, 298–301.

[53] *Rawl. MSS. A.* 194, f. 278.

[54] *Rawl. MSS. A.* 178, ff. 134, 136; *A.* 194, f. 278; *Howarth* 144.

[55] *Pepysian MS.* No. 2612, ff. 531–613; *Naval Minutes* 136, 148–9; *Pearce* 112.

[56] *Naval Minutes* 136, 148–9; *Pepysian MS.* No. 2612, ff. 575, 613, 722; *J. R. Tanner, Mr Pepys* (1925) 259; *Davey*, Item 2871; *Smith* I, 301–3; *Rawl. MSS. A.* 178, f. 153.

[57] *Smith* I, 303–6; *Wood, Athenae Oxonienses; Rawl. MSS. A.* 178, f. 18; *A.* 194, f. 280; *Howarth* 144–6.

[58] *Rawl. MSS. A.* 194, ff. 283–4; *Howarth* 146–9; *Smith* I, 311–18.

[59] *Rawl. MSS. A.* 171, ff. 148–53; *A.* 174, f. 377; *A.* 178, f. 108; *A.* 179; ff. 20–1; *A.* 181, f. 102; *A.* 183, f. 242; *A.* 194, ff. 236, 256, 270v, 285v–6.

[60] *Smith* I, 306–7; *Rawl. MSS. A.* 178, ff. 122, 135; *A.* 194, ff. 280 v–2; *Howarth* 145; *Pepysian MS.* No. 2141; *Naval Minutes* 148–87.

[61] *Naval Minutes* 125, 153, 156, 162–3, 166–8, 170–2, 191.

[62] *Naval Minutes* 155–6, 166–7, 176–7.

[63] *Naval Minutes* 180, 183, 187, 196, 237.

[64] *Naval Minutes* 192–3; *C.P. MSS.* I, 61; *Tangier Papers* 319.

[65] *Naval Minutes* 210–11; *A. Bryant, Charles II* 333–6; *Rawl. MSS. A.* 178, ff. 264–9; *C.* 859, ff. 146v, 153v, 154v.

[66] *H.M.C. Dartmouth* I, 83–5; II, 39–40.

[67] *Rawl. MSS. C.* 859, ff. 151–3; *Tangier Papers* 252; *Smith* II, 150; *D.* I, xliv.

[68] *Rawl MSS. C.* 859, ff. 151v, 217–19; *Tangier Papers* 3; *H.M.C. Dartmouth* III, 39.

[69] *Rawl MSS. C.* 859, ff. 217–19; *Tangier Papers* 3; *H.M.C. Dartmouth* III, 39; *Smith* II, 150.

[70] *Tangier Papers* 3; *Howarth* 151–7; *Rawl. MSS. A.* 190, f. 10.

[71] *Tangier Papers* 4.

[72] *Tangier Papers* 6–7; *Howarth* 156–7; *Rawl. MSS. A.* 190, ff. 25, 29, 41, 49–52.

[73] *Rawl. MSS. A.* 190, ff. 49–52

[74] *Rawl. MSS. A.* 190, f. 56.

[75] *Rawl. MSS. A.* 190, f. 58; *Tangier Papers* 7.

[76] *Tangier Papers* 7.

Index

Index 349

S.P.Y.P.—20